A Guide to Advancing Graduate Medical Education for All

A Guide to Advancing Graduate Medical Education for All

Bonnie Simpson Mason, MD
Medical Director, Inclusive Excellence
American College of Surgeons

Pilar Ortega, MD, MGM
Vice President, Diversity, Equity, and Inclusion
Accreditation Council for Graduate Medical Education

William McDade, MD
Chief Diversity, Equity, and Inclusion Officer
Accreditation Council for Graduate Medical Education

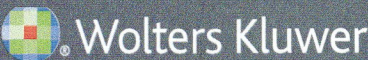 Wolters Kluwer

Philadelphia · Baltimore · New York · London
Buenos Aires · Hong Kong · Sydney · Tokyo

ACGME

Acquisitions Editor: Matt Hauber
Development Editor: Deborah Bordeaux
Editorial Coordinator: Ann Francis
Editorial Assistant: Parisa Saranj
Marketing Manager: Kirsten Watrud
Senior Production Specialist: Bridgett Dougherty
Manager, Graphic Arts & Design: Stephen Druding
Art Director, Illustration: Jennifer Clements
Manufacturing Coordinator: Margie Orzech
Prepress Vendor: S4Carlisle Publishing Services

Copyright © 2026 Accreditation Council for Graduate Medical Education.

All rights reserved. This book is protected by copyright. No part of this book may be reproduced or transmitted in any form or by any means, including as photocopies or scanned-in or other electronic copies, or utilized by any information storage and retrieval system without written permission from the copyright owner, except for brief quotations embodied in critical articles and reviews. Materials appearing in this book prepared by individuals as part of their official duties as U.S. government employees are not covered by the above-mentioned copyright. To request permission, please contact Wolters Kluwer at Two Commerce Square, 2001 Market Street, Philadelphia, PA 19103, via email at permissions@lww.com, or via our website at shop.lww.com (products and services).

9 8 7 6 5 4 3 2 1

Printed in the United States of America

Library of Congress Cataloging-in-Publication Data

ISBN-13: 978-1-975226-41-1

Cataloging-in-Publication data available on request from Publisher.

This work is provided "as is," and the publisher disclaims any and all warranties, express or implied, including any warranties as to accuracy, comprehensiveness, or currency of the content of this work.

This work is no substitute for individual patient assessment based upon healthcare professionals' examination of each patient and consideration of, among other things, age, weight, gender, current or prior medical conditions, medication history, laboratory data and other factors unique to the patient. The publisher does not provide medical advice or guidance and this work is merely a reference tool. Healthcare professionals, and not the publisher, are solely responsible for the use of this work including all medical judgments and for any resulting diagnosis and treatments.

Given continuous, rapid advances in medical science and health information, independent professional verification of medical diagnoses, indications, appropriate pharmaceutical selections and dosages, and treatment options should be made and healthcare professionals should consult a variety of sources. When prescribing medication, healthcare professionals are advised to consult the product information sheet (the manufacturer's package insert) accompanying each drug to verify, among other things, conditions of use, warnings and side effects and identify any changes in dosage schedule or contraindications, particularly if the medication to be administered is new, infrequently used or has a narrow therapeutic range. To the maximum extent permitted under applicable law, no responsibility is assumed by the publisher for any injury and/or damage to persons or property, as a matter of products liability, negligence law or otherwise, or from any reference to or use by any person of this work.

shop.lww.com

DEDICATION

To the many current and aspiring leaders, persistent advocates, and dedicated medical educators committed to fostering diversity, equity, inclusion, and antiracism for all physician learners so they will continue their efforts to improve population health and eliminate health disparities.

ACKNOWLEDGMENTS

We extend our deepest gratitude to each of the volunteer contributing authors whose dedication, professional expertise, and personal lived experiences have been invaluable in bringing *A Guide to Advancing Graduate Medical Education for All* to life. Their commitment to advancing diversity, equity, inclusion, and antiracism in medical education has shaped every page of this textbook.

For his steadfast support and vision in championing diversity, equity, and inclusion efforts across the organization and throughout the medical education community, our sincere thanks also go to Thomas J. Nasca MD, MACP, President Emeritus, Senior Fellow, and Administrative Director of the Center for Professionalism and the Future of Medicine of the Accreditation Council for Graduate Medical Education. His leadership continues to inspire meaningful change and growth within the field.

We also acknowledge with special appreciation, our colleague Allison Cox-Simpson, for her tireless efforts behind the scenes. Her meticulous attention to detail and unwavering support have been instrumental in creating this resource.

We know firsthand that participating in efforts to advance diversity, equity, inclusion, and antiracism can be challenging and exhausting, not only professionally, but also personally. Yet, even in the face of adversity, we are filled with an overwhelming sense of purpose, thanks to the authenticity and deep passion, contagious energy, academic rigor, and collective strength reflected in these pages by the many individuals who have made this volume possible.

DISCLAIMER

The statements in each of the chapters of this book are those of the respective author(s) of each chapter and do not represent, nor should they be attributed to, author-affiliated institutions or the ACGME.

The execution of any strategies or other statements expressed in this book does not guarantee substantial compliance with ACGME requirements for accreditation. The determination of substantial compliance is made solely by the ACGME. Readers are urged to consult their own attorneys regarding the potential execution of any strategies or other statements in this book.

FOREWORD: JEROME ADAMS, MD, MPH

Jerome Adams, MD, MPH
Distinguished Professor and Executive Director of Health Equity, Purdue University
20th United States Surgeon General

To improve public health, we must center the education of future physicians around the needs of our diverse populations. The goal of graduate medical education (GME) is to cultivate skilled, compassionate, and inclusive physicians who are equipped to deliver high-quality patient care in all circumstances. By adhering to rigorous standards that guide both knowledge acquisition and clinical experience, GME programs prepare residents and fellows to meet the evolving challenges of health care, including public health emergencies like pandemics and natural disasters.

The Accreditation Council for Graduate Medical Education (ACGME) plays a crucial role in upholding the social contract between the medical profession and society, ensuring that physicians are educated and trained to provide equitable, high-quality care. By monitoring compliance with educational standards, the ACGME is dedicated to improving population health and addressing the disparities that persist within our health care system. As a former Surgeon General of the United States and Health Commissioner of Indiana, I am proud to lend my perspective to *A Guide to Advancing Graduate Medical Education for All*, a vital initiative undertaken by the ACGME.

My own experiences in medical education and training have profoundly shaped my understanding of these issues. During my internship, I participated in an environmental health rotation in the Rio Grande Valley where I witnessed the unique challenges faced by border communities. Language barriers, fears of deportation, and air and water pollution all worked in opposition to community and provider goals for better health. In my anesthesia residency, rotations at an inner-city Level 1 trauma center exposed me to additional societal barriers—such as transportation, housing, and legal issues—that affect patient outcomes. These experiences reinforced the importance of preparing physicians to deliver care that is responsive to the complexities of real-world situations, where individual patients may not fit neatly into the textbook scenarios we are taught in medical school.

Despite significant medical advancements over the past several decades since my own experience as a resident, our society still grapples with disparities in health care access and outcomes, particularly affecting marginalized populations. During my tenure as Surgeon General from 2017 to 2021, the COVID-19 pandemic highlighted these enduring inequities and the severe consequences of preventable diseases on vulnerable communities. To mitigate such impact, we must confront the social determinants of health—the conditions in which people live, learn, and work. Addressing factors such as housing, education, income, and access to nutritious food is not only ethical; it is essential for achieving health equity. Our interventions must be inclusive, ensuring that health care advancements benefit everyone.

Imagine a future where diversity is celebrated as a strength rather than viewed as a barrier. Research consistently shows that a physician workforce representative of the populations they serve can lead to improved clinical outcomes. While achieving perfect concordance may be challenging, it is crucial to train all health care providers to recognize, respect, and respond to the diversity within their communities. The chapters in this volume offer a roadmap for realizing this vision.

Now, more than ever, we must address the shifting attitudes within the US public. Despite growing awareness of health disparities and the necessity for equitable health care, we face increasing resistance to diversity, equity, inclusion, and antiracism initiatives, with some viewing these efforts as divisive. The content of *A Guide to Advancing Graduate Medical Education for All* reminds us that these efforts are not optional; they are essential for creating a high-quality and low-cost health care system for all. Regardless of the challenges we encounter, we must remain steadfast champions for a future that is inclusive, healthier, and equitable—one where everyone has the opportunity to thrive, regardless of their background.

This book is critical reading for anyone involved in patient care or medical education. It is our responsibility as health care professionals and educators to cultivate an equitable health care system and learning environments that foster new generations of physicians committed to these values. Together, we can build a future where diversity, equity, inclusion, and antiracism are at the forefront of medical education and practice.

FOREWORD: REGINA M. BENJAMIN, MD, MBA

Regina M. Benjamin, MD, MBA
18th United States Surgeon General
Founder and CEO BayouClinic, Inc

The practice of medicine is deeply connected with social justice. Physicians have the unique opportunity to not only treat patients but also address broader inequities that affect public health. We can play a major role in creating a more just and humane society. My experiences as both US Surgeon General and a family physician have shown me how public health serves as a foundation for addressing the social determinants of health. Early on at my clinic in rural Alabama, I learned that my prescription pad was not always enough to solve my patient's problems. I had to address other facets of life such as basic literacy, employment, transportation, clean water, and healthy foods.

Diversity, equity, inclusion, and antiracism are essential to our professional calling. By embracing physician workforce diversity, we acknowledge the proven benefits to excellence and quality brought forth by diverse perspectives, life experiences, and skill sets in the health care environment. By fostering educational and health equity, we reiterate our commitment to ensuring that health care is accessible to the entire US public and that children from all communities can aspire to becoming physicians.

The journey to becoming a physician is a lifelong process that can be greatly facilitated by structured support and intentional inclusion. Growing up, I had never seen a black physician until I got to college. Although I had good grades, loved science, and was very bright, the thought of being a doctor never entered my mind. Were it not for an on-campus pre-college summer program designed to get minority students interested in health careers, I may never have gone into medicine. In medical school and residency I also credit intentional structured programs and strong mentors (both Black and White) for advising me through a world that was very foreign to me.

The reality for some individuals, is that they are constantly going against the grain in order to succeed. They are constantly fighting stereotypes or assumptions that they are not fit for a career as a physician, a health care leader, or a scientist. Such situations need not exist. Faculty members, administrators, and everyone involved in medical education can take clear and decisive action to create learning environments where all learners can thrive. This book underscores the importance of these elements with chapters such as "Building Institutional Cultures of Safety and Accountability to Support Graduate Medical Education," and "Building an Inclusive Environment for Residents and Fellows from First-Generation College Graduate and Low-Income (FGLI) Backgrounds," which offer actionable strategies for creating inclusive learning environments.

Through inclusion, we can adopt practices in our workplaces, educational institutions, and consultation rooms to make everyone feel that they belong and that their voice will be heard. This book provides not only a conceptual and historical backdrop for the inequities that still plague US health care and graduate medical education; it also outlines practical ways in which we demonstrate our commitment to creating a health care system where all persons, regardless of their background, can achieve optimal health outcomes.

Each chapter that follows will illuminate the systemic barriers faced by minority physician learners. You will notice that some barriers affect certain groups differently or disproportionately, and you will also notice common threads woven through the lived experiences across identity groups. *A Guide* addresses these challenges and provides readers with actionable tools to dismantle these barriers and create a more equitable health care system.

This book serves as a call to action for residents and fellows, faculty members, staff, and all leaders to not simply read its lessons but to implement *real* change. It challenges readers to think beyond the topics presented and consider tangible ways they can implement diversity, equity, inclusion, and antiracism principles in their own programs. Through embracing this responsibility, we can contribute to public health that is truly *for all*.

After reading this book, I hope you feel empowered to take concrete steps to foster an equitable health care setting. I encourage you to choose at least two actions you can incorporate into your daily practice—whether you are physician, educator, learner, or leader. These actions can include mentoring, advocating for policies that promote diversity, creating clear and responsive reporting mechanisms for those who experience discrimination or other forms of mistreatment, or launching community outreach programs. The knowledge gained from this book will only reach its full potential when translated into action; consistent efforts will collectively drive meaningful and lasting change.

Imagining the future, I remain hopeful and optimistic. I see a path where all persons, regardless of their background, can access the care they need to live their healthiest, most fulfilling lives. This vision of equitable health care is within reach if we all come together and do the work. We must remain committed to diversity, equity, inclusion, and antiracist practices in medical education and in every facet of health care.

INTRODUCING *A GUIDE*: WHY WE WROTE IT AND HOW TO USE IT

A Guide to Advancing Graduate Medical Education for All is an educational tool that provides multiple perspectives on a variety of topics related to diversity, equity, inclusion, and antiracism in the context of graduate medical education (GME). Each of the authors are preeminent thought leaders in medical education from across the country who volunteered their scholarship to further diversity in medicine and to ensure that physician learners are treated equitably as well as made to feel included during their formative years.

The text moves beyond calling attention to historical and current injustices in GME. Through its case-driven examples, it invites readers to action through recommendations on how to analyze educational and clinical cultures, assess learner and patient needs, and implement effective change. Each author is a subject matter expert, the majority of whom have engaged in diversity, equity, and inclusion (DEI) efforts. Their personal investment arises from their lived experience and their unwavering commitment; they have contributed to improving the DEI space for many years and are poised to continue doing so for years to come. The topics covered are not exhaustive and may not be universally relevant to all groups that, sadly, have been or are excluded from health care and medical education. They represent an extension of the topics addressed in *ACGME Equity Matters*® online learning resources, currently presented as a video library and toolkits at Learn at ACGME on the ACGME website.[1] The scholarship represented in this text will continue the dialogue necessary to advance the critical work in DEI and antiracism accomplished thus far.

A Guide is designed for anyone interested in or involved with efforts to increase physician workforce diversity, build safe and inclusive environments, and promote health equity by addressing health care disparities and enhancing overall population health. From leaders vested in DEI and antiracism at the executive level to faculty members, residents, and fellows—all represent potential readers and learners.

Central to *A Guide* are the terms diversity, equity, and inclusion, and antiracism. Diversity refers to valuing individual differences (ie, race, ethnicity, gender, sexual orientation, class, age, country or language of origin, education, religion, geography, physical or cognitive abilities) as an asset and striving for representation.[2] Equity is defined as "fairness and justice and focuses on outcomes that are most appropriate for a given group, recognizing different challenges, needs, and histories."[2] Equity differs from equality which suggests uniform treatment, and instead focuses on a dynamic approach based on the given group. Inclusion extends beyond diversity and equity; inclusion refers to full participation with access to opportunities.[2] Antiracism has been included specifically because it is a process unto itself, referring to actively identifying, opposing, confronting, and dismantling racist systems.

The concepts of diversity, equity, and inclusion are also, most importantly, among the ACGME's foundational values. Thus, *A Guide* represents an effort to fulfill the ACGME's Mission to improve health care and population health by assessing and enhancing the quality of resident and fellow physicians' education through advancements in accreditation and education.[3]

HOW *A GUIDE* IS ORGANIZED

A Guide is organized into the four sections listed below. An essay introduces the topic of each section and also includes the title chapters, authors, and a summary of each chapter. Each section and the chapters therein build upon the next.

- Section 1: Historical Foundations and Basic Principles of Diversity, Equity, and Inclusion in Graduate Medical Education
- Section 2: On Racial and Ethnic Experiences in Graduate Medical Education

- Section 3: Ethnocultural, Immigrant, Multilingual, and Religious Experiences in Graduate Medical Education
- Section 4: Gender and Sexual Identity, Disability, and Age in Graduate Medical Education

The chapters are intentionally brief; each could easily form the basis for its own textbook. The intent is to introduce an aspect of diversity, equity, inclusion and antiracism, breathe life into it through use of a case study crafted by the authors, and to elaborate on elements of the case study in the context of that particular subject. Many more areas could obviously have been included for discussion; however, to make the volume accessible and to stimulate further thinking on each subject, the references at the end of each chapter will be helpful to the readers if they wish to pursue further study.

HOW TO USE A GUIDE

In keeping with its purpose as an educational tool, each chapter in A Guide begins with learning objectives. Each case study that follows is accompanied by an illustration to help bring life to the situation described in the case. While it is impossible for any single graphic to fully represent all aspects of the situation or all aspects of DEI depicted, the illustrations nonetheless are an intentional effort to thoughtfully and inclusively depict key themes highlighted in the cases as starting points for further reflection, discussion, and learning. For example, an illustration could be used to initiate a conversation in a small group by asking open-ended questions such as inviting participants to share what they observe in the image.

Call-out boxes included throughout the text underscore the key teaching points of each chapter's case and provide principles for readers to apply in their own clinical learning environments. "Take Home Points" and "Questions for Further Thought" provide additional opportunities for readers to guide whether and how they have achieved the objectives for each chapter.

Additionally, each chapter of the volume incorporates keywords relevant to its specific subject matter to ensure readers are familiar with essential terminology. These key terms are bolded within the text of the chapter in which they are introduced to emphasize their importance and to provide meaning and context to enhance understanding. The terms are compiled and fully defined within the volume's Glossary located at the back of the book, providing a useful tool for readers as they engage with the content.

BEYOND A GUIDE

A Guide is, ultimately, an exploration of DEI and antiracism within GME—including concepts foundational to creating an inclusive and supportive learning environment for all individuals, including learners, faculty members, staff members, and also extends to its diverse patient populations. The dominant culture in health care and GME often reflects traditional norms and values that can marginalize individuals whose identities diverge from these norms. Through this exploration, the ACGME and the authors who have contributed to this text aim to equip readers with the knowledge and tools necessary to recognize and address the systemic inequities that exist in GME.

Following the murder of George Floyd, there was a heightened interest in racial understanding and an explosion of scholarship that had heretofore been suppressed. The observation that cycles of interest ebb and flow in terms of progress towards racial equity has been made by many authors, but none more clearly than Cato T. Laurencin, MD, PhD, in his 2020 address upon receiving the Herbert W. Nickens Award from the Association of American Medical Colleges. In his comments, Dr Laurencin documented the level of interest in racism as a function of time in online searches and described the historical waves of progress in terms of racial change in the US.[4] However, what seemed like a sea change in racial understanding only a few years ago has recently been met with fierce and distorted opposition to DEI education and training; banning of books, terms, and concepts central to understanding racism; and, dismantling of DEI Offices in institutions to further undermine equitable and inclusive environments across all facets of DEI. That is why an enduring piece of work was needed to help address DEI and antiracism in our GME learning environments. Efforts at achieving diversity in our workforce, equity and inclusion in our workplaces, and antiracism in society writ large must be ongoing. Backtracking on this commitment is unacceptable. A diverse workforce is vital to the interests of public health in the US.

* * *

On behalf of the ACGME, we extend our gratitude and admiration to the authors who have contributed their time and talent over many months in preparing *A Guide to Advancing Graduate Medical Education for All*. And, we extend that gratitude to you, the readers, who commit to exemplifying, innovating, and advancing diversity, equity, inclusion, and antiracism efforts in your workplace and communities.

**William McDade, MD, PhD, Chief, Diversity, Equity, and Inclusion,
Accreditation Council for Graduate Medical Education**

**Pilar Ortega, MD, MGM, Vice President, Diversity, Equity, and Inclusion,
Accreditation Council for Graduate Medical Education**

REFERENCES

1. Accreditation Council for Graduate Medical Education. Learn at ACGME. Accessed July 26, 2024. https://dl.acgme.org/
2. The Center for Racial Justice Innovation. Race Reporting Guide. Race Forward, 2015. Accessed August 28, 2024. https://www.raceforward.org/sites/default/files/Race%20Reporting%20Guide%20by%20Race%20Forward_V1.1.pdf
3. Accreditation Council for Graduate Medical Education. Mission, vision, values. Accessed July 26, 2024. https://www.acgme.org/about/overview/mission-vision-and-values/
4. Laurencin CT. Black lives matter in science, engineering and medicine: Cato T. Laurencin, MD, PhD: Winner of the 2020 Herbert W. Nickens Award of the Association of American Medical Colleges, Acceptance Remarks. *J Racial Ethn Health Disparities*. 2020;7(6):1021-1034. doi:10.1007/s40615-020-00924-2

LIST OF CONTRIBUTORS

Jerome Adams
Ngozi F. Anachebe
David Ansell
Michael S. Argenyi
Anne Knox Averitt
Santiago Avila
Keisha Bell
Regina M. Benjamin
Anita Blanchard
Natasha Bray
Helen Burstin
Alec Calac
Allison Cox-Simpson
Daniel Eisenberg
Wendi El-Amin
Ted Epperly
Tonya L. Fancher
Nicole Franks
Monique Gary
Leila E. Harrison (née Diaz)
Dionne Hart
Catherine Havemann
Sandra E. Hodgin
Jessica Elizabeth Isom
Brittani James
Camara Phyllis Jones
Deena Kishawi
Alden Landry
Rosa Lee
Itzel López-Hinojosa
Mario Lorenzana De Witt
Monica Lypson
Jasmine R. Marcelin
Roselande Marcellon
Aletha Maybank
William McDade
David F. McIntosh
Lisa M. Meeks
Priya M. Mehta
Christopher J. Moreland
Linda Rae Murray
Sunny Nakae
Mytien Nguyen
Oluwaferanmi O. Okanlami
Jamieson O'Marr
Pilar Ortega
Holly Pilson
Susan M. Pollart
Vidhya Prakash
Maria J. Ruiz
Nelson Sánchez
Maurice Sholas
Julie K. Silver
Bonnie Simpson Mason
Jill Strachan-Batson
Nichole Taylor
Monica Taylor-Desir
Monica Vela
Iris Vuong
Valencia P. Walker
Tracy Wallowicz
Chana Weinstock
Sidney S. Welch
Siobhan Wescott
J. Corey Williams
Tyree M.S. Winters
Clyde W. Yancy

CONTENTS

Dedication .... *v*
Acknowledgments .... *vii*
Disclaimer .... *ix*
Foreword: Jerome Adams, MD, MPH .... *xi*
Foreword: Regina M. Benjamin, MD, MBA .... *xiii*
Introducing A Guide: Why We Wrote It and How to Use It ... *xv*
List of Contributors .... *xix*

SECTION 1: HISTORICAL FOUNDATIONS AND BASIC PRINCIPLES OF DIVERSITY, EQUITY, AND INCLUSION IN GRADUATE MEDICAL EDUCATION

1. The Intersection of Race in Medicine: A Difficult Past, a Challenging Future 5
2. Naming Racism and Moving to Action 13
3. Intersectionality: A Framework for Advancing Patient and Professional Equity in Medicine 21
4. Geographic Location as a Determinant of Health 29
5. Building Institutional Cultures of Safety and Accountability to Support Graduate Medical Education 41
6. Federal Employment Laws: Resident and Fellow Rights and Institutional Accountability 51
7. Navigating the ACGME Institutional and Program Requirements for Due Process 61

SECTION 2: ON RACIAL AND ETHNIC EXPERIENCES IN GRADUATE MEDICAL EDUCATION

8. American Indian and Alaska Native Presence in Medicine 79
9. Asian, Pacific Islander, Native Hawaiian and Asian Pacific Islander American Experience 89
10. Aspects of the Black Experience in Graduate Medical Education 97
11. The Graduate Medical Education Experience of Individuals Who Identify as Latino, Hispanic, or of Spanish Origin 107
12. Reimagining Graduate Medical Education by Contextualizing "Whiteness" 115
13. Health Disparities in Correctional Medicine and the Justice-Involved Population: Impact on Physician Education and Training 123

SECTION 3: ETHNOCULTURAL, IMMIGRANT, MULTILINGUAL, AND RELIGIOUS EXPERIENCES IN GRADUATE MEDICAL EDUCATION

14. Building an Inclusive Environment for Residents and Fellows from First-Generation College Graduate and Low-Income Backgrounds 135
15. Pathways to Graduate Medical Education for Foreign National Physicians and DACA Recipients 143
16. Creating an Inclusive Environment for Multilingual Learners and Faculty Members 153
17. Creating Inclusive Environments for Muslim Residents and Fellows 163
18. Creating Inclusive Environments for Orthodox Jewish Learners in Graduate Medical Education 173

SECTION 4: GENDER AND SEXUAL IDENTITY, DISABILITY, AND AGE IN GRADUATE MEDICAL EDUCATION

19 Women in Academic Medicine: Optimizing Equity, Inclusion, and Belonging 187
20 Transgender and Gender-Diverse Patients, Physician Learners, Clinicians, and Staff: Improving Inclusion, Equity, and Belonging 197
21 Inclusion and Health Equity for Sexual Minorities................................... 209
22 Creating Inclusive Working and Learning Climates for Residents and Fellows with Disabilities in Graduate Medical Education........................... 217
23 Remaining Inclusive of and Supporting Non-traditionally Aged Residents 231

Glossary... *239*
Index *247*

Historical Foundations and Basic Principles of Diversity, Equity, and Inclusion in Graduate Medical Education

Linda Rae Murray, MD, MPH, Retired Chief Medical Officer, Cook County Department of Public Health; Adjunct Assistant Professor, University of Illinois School of Public Health

Aletha Maybank, MD, MPH, Senior Vice President and Chief Health Equity Officer, American Medical Association

Helen Burstin, MD, MPH, MACP, Chief Executive Officer, Council of Medical Specialty Societies

Allison Cox-Simpson, MA, Diversity, Equity, Inclusion Communications Liaison, Accreditation Council for Graduate Medical Education

More than 20 years have passed since the publication of *To Err Is Human,*[1] *Crossing the Quality Chasm,*[2] and *Unequal Treatment: Confronting Racial and Ethnic Disparities in Health Care*[3]—landmark reports by the Institute of Medicine using rich empirical data and extending urgent messages for everyone working in health care quality and equity. In these 20-plus intervening years since their publication, significant progress has been made in addressing health care quality; yet, to considerable dismay among clinicians and patients alike, the same cannot be said for reducing inequities in health care.

In particular, the fundamental issue raised in *Unequal Treatment*—the differences in care received by racially and ethnically minoritized patients—continues to plague the US health care system. *Unequal Treatment* emphasized that differences in the quality of care provided to minoritized patients were driven largely by discrimination (including biases, prejudices, and harmful stereotypes) as well as the operation of the health care system, together with the legal and regulatory climates at the time. Today, however, significant inequities in major indicators of health and health care continue. While a more nuanced appreciation of the social and structural drivers of health has been developed, only 20% of a person's health is attributable to health care services, and factors such as community-level social determinants of health (including poverty and the physical environment) and health behaviors (themselves constrained by context) drive the vast majority of adverse outcomes. Strong and persistent correlations exist among poverty, place, and all-cause mortality in the United States.

Section One of *A Guide* explores the historical, conceptual, and geographic underpinnings of race, gender, and other domains of diversity in medicine so that practicing physicians, residents, and fellows—and those responsible for the clinical and learning environments in which they treat patients—grasp the reasons why certain practices, policies, and procedures have been and continue to be based on systems of oppression of minoritized and marginalized groups. Societal influences, including racism, homophobia, sexism, isolationism, ableism, among other destructive "-isms," may result in reduced opportunities for affected individuals in the graduate medical education (GME) setting. The chapters in this section provide the context for why, in particular, these groups matter in GME.

The concepts presented in *A Guide* are grounded in a commitment to equity derived from the framework for equity developed by Camara Jones, MD *(see Chapter 2)* that calls for assurance of the conditions for an optimal educational environment in GME extending to all learners, faculty members, and staff. Dr Jones' framework requires valuing all individuals and populations equally, recognizing and rectifying historical injustices, and providing resources according to need.[4]

As presented in the introduction to this volume, diversity, equity, inclusion (DEI), and antiracism are terms that are foundational to the forthcoming work. Taking those foundational concepts as a starting point, the chapters encourage readers to explore their understanding more deeply. Furthermore, these concepts should be viewed as part of a continuum of understanding and learning rather than as a fixed goal.

Subsequently, those who treat and those who lead can and will identify opportunities to identify, rectify, and dismantle current and ongoing inequities in medical education and in health care delivery today. With a new level of enlightenment based on facts and data, this first section highlights the rationale for understanding the concept of privilege and examining implicit bias. When developing curricula for learners, the fundamental principles in these chapters form the bedrock of understanding why we treat people differently, based on their identities and the impact of such treatment when understanding is biased, stereotyped, or flawed in other negative ways.

* * *

Chapter 1: The Intersection of Race in Medicine: A Difficult Past, a Challenging Future
Priya M. Mehta, MD; Clyde W. Yancy, MD, MSc

Data continually point to disparities in access to and delivery of health care as well as to social determinants of health; these disparities start early in the lives of Black persons. Yancy and Mehta describe the impact of history on medical education and the physician workforce along with its implications for the delivery of patient care. Beginning with the adverse impact of the Flexner report on the closure of minority-serving medical schools, the Tuskegee experiment, the painful story of Henrietta Lacks, and through to the COVID-19 pandemic, they reflect on the false accommodation of race in medicine.

The authors point to structural racism as the source of why and how these inequities develop at the community level, also pointing to the fact that not every racial or ethnic difference qualifies as a disparity. However, when bias, prejudice, or stereotyping exists, these factors affect how systems are configured and how decisions are made, thus resulting in the racial disparities that are exemplified throughout the case studies in *A Guide*. Their recommendations focus on how systemic decisions should not rely on diversity itself as being the solution, but rather they suggest that diversity of thought and leadership, nurtured during the formative years for physician learners, will result in lasting change so that effective solutions for these complex problems may gradually emerge and take hold.

Chapter 2: Naming Racism and Moving to Action
Brittani James, MD; Camara Phyllis Jones, MD, MPH, PhD; J. Corey Williams, MD, MA

James et al expand on the history of race in US medicine and medical education in Chapter 1 by using the framework of the contributing author, Dr Jones, to conceptualize the understanding of racism. They provide definitions for the forms of racism and other key terms that will prove useful as the reader progresses through each section of *A Guide*.

The Healing ARC (*acknowledgment, redress, closure*) Network and institutional strategies for antiracist change described by the authors support efforts to move toward equity for physician learners as well as for patients. Making firm commitments, recognizing history at work both in the wider environment and at a local level, and identifying the shift from race-based to race-conscious medicine, are among the practical strategies they suggest for "moving to action" in eliminating bias and targeting structural racism rather than only emphasizing individual-level interventions.

Chapter 3: Intersectionality: A Framework for Advancing Patient and Professional Equity in Medicine
Oluwaferanmi O. Okanlami, MD, MS; Valencia P. Walker, MD, MPH, FAAP

Building on Chapters 1 and 2, Okanlami and Walker continue to raise awareness of the effects of discrimination perpetuated by structural racism in the clinical learning environment by introducing the conceptual framework of intersectionality. Those medical students, residents, and fellows often marginalized in medicine also have intersecting marginalized identities that make them especially vulnerable as the following chapters in *A Guide* will proceed to describe. The authors also use the concept of Professional Identity Formation (PIF) to illustrate how societal and cultural beliefs can be normalized around a very small range of identity and expression. Marginalized residents and fellows often find themselves excluded from support networks open to their peers or even doubting their own professional identity in medicine, an experience that can affect them both personally and professionally throughout their years in practice, exemplified in other chapters throughout *A Guide*.

Evaluating and addressing the institutional climate of culture and belonging, engaging in discussions about redefining professionalism, and tracking progress about the intersection of multiple identities among cohorts of physician learners are among the strategies proposed by the authors to include intersectionality and PIF in local efforts to address racism in its many forms, address disparities and inequities, and create more inclusive learning environments.

Chapter 4: Geographic Location as a Determinant of Health
David Ansell, MD, MPH; Ted Epperly, MD

The influence of geography should not be overlooked as a possible determinant of health outcomes. Ansell and Epperly focus on the impact of location on health for both rural/frontier and urban areas, providing examples from both and comparing similarities and differences between them. Lack of timely access to medical and behavioral health care in either area increases morbidity and mortality, demonstrated by data related to acute, chronic, preventive, and maternal/neonatal conditions. Geography can also intersect with race and poverty to influence health outcomes. The authors provide valuable information to assist programs in helping physician learners understand how Health Professional Shortage areas and Medically Underserved areas are defined and how they impact the health status of their respective socially, racially, and economically isolated populations.

The authors also outline the important implications that recognizing the challenges of providing health care in rural, frontier, and underserved urban or exurban areas has for GME. They provide potential solutions for how to address the need for GME curricula that aims to enhance population health outcomes defined and influenced by geography.

Chapter 5: Building Institutional Cultures of Safety and Accountability to Support Graduate Medical Education
Nicole Franks, MD; Jessica Elizabeth Isom, MD; Sunny Nakae, PhD, MSW; Bonnie Simpson Mason, MD

Defining key concepts of quality, safety, well-being, and equity is central to understanding and assessing their impact on the clinical learning environment and on entire institutional culture. Franks et al continue the discussion of the principles of DEI and antiracism in this section by characterizing a safe and equitable institutional culture that extends beyond medical education and to the well-being of the health care workforce. At a time when issues such as clinician shortages, learner attrition, and death by suicide are growing concerns in the health care workforce, the authors show how these challenges must be examined and addressed, especially in GME.

The authors also demonstrate how addressing disparities and inequities in GME, in health care institutions, and in health care delivery is central to building a safe and equitable learning environment for all physician learners and central to the message of each chapter in *A Guide*.

Chapter 6: Federal Employment Laws: Resident and Fellow Rights and Institutional Accountability
Sandra E. Hodgin, PhD, MEd; Anne Knox Averitt, JD

The clinical learning environment also presents a context in which physician learners are employees. The work by Hodgin and Averitt demonstrates how, by protecting employees' federal rights, Sponsoring Institutions and GME programs build the institutional cultures of safety and accountability described in Chapter 5. Such cultures support residents' and fellows' well-being and their ability to thrive in the physician workforce. Equitable application of basic employment laws and the best practices by institutions noted by the authors also exemplify DEI principles of inclusivity and equity central to improving the clinical learning environment for physician learners and patients alike.

Chapter 7: Navigating the ACGME Institutional and Program Requirements for Due Process
Sidney S. Welch, JD, MPH

Through its Institutional and Common Program Requirements, the ACGME sets and monitors voluntary professional educational standards. In particular, due process standards relate to processes of resident promotion, appointment renewal, and dismissal for GME programs and Sponsoring Institutions in the United States. They are designed to protect the rights of residents and fellows as employees and as physician learners in educational settings. Within this section, Welch outlines the GME processes leading to discipline or termination of resident contracts, the role of the ACGME, and practical advice for institutional and program leadership to consider before and during these processes. This chapter is also of value to physician learners to build awareness of their rights, as well as to be aware of their responsibilities, during these critical processes in GME. As in the case of the federal regulations described in Chapter 6, each of these processes, when applied to local situations in compliance with the Requirements, provides assurance of fairness. In turn, that fairness supports confidence in an equitable and inclusive clinical learning environment where residents' and fellows' voices are respected, even during times when they feel vulnerable.

REFERENCES

1. Institute of Medicine (US) Committee on Quality of Health Care in America; Kohn LT, Corrigan J, Donaldson MS, eds. *To Err Is Human: Building a Safer Health System*. National Academies Press; 2000. https://www.ncbi.nlm.nih.gov/books/NBK225182.
2. Institute of Medicine (US) Committee on Quality of Health Care in America. *Crossing the Quality Chasm: A New Health System for the 21st Century*. National Academies Press; 2001.
3. Institute of Medicine (US) Committee on Understanding and Eliminating Racial and Ethnic Disparities in Health Care; Smedley BD, Stith AY, Nelson AR, eds. *Unequal Treatment: Confronting Racial and Ethnic Disparities in Health Care*. National Academies Press; 2003.
4. Jones CP. Systems of power, axes of inequity: parallels, intersections, braiding the strands. *Med Care*. 2014;52(10 Suppl):S71-S75. doi: 10.1097/mlr.0000000000000216.

The Intersection of Race in Medicine: A Difficult Past, a Challenging Future

Priya M. Mehta, MD, Internal Medicine, Northwestern University Feinberg School of Medicine, Chicago, IL

Clyde W. Yancy, MD, MSc, Vice Dean for Diversity and Inclusion, Chief of the Division of Cardiology, Northwestern University Feinberg School of Medicine, Chicago, IL

CHAPTER SUMMARY

This chapter examines race in medicine, its historical context, and its impact on health care disparities. We begin by emphasizing the known and difficult history of race in medicine. This history not only impacts clinical outcomes but especially the experience of racialized groups in medical research, education, and practice. Our chapter highlights the necessity for graduate medical education (GME) to address the critical and continuous examination of race in health care and to make a firm commitment not only to address health care disparities but also to work toward attaining health equity.

LEARNING OBJECTIVES

1. Describe the historical intersection of race and medicine.
2. Recognize the impact of structural bias on health care disparities.
3. Evaluate the role of bias, implicit and explicit, in community health outcomes.
4. Propose strategies to address the intersection of race and medicine in GME.

Case Study

As the medical team begins pre-rounds for the day, the senior resident, Lily, arrives and informs the first-year resident, Jessica, that she will be picking up the overnight admission. Jessica begins reading about her new patient who presents to the hospital for a recurrent heart failure exacerbation. Upon reading the patient's history of present illness, she notes this is the patient's third hospitalization for the same problem in 2 months. She discusses the medical case with her third-year medical student, Bryan, and directs him to interview the patient prior to presenting on rounds with the attending. Bryan asks the patient if he has been taking his diuretic agents and the patient responds that he missed four doses over the past week.

On morning rounds, Bryan presents his assessment and plan for his new patient. When discussing the trigger for the patient's recurrent heart failure exacerbation, Bryan concludes that the patient was non-compliant with his diuretic agents, low-salt diet, and the goal-directed medical therapies with which he was discharged during his last hospitalization. After Bryan concludes his presentation, the team enters the patient's room. Jessica asks

(continued)

if she could try to obtain some additional history from the patient herself and the patient and team agree. Jessica asks the patient why he has not been taking his diuretics; what his understanding is of the purpose for the diuretics; whether he can afford his medications; whether he has the capability to pick them up from the pharmacy; and if he has grocery stores near him to buy fresh food. The patient demonstrates medical literacy and understands that he needs the diuretics to maintain his volume status. He explains, however, that he has been skipping doses to make the medications last longer because he cannot afford to keep buying them. Further, he notes that although he tries to maintain a low-salt diet, there is only one grocery store in his neighborhood that is too expensive for him, and fast food is substantially cheaper.

The team finishes obtaining the remainder of the subjective and exits the room. Bryan feels embarrassed that he dismissed the patient as non-compliant without realizing his social situation. Jessica shares that she volunteered at a free student clinic while attending a minority-serving medical school. During this time, she cared for a significant number of patients who were unable to afford their medications or a healthy lifestyle, which led to disproportionately higher rates of recurrent hospitalization and poor patient outcomes. Jessica then reassures Bryan that every patient is a learning opportunity and commends him on his self-reflection and plan to perform a more thorough history in the future. The team calls a social work consult for the patient and sets a goal for the remainder of the month to identify how every patient's social context affects their medical care.

Case Discussion

Black or African American patients suffer disproportionately higher rates of heart failure incidence, hospitalization rates, and mortality rates. Epidemiological studies propose that the root cause of these disparities in heart failure are grounded in structural racism, emerging early in life for Black persons and further magnified by social determinants of health as well as a disparity in the access to and the delivery of care.[1] This case not only demonstrates the importance of understanding how racial disparities impact medical outcomes; it also highlights the critical value of a diverse medical team that intentionally maintains awareness of a patient's social context. In this chapter, we explore root causes of disparate care and health inequities and bring attention to pathways forward. For established care providers, much of this movement forward requires an active process of unlearning, but for residents and fellows, these strategies offer an opportunity to effectively address health care disparities and health inequities and more importantly, to pre-empt future disparate care.

INTRODUCTION

Individuals from racially and ethnically minoritized communities remain underrepresented in GME relative to their proportion in the general population.[2] The lack of diversity in GME drives a resulting lesser presence in medicine and life sciences and leads to a dearth of diverse ideation. Lack of diverse perspectives, in turn, leads to the perpetuation of adverse historical events limiting health and health outcomes in minoritized communities. While bias and racism are phenomena experienced at a personal and direct level, they can also occur at an institutional and educational level. To effectively address these structural issues,

GME must prioritize equity in medicine. Such conversations are far-reaching, with societal, medical, and educational implications.

The historical context behind race in medicine, driven by significant events, establishes a space for discussion about our past but also points to how these events impact the culture of health care as we know it today. This historical context impacts clinical health outcomes, defines the experience of racialized groups in medical research, and accentuates the invaluable role of GME to provide guidance for health care and research. Without understanding the path already traversed, the fate of GME is likely to replicate the past and miss the opportunity to lessen the health care gap caused by disparities and to work toward equity.

HISTORICAL EVENTS

Throughout history, the struggles of race in medicine mirror those in the greater society. The historical legacy of racism in medicine, exemplified by events like the closure of minority-serving medical schools following the Flexner Report of 1910, continues to shape the current lack of diversity in the health care workforce. Ostensibly serving to raise the educational standards for medical education, the Flexner Report had an outsized negative effect on GME sourced by minority serving medical schools. Prior to the Flexner Report, a host of minority-serving medical schools in the US were deemed suitable by contemporary scholars. However, an outcome of the otherwise transformative Flexner Report was an act by fiat to close all but two of these institutions. The premise of lesser academic standards was never validated, but the generational impact of the disproportionate closure of minority-serving medical schools persisted for decades to follow. Using conservative estimates of missed opportunities, investigators found a deficit of *35,000 physicians* in the 20th century alone, with almost certain carryover into the 21st century. It is not an unreasonable supposition that this core of physicians might have capably served minority communities providing a buffer against disparate care and serving as leaders to advocate for health and health equity.

Understanding the racialized context behind historical decisions such as the Flexner Report is imperative. By definition, racism is a belief that "all members of each race possess characteristics or abilities specific to that race, especially so as to distinguish it as inferior or superior to another race or races."[3] The archetype of racism yields several actualized dimensions. Of those several dimensions, the one most relevant to GME is institutional racism whereby systemic models, usually preserved by infrastructure and leadership hierarchies, provide advantages to one group while disadvantaging another group. Once these structures are cemented in the ecosystem of institutions, the pernicious and lingering effects of racism persist, and result in intransigent inequities in health and outsized vulnerability to diseases with overtly disparate health outcomes.

The result of applying these scholarly definitions, however, is cerebral; "racism" is a disruptive and emotive term. Historical events have repeatedly proven this fact, demonstrating the painful intersection between race and medicine and among the most notable: the Tuskegee experiment.[4] This egregious experiment intentionally exposed unknowing Black men and their families to untreated syphilis as a natural history exercise to ascertain the consequences of syphilitic infection. The full gamut of cardiovascular and neurological disease occurred with infections transmitted to spouses and next generation family members. Progeny of the descendants of the Tuskegee experiment *remain alive* and offer a living history of one of the darkest chapters in the public health history of the US. The wound of mistrust impacts not only the willingness of under represented minorities to participate in research but also a skepticism for all things emanating from medicine.

The story of the HeLa cells demonstrates yet another painful chapter in the history of American medicine.[5] Cells harvested from Henrietta Lacks at the time of her cervical cancer diagnosis, and without her informed consent, were noted to perpetually divide ex vivo—a previously unrecognized phenomenon and an opportune resource to facilitate the study of cancer at the cellular level. Yet, Ms Lacks never agreed to such use of her cells and not until long after her death was this unauthorized use made known to her family. While these cells have been an extraordinary resource for life sciences and biomedical investigators and pivotal in a number of life-enhancing research discoveries, the unauthorized use of her cells has been a stain on the enterprise of research.

These chapters in the history of US medicine clearly delineate a challenged and regrettable history, and a disingenuous accommodation of race in medicine.

LESSONS FROM COVID-19

The COVID-19 pandemic of 2020-2022 exposed important evidence of deeply embedded health inequities resulting in historic disparities. Data aggregated throughout the pandemic by the American Public Media Research Lab identified the burden of deaths due to COVID-19 by race and ethnicity. The early phase data suggested that as many as 1 in every 264 Black or African American residents (or 379 deaths per 100,000) in the US died due to COVID-19.[6] These deaths were largely attributable to health inequities and poor access to care at the community level.

Through mid-May 2023, nationwide crude mortality rates from COVID-19 data (aggregated from all available US states and the District of Columbia) for all race groups since the start of the pandemic showed that Indigenous, Hispanic/Latinx, Pacific Islander, and Black Americans all had significantly higher COVID-19 age-adjusted mortality rates than either White or Asian Americans, particularly early in the pandemic and at the height of vulnerability.[7] No racial group has been spared but some groups have been disproportionately impacted, showing a repetition of our country's known history of inequity in health and health outcomes. COVID-19 exposed deep fissures in the life and living circumstances of many and especially those living in minoritized communities. Infections due to COVID-19 disproportionately impacted African Americans and served as a bellwether event illuminating the extent of health and health care inequities. There could be no more poignant starting point to yield further conversations about the origin of these health care disparities in the past and how they affect contemporary events today. GME holds an enormous duty to seize this teachable moment and enlighten generations to come about the intersection of race and medicine and the association of poor health with disease vulnerability and measurement of disparate health outcomes.

UNDERSTANDING DISPARITIES

The National Academy of Medicine defines **health disparities** as racial or ethnic differences in health care that are not due to access related factors, clinical needs, patient preferences, or the appropriateness of the intervention.[8] It is not simply the difference between groups, as evident differences are at times appropriate and not every difference as a function of race or ethnicity qualifies as a disparity. A disparity between groups is appropriately recognized when bias, prejudice, or stereotyping affects how a system is configured or how decisions are made.

Similarly, it is imperative to broaden our viewpoint and understand why health care inequity develops at the community level. This inequity is often derived from **structural bias or racism**, which as defined by the Aspen Institute, is a system in which public policies, institutional practices, cultural representations, and other norms work in various, often reinforcing ways, to perpetuate racial group inequity.[8]

This concept is clearly illustrated by the historical phenomenon of "**redlining**." After World War I, a housing crisis developed in the US. To combat this, the Home Owners' Loan Corporation was developed in the 1930s with seemingly good intentions to assign credit worthiness to different communities and to ultimately determine allotment of federally backed mortgages. A red line circumscribed those communities deemed to have the lowest credit worthiness. Unfortunately, this practice was heavily influenced by segregation, with the city of Chicago as a case in point.[9] Because of fierce segregation, Black or African American citizens emigrated into higher credit risk communities, which were later the target of social disinvestment yielding an environment prone to poor health variables and vulnerable to high-risk diseases. It is presumed these circumstances underpinned the dramatic disproportionate early mortality due to COVID-19 in formerly red-lined communities in Chicago and elsewhere. Such an overt example is a necessary case study to provoke discussion and ideate new policies addressing health communities. Incorporating such content in future GME curricula might raise awareness regarding structural bias and mitigate future outsized vulnerabilities.

EXAMINING SOCIAL RISK IN COMMUNITIES

There are various ways to understand the risk profile of communities. One of the emerging schemes is to consider the Social Vulnerability Index.[10] Aggregated from 15 variables in the US census, this index is intended to identify those communities with deep resilience for external disruptions, such as the pandemic, or those communities that have great vulnerability. The scale ranges from zero, or communities with the greatest resilience and lowest vulnerability, to one, or communities with the lowest resilience and highest vulnerability. Similarly, the Area Deprivation Index[11] and Distressed Communities Index[12] allow for rankings and comparisons of communities by socioeconomic disadvantage and can be used to inform health delivery and policy. These several indices represent yet another educational opportunity for GME and allow conversations to extend beyond the rather vague model of "the social construct" and delve into a more detailed discussion of the social determinants of health and the use of various scoring paradigms.

RETHINKING THE USE OF RACE IN MEDICINE: STRATEGIES AND RECOMMENDATIONS FOR GME

The history of race in medicine, though difficult to revisit, is important to comprehend as it drives so much of health and health care. Now is not the time to use a muted voice about this history, but instead, to overtly recognize the history and use GME as a platform to raise awareness. However, an important question remains for consideration by all with an investment in GME, and in turn health equity: how should we use race in medicine?

It is important to appropriately calibrate how we use race in medical research. We believe the most pressing reason to maintain race in the conversation is to allow for continual investigation of existing health inequities; however, race is not a proxy for biology, nor a proxy for genetics; it is a poor proxy for the social construct. Genomic studies, *independent of race,* identify the limited but appropriate genetic markers pertaining to ancestry and associated with diseases, but such studies are not the default; rather, genomic associations are separate analyses based on appropriate genetic risk assessment and subsequent screening.[13] Importantly, the emerging social variables as discussed previously are measurable (eg, Social Vulnerability Index) and allow a semi-quantitative assessment of the burden of risk. This interconnectedness of health and society as demonstrated by COVID-19 infection reflects a new public health reality.

Table 1.1 summarizes the prior descriptions chronicling both the history and consequences of race in medicine.

Table 1.1 History and Consequences of Race in Medicine

Historical Event	Description	Impact on Racial Disparities
Flexner Report (1910)	Closed many minority-serving medical schools	Reduced diversity in health care workforce, perpetuating disparities
Tuskegee Experiment	Unethical study withholding treatment from Black men with syphilis	Eroded trust in medical research among minority communities
HeLa Cells Case	Henrietta Lacks' cells used in research without informed consent	Raised ethical concerns about exploitation in medical research

It is important to ascertain how communities move forward toward health equity. Table 1.2 summarizes suggested strategies to support our belief that diversity in medical education enabled by GME can pave the way forward.

Diversity, not in and of itself as a solution, but as a means of diversity of thought and leadership, ultimately enables new policies and designs new systems.[16] With explicit steps to correct the inequities in the workforce, a more diverse workforce may allow for more diverse ideas to be considered, offer opportunities for more diverse leadership to evolve, and help create policies that reflect the emerging diversity of the communities in which we live. It is a major challenge since the most important pivot is culture change. Such change will all take time, but no effective solution for any complex problem is either simple or quick.

> Health equity is the inarguable goal and requires an active process of unlearning and relearning best strategies to practice intentional inclusion and leverage diverse ideation.

> The COVID-19 pandemic magnified health disparities for racially and ethnically minoritized groups, presenting a key recent example of the intersection of race and medicine and its impact on population health outcomes.

Table 1.2 Strategies to Support Diversity in Medical Education

Strategy	Example
1. Review the GME curriculum and evaluate content that addresses race per se and social determinants of health.	Emphasize incorporation of social determinants of health in patient assessments, including both the history and physical documentation and within the electronic health record.
2. Review clinical practice algorithms, in partnership with clinical services where residents/fellows rotate, and critically evaluate and, when possible, expunge race-based algorithms for care or risk assessment.	The Critical Appraisal of Race in Medical Literature (CARMeL) tool was developed for teaching physician learners to critically evaluate the literature for race-based algorithms.[14] The AHA PREVENT CVD risk assessment tool is now race-agnostic.[15]
3. Incorporate critical appraisal of clinical practice algorithms as well as historically expunged race-based algorithms into medical education conferences.	Create a longitudinal weekly noon conference schedule on critical appraisal of clinical practice algorithms as well as other subjects within diversity, equity, and inclusion (DEI).
4. Incorporate holistic review practices for resident/fellow recruitment to identify individuals aligned with the program and institutional mission.	Emphasize narrative construct of life journeys and the impact of either a marginalized or minoritized acculturation on medical education and institutional mission.
5. Create mentorship and leadership opportunities within DEI for residents/fellows to further advocate, educate, and engage the institutional and greater medical community on the intersection of race in medicine.	A program can inquire interest in DEI engagement upon candidate matriculation, and subsequently assign a mentor with similar interests or background.

Data from Khan SS, Coresh J, Pencina MJ, et al. Novel prediction equations for absolute risk assessment of total cardiovascular disease incorporating cardiovascular-kidney-metabolic health: a scientific statement from the American Heart Association. *Circulation.* 2023;148(24):1982-2004. doi: 10.1161/CIR.0000000000001191

Take Home Points

- Race is a social construct and does not infer biology.
- Social models are measurables; when appropriate, genetic analyses, independent of race/ethnicity, may further illuminate differences in disease.
- Active education, including GME, affords an opportunity to highlight the importance of persistent health inequities and the necessity for meaningful interventions.

QUESTIONS FOR FURTHER THOUGHT

1. What are the short- and long-term outcomes for Black or African American patients suffering from heart failure? Consider another disease or condition in your practice and describe whether and how race and medicine have historically intersected with regard to the outcomes for patients.
2. In what ways does your GME program and clinical learning environment currently apply race-based algorithms in education or clinical practice? In what ways have those algorithms been examined, revisited, or edited over time?

Acknowledgments
We would like to thank the ACGME for providing a forum to host major discussions addressing the role of GME in narrowing disparities and working towards health equity.

REFERENCES

1. Roger VL. Epidemiology of heart failure: a contemporary perspective. *Circ Res.* 2021;128(10):1421-1434. doi:10.1161/CIRCRESAHA.121.318172
2. Mabeza RM, Christophers B, Ederaine SA, Glenn EJ, Benton-Slocum ZP, Marcelin JR. Interventions associated with racial and ethnic diversity in us graduate medical education: a scoping review. *JAMA Netw Open.* 2023;6(1):e2249335. doi:10.1001/jamanetworkopen.2022.49335
3. Clair M, Denis JS. Sociology of racism. In: Wright JD, ed. *The International Encyclopedia of the Social and Behavioral Sciences.* Vol. 19. Elsevier;2015:857-863.
4. Mcvean A. 40 Years of Human Experimentation in America: The Tuskegee Study. Office for Science and Society; McGill University. Published January 25, 2019. Accessed June 5, 2023. https://www.mcgill.ca/oss/article/history/40-years-human-experimentation-america-tuskegee-study
5. Skloot R. *The Immortal Life of Henrietta Lacks.* Crown Publishers; 2010.
6. APM Research Lab. The color of coronavirus: COVID-19 deaths analyzed by race and ethnicity in the U.S.: key findings. APM Research Lab. Updated October 19, 2023. https://www.apmresearchlab.org/covid/deaths-by-race
7. Institute of Medicine (US) Committee on Understanding and Eliminating Racial and Ethnic Disparities in Health Care. *Unequal Treatment: Confronting Racial and Ethnic Disparities in Health Care.* In: Smedley BD, Stith AY, Nelson AR, eds. National Academies Press; 2003.
8. The Aspen Institute. Glossary for Understanding the Dismantling Structural Racism/Promoting Racial Equity Analysis. Accessed June 5, 2023. https://www.aspeninstitute.org/wp-content/uploads/files/content/docs/rcc/RCC-Structural-Racism-Glossary.pdf
9. Nightengale CH. *Segregation: A Global History of Divided Cities.* University of Chicago Press; 2012.
10. Agency for Toxic Substances and Disease Registry. CDC/ATSDR Social Vulnerability Index. Last reviewed June 14, 2024. Accessed June 5, 2023. https://www.atsdr.cdc.gov/placeandhealth/svi/index.html
11. Center for Health Disparities Research; University of Wisconsin School of Medicine and Public Health. About the Neighborhood Atlas®. Accessed June 5, 2023. https://www.neighborhoodatlas.medicine.wisc.edu
12. Economic Innovation Group. Distressed Communities Index. Accessed June 5, 2023. https://eig.org/distressed-communities/

13. Ioannidis JPA, Powe NR, Yancy C. Recalibrating the use of race in medical research. *JAMA*. 2021;325(7):623-624. doi:10.1001/jama.2021.0003
14. Garvey A, Lynch G, Mansour M, Coyle A, Gard S, Truglio J. From race to racism: teaching a tool to critically appraise the use of race in medical research. *MedEdPORTAL*. 2022;18:11210. doi:10.15766/mep_2374-8265.11210
15. Khan SS, Coresh J, Pencina MJ, et al. Novel prediction equations for absolute risk assessment of total cardiovascular disease incorporating cardiovascular-kidney-metabolic health: a scientific statement from the American Heart Association. *Circulation*. 2023;148(24):1982-2004. doi: 10.1161/CIR.0000000000001191
16. Gomez LE, Bernet P. Diversity improves performance and outcomes. *J Natl Med Assoc*. 2019;111(4):383-392. doi:10.1016/j.jnma.2019.01.006

Naming Racism and Moving to Action

Brittani James, MD, Medical Director, Inner City Muslim Action Network, Site Medical Director, Insight Hospital Internal Medicine Residency, Chicago, IL

Camara Phyllis Jones, MD, MPH, PhD, 2021-2022 UCSF Presidential Chair, University of California, San Francisco, CA

J. Corey Williams, MD, MA, Assistant Professor of Clinical Psychiatry, Co-Director of Recruitment, Retention, and Development, Medstar-Georgetown University Hospital, Washington, DC

CHAPTER SUMMARY

Racial health disparities in the US are longstanding and well-documented. Despite this fact, and in the context of overall improvements in population health over time, many disparities have not only remained persistent, but in some instances, have widened. For many, racism is primarily understood to exist as interpersonal instances of prejudice and discrimination based on race. While accurate, understandings such as these fail to adequately capture the complexity of racism. In this chapter, we aim to help graduate medical education (GME) leaders understand the structural nature of racism and its impact on population health. We will highlight key examples of structural racism within health care and provide strategies for antiracist change within GME programs and their health care institutions.

LEARNING OBJECTIVES

1. Define internalized, interpersonal, and structural racism.
2. Identify manifestations of structural racism within and outside of health care.
3. Develop strategies for antiracist change at the institutional level.

Case Study

Mr Moreno is a 36-year-old, Spanish-speaking male who identifies as Afro-Dominican. He arrives at his local emergency department with severe chest pain. The pain came on suddenly, about 5 hours earlier while he was rearranging some furniture in his home. It is accompanied by nausea, shortness of breath, and diaphoresis. Given the severity of his chest pain, Mr Moreno initially considered calling for an ambulance but changed his mind because he was worried about the cost. It took him several hours to find someone willing to drive him to the emergency department; the nearest one to his home was almost an hour away.

On arrival at the emergency department, Mr Moreno was seen by a triage nurse who evaluated him as "low acuity" because he did not appear uncomfortable. After waiting several hours, he was able to see a resident who spoke limited Spanish. Even so, Mr Moreno still had difficulty understanding some of the resident's questions and, as a result, was unable to share the exertional nature of his chest pain. Mr Moreno was not offered an interpreter. After performing a history and physical, blood work, and other testing, the resident concluded that Mr Moreno's chest pain was most likely musculoskeletal in origin. The resident wrote Mr Moreno a prescription

(continued)

for ibuprofen and advised him to follow up with his primary care physician in the next week. Mr Moreno failed to mention he did not currently have a primary care provider due to his lack of insurance. He felt concerned about finding a doctor so quickly. He also worried about finding transportation to an appointment, even if he was able to make one.

Case Discussion

Mr Moreno's experience highlights how structural racism can be found not only within the health care system, but also in other institutional forms that reinforces and compounds itself to create racial health inequities. Decades of racist laws and policies mean that Mr Moreno is more likely to live in an under-resourced community, which lacks health care resources such as a closer emergency department, access to fresh fruits and vegetables, and safe, walkable spaces that would support good baseline health. In instances where racially and ethnically minoritized people like Mr Moreno can access care, they are more likely to be uninsured, under-insured, or covered by a government program such as Medicare or Medicaid. The hospitals and clinics to which they have access are more likely to be underfunded than those attended by their White counterparts. Structural racism also means that Mr Moreno is less likely to have the financial resources to afford the cost of an ambulance, medication, or transportation to appointments and less likely to have reliable access to primary care. When it comes to the care he received, Mr Moreno is more likely to have his pain undervalued and less likely to receive analgesic medication for that pain. All these factors, and others, conspire to produce poor health in racially and ethnically minoritized people like Mr Moreno. As you review this chapter, consider what aspects of GME might be changed to ensure that Mr Moreno receives excellent quality care. Additionally, think about how your GME program prepares physicians to recognize and effectively address the health care needs of Mr Moreno and other patients in similar circumstances.

NAMING RACISM

Racial health disparities in the US are longstanding and well-documented. Despite this fact, and in the context of overall improvements in population health over time, many disparities have not only persisted, but in some instances, widened.[1] Data from the 2023 Kaiser Family Foundation Survey on Racism, Discrimination, and Health show that racially and ethnically minoritized people fared worse than their White counterparts across a range of health measures including infant mortality, prevalence of chronic disease, and overall physical and mental health (Figure 2.1).[2] Understanding and eradicating racism is critical to closing racial health gaps.

For many, racism is primarily understood to exist as interpersonal instances of prejudice and discrimination based on race. While accurate, such understandings fail to adequately capture the complexity of racism. In the context of health care, racism is more accurately described as a system of structuring opportunity and assigning value to communities based on the social interpretation of "how one looks"[3] that unfairly disadvantages some individuals and communities, and unfairly advantages other individuals. In this context, racial bias in our individual interactions should be understood to be a symptom of a more fundamental system of racism.

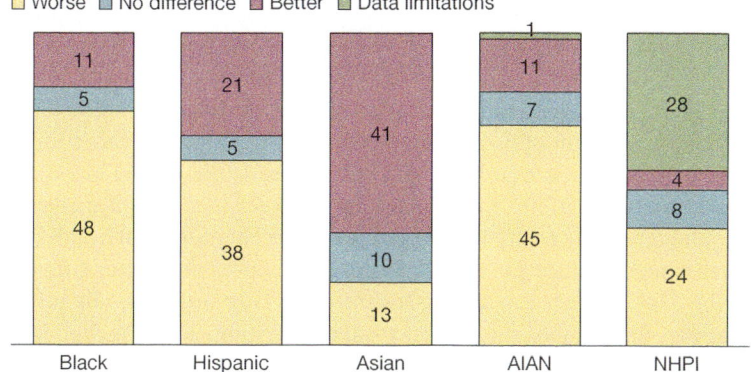

FIGURE 2.1 Number of health status measures for which racially and ethnically minoritized people fared better, the same, or worse compared to White counterparts. AIAN, American Indian or Alaskan Native; NHPI, Native Hawaiian or Pacific Islander. (Ndugga N, Hill L, Artiga S. *Key Facts on Health and Health Care by Race and Ethnicity*. Kaiser Family Foundation; 2024. Accessed June 23, 2024. https://www.kff.org/report-section/key-facts-on-health-and-health-care-by-race-and-ethnicity-health-coverage-and-access-to-and-use-of-care)

Racism saps the entire society. Given its scale and influence on health, it represents, perhaps, one of the largest public health crises of our time. It is incumbent upon each of us to dismantle it. First, however, we must learn to recognize when and how it is at work, including within GME programs and health care institutions.

THE LEVELS OF RACISM

In her key theoretical framework, Camara Phyllis Jones (2000) conceptualizes racism as existing in three forms: internalized, personally mediated, and institutionalized or structural.[4]

In her framework, Dr Jones defines **internalized racism** as acceptance of negative messages about their own abilities and intrinsic worth by members of the stigmatized races, and acceptance of the inherent superiority of their abilities and intrinsic worth by members of structurally advantaged races. Internalized racism by racially and ethnically minoritized people leads them to accept limitations on their full humanity. Internalized racism is significantly related to negative mental and physical health outcomes in racially and ethnically minoritized people. For example, internalized racism may contribute to poor health outcomes through demonstrating mental health symptoms of depression or anxiety, as well as limiting expectations to function with healthy behaviors based on racial group membership.[5]

Personally mediated or **interpersonal racism** is identified by Dr Jones as prejudice and discrimination, wherein **prejudice** means differential *assumptions* about the abilities, motives, and intentions of others according to their race, and **discrimination** indicates differential *actions* toward others according to their race. Examples include the disproportionate police brutality experienced by Black Americans and teacher devaluation of students of color.

Finally, Dr Jones describes **institutionalized** or **structural racism** as differential access to the goods, services, and opportunities of society by race including the disparate access to housing, education, employment opportunity, medical facilities, and other resources experienced by people of different races. Institutionalized racism explains the association between social class and "race."

Alternative frameworks describe institutional racism as occurring solely within institutions and systems of power such as schools or workplaces. In these cases, a fourth level of racism is often identified and described by the terms structural racism or systemic racism. Institutional, systemic, and structural racism all indicate forms of racism that are pervasively and deeply embedded in and throughout systems, laws, written or unwritten policies, entrenched practices, and established beliefs and attitudes that produce, condone, and perpetuate widespread unfair treatment of racially and ethnically minoritized people.[6] These terms—institutional, systemic, and structural racism—are often used interchangeably.

STRUCTURAL RACISM IN HEALTH CARE

Race-associated differences in health outcomes are a consistent feature of life in the US, despite the nation spending a disproportionate amount of its gross domestic product on health care compared to economically similar countries. Structural racism is the fundamental cause of these differences, since US health care policy advantages the White population—the racial group in power—and disadvantages racially and ethnically minoritized populations.[7] This reality is mirrored at the level of individual health care institutions and GME programs as well, since the rules, policies, practices, procedures, and cultural norms of these settings similarly advantage the White population and disadvantage racially and ethnically minoritized people. In this section, we will review key components of structural racism in medicine, including the propagation of biological racism, workforce diversity and career progression, and health care segregation.

Propagation of Biological Racism

Since the earliest days of America, scientific authority has been co-opted to justify racial inequity. Scientific or **biological racism** is the pseudoscientific belief that objective empirical evidence exists for races to be considered as biologically distinct entities. While modern scientific consensus rejects the notion that humankind can be divided into biologically distinct groups by race, nonetheless, race-based science continues to dominate medical research, education, and clinical practice.[8,9] Evidence of this finding is demonstrated by everything from racially tailored clinical practice guidelines such as the Eighth Joint National Committee (JNC 8) guidelines for hypertension in adults, to the implicit and explicit messages given to physician learners that certain racial groups are inherently diseased, to basic research studies that link race with biology, to the marketing of race-specific drugs, such as a brand name combination pill of isosorbide dinitrate and hydralazine.[10,11]

Workforce Diversity and Career Progression

The Flexner Report of 1910 not only transformed medical education by establishing the biomedical model as the gold standard for medical education but also had a direct negative impact on the success rate of historically Black medical schools.[12] It ultimately led to the closing of 7 out of 10 medical schools training Black doctors at the time, and a significant drop in the number of Black physicians produced in the US. History has shown little has occurred to alter the course of structurally racist policy stemming from the Flexner Report as well as other factors such as low-quality secondary education, limited financial support, and caustic educational environments. We continue to observe disproportionally low numbers of Black, Latino, Latina, Latinx, Latine, Hispanic, or Spanish (LHS+), and Native Americans applying to, getting accepted to, and graduating from health professional schools.[13] Furthermore, individuals underrepresented in medicine have high rates of attrition from their residency programs and are less likely to attain academic and general hospital leadership positions (Figure 2.2).[14,15]

Health Care Segregation

Similar to other forms of segregation, health care segregation was initially encoded into law. The 1963 US Supreme Court decision in *Simkins v. Moses H. Cone Memorial Hospital*, followed thereafter by *Cypress v. Newport News Hospital* in 1967, reaffirmed the federal government's application of Medicare certification guidelines to hospitals receiving government funds or utilizing Medicare or Medicaid in such a way that allowed for the slow process of hospital desegregation to begin.[16]

Although legal segregation of hospitals by race ended in 1967, it continues to exist, de facto, to this day. The racial segregation of the US hospital system is supported by the fee-for-service system, under which hospitals make higher profits for costly, high technology, specialist level care and receive higher reimbursements for patients with private insurance as compared to Medicare or Medicaid. As Black and LHS+ people are more

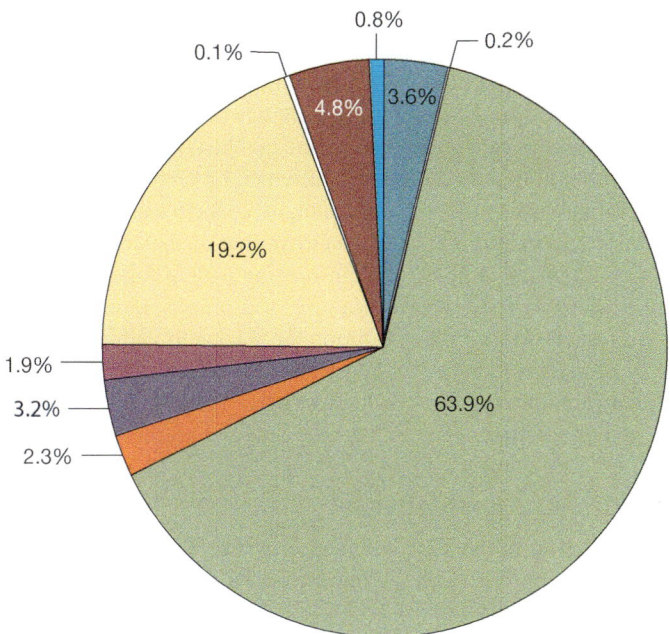

Click on legend item below to add or remove a section from the report.

- American Indian or Alaska Native (274)
- Hispanic, Latino, or of Spanish Origin (5,734)
- Native Hawaiian or Pacific Islander (141)
- Unknown (8,511)
- Asian (34,015)
- Multiple Race - Hispanic (3,978)
- Others (1,456)
- Black or African American (6,288)
- Multiple Race - Non-Hispanic (3,441)
- White (112,894)

FIGURE 2.2 Percentage of full-time US medical school faculty by race/ethnicity, 2018. (Association of American Medical Colleges. Percentage of full-time U.S. medical school faculty by race/ethnicity, 2018. Diversity in Medicine: Facts and Figures 2019; 2019. https://www.aamc.org/data-reports/workforce/interactive-data/figure-15-percentage-full-time-us-medical-school-faculty-race/ethnicity-2018)

likely to be uninsured, under-insured, or covered by a government program such as Medicare or Medicaid, they are structurally primed to receive care at frequently under-resourced safety net hospitals and clinics. This reality is particularly devastating given that Black, LHS+, Native American people, and other racially and ethnically minoritized people are more likely to have underlying poor health and chronic conditions than those at better-resourced hospitals. De facto health care segregation exacerbates racial health disparities.

Beyond reimbursement, racially and ethnically minoritized people may avoid certain hospitals and health centers for feeling mistreated or expecting to be mistreated therein due to their race.[17]

STRATEGIES FOR ANTIRACIST CHANGE IN HEALTH CARE

Despite the reality that racism is deeply embedded in our society and is resistant to efforts toward its eradication, it is critical to recognize that we each have the power by our actions to dismantle its pervasive hold on the health care system.

The Healing ARC Framework

In 2019, a group of physician researchers analyzed 10 years of heart failure data at their large academic referral center. They found that Black and LHS+ patients were less likely to be admitted to cardiology for heart failure care despite improved health outcomes for those receiving this specialized care when needed.[18] Group members began to advocate for change within their institution. They designed a pilot initiative utilizing a reparation framework of *acknowledgement, redress,* and *closure* (ARC) at an institutional level, with initiatives for all three components. That is, within the Healing ARC framework, GME programs and health care institutions must acknowledge how racism has contributed to unequal health outcomes; redress the damage by providing restitution to the population that has been harmed, which involves offering pathways for access to services and care that have historically been denied; and facilitate reconciliation with the community that has been harmed by the health care system and reaching agreement that the harm has been redressed.

In the case cited here, *acknowledgement* came through informing patients about the heart failure findings at their hospital, claiming responsibility and incorporating community ideas for redress. *Redress* in their initiative meant providing a preferential admission option for Black and LHS+ heart failure patients to their specialty cardiology service. To achieve *closure* in their Healing ARC, the team posits that community and patient stakeholders and institutional representatives must agree that the institutional debt has been paid and that a new system is in place to ensure that the problem will not reemerge.

Institutional Strategies for Antiracist Change

In addition to the approach described in the Healing ARC framework, the following are strategies GME programs and health care institutions should employ as they work to move the needle toward racial health equity, many of which reflect expectations associated with Systems-Based Practice, one of the six core competencies outlined in the ACGME Common Program Requirements[19]:

1. *Make a commitment to acting for racial equity.*
   While some institutional stakeholders are ready advocates for the work of dismantling structural racism within their organizations, others may be resistant to formal antiracist change. In the latter instances, it will be important for health equity champions to build necessary alliances and form a strategic approach to gain a philosophical and financial commitment by departmental or institutional stakeholders to racial health equity. For example, a GME program may commit to measuring and reviewing patient care data including health outcomes by race and performing quality improvement initiatives to address any racial health gaps identified in the process. The program may also present this data to broader institutional leadership and advocate for greater resources and support from institutional leadership to address any noted inequities.
2. *Get grounded in history and learn the local context.*
   It is important that GME leaders understand the local demographics of the areas they serve. As programs work to understand the local context, this knowledge search should move beyond journal articles and books. Programs can engage in efforts to support community organizations through attending their events, speaking with community elders, and experiencing the places around them directly. It is important that those embarking on antiracist action also understand the legal and political history, which has made their community and institution what it is today. A GME program can do this, for example, by inviting community leaders to lecture during scheduled didactic sessions for learners. Of note, any community member assisting in the teaching of residents and fellows should be appropriately compensated for their time, experience, and generosity.
3. *Aim to intervene on an institutional level.*
   To date, antiracism work in health care settings has disproportionately emphasized interpersonal interventions rather than interventions that target structural racism. For example, implicit bias training programs, which purport to expose people to their unconscious biases and provide tools to adjust and ultimately eliminate automatic, racially biased patterns of thinking and behaving, fail to address racism at the institutional level. In envisioning and working to advance racial health equity, it is important to aim for change at the level where the greatest amount of harm is produced. GME programs can start by analyzing the mission and values of their institutions, noting whether an explicit commitment to racial health equity exists. Where there is none, programs can advocate for an update. Where such a

commitment is already written into an institution's mission and values, GME programs can spearhead efforts at understanding how well the institution is upholding its commitment, as well as what advocacy efforts should be in place if the need arise to bring about antiracist change.

4. ***Identify opportunities and processes to shift from race-based to race-conscious medicine.***

    Race-based medicine should be explicitly denounced by GME leadership. Institutions should strive to evaluate where racist, racially tailored practices and guidelines are employed and work to eliminate them. Such an effort includes the elimination and replacement of race-based tools such as estimated glomerular filtration rate and spirometry. Racial health inequities should be taught as a consequence of racism rather than a result of an inherent biological difference between different races. For example, GME programs may review and discuss the primary literature on which purportedly racially tailored clinical guidelines and lab studies are based, and in doing so, assist residents/fellows in honing their ability to detect racial bias in biomedical and other forms of research.

5. ***Form deep partnerships with affected communities.***

    The people who are closest to injustice are closest to the solutions for that injustice. It is critical that communities that have been harmed are included early in efforts and have a central role in determining how harms are redressed. As communities of color are called to interact with the institution that has harmed them, it is important to avoid recreating racist power dynamics that led to their initial harm. Care should be taken to ensure that community partners are treated with respect, dignity, and fairness. They should be appropriately compensated, including financially, for any physical, mental, or emotional labor they provide. For example, a GME program could provide such assistance by cultivating longitudinal partnerships with community organizations working to improve the well-being of communities of color and supporting these organizations in the execution of their mission.

> Racial health inequities, at their root, are caused by structural racism.

> Racism is not just the problem of racially and ethnically minoritized people; racism saps strength from the entire society.

Take Home Points

- Racial health disparities in the US are longstanding and well-documented.
- Structural racism in health care presents as biological racism, de facto health care segregation by race, and barriers to medical education and career progression by race in addition to other forms of racism.
- We have the power by our actions to dismantle racism.
- Efforts toward antiracist change should be advocated for and sustained over time, with a specific focus on institutional-level interventions, rather than interpersonal-level interventions alone.

? QUESTIONS FOR FURTHER THOUGHT

1. Has your institution made a formal commitment to pursue racial health equity? If not, what steps can you take to ensure one is achieved?

2. What are some reasons that structural racism in health care is rarely discussed in medicine? How does the lack of understanding and discourse of structural racism contribute to its propagation?

3. In considering the opening case study, what action could Mr Moreno's hospital take to mitigate the structural racism influencing the care he received? What antiracist steps should be undertaken by residency and fellowship programs and health care institutions where residents and fellows are educated?

REFERENCES

1. Institute of Medicine (US). *How Far Have We Come in Reducing Health Disparities? Progress since 2000: Workshop Summary*. National Academies Press; 2012. doi:10.17226/13383
2. Ndugga N, Hill L, Artiga S, *Key Data on Health and Health Care by Race and Ethnicity*. Kaiser Family Foundation; 2024. Accessed June 23, 2024. https://www.kff.org/report-section/key-facts-on-health-and-health-care-by-race-and-ethnicity-health-coverage-and-access-to-and-use-of-care
3. Jones CP. Confronting institutionalized racism. *Phylon*. 2002;50(1/2):7-22. https://stacks.cdc.gov/view/cdc/104986
4. Jones CP. Levels of racism: a theoretic framework and a gardener's tale. *Am J Public Health*. 2000;90(8):1212-1215. doi:10.2105/ajph.90.8.1212
5. Gale MM, Pieterse AL, Lee DL, Huynh K, Powell S, Kirkinis K. A meta-analysis of the relationship between internalized racial oppression and health-related outcomes. *Couns Psychol*. 2020;48(4):498-525. doi:10.1177/0011000020904454
6. Bonilla-Silva E. Rethinking racism: toward a structural interpretation. *Am Sociol Rev*. 1997;62(3):465-480. https://www.jstor.org/stable/2657316
7. Yearby R. Structural racism and health disparities: reconfiguring the social determinants of health framework to include the root cause. *J Law Med Ethics*. 2020;48(3):518-526. doi:10.1177/1073110520958876
8. The American Society of Human Genetics. ASHG denounces attempts to link genetics and racial supremacy. *Am J Hum Genet*. 2018;103(5):636. doi:10.1016/j.ajhg.2018.10.011
9. Cerdeña JP, Plaisime MV, Tsai J. From race-based to race-conscious medicine: how anti-racist uprisings call us to act. *Lancet*. 2020;396(10257):1125-1128. doi:10.1016/S0140-6736(20)32076-6
10. Brody H, Hunt LM. BiDil: assessing a race-based pharmaceutical. *Ann Fam Med*. 2006;4(6):556-560. doi:10.1370/afm.582
11. Savitt T. Abraham Flexner and the black medical schools. 1992. *J Natl Med Assoc*. 2006;98(9):1415-1424. PMID: 17019906
12. Salsberg E, Richwine C, Westergaard S, et al. Estimation and comparison of current and future racial/ethnic representation in the US health care workforce. *JAMA Netw Open*. 2021;4(3):e213789. doi:10.1001/jamanetworkopen.2021.3789
13. Kamran SC, Winkfield KM, Reede JY, Vapiwala N. Intersectional analysis of U.S. medical faculty diversity over four decades. *N Engl J Med*. 2022;386(14):1363-1371. doi:10.1056/nejmsr2114909
14. American Hospital Association and Institute for Diversity in Health Management. Diversity and disparities: a benchmark study of U.S. hospitals. June 2012. https://www.aha.org/ahahret-guides/2012-06-01-diversity-and-disparities-benchmark-study-us-hospitals
15. Reynolds PP. Professional and hospital discrimination and the US court of appeals fourth circuit 1956–1967. *Am J Public Health*. 2004;94(5):710-720. doi:10.2105/ajph.94.5.710
16. Grady M, Edgar T. Appendix D: Racial disparities in health care: highlights from focus group findings. In: Smedley BD, Stith AY, Nelson AR, eds. *Unequal Treatment: Confronting Racial and Ethnic Disparities in Health Care*. Institute of Medicine; The National Academies Press; 2003. https://nap.nationalacademies.org/catalog/12875/unequal-treatment-confronting-racial-and-ethnic-disparities-in-health-care
17. Eberly LA, Richterman A, Beckett AG, Wispelwey B, et al. Identification of racial inequities in access to specialized inpatient heart failure care at an academic medical center. *Circ Heart Fail*. 2019;12(11). doi:10.1161/circheartfailure.119.006214
18. Feagin JR, Ducey K. *Racist America: Roots, Current Realities, and Future Reparations*. Routledge; 2018.
19. Accreditation Council for Graduate Medical Education. Common program requirements (residency). Accessed June 23, 2024. https://www.acgme.org/globalassets/pfassets/programrequirements/cprresidency_2023.pdf

Intersectionality: A Framework for Advancing Patient and Professional Equity in Medicine

Oluwaferanmi O. Okanlami, MD, MS, Assistant Professor of Family Medicine, Physical Medicine and Rehabilitation, Urology, and Orthopaedic Surgery, University of Michigan Medical School, Ann Arbor, MI

Valencia P. Walker, MD, MPH, FAAP, Vice Dean for Health Equity and Inclusion, Geisinger Commonwealth School of Medicine, Scranton, PA

CHAPTER SUMMARY

This chapter defines the conceptual framework of intersectionality and highlights its relevance to the medical profession. The use of the intersectionality framework in this context presents a scholarly rationale for transforming the process of professional identity formation (PIF) experienced by medical students, residents, and fellows, particularly those frequently, but incompletely, described as "underrepresented in medicine." In addition, acquiring a more nuanced and critical understanding of intersectionality can facilitate the process of identifying various scenarios where patients and physician learners with marginalized identities are made vulnerable within the health care system. Establishing metrics of accountability to address barriers, harms, and mistreatment experienced by people with intersecting marginalized identities in health care and medical education supports the goal of achieving equitable outcomes for patients and learners.

LEARNING OBJECTIVES

1. Describe the concept of intersectionality.
2. Discuss examples of inequities in the health care system and workforce experienced by individuals with multiple intersecting marginalized identities.
3. Define the concept of Professional Identity Formation (PIF).
4. Develop strategies that support PIF for those with intersectional identities in the graduate medical education (GME) workforce, professional health care environments, and clinical care.

Case Study

Sam Jones is a 65-year-old man who develops abdominal pain while being out of town visiting his partner, Chris. Sam identifies as a transgender man and uses he/him pronouns. He has never been seen in this Emergency Department (ED) prior to tonight; therefore, there are no notes in his chart. When he arrives in the ED, he is not given an opportunity to share his pronouns. He is accompanied by his partner, Chris, who is in his 30s.

(continued)

Chris has stepped out to use his phone when an emergency medicine resident enters the room, and who greets Sam in the following manner:

"Good afternoon, ma'am, what brings you in tonight?"

"Hi doctor, I suddenly started feeling this terrible pain in my abdomen, and please don't call me ma'am, I prefer Sam," he says, visibly wincing in pain with each word.

"Ok, Sam, but you look to be about my mother's age, so I was only saying that out of respect."

At that moment, Chris knocks on the door and re-enters the room.

The resident turns to acknowledge Chris and says, "Oh, hello there. I was just about to start asking your mother a few questions about her symptoms. Maybe you can help because she appears to be in a lot of pain."

Sam frustratingly responds by saying, "Chris is not my child. I would appreciate it if you would use he/him pronouns to address me, and I am perfectly capable of speaking for myself. Thank you."

The resident, looking flustered, clicks through a few pages on the computer screen before responding to Sam. "Well, ma'am... I'm sorry... sir, there are a few questions I need to ask you in order to identify the cause of your pain." The resident proceeds to take a history, but completely omits any questions related to Sam's sexual history. The resident does not perform a physical examination and concludes the assessment by saying, "I am going to run a few tests first and will be back in to chat with you once the results are available."

Case Discussion

This scenario highlights multiple instances where improved communication about Sam's identities could have led to a better clinical encounter for the patient and critical information-gathering for the resident. It is important to note that the missed opportunities for accurate communication were not simply caused by the resident's desire to intentionally discriminate. First, this was Sam's first visit to this particular clinical site; hence, there was a lack of information in Sam's medical record that could have helped guide the resident prior to the encounter. Once the encounter started, the resident made assumptions about Sam's identity that could have been avoided by merely asking open-ended questions and listening to how Sam identified himself. The resident then makes an assumption about the relationship between Sam and Chris. He also continues to misgender Sam by repeating the use of the term "ma'am," despite being asked by Sam not to use the term.

This clinical scenario could have led the resident to assume that Sam was not sexually active given his perceived older age, and to skip over questions one would routinely ask when an individual presents with abdominal pain. Furthermore, after learning about Sam's gender identity, the resident did not ask Sam about sexual preferences or activity, possibly relying on unspoken and inaccurate assumptions. Even in scenarios where physicians are not overtly bigoted, the inability to consider how older age and gender identity may intersect can lead to poor history-taking, inadequate physical examinations, and an overall subpar clinical encounter, such as in this case study. As you review the chapter, consider what steps you personally take or omit to learn a patient's identities before making assumptions. What if the roles were reversed and the resident in the scenario was the transgender man who is of non-traditional age interacting with a patient who continually misgenders him during the conversation? Or what if the transgender physician was a resident being repeatedly belittled by a colleague or supervisor?

DEFINING INTERSECTIONALITY

Intersectionality, a term coined by legal scholar Kimberlé Crenshaw (1989), is much more than a mere buzzword; rather, it is a theoretical framework deeply rooted in Black feminist culture. Crenshaw explains that "intersectionality is a lens through which you can see where power comes and collides, where it interlocks and intersects."[1] At its core, intersectionality allows us to understand how various systems of oppression intersect to shape the experiences of marginalized individuals. Rather than viewing identities as separate or additive, intersectionality recognizes their interconnectedness.

Intersectionality highlights the compounding effects of oppression on those individuals with multiple marginalized personalities. It is a concept that has been pivotal in broadening the scope of feminist theory by acknowledging that women can be affected by other forms of oppression aside from gender. Patricia Hill Collins (2000) expands this view by stating, "Intersectionality is not just about identities, but rather, about the institutions that use identity to exclude and privilege."[2] The notion of multiple layers of identity challenges traditional sociological structures which tend to place people into single category boxes. Intersectionality means we must acknowledge that social systems are complicated and that multiple forms of oppression, such as racism, sexism, and ageism might be present and active at the same time in someone's life. Most attempts to create equitable systems fail to acknowledge this fact and, therefore, focus on merely one form of discrimination. While a young, White, non-disabled woman may benefit from gender equality protections, an older, Black, disabled, queer woman may continue to feel the impacts of racism, ageism, ableism, and homophobia.

Intersectionality recognizes that individual forms of oppression exist, but its power is in understanding how such forms change in combination with one another, compounding the experience of oppression (Figure 3.1).

FIGURE 3.1 A Venn diagram illustrating the concept of intersectionality, with identities being more than the sum of their parts but forming something new at the intersections of multiple identities. (**Source:** Openclipart. tango-rgb. Accessed May 31, 2024. https://openclipart.org/detail/27210/tangorgb#google_vignette)

Intersectionality requires us to listen to one another. It is an essential framework that engages with issues of power and privilege, bringing them into open discussion about our own privileges and how others may be excluded or negatively impacted by our work. Ultimately, for graduate medical education (GME), it means that educational leaders, faculty members, physician learners, and staff must take specific actions not only to invite, but to actively include and center, the voices of the marginalized and minoritized individuals within our communities.

PROFESSIONAL IDENTITY FORMATION

Professional identity formation (PIF) can be defined as "the integration of the knowledge, skills, values, and behaviors of a profession with one's preexisting identity and values."[3] Similar to defining intersectionality as a framework, applying the concept of PIF requires us to discuss what is meant by the word "professional." When someone identifies as being part of a profession, there is an expectation of professionalism which refers to the conduct, aims, and qualities that characterize not only each individual *professional*, but also the *profession* itself. When one thinks about a physician, a lawyer, or a minister, for example, without consciously realizing, certain images likely appear in one's mind. These images are rooted in ideas formed by the normalization of societal and cultural beliefs. But what happens if these ideas and images are normalized around a very narrow range of identity and expression?

As a simple experiment, the authors conducted an internet image search for "business professional hairstyles"; the results displayed a fairly homogeneous group of images, with predominantly White and masculine-presenting individuals. When a similar search was done for "unprofessional hairstyles," the results presented a stark contrast. The "unprofessional" examples looked very similar to the manner in which hair grows naturally from the heads of individuals with whom we, the authors, more closely identify. While this example may seem trivial, certain images and symbols of the profession stand out when discussing professionalism in medicine, such as the stethoscope and the white coat. When considering PIF in medicine, we must acknowledge that becoming a physician requires a transformation. We do not simply learn the clinical protocols and guidelines, the pharmacology, or the physiology. We also strive to become members of this profession, which may also involve striving to embody the societal or cultural attributes of the "normative" physician. Yet, to what degree do those norms and attributes that represent the PIF in physicians accurately represent all physicians, particularly those with marginalized characteristics?

The process of PIF in medicine is not typically linear and can often take a toll on different people in different ways. Many residents and fellows "must reconcile the dissonance between the stated values of the medical profession and the realities of medicine as practiced in the real world."[4] For some, it can raise serious issues and questions about past experiences and struggles with personal identity versus what is demanded of the profession. Effective PIF requires acknowledging and valuing the diverse backgrounds and perspectives that individuals bring to the medical field, rather than expecting them to conform to a narrow standard of professionalism.

GME STRATEGIES TO SUPPORT INTERSECTIONALITY IN PIF

In light of the complexities surrounding intersectionality and PIF, we propose several strategies for Sponsoring Institutions and GME programs to create inclusive health care and medical education environments.

1. *Evaluate and address the institutional climate of culture and belonging.*

    Education and health care leaders should recognize that many learners are asked to enter spaces and situations that historically were not developed directly for them or were not developed with them in mind; at the same time they should not be overcome by shame or guilt about such history of which they were not a part. To address such a situation, leaders should commit to doing things differently, to create a new history, by intentionally evaluating the institutional climate of culture and belonging.

One example of how this strategy can be accomplished includes hiring an outside firm to conduct an analysis or a survey of current learners, faculty members, and staff. Another example is to implement exit interviews for graduating residents, fellows, and departing staff to gather feedback on their experiences and to identify areas for improvement. However, evaluating and then identifying climate concerns is not sufficient. What follows must be a leadership commitment to promote a culture of belonging through policies, actions, and resource allocation. Creating support networks and affinity groups for underrepresented and marginalized physician learners is one way to foster a sense of community and belonging. Establishing mentorship programs to pair them with diverse faculty mentors could provide additional guidance and support; and regularly reviewing and updating policies to ensure that they continue to promote equity and address barriers to inclusion should be an ongoing practice as well.

Another key strategy in evaluating and addressing the institutional climate of culture and belonging involves making trauma-informed care part of the expected culture of care at health care institutions. Trauma-informed care is an approach that responds to the impact of trauma on individuals which emphasizes understanding, recognizing, and responding to the effects of all types of trauma. Trauma-informed care seeks to provide support services in manner that is accessible and sensitive to the needs of individuals who have experienced trauma.[5] Some key principles of trauma-informed care include:

- *Safety*: ensuring physical and emotional safety for patients, residents, fellows, faculty members, and staff;
- *Trustworthiness and Transparency*: building trust through transparent actions, policies, procedures, and decision-making;
- *Peer Support*: integrating the lived experiences of peers who have experiences trauma into the support process;
- *Collaboration and Mutuality*: emphasizing partnership and leveling power differences between individuals within the institution or organization;
- *Empowerment, Voice, and Choice*: prioritizing client autonomy and strengths, and supporting individuals in making their own decisions; and
- *Cultural, Historical, and Gender Issues*: acknowledging and incorporating cultural, historical and gender considerations into care.[6]

A trauma-informed approach is designed to avoid re-traumatization and to promote recovery and healing for those who have experienced trauma.

Trauma-informed care and intersectionality are closely related concepts; both emphasize the importance of understanding and addressing the complexities of individual experiences and identities. By practicing trauma-informed care, an understanding of the principle of intersectionality allows one to acknowledge that trauma can be compounded by intersecting identities. For example, a physician learner who is both a person of color and a survivor of domestic violence may face distinct challenges that differ from someone who experiences only one of those identities. Intersectionality and trauma-informed care highlight the importance of how cultural, historical, and social contexts shape an individual's experience. Historical traumas such as systemic racism, ableism, or colonization have a profound effect on both individuals and communities; therefore, one's PIF is also likely to be impacted by whatever traumas they have experienced that are specific to the identities they occupy. In light of this knowledge, adequately supporting residents' and fellows' PIF requires an understanding of both intersectionality and trauma-informed care in order to provide more comprehensive and compassionate support.

> Racial identity and disability are characteristics that may uniquely intersect in a physician learner. If a learner identifies both as a person from a minoritized racial group and as disabled, they may be subject to stereotyping, microaggressions, or other harms based on one or both of those aspects of their identity.

2. ***Engage in discussions and scholarly discourse about redefining professionalism in medicine.***

   Historically, characteristics such as grit and resilience have been considered core attributes of the physician profession. However, this approach has been criticized since the individual behaviors of grit and resilience cannot overhaul harmful systems and structures and may inadvertently sustain larger systemic problems by creating "band aid" solutions at the individual level and ignoring core structural issues.[7] Redefining professionalism in medicine provides an opportunity to highlight desirable qualities that are linked to improved health outcomes, such as altruism, effective communication, and a motivation to care for underserved populations. By including an intersectionality framework in conversations around professionalism in medicine, we have an opportunity to account for a more nuanced approach to what professionalism means and how it can be informed by the perspectives of individuals with one or more marginalized identities.

   > Intersecting religious and gender identities may affect how physician learners are perceived by others while doing their job. For example, a surgery resident who is a Muslim woman wearing a *hijab* may experience discrimination from a patient based on religion, and on the same day may be assumed to be a nurse by a staff member in the operating room.

3. ***Collect data about multiple aspects of individuals' identities and track progress not only about individual demographic characteristics but also about the intersection of multiple identities.***

   Addressing systemic and structural barriers that have perpetuated and continue to perpetuate health care and educational inequities will require data-driven goals and metrics. Metrics are key to establishing an expectation of accountability for a climate and culture of belonging. An individual who identifies with a particular race, for instance, is not fully captured as being a member of a particular racial group. By layering and appreciating the multiple identities carried by that individual, data can be enriched and conclusions drawn from the data can be more nuanced. An example of the value of analyzing intersecting characteristics is the analysis of medical school matriculation data by race/ethnicity and gender. Recognizing a particularly salient gap in the number of Black men matriculating in medical schools, the Association of American Medical Colleges (AAMC) created the Action Collaborative for Black Men in Medicine to evaluate the reasons for this finding and to address the problem.[8] Looking at gender data alone or race/ethnicity data alone would not have identified this intersectional gap affecting the profession. Another critical example of intersectional data analysis involves exploring the impact of race/ethnicity and disability. A recent analysis showed a 3-fold higher rate of burnout among medical students with multiple disabilities who also identified as Asian or underrepresented in medicine, compared to White students without a disability.[9] Several studies also highlight the importance of addressing the intersectional challenges faced by LGBTQIA+ students of color in educational settings. These students often experience unique and compounded forms of bullying and harassment based on both their race and sexual orientation or gender identity, significantly impacting their academic performance, mental health and overall school experience.[10]

4. ***Consider intersectionality as an aspect of holistic review.***

   One strategy to apply data-driven metrics to recruitment and retention of learners, faculty members, and staff is holistic review. Holistic review in an application process is an evaluative approach that considers the whole applicant, not just their academic achievements or test scores; it accounts for multiple, potentially intersecting attributes of an applicant's profile, such as their relevant skills and experiences as aligned with an institution's mission or population. This comprehensive method aims to understand applicants in a broader context, considering various factors that reflect their potential, experiences, and contributions. Holistic review promotes diversity among residents and fellows, faculty members, and staff by valuing a range of experiences and backgrounds, acknowledging that not all applicants have had the same opportunities and resources and allowing for a more equitable assessment process. It identifies candidates who not only meet the technical requirements for a role, but who also align with the organization's values and culture. Holistic review processes ensure that institutions and organizations recruit and retain candidates who will contribute positively to the community and show promise beyond their test scores alone, such as those who have demonstrated leadership, creativity, resilience, and a commitment to service. Holistic review is about seeing applicants as whole individuals and valuing their unique contributions, experiences, and potential for growth.

CONCLUSION

Intersectionality and PIF are integral components of creating equitable and inclusive health care systems. By embracing the principles of intersectionality and prioritizing strategies for supporting intersecting identities, GME programs can work toward dismantling systemic barriers and promoting equitable and inclusive work environments. Such efforts will not only improve the quality of care provided to patients but also will foster a professional community that genuinely reflects the diversity of the societies it serves.

Take Home Points

- Intersectionality is a conceptual framework that highlights the complex and interwoven identities of individuals and describes how various systems of oppression may differentially impact marginalized individuals and populations.
- The intersectionality framework characterizes the integrated and inseparable manner in which multiple marginalized identities may exist for a single person.
- PIF is the integration of the knowledge, skills, values, and behaviors of a profession with one's preexisting identity and values.
- Prioritizing an inclusive culture, practicing trauma-informed care, analyzing data in an intersectional manner, and conducting holistic review are key strategies for optimizing successful outcomes in both the education and development of residents and fellows and the care of patients.

ⓘ QUESTIONS FOR FURTHER THOUGHT

1. How can disaggregated data drive diversity, equity and inclusion metrics of accountability and institutional goals without paradoxically disadvantaging those with intersecting marginalized identities?
2. What metrics, if any, does your GME program, hospital, or institution use to track the effectiveness of your recruitment and retention efforts to address the needs of your population and achieve the institutional mission? How can the conceptual framework of intersectionality be applied to enhance your current strategies for recruitment and retention of residents, faculty members, and staff?

REFERENCES

1. Crenshaw K. Demarginalizing the intersection of race and sex: a black feminist critique of antidiscrimination doctrine, feminist theory and antiracist politics. *Univ Chic Leg Forum*. 1989;140(1):139-167. https://chicagounbound.uchicago.edu/uclf/vol1989/iss1/8
2. Collins PH. *Black Feminist Thought: Knowledge, Consciousness, and the Politics of Empowerment*. 2nd ed. Routledge; 2000.
3. Mount GR, Kahlke R, Melton J, Varpio L. A critical review of professional identity formation interventions in medical education. *Acad Med*. 2022;97(11S):S96-S106. doi:10.1097/ACM.0000000000004904
4. Wald HS, Anthony D, Hutchinson TA, Liben S, Smilovitch M, Donato AA. Professional identity formation in medical education for humanistic, resilient physicians: pedagogic strategies for bridging theory to practice. *Acad Med*. 2015;90(6):753-760. doi:10.1097/ACM.0000000000000725

5. Roche P, Shimmin C, Hickes S, et al. Valuing all voices: refining a trauma-informed, intersectional and critical reflexive framework for patient engagement in health research using a qualitative descriptive approach. *Res Involv Engagem*. 2020;6:42. doi:10.1186/s40900-020-00217-2
6. Substance Abuse and Mental Health Services Administration. *SAMHSA's Concept of Trauma and Guidance for a Trauma-Informed Approach*. U.S. Department of Health and Human Services; Published July 2014. Accessed July 3, 2024. https://ncsacw.acf.hhs.gov/userfiles/files/SAMHSA_Trauma.pdf
7. Datu JAD. Beyond passion and perseverance: review and future research initiatives on the science of grit. *Front Psychol*. 2021;11:545526. doi:10.3389/fpsyg.2020.545526
8. Association of American Medical Colleges; National Medical Association. Action collaborative for Black men in medicine. Association of American Medical Colleges; 2024. Accessed May 31, 2024. https://www.aamc.org/about-us/equity-diversity-inclusion/action-collaborative-black-men-medicine
9. Nguyen M, Meeks LM, Pereira-Lima K, et al. Medical student burnout by race, ethnicity, and multiple disability status. *JAMA Netw Open*. 2024;7(1):e2351046. PMID: 38198142
10. Truong NL, Zongrone AD, Kosciw JG. *Erasure and Resilience: The Experiences of LGBTQ Students of Color; Black LGBTQ Youth in U.S. Schools*. Gay, Lesbian and Straight Education Network (GLSEN); 2020.

ADDITIONAL RESOURCES

McCall L. The complexity of intersectionality. *Signs J Women Cult Soc*. 2005;30(3):1771-1800. https://www.journals.uchicago.edu/doi/10.1086/426800

Bilge S. Introduction to intersectionality. In: Bilge S, ed. *Intersectionality: From Theory to Practice*. Oxford University Press; 2010:1-17.

Davis AY. *Women, Race & Class*. Vintage Books; 1983.

Cho S, Crenshaw KW, McCall L. Toward a field of intersectionality studies: theory, applications, and praxis. *Signs J Women Cult Soc*. 2013;38(4):785-810. https://psycnet.apa.org/doi/10.1086/669608

Carastathis A. The concept of intersectionality in feminist theory. *Philos Compass*. 2014;9(5):304-314. doi:10.1111/phc3.12129

Crenshaw K. Mapping the margins: intersectionality, identity politics, and violence against women of color. *Stanford Law Rev*. 1991;43(6):1241-1299. https://www.jstor.org/stable/1229039

Bhatia-Lin A, Wong K, Legha R, Walker VP. What will you protect? Redefining professionalism through the lens of diverse personal identities. *MedEdPORTAL*. 2021;17:11203. doi:10.15766/mep_2374-8265.11203

Sarraf-Yazdi S, Teo YN, How AEH, et al. A scoping review of professional identity formation in undergraduate medical education. *J Gen Intern Med*. 2021;36(11):3511-3521. doi:10.1007/s11606-021-07024-9

Sharpless J, Baldwin N, Cook R, et al. The becoming: students' reflections on the process of professional identity formation in medical education. *Acad Med*. 2015;90(6):713-717. doi:10.1097/ACM.0000000000000729

Kim DT, Applewhite MK, Shelton W. Professional identity formation in medical education: some virtue-based insights. *Teach Learn Med*. 2024;36(3):399-409. doi:10.1080/10401334.2023.2209067

Voith LA, Hamler T, Francis MW, Hyunjune L, Korsch-Williams A. Using a trauma-informed, socially just research framework with marginalized populations: practices and barriers to implementation. *Soc Work Res*. 2020;44(3):169-181. doi: 10.1093/swr/svaa013

Geographic Location as a Determinant of Health

David Ansell, MD, MPH, Senior Vice President Community Health Equity, Rush University Medical Center; Endowed Professor, Department of Internal Medicine, Rush University Medical Center, Chicago, IL

Ted Epperly, MD, President, CEO, DIO, Full Circle Health, Boise, ID; Clinical Professor of Family Medicine, University of Washington School of Medicine, Seattle, WA

CHAPTER SUMMARY

In this chapter, we discuss the influence of geographic location on health and disease. We examine how geography itself can be a determinant of health outcomes and focus on the impact of place on health for both rural/frontier and urban areas, providing examples from both and comparing similarities and differences. In medical education, particularly when considering the mechanisms of disease and mortality, the issue of geography and its impact on health is rarely considered outside of the realm of tropical diseases. We argue that the impact of geographic location as a determinant of health should be taught in graduate medical education (GME) to prepare physicians to appropriately identify and address health disparities in the populations they serve. Finally, this chapter presents potential solutions to these complicated issues.

LEARNING OBJECTIVES

1. Recognize that lack of timely access to medical and behavioral health care in rural areas leads to increases in morbidity and mortality in acute, chronic, preventive, and maternal/neonatal conditions.
2. Identify how geography (place) can influence health outcomes and how it can intersect with race and poverty to influence health outcomes.
3. Develop potential strategies for GME programs and institutions to address physician workforce geographic shortages and increase geographic-related health equities.

Case Study: A Rural Emergency Department

After seeing many patients in her clinic earlier in the day, Dr Smith, a third-year family medicine resident, is now involved in her fourth emergency department visit on her busy call night. She is on call with the family medicine physician attending in her rural Idaho critical access hospital. She was hoping to get to bed at a reasonable time as her clinic was booked with patients the next morning. Those were her thoughts when her pager went off, calling her emergently to Labor and Delivery where a woman with minimal prenatal care had just walked in with a prolapsed umbilical cord protruding from her vagina after her bag of waters ruptured 15 minutes prior with meconium-stained fluid. Fetal heart tones were present at 80 beats/min. The mother had a temperature of 102.4°F and heart rate of 115. This was her and her husband's first child; they were both frightened and anxious. Dr Smith knew it was her and her family medicine physician attending to care for this patient since there was no obstetrician, general surgeon, or anesthesiologist for 60 miles. "It's time to get to work," she said to herself as she prepared for the skilled work ahead.

Case Study: An Urban Emergency Department

Dr Gupta, a harried third-year emergency medicine resident at a south side Chicago community hospital, sees a 60-year-old, unemployed, uninsured Black woman with a new, tender breast lump. The attending physician is busy with a caseload of patients. The emergency medicine resident suspects an infection and discusses the case quickly with the attending who agreed with the suggestion of antibiotics but did not examine the patient. Dr Gupta did not know where to refer the woman for follow-up since there was no breast surgeon on staff. Besides, without insurance, the patient would be unable to get an appointment. Dr Gupta reassured the patient the best she could and discharged her with the recommendation for a mammogram. However, as a rotating resident at this hospital, Dr Gupta was unaware that there was no breast imaging center in the patient's neighborhood, nor did she know of free mammography resources. The patient took the reassurances of the doctor to mean there was nothing to worry about, but when the lump grew, the patient was finally able to obtain a mammogram far from her neighborhood. The mammogram revealed possible breast cancer.

Case Discussion

While taking place in very different geographic settings, one rural and one urban, both cases illustrate the life-threatening challenges to health care access that can be posed by geographic location. Dr Smith's situation highlights the challenges inherent in the delivery of medical, maternal, and neonatal care that can occur in rural and frontier areas. Lack of timely access to care can present multiple challenges that can suddenly present as full-blown emergencies and crises in resource-constrained locations. Dr Gupta's case illustrates that even in densely populated urban areas, access to high quality care can be a challenge and can affect health outcomes. As you read the chapter, consider how your GME program or Sponsoring Institution's geographic location influences the resources to which your patients and physician learners have access. Consider whether more poorly resourced hospitals and other GME-participating sites near you may be in need of assistance and partnership.

INTRODUCTION

The issue of access to high-quality health care has national implications across rural, frontier, urban, and state geographies. For those of us trained in biomedical science, it is almost inconceivable that geography or place can be a determinant of health. However, researchers have increasingly noted the relationship between geography and health.[1] In this chapter, we will illustrate these associations in data showing geographical variation in health outcomes at the national and the local levels.

For many diseases, geographical access to resources is among the most critical of the **social and structural determinants of health** that can influence disease severity and ultimately life expectancy. Three major and intersectional reasons account for why geography can impact health outcomes. The first is the lack of timely access to high-quality medical care. The second is the impact of poverty on a broad set of health determinants (eg, education, housing, food access, jobs, trauma) that can have cumulative deleterious health impacts across communities in rural/frontier and urban areas. Lastly, structural racism has an independent and enduring negative influence on health often mediated through historic patterns of residential and geographic segregation and reflected in the health and social care resources available in socially, racially, and economically isolated communities.

There are many medically underserved regions of the country where the lack of timely access to medical care can influence outcomes. **Rural**, **frontier**, **urban**, and **exurban** areas have widely varying access to health care depending on the concentration of physicians, clinics, hospitals, and pharmacies. The federal government has designations for **Health Professional Shortage areas** (Figure 4.1)[2] and **Medically Underserved areas**, which are geographic areas in which persons lack access to health care. The federal designation of an area as medically underserved is based upon four factors: (1) the number of primary care physicians per 1,000 persons; (2) the percent of the population below the poverty level; (3) the infant mortality rate; and/or (4) a large elderly population. Populations who live in medically underserved areas have disease and mortality rates that greatly exceed those neighborhoods not designated as shortage areas.

RURAL AND FRONTIER AREAS

The most significant health-related obstacle faced by persons in rural and frontier areas is timely access to care. Approximately 20% of the US population lives in rural areas (any area outside of a Metropolitan Statistical Area [MSA] with less than 500 people per square mile)[3] and frontier areas (an area where there are less than six people per square mile). However, only 9% of the US physician workforce is represented in these two areas, resulting in a reduced physician-to-patient ratio.[4] Most of the clinicians in these areas are primary care physicians, and most are family medicine physicians who have the breadth of education and training to handle issues ranging from pediatrics to obstetrics to adult medicine, including inpatient, outpatient, and emergency care within their scope of practice. A wide margin of variability exists among family medicine residency programs, which may affect these graduates' readiness for rural or urban under-resourced care. Because of the lack of timely access and the resource constraints that exist in these areas, the people who live within them live sicker and die younger.[1] In fact, health care disparities and health inequities have increased over time as less of the physician workforce practices in these areas. Chronic diseases and diseases of despair, including alcoholism, opioid drug addiction, overdose deaths, and suicides, are all higher in these locations compared to urban areas.[1,5] Life expectancy in these areas is dropping, particularly among the non-college educated population.[5-8]

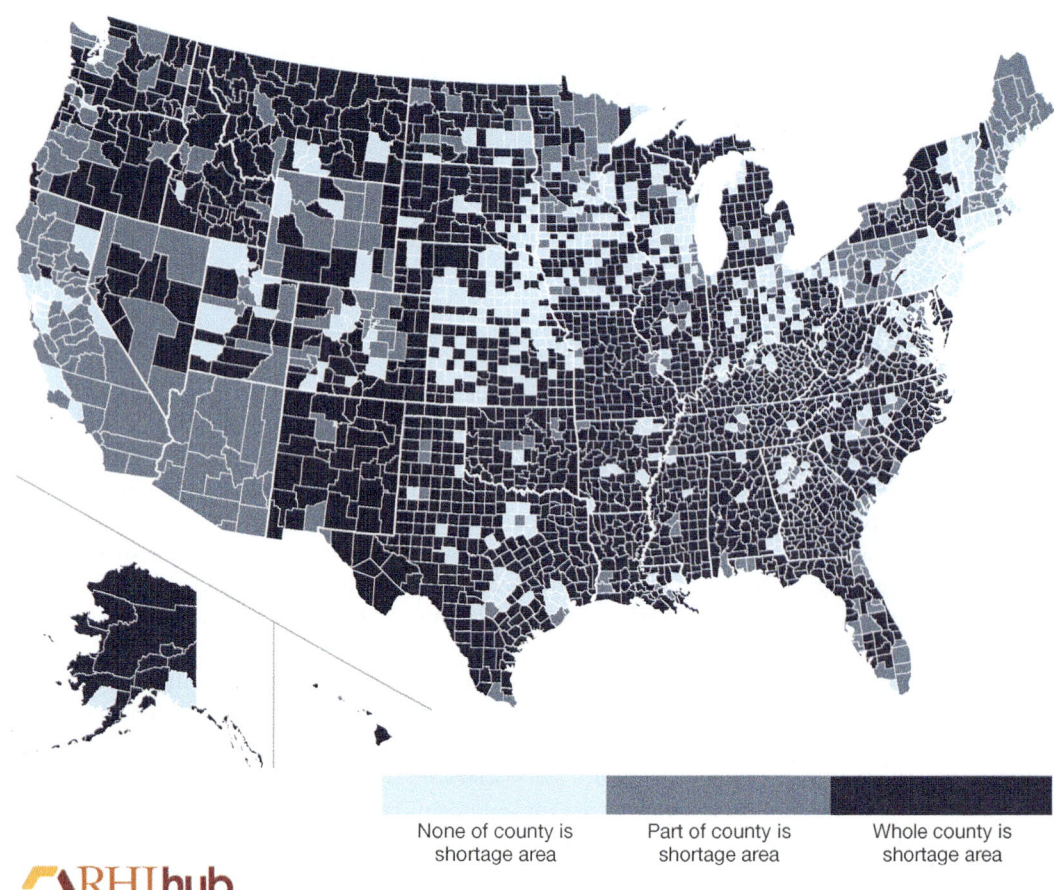

FIGURE 4.1 Map of primary care health professional shortage areas.[2] (**Source:** US Health Resources and Services Administration. Health professional shortage areas: primary care, by county. October 2024. https://www.ruralhealthinfo.org/charts/5)

Part of the reason only 9% of the physician workforce can be found in rural and frontier areas is that only 1% of the physician workforce trains in them. It is extremely difficult to recruit and retain physicians to practice in these locations if they are not familiar with them through their educational experiences. Not only is there a lack of primary care physicians (Figure 4.1)[2] and prenatal/maternity care clinicians (eg, pediatricians and obstetricians), but there is also a lack of other health care staff and the services they provide, including nurses, pharmacists, social workers, psychologists, community health workers, behavioral health clinicians, and surgeons. All these deficits lead to lack of timely access as the central problem.

Also contributing to the increasing morbidity and mortality in rural and frontier areas is the closure of many hospitals, including critical access hospitals, in these locations. This fact has been especially true following the onset of the COVID-19 pandemic. Difficulties related to transportation and distance that lead to less-than-timely access for all sorts of acute, chronic, and preventive health care compound the impact of increasing closures. The socioeconomic status and finances of people living in these areas are also barriers to their care. It is, therefore, evident that persons living in rural and frontier areas experience many barriers to health care access due to social and structural determinants of care, including the relative lack of timely access to primary care and subspecialty physicians, transportation issues, finance issues, timely access, and other critical resources.

Challenges to health experienced by patients in rural and frontier areas intersect with GME in important ways. Some examples include how much time residents and fellows spend in obstetrics, emergency medicine and procedural training (eg, endoscopy, ultrasound and women's reproductive health care). All these findings provide evidence of the intersectional problems around physician workforce deficits and health care outcomes for persons living in the rural and frontier US.

THE IMPACT OF POVERTY ON ACCESS TO CARE

Beyond federal designations pertaining to physician shortage or medically underserved areas, the general availability of medical services is often predicated on the income levels and concentration of poverty within a geographic area. Hospitals and clinics that serve low-income neighborhoods and regions often face financial difficulties in rural or urban areas. The quality of care delivered in low-income medically underserved areas often is not the same as in wealthier geographies. Studies have shown that quality of care varies widely between hospitals and clinics that serve the poor and those that serve middle class populations. For example, the Centers for Medicare & Medicaid Services (CMS) publishes hospital quality ratings that range from one to five to provide more transparent and useable quality information to patients and stakeholders.

Intersection of Race/Ethnicity, Poverty, and Geography

Based on these hospital quality ratings, researchers have found that hospitals with higher quality ratings are less likely to be found in communities with higher Black/African American, Hispanic/Latinx or American Indian/Alaska Native populations, or in lower income communities. Moreover, living in neighborhoods of concentrated poverty can have profound implications for health outcomes on these populations, often because of intersectionality with related multiple influences such as structural racism, poverty, lack of access to and provision of health care, dental and behavioral health care, food, housing, and exercise facilities. When these negative influences of health are concentrated geographically, health outcomes are particularly affected. The biological mechanisms by which exposure to the ongoing stressors of poverty and racism have been explored and increasingly described in the medical literature.[1,9] They seem to accumulate over a lifetime of exposure and have a profound, negative impact on human biology and aging, even affecting the length of, often shortening, chromosomal telomeres in a process called biological weathering.

A growing body of literature demonstrates the intersectional impact of race/ethnicity and geography on mortality. Figure 4.2[10] displays mortality from treatable diseases by race and ethnicity for each of the 50 states in the US. This data highlights the critical role that geography (place) plays in overall mortality and in racial/ethnic mortality gaps. Importantly, in all 50 states, Black and American Indian/Alaska Native people have higher mortality for treatable conditions compared to Whites. This finding illustrates the impact of the legacy of racial/ethnic residential segregation, racial/ethnic segregation in the health care delivery system, and geographically concentrated exposures to the toxic impact of social and structural determinants of health (eg, food access, health care access, educational attainment, housing, exercise, and financial resources). Across the 50 states, White and Black mortality rates from treatable conditions vary greatly. In general, in states with high Black mortality from treatable conditions, such as Mississippi and Oklahoma, the White mortality from treatable conditions is also high. Similarly, in the states with the lowest White mortality from treatable conditions, such as Massachusetts and Oregon, the Black mortality also trends lower. State-by-state mortality variations may be related to the rising mortality rates across the nation for people without college educations–a trend that is thought to be related to the growing poverty levels in this subgroup. This finding suggests that public policies that promote health and wealth creation, and that vary widely between states, might be contributing to geographic variations in mortality.

Data also show that as wealth decreases, there is a profound impact of place on mortality. If one's earnings are in the top 5% of US income, where one lives has no impact on mortality. But as income drops below the US median, where one lives has a profound impact on life expectancy. The divergence in mortality by location is greatest for those in the lowest 5% income bracket. For the poorest individuals, life expectancies are 6 years higher in New York City than in Detroit; by contrast, for those in the wealthiest subset, the difference is less than 1 year. Hence, while wealth alone is highly correlated with life expectancy, geography also has a profound impact, likely mediated through public policies that create expanded access to health and social care.

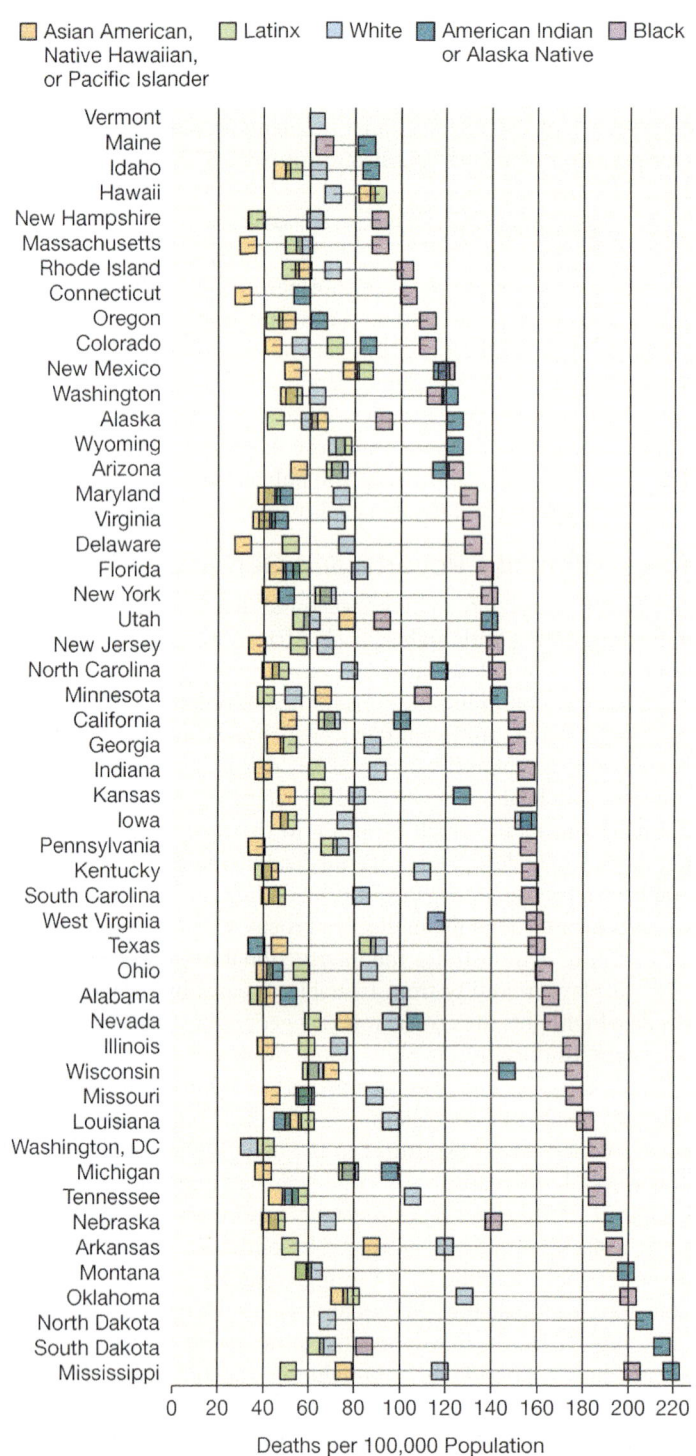

FIGURE 4.2 Deaths from conditions that are treatable with timely access to high-quality health care. Note: Missing squares for a particular group indicate that there are insufficient data for that state. States are arranged in rank order based on the highest death rate in each state. (Radley DC, Baumgartner JC, Collins SR, Zephyrin L, Schneider EC. Achieving racial and ethnic equity in U.S. health care: a scorecard of state performance. *Commonwealth Fund*. November 18, 2021. https://www.commonwealthfund.org/publications/scorecard/2021/nov/achieving-racial-ethnic-equity-us-health-care-state-performance)

Close Proximity of Geographic Areas with Disparate Health Outcomes

In addition to regional and state distributions, local geographic patterns can have a profound impact on health outcomes. Life expectancy data across Chicago neighborhoods is an example of staggering health disparities within a single city. For example, if you live on the Magnificent Mile by Chicago's lakefront, life expectancy is well into the eighties, among the highest in the world. However, if you travel seven stops down the Chicago Transit Authority Blue Line into Garfield Park, life expectancy plummets to 66 years. If Garfield Park in Chicago were a county, it would be one of the lowest life expectancy counties in the US. The number one cause of premature mortality in this neighborhood is heart disease, and the death rates from cardiovascular disease are nearly twice the heart disease death rates on the lakefront neighborhoods 5 miles away.

The longstanding patterns of racial/ethnic segregation in Chicago make the racial and ethnic gaps in life expectancy a story of neighborhoods. Chicago has the largest dissimilarity index–72%–of all large cities in the US; this index means that 72% of Blacks and Whites would need to move to a different neighborhood to achieve residential integration. With over one-third of Black Chicagoans living in poverty also live in neighborhoods of concentrated poverty; thus, they are negatively impacted by multiple social influencers of health throughout their lives. Structural racism and the impact of past and current practices of residential neighborhood segregation and economic disinvestment have resulted in these wide--and widening–lifespan gaps between neighborhoods, not just in Chicago but across the nation. There are likely multiple mediating factors such as lack of access to healthy foods, safe walking, educational attainment, low wage jobs, hospitals and health care resources, and a myriad of other factors that are concentrated in certain geographic areas.

Figure 4.3[11] is a map of Chicago that shows the distribution of communities with high breast cancer mortality and the location of hospitals with American College of Surgeons Commission on Cancer accreditation. The highest mortality neighborhoods for breast cancer are in the Black, racially segregated west and south sides of the city, while the hospitals with accredited cancer programs are concentrated in lower

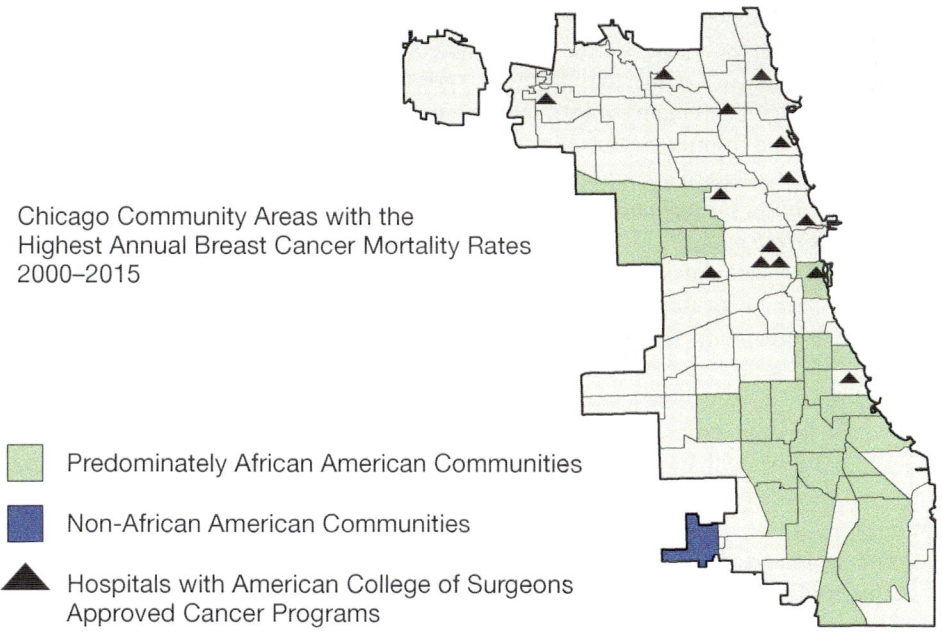

FIGURE 4.3 The geography of breast cancer mortality and accredited cancer hospitals in Chicago. (Reprinted by permission from Springer Nature. Ansell D, Grabler P, Whitman S, et al. A community effort to reduce the black/white breast cancer mortality disparity in Chicago. *Cancer Causes Control*. 2009;20:1681–1688. doi: 10.1007/s10552-009-9419-7)

mortality, largely White northside neighborhoods. The maldistribution of quality resources by geography contributes to geographical and racial mortality gaps from breast cancer in Chicago and across the nation.

IMPLICATIONS FOR GME

Providing health care in rural, frontier, and underserved urban or exurban areas has important implications for GME programs, residents/fellows, and faculty. Finding medical care in these under-resourced settings often requires access to social care resources that can help patients navigate through complex care systems. Physician learners, rotating from site to site, are often unaware of the resources available to patients and their families, and this lack of knowledge can contribute to adverse outcomes. Even if they are aware, these services are often inadequate or difficult to access. Advocacy by physician learners for individual patients sometimes is the last thread in a tattered social and medical safetynet. Systems-Based Practice, one of the six ACGME Core Competencies addressed in the ACGME Common Program Requirements, addresses the need for programs to focus on the social and structural drivers of health which, should emphasize the unique community needs and influences based on a specific clinical learning environment. In addition, this same competency requires residents and fellows should be educated to work within the construct of an integrated care team in collaboration with community health workers, navigators, nurses, and social workers who can help patients access the care they need.

POTENTIAL SOLUTIONS

Academic centers that educate physicians have an opportunity to take action to reduce the existing problems of disease and mortality gaps in rural, frontier, and underserved urban or exurban areas. We propose six potential solutions:

1. ***Develop a pathway of learners from rural, frontier, and urban underserved areas.***
   By creating and maintaining pathway programs to support students entering the health care professions from rural, frontier, and urban or exurban underserved areas, the physician workforce can, over time, better reflect the populations who are currently geographically underserved. If we can educate physicians, nurses, psychologists, social workers, and other key health care personnel from these areas, the likelihood that they will return to these areas is greatly enhanced. We must encourage and incentivize the concept of "train to remain" as a strategy to reduce the physician shortage. This recommendation is as true for rural and frontier areas as it is for urban neighborhoods serving racial/ethnic minoritized groups or other marginalized communities.
2. ***Increase opportunities for residents and fellows to experience rural, frontier, and urban health settings for some portion of their GME.***
   When recruiting candidates who come from underserved areas themselves, it is particularly critical that they learn in these locations for some part of their education. Physicians are unlikely to settle in rural, frontier, or urban underserved areas if they are not educated there. "If they can't see it, then they can't be it." Evidence demonstrates that up to 50% of physicians will settle within 75 miles of the geographic area in which they complete their postgraduate education.[1] Therefore, we must develop more residency and fellowship programs and other health learner professional programs in rural and frontier areas. By contrast, while many GME programs have participating sites located in urban underserved areas, greater incentives are needed for professionals to remain there after completing their medical education.
3. ***Reduce financial barriers for physician learners through scholarships, loan repayment, and government partnerships as an incentive to training and remaining in underserved areas.***
   To reduce the barriers that may prevent health care professionals from training or practicing in resource-constrained areas, we must further develop scholarship programs on the front end of the pathway and loan repayment programs on the back end of the pathway. These incentives can alleviate financial burdens and may increase the number of current and future physicians moving into medically underserved areas. Robust scholarships and loan repayment to the National Health Service Corps, as well

as state-based programs, must be increased to help solve health disparities in physician shortage areas. Additionally, there must be greater partnerships between the federal government and the State Offices of Rural Health to help such programs thrive. In urban underserved areas, we need to create integrated delivery systems between federally qualified health centers, Sponsoring Institutions, and GME programs to enhance both the physician workforce pathway and access to care for patients and communities.

4. *Evaluate institutional priorities and values for alignment with population health and advocate for systemic change.*

    Universal access to health care is a foundational value to improve health outcomes. Within the current US health care system, we recommend an evolution of the payment model to a value-based population health model that would focus on keeping the population healthy and maintaining sustainable practices. This model would move away from fee-for-service productivity payments to a capitation-based payment based on the number of patients in the area whom health care professionals will serve. Such a model can provide an annual fixed amount of payment per person along with some fee-for-service quality payments and shared savings, and can be paid to team-based practices based on health care outcomes so that achieving a healthier population is valued and incentivized.

    Changes to the payment model must ensure that physicians and centers that care for underserved patients are not inadvertently penalized. For this reason, advocacy for systemic change must include reform to Medicaid and other payors such that the financial incentives to care for the underserved are enhanced. We also need more robust social support systems included in payment models to screen for and address the social and structural determinants of health. Access to food, transportation, safe housing, and other factors should be included within the payment models in order for population health to be enhanced beyond traditional access to health care.

5. *Leverage health care technology to enhance accessibility of health care services and information to underserved geographic areas.*

    Health care technology must be leveraged to help care for people as close to their homes as is possible. For example, telehealth systems and patient biometric data are important tools that can be managed remotely and input into a team-based practice. Additionally, technology can facilitate access to appropriate patient education materials. Training physicians in use of such technologies and in patient education related to technological access is key. GME programs should incorporate opportunities for residents and fellows to learn to use these technologies and to stay current on the rapidly evolving field. It is worth noting that patients in underserved geographic areas may also have difficulty accessing Wi-Fi as one-fourth of the rural population lacks access to fixed broadband services necessary for telehealth services. In addition, some populations may not have access to electronic devices, or may not know how to use them due to limited health literacy or educational status. Assessing for technology accessibility issues should be an important step for GME programs and health care teams hoping to leverage technology to provide effective care to underserved patients.

    > Although 20% of the US population lives in rural and frontier areas, only 9% of the physician workforce is both located in and educated in these areas. "You can't be it if you don't see it."

6. **Enhance GME that focuses on health and health promotion and promotes team-based care.**

    There must be enhanced education and training in the generalist disciplines of family medicine, internal medicine, pediatrics, geriatrics, surgery, and psychiatry, with a specific emphasis on team-based care in rural and frontier areas. This approach aims to widen the vision of providing holistic care to underserved populations in a way that moves our gaze from disease and sick care only and more toward health and health promotion.

    > While urban areas are physician-dense, unlike rural and frontier regions, there are urban neighborhoods of concentrated poverty that are highly medically underserved and lack easy access to primary and advanced specialty care and social care.

All GME programs should provide residents and fellows with experience on interdisciplinary team-based models with nurses, medical assistants physician assistants, nurse practitioners, social workers, psychologists, pharmacists, community health workers, and others.[9] This training must start as early as possible, including both in undergraduate medical education and GME. Rural and frontier health care will particularly benefit from a new model focused on team-based care. All health care is local. If teams can work effectively together to lessen morbidity and mortality and improve health care outcomes, they will not only elevate patient satisfaction and timely access but will also lessen the burnout that occurs to many clinicians in underserved locations.

Take Home Points

- Timely access to acute, chronic, and preventive health care is the key to better health care outcomes in rural and frontier areas.
- Team-based interdisciplinary health care and medical education models are needed to provide the resources and bandwidth necessary to tackle geographic location-related challenges to access.
- Across states and in urban areas, there are wide geographic differences in mortality, races, and ethnicities for treatable conditions.
- Controlling for race, large geographic differences in life expectancy exist for low-income individuals in urban areas.
- There are large gaps in health outcomes and life expectancy in geographic areas that are short distances apart due to the unequal and inequitable distribution of social and health resources.

QUESTIONS FOR FURTHER THOUGHT

1. When considering the case study about a patient with complex urgent health care needs arriving at a rural medical setting for care, how could more resources (eg, surgical, obstetric, pediatric, and anesthesia) have been developed in advance?
2. What institutional partnerships or collaborations at geographic settings different from yours could be beneficial to the education and training of your program or institution's physician learners?
3. What is the role of public policy in addressing the geographic life expectancy and mortality gaps in urban areas? Think through what policies around social needs, health care insurance access, housing, and education might improve geographic and income variability.
4. How is geographic social disadvantage incorporated into the learning content of resident/fellow physicians at your institution? If geographic location is not currently being addressed, what are possible opportunities in your curriculum where this topic could be taught?

REFERENCES

1. Council on Graduate Medical Education (COGME) 24th Report. Strengthening the rural health workforce to improve health outcomes in rural communities. 2022. https://www.hrsa.gov/sites/default/files/hrsa/advisory-committees/graduate-medical-edu/reports/cogme-april-2022-report.pdf
2. US Health Resources and Services Administration. Health professional shortage areas: primary care, by county. October 2024. https://www.ruralhealthinfo.org/charts/5
3. America Counts Staff. America Counts: Stories–What is rural America? United States Census Bureau. 2017. Accessed June 23, 2023 https://www.census.gov/library/stories/2017/08/rural-america.html
4. Rabinowitz HK, Diamond JJ, Markham FW, Wortman JR. Medical school programs to increase the rural physician supply: a systematic review and projected impact of widespread replication. *Acad Med*. 2008;83(3):235-243. doi: 10.1097/ACM.0b013e318163789b

5. Hoffman A, Holmes M. Regional differences in rural and urban mortality trends. North Carolina Health Research Program. Findings Brief: North Carolina Rural Health Research and Policy Analysis Center. 2017. Accessed June 23, 2023. https://www.shepscenter.unc.edu/wp-content/uploads/dlm_uploads/2017/08/Regional-Differences-in-Urban-and-Rural-Mortality-Trends.pdf
6. Lister JJ, Weaver A, Ellis JD, Himle JA, Ledgerwood DM. A systematic review of rural-specific barriers to medication treatment for opioid use disorder in the United States. *Am J Drug Alcohol Abuse*. 2020;46(3):273-288. doi:10.1080/00952990.2019.1694536
7. Villapiano N, Iwashyna TJ, Davis MM. Worsening rural-urban gap in hospital mortality. *J AM Board Fam Med*. 2017;30(6):816-823. doi:10.3122/jabfm.2017.06.170137
8. Skinner L, Wong, S, Colla C. Rethinking rurality: using hospital referral regions to investigate rural-urban health outcomes. *BMC Health Serv Res*. 2022;22(1):1312. doi:10.1186/s12913-022-08649-0
9. National Academies of Sciences, Engineering, and Medicine. *Implementing High-Quality Primary Care: Rebuilding the Foundation of Health Care*. The National Academies Press; 2021. doi:10.17226/25983
10. Radley DC, Baumgartner JC, Collins SR, Zephyrin L, Schneider EC. Achieving racial and ethnic equity in U.S. health care: a scorecard of state performance. *Commonwealth Fund*. November 18, 2021. https://www.commonwealthfund.org/publications/scorecard/2021/nov/achieving-racial-ethnic-equity-us-health-care-state-performance
11. Ansell D, Grabler P, Whitman S, et al. A community effort to reduce the black/white breast cancer mortality disparity in Chicago. *Cancer Causes Control*. 2009;20:1681-1688. doi:10.1007/s10552-009-9419-7

Building Institutional Cultures of Safety and Accountability to Support Graduate Medical Education

Nicole Franks, MD, Professor of Emergency Medicine, Emory School of Medicine; Interim Chief Quality Officer, Emory Healthcare, Atlanta, GA

Jessica Elizabeth Isom, MD, Clinical Instructor, Department of Psychiatry, Yale School of Medicine, New Haven, CT

Sunny Nakae, PhD, MSW, Senior Associate Dean for Diversity, Equity, Inclusion, and Partnership, Associate Professor of Medical Education, California University of Science and Medicine, Colton, CA

Bonnie Simpson Mason, MD, Medical Director, Diversity, Equity and Inclusion, American College of Surgeons, Chicago, IL; Associate Adjunct Professor, Department of Orthopedic Surgery and Rehabilitation, University of Texas Medical Branch, Galveston, TX

CHAPTER SUMMARY

This chapter focuses on basic principles and actions to guide development of a safe and equitable institutional culture that promotes the well-being of the health care workforce. Such a culture is necessary in order to decrease inequities at all levels with the ultimate goal of achieving excellent patient care delivery. Its development requires commitment and accountability from leadership who can achieve these goals strategically by understanding the key unique and overlapping elements of quality, safety, well-being, and equity. Through its Clinical Learning Environment Review (CLER) program, the ACGME has provided the foundation for recognizing how these elements interact to support excellence in the clinical learning environment (CLE) for graduate medical education (GME) and to provide high quality patient care. Our goal here is to offer additional information that emphasizes how the continuum of medical education permeates the overall institutional culture in Sponsoring Institutions and GME programs and affects the entire health care workforce.

LEARNING OBJECTIVES

1. Define the key concepts of quality, safety, well-being, and equity.
2. Describe the integral relationship between quality, safety, well-being, and equity and their impact on the overall learning environment and institutional culture.
3. Outline recommendations for leaders, faculty members, residents, fellows, and staff regarding how each can contribute to a culture of safety within their learning environments.

Case Study

Dr Sims, a first-year general surgery resident, is pre-rounding on post-operative surgery patients before the team arrives at 7:00 AM. Upon entering Patient X's room and introducing herself to the patient, the patient responds to Dr Sims, "Absolutely not. I do not want a Black person seeing me." Dr Sims tries to explain that she is part of the surgical team and just needs to examine her quickly. Patient X doubles down, saying, "No. I do not want a Black person seeing me." Dr Sims leaves Patient X's room surprised, hurt, and now fearful that, because of the patient's refusal, she will not be prepared for rounds.

At 7:00 AM., the team gathers at the nursing station for rounds. Once the team reaches Patient X's room, Dr Sims presents Patient X's vitals and labs. The chief resident, Dr Schneider, then queries Dr Sims about the status of Patient X's wound, and Dr Sims hesitantly shares that she did not perform a physical examination on Patient X because the patient refused to have a Black doctor examine her. Without hesitation, Dr Schneider tells the team to follow him into Patient X's room. Once there, Dr Schneider greets the patient then states to the patient, "Dr Sims is a member of our surgical team, and she is here to deliver excellent surgical care to you. If you do not want her to provide care for you as a part of our surgical team, then you can seek care elsewhere."

Case Study Discussion

Dr Schneider took immediate steps to address the racist remarks by a patient directed toward his junior team member. This action may serve to mitigate the trauma experienced by Dr Sims upon being rejected and demeaned by a patient because of her race. Such allyship helps to create a sense of safety and community, potentially quelling the sense of isolation that Dr Sims felt as a result of the patient's statement. This psychological safety extended not just to Dr Sims, but also to the entire surgical team who benefited from the modeling by Dr Schneider of how to create a safe space for the team in a clinical learning environment (CLE).

Alternatively, had Dr Schneider chosen to ignore Patient X's statement, the traumatizing experience could have been perpetuated. It would have further isolated and marginalized Dr Sims, increasing her stress level, potentially serving as a distraction, decreasing her ability to concentrate, or perhaps, even creating undo anxiety, which could potentially impact her ability to care effectively for other patients. It would have also demonstrated a passive reaction to such an event by a leader of the team and possibly perpetuated affirmation of such behavior.

INSTITUTIONAL CULTURE AND GME

Building safe and courageous spaces begins with examining an organization's culture. The importance of culture in all its dimensions as it impacts workforce—environmental, professional, interpersonal—has been well-recognized across various industries. For example, the business sector has demonstrated the effect of culture on productivity, workforce stability/growth, revenues, profits, and sustainability. The state of an organization's culture has a significant impact on the ability of the organization to achieve its mission or to meet any of its stated goals. In fact, business consultant Peter Drucker is believed to have coined the widely accepted business concept, "Culture eats strategy for breakfast," meaning that the best efforts can be thwarted if the organization's culture (ie, its foundation) is negative or toxic.

Similarly, the culture of medicine has come under scrutiny as issues affecting the health care workforce, such as clinician shortages, learner attrition, and death by suicide, are growing concerns. As a result, challenges facing the current workforce, especially in GME, must be examined. The institutional culture in which GME occurs in Sponsoring Institutions and programs may serve as the key to stabilizing and growing the physician and health care workforce to meet a rapidly growing US population in need of care.

UNDERSTANDING THE EFFECTS OF CULTURE—AN ANALOGY

The culture of the CLE in every configuration is critical to either the proliferation of or detriment to all those who learn and work in this environment. Among physicians, negative and even toxic cultures, defined as settings where harassment, mistreatment, and discrimination are permitted to occur, have led to increased burnout, attrition, and death by suicide at all levels along the continuum of medical education.[1]

To help define and contextualize the impact of institutional culture on GME, we offer an analogy from microbiology. Microbiology experiments are conducted to observe the proliferation of microorganisms, or a lack thereof, by pipetting the organisms into a petri dish filled with agar (Figure 5.1a). The role of the observer is to watch for and document whether or not there is proliferation of microorganisms in the culture (Figure 5.1b). The culture's composition is the primary determinant of the microorganism's proliferation or non-proliferation. More specifically, the components of the culture rather than the characteristics of the microorganisms themselves have a greater impact in determining whether the microorganism grows (Figure 5.1c). In other words, the microorganisms themselves are not the sole or primary determinants of their ability to survive and proliferate in a particular culture; rather, the culture largely determines whether or not the microorganisms will thrive. In order to survive despite inhospitable circumstances (eg, the presence of antibiotics), some bacteria develop special features that allow them to proliferate. Examples include Methicillin-Resistant *Staphylococcus aureus* (MRSA) or Vancomycin Resistant Enterococcus (VRE).

Similarly, in an institution, workforce at all levels cannot thrive and grow in toxic cultures. Residents and fellows, in particular, should not have to exhibit the characteristics of MRSA or VRE in order to successfully navigate each level of their respective GME programs. This is especially true for minoritized learners and practicing physicians who experience discrimination in the workplace. Those who have the power, authority, and access to resources to determine the composition of the culture in their respective learning environments have the responsibility for and should be held accountable for developing safe and equitable settings that benefit the workforce and their patients.

THE CULTURE OF THE LEARNING ENVIRONMENT

Just as the institution has a culture of its own, likewise, the learning environment has a culture that can have a positive or negative impact on physician learners and faculty members, both in clinical and research settings. Its influence has been well documented:

1. Well-being: Significant environmental threats to mental health and well-being occur in the transition to and in the first year of residency.[2]
2. Burnout: Hu et al have documented that almost 40% of surgical residents surveyed report weekly burnout symptoms.[3]
3. Mistreatment: Approximately 70% of surgical residents from minoritized gender or racial/ethnic backgrounds report mistreatment in surgical training.[3]
4. Resident transitions, including attrition: Haruno et al report disparate attrition rates have been reported with an overrepresentation from minoritized gender and racial/ethnic backgrounds in every surgical subspecialty.[4]
5. Suicidality: Exposure to discrimination, abuse, or harassment greater than 2 times per month found that residents were almost 3 times as likely to have symptoms of burnout and were more than 3 times more likely to have suicidal thoughts compared to those with no reported mistreatment exposures.[1]

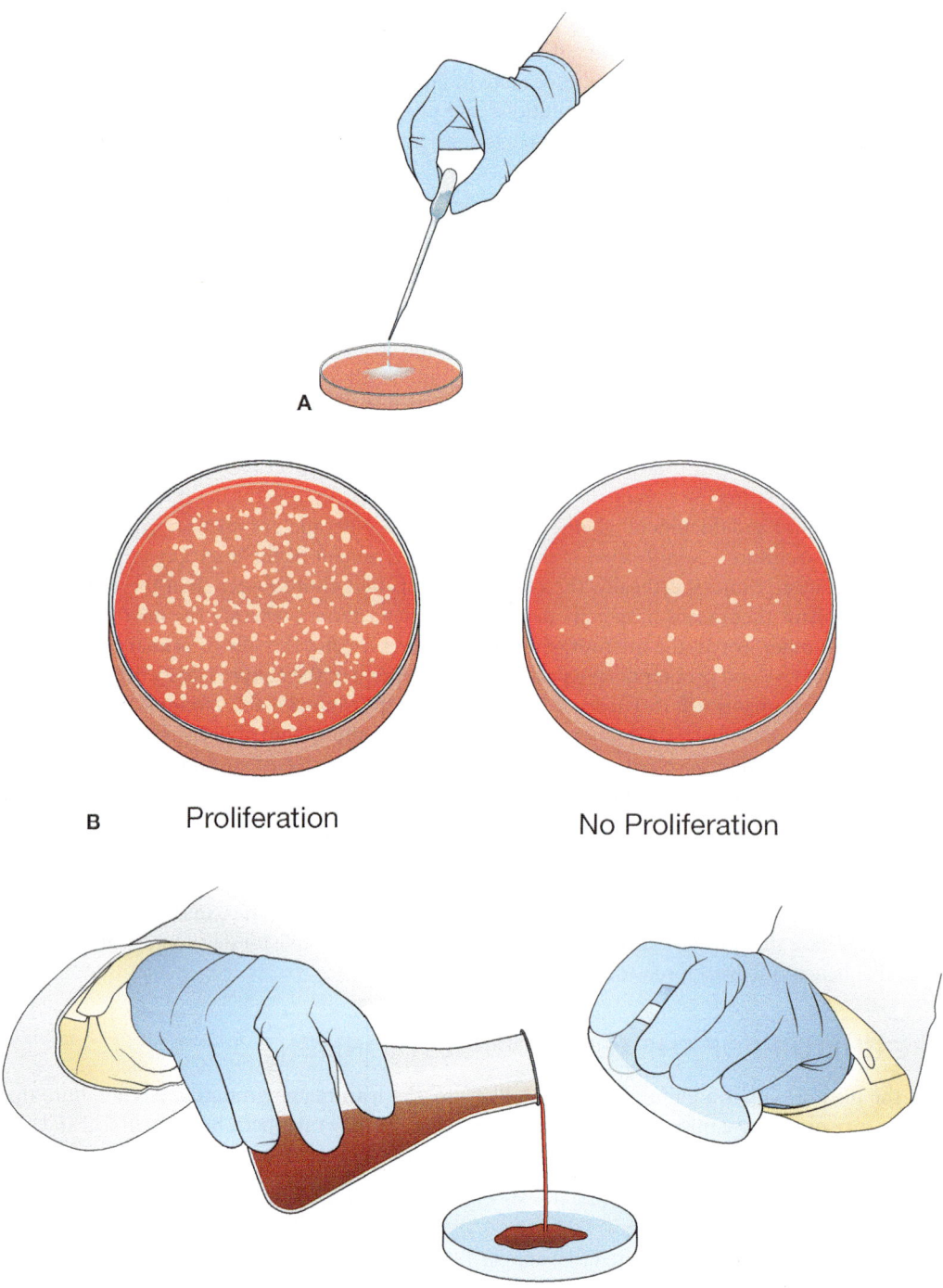

FIGURE 5.1 The culture for growth of microorganisms can serve as an analogy for institutional culture. (A) Pipetting of microorganisms into a petri dish with agar (the culture medium)—residents and fellows are acculturated into an existing learning environment. (B) Resulting proliferation or non-proliferation of microorganisms over time—ongoing observation and assessment of the learners and how cultural determinants may be at work in their growth or lack thereof. (C) The culture medium being poured into the petri dish—the learners are not the sole determinants of their ability to survive; the culture largely determines whether they will thrive.

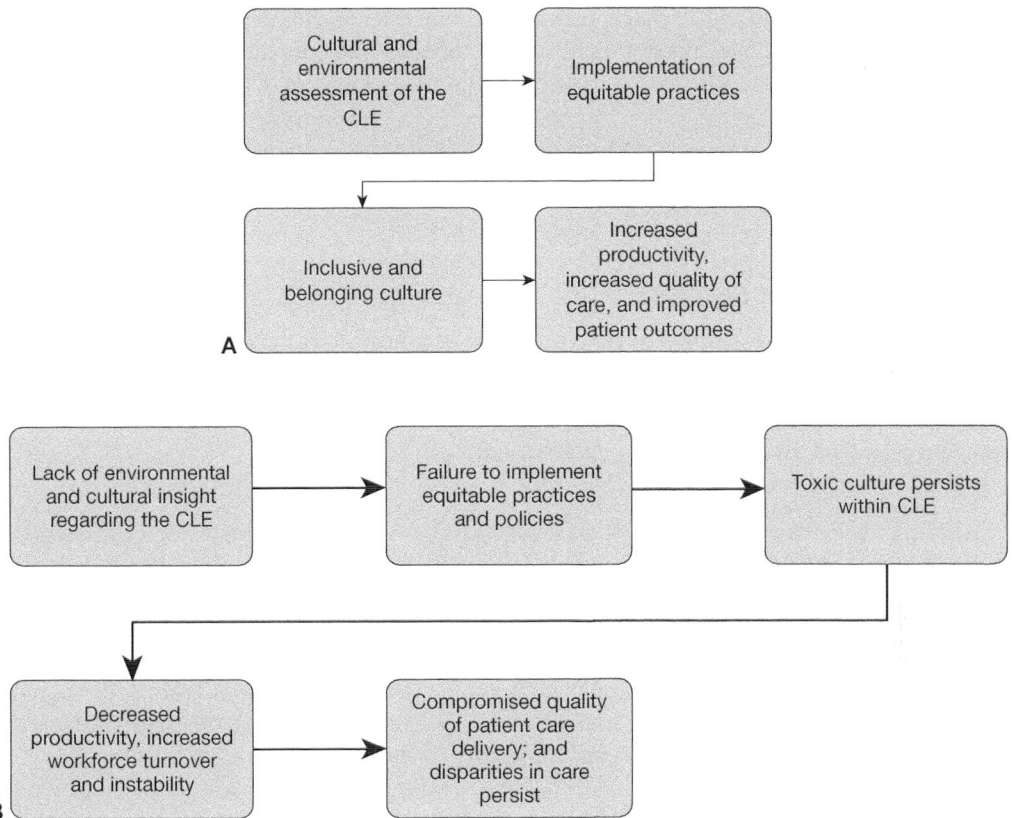

FIGURE 5.2 (A) Positive results from ongoing assessment of the CLE. (B) Negative outcomes from a lack of environmental and cultural insight in the CLE.

Figure 5.2a and b provides a flow diagram of the positive result from ongoing assessment of the CLE and the negative outcome when environmental and cultural insight into the CLE is lacking, respectively.

Heretofore, most diversity, equity, and inclusion efforts have focused downstream on the lack of preparation, understanding, or resilience of residents, fellows, or patients from minoritized or marginalized backgrounds. Extensive literature exists on the need to strengthen the academic readiness and professional development of physician learners in the pathway to and through the continuum of medical education. Similarly, regarding diverse populations, their knowledge, education levels, access to resources, health, and financial literacy have been examined and assessed as factors contributing to ongoing and worsening health disparities nationwide. If institutions solely focus on the downstream strategies, they may inadvertently single out the characteristics of marginalized individuals as being responsible for the health disparities or educational inequities they experience.

However, a paucity of literature examines and holds accountable the systems and structures that determine the educational policies and carry out the health care practices that limit access to quality care. Organizational leadership is responsible for developing cultures within health care and medical education that can contribute to inclusion, belonging, and safety. Cultures of inclusion, belonging, and safety may, in turn, support the well-being of the current and burgeoning workforce. A well-supported workforce would subsequently be well positioned to deliver excellent care to all patients, including those from marginalized backgrounds. In 2001, the Institute of Medicine (IOM) identified that across all chronic conditions, Black Americans fared worse in all chronic disease categories compared to White Americans, even after controlling for social and financial factors.[5] Studies by Lucas et al confirm persisting health disparities among marginalized groups.[6] These poorer outcomes were attributed to providing poorer care due to physician and provider bias. The IOM, now the National Academy of Medicine, subsequently identified equity as the sixth aim of quality care delivery in 2002 as part of its recommendations on improving the quality and safety of US health care.[7]

THE FUTURE (IDEAL) STATE OF MEDICAL EDUCATION

Building a Culture of Equity

Dr Camara Jones explains that **equity** aims to provide "the assurance of the conditions for optimal health for all people, which requires:

- valuing all individuals and populations equally;
- recognizing and rectifying historical injustices; and,
- providing resources according to need."[8]

When these elements of equity are met, individuals feel a sense of belonging within the environment, which fosters inclusion and psychological safety, subsequently increasing productivity and performance, which, in turn, translates to the provision of quality care to patients. Moreover, this sense of belonging provides a foundation for continued connection for all those who function within that environment, increasing work satisfaction and preventing burnout. Through the provision and intentional development of a culture that prioritizes optimizing the workplace, all can thrive. In GME, the setting includes both learning and clinical workplace environments, and the individuals who stand to benefit from the environmental culture include all those who work or deliver care, including learners, faculty members, and staff members.

Building a Culture of Well-Being

Individual **well-being** can be defined as the extent to which people experience happiness and satisfaction and are able to realize their full potential. Situating these efforts in the workplace context is important because achieving individual well-being in the workplace—workplace well-being—is inextricably connected to having safe spaces.

Organizational policies and programming should support all health care workforce while ensuring that those who have been marginalized in the workplace are at the center of these efforts. This approach acknowledges that social positioning affects every aspect of the life experiences of all colleagues, both within and outside of the workplace. Institutional engagement in building a culture of well-being also acknowledges how dominant culture, power, privilege, and oppression shape opportunities and impact their well-being. Applying the concept of **psychological safety**, the shared belief that it is safe to discuss ideas, experiment, take risks, and give feedback, may help shift institutions closer to equitable interventions.

Building a Culture Prioritizing Delivery of Quality Care

Care must be delivered with attention to patient safety to provide quality care that ultimately results in optimal outcomes. Advancing quality and patient safety in health care is a journey that requires continuous improvement by all health care team members to yield positive results.

The impetus for health care to focus on quality and patient safety began over 20 years ago with a self-assessment of health care practice in the Institute of Medicine report *To Err is Human*.[9] This report revealed that quality patient care was not happening, not happening consistently, or not happening as intended, resulting in harm. The report highlighted the unintended consequences of actions or inactions when medical practice goes unchecked. The follow-up report *Crossing the Quality Chasm*[7] responded to this call to action by defining quality care with six domains:

1. Safety
2. Timeliness
3. Efficiency

4. Effectiveness
5. Patient centeredness
6. Equity

These reports form the foundation of the intentional movement in medicine to prevent harm and improve patient outcomes. That same intentional movement set the stage for the ACGME CLER program. At present, through its National Reports of Findings, CLER provides an annual national data profile for how these domains, with the addition of physician well-being, are the focus of how Sponsoring Institutions engage residents and fellows in the CLE to address patient safety and quality.

In a complex health care system, analyzing outcomes data or harmful events requires a balanced approach that considers human factors, just culture, competency, and system structure. Human factors, such as implicit or explicit bias, test burden, or the physical condition of the involved individual, reveal contributors to decision-making. Just culture evaluates the individual's intention in any event or process. Finally, system structure that includes policy, technology, or environmental factors can be contributing causes when a trend is identified or an event has occurred. Using improvement tools for systematic analysis creates a safe space for care team members to explore concerns in the context of just culture, principles, competency, human factors, and system structure. Examples of such tools that can be applied in a health care or GME setting to identify the root cause of a problem or event include the following: process maps, asking the five whys, or value stream analysis.

Quality and patient safety require continuous improvement to ensure the right solution is planned and implemented with constant checking for sustainment. The solution must be targeted and based on these analyses, as generalized interventions do not always achieve equitable results. Although education and training are important components of change, sustainment of change involves using reliable methods such as checklists, visual management, audits, and feedback or automation. Data should be used to evaluate practices and anonymous reporting of harmful events should be facilitated. Finally, building in-progress checkpoints and debriefing meetings or discussions help to manage the difficulty of change. Committing to continuous improvement and honoring the difficulty of change are key for the sustainment of targeted solutions.

Building a Culture of Safety

We have reviewed the critical components necessary to build safe and equitable cultures in Sponsoring Institutions and GME programs that prioritize workforce well-being in pursuit of optimizing delivery of quality and safe patient care. Significant overlap exists in the cultural components of CLEs that promote and prioritize (1) delivering safe and quality care; (2) ensuring well-being for residents, fellows, and practicing physicians; and, (3) implementing equitable practices to create safe and inclusive learning environments for each level of the clinical workforce. Ellis et al offer a framework for improving the clinical, academic, and professional experiences of learners in need of support, which includes assessing and examining the culture of a CLE at a departmental, institutional, and organizational level that can lead to clues as to the viability and productivity of the workforce and learners within that environment.[10] These characteristics are cultural indicators of CLEs that, when instituted by program, institutional, or organizational leadership, can support workforce well-being and retention (Table 5.1).

It is important to recognize the steps that leaders can take to operationalize a culture of safety in GME environments. Figure 5.3 provides a sequential approach to actionable steps for leaders.

> Developing organizational cultures that are accountable for safe and equitable learning environments is the responsibility of leadership across the continuum of medical education, not only at the level of the individual learner or faculty member.

> According to *Crossing the Quality Chasm*, the six aims of quality care include the following: safety, timeliness, efficiency, effectiveness, patient centeredness, and equity.

Table 5.1 Key Indicators of a Culture of Safety in Clinical Learning Environments

Key Indicators of a Culture of Safety in the Clinical Learning Environment	Quality and Safe Care Delivery	Well-Being of Individuals	Equitable Practices Leading to Belonging
Faculty members	Faculty integrate the six domains of quality into the core competencies and milestones within teaching curricula.	Faculty receive training and support in the pursuit of physical, mental, and psychological health.	Faculty are taught to build cultural humility skills and recognize and address their own biases.
Residents/fellows	Learners are educated on the six domains of quality and safe care and implement health equity quality improvement projects.	Institutions actively seek input from learners regarding their well-being and their assessment of psychological safety within the learning environment; ongoing resources are available to support resident/fellow well-being.	Learners are queried and receive academic, clinical, and professional development support according to need.
Patients	Feedback is solicited regarding quality of care received, including their perception of safety in health care environment.	Patients give feedback on communication skills and responsiveness of the health care team.[11]	Patients are provided with care and resources to address their specific cultural, language, or other specific needs.[11]

Reprinted from Allar BG, Ortega G, Chun MBJ, et al. Changing surgical culture through surgical education: introduction to the pacts trial. *J Surg Educ.* 2024;81(3):330-334. doi: 10.1016/j.jsurg.2023.11.018, with permission from Elsevier.

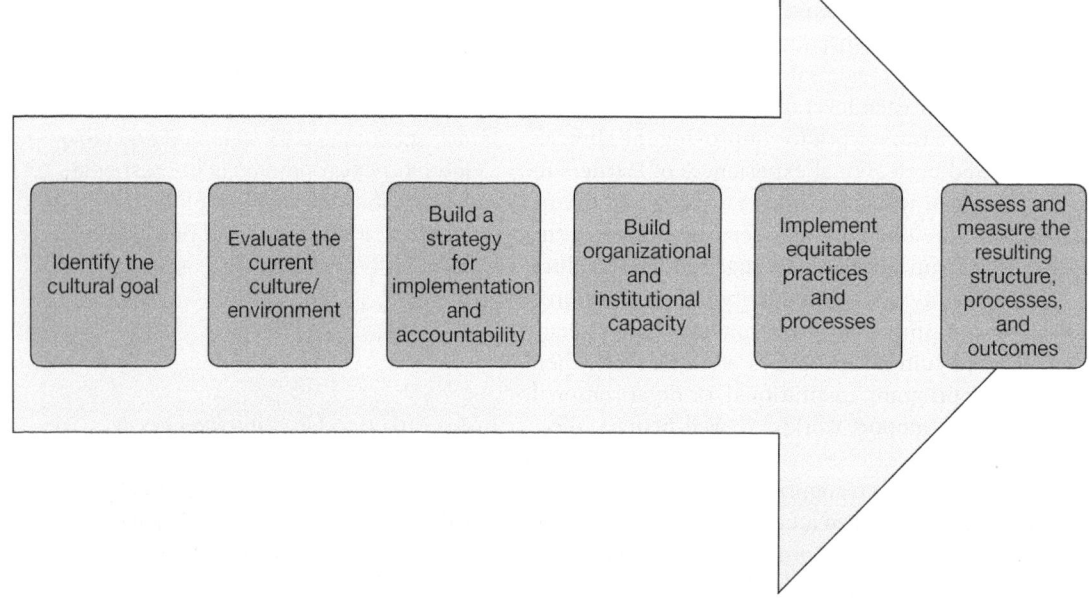

FIGURE 5.3 Actionable steps leaders can take to build a safe and equitable culture in medical education.

When institutional leaders, program directors, designated institutional officials, and all leaders in health care institutions and programs across the continuum of medical education are conscious of and commit resources to creating cultures that promote safety and workforce well-being, then all in the workforce have the opportunity to prosper via improved well-being, patients will benefit, and health equity can be achieved.[12]

Ensuring that the CLE that supports medical education is both safe and equitable is critical to the development of future physicians and the entire health care workforce if they are to provide the highest quality of care to patients. There is no patient safety without physician safety.

Take Home Points

- Negative and even toxic cultures, defined as settings where harassment, mistreatment, and discrimination are permitted to occur, have led to increased burnout, attrition, and death by suicide in the physician workforce at all levels of medical education.
- Like in microbiology petri dish cultures, institutional culture more significantly impacts whether individuals will thrive compared to the characteristics of each individual.
- The extent to which the culture of the learning environment is positive or negative has a substantial impact on well-being, burnout, mistreatment, attrition, and suicidality.
- Prioritizing quality and patient safety is a critical piece of creating a culture of safety in GME settings and requires continuous improvement and sustainability efforts.
- Leaders can take multiple actionable steps to build a safe and equitable institutional culture that will support excellence in GME.

QUESTIONS FOR FURTHER THOUGHT

1. What, if any, foundational aspects of equity, well-being, and quality are integrated in the curriculum at your GME program or Sponsoring Institution?
2. What specific educational modalities and resources are being used to teach foundational concepts related to equity, well-being, and quality? What elements have you found to be effective or ineffective?
3. In what ways does your GME program or Sponsoring Institution measure equity, well-being, and quality? If there are metrics not currently being collected that you would like to see considered in the future, please explain.

REFERENCES

1. Engelhardt KE, Bilimoria KY, Johnson JK, et al. A national mixed-methods evaluation of preparedness for general surgery residency and the association with resident burnout. *JAMA Surg*. 2020;155(9):851-859. doi:10.1001/jamasurg.2020.2420
2. Slavin S, Cheong J, Bienstock J, Bernstein C. Overcoming barriers to mental health care for residents. *J Grad Med Educ*. 2024;16(3):374-378. doi:10.4300/JGME-D-24-00409.2
3. Hu YY, Ellis RJ, Hewitt DB et al. Discrimination, abuse, harassment, and burnout in surgical residency training. *N Engl J Med*. 2019;381(18):1741-1752. doi:10.1056/NEJMsa1903759
4. Haruno LS, Chen X, Metzger M, et al. Racial and sex disparities in resident attrition among surgical subspecialties. *JAMA Surg*. 2023;158(4):368-376. doi:10.1001/jamasurg.2022.7640
5. Institute of Medicine (US) Committee on Understanding and Eliminating Racial and Ethnic Disparities in Health Care. Understanding and eliminating racial and ethnic disparities in health care; background paper racial and ethnic disparities in health care: a background and history. In: Smedley BD, Stith AY, Nelson AR, eds. *Unequal Treatment: Confronting Racial and Ethnic Disparities in Health Care*. National Academies Press (US); 2003.

6. Lucas FL, Stukel TA, Morris AM, Siewers AE, Birkmeyer JD. Race and surgical mortality in the United States. *Ann Surg.* 2006;243(2):281-286. doi:10.1097/01.sla.0000197560.92456.32
7. Institute of Medicine (US) Committee on Quality of Health Care in America. *Crossing the Quality Chasm: A New Health System for the 21st Century*. National Academies Press (US); 2001.
8. Jones CP, Holden KB, Belton A. Strategies for achieving health equity: concern about the whole plus concern about the hole. *Ethn Dis.* 2019;29(suppl 2):345-348. doi:10.18865/ed.29.S2.345
9. Institute of Medicine (US) Committee on Quality of Health Care in America, Kohn LT, Corrigan JM, Donaldson MS, eds. *To Err Is Human: Building a Safer Health System*. National Academies Press (US); 2000.
10. Ellis J, Otugo O, Landry A, Landry A. Dismantling the overpolicing of black residents. *N Engl J Med.* 2023;389(14):1258-1261. doi:10.1056/NEJMp2304559
11. Allar BG, Ortega G, Chun MBJ, et al. Changing surgical culture through surgical education: introduction to the pacts trial. *J Surg Educ.* 2024;81(3):330-334. doi:10.1016/j.jsurg.2023.11.018
12. Nasca BJ, Cheung EO, Eng JS, et al. National comparison of program director perceptions vs. resident reports of the learning environment and well-being. *J Surg Educ.* 2023;80(1):72-80. doi:10.1016/j.jsurg.2022.08.016

Federal Employment Laws: Resident and Fellow Rights and Institutional Accountability

Sandra E. Hodgin, PhD, MEd, Founder and CEO of Title IX Consulting Group, Chino Hills, CA

Anne Knox Averitt, JD, Attorney, Bradley Arant Boult Cummings LLP, Birmingham, AL

CHAPTER SUMMARY

It is critical for residents and fellows, faculty members, and leadership at Sponsoring Institutions and graduate medical education (GME) programs to understand Title VII and other federal employment laws that are in place to protect residents and fellows from unfair treatment in the workplace, entitle them to reasonable leaves of absence, and ensure they have full access to educational opportunities. This chapter serves to provide foundational knowledge on basic federal employment laws and outline best practices for institutions.

LEARNING OBJECTIVES

1. Outline the basic federal employment laws for equal employment opportunity.
2. Describe the protections employees enjoy under those laws and the available remedies for an alleged employer violation.
3. Describe scenarios in which issues might arise under those laws.
4. Review strategies for hospital accountability on compliance with federal employment laws and ACGME requirements that impact the graduate medical education (GME) learning environment.

Case Study

Patrick and Ellen are both new residents. Ellen tells Patrick that one of her supervising attending physicians has made her feel uncomfortable and gives details about her interactions with the physician. Patrick is concerned about what Ellen shares with him, but he is unsure of what to do or what to advise.

The supervising physician is Dr Hellman, a well-established attending physician who is known to play a key role in helping program graduates obtain their desired fellowships and job opportunities. Ellen shares with Patrick that during spring break, she attended an informal gathering at his home, to which Dr Hellman had invited several residents. Dr Hellman served alcohol throughout the night, and Ellen became dizzy after a couple of drinks. As the gathering ended, Dr Hellman offered to take Ellen home so that she would not have to drive. Ellen accepted the offer, and as they walked to his vehicle, he grabbed her waist to ensure she maintained her balance. Ellen describes feeling surprised, but initially thought he was trying to help her from falling. Once they were in the car, however, Dr Hellman told Ellen she was attractive and that he was interested in helping

(continued)

her career. Dr Hellman then placed his hand on the inside of her thigh and began to run his hand up her leg; Ellen pulled her leg away. Soon after, they arrived at her home and she rushed inside. Following that evening, Dr Hellman has stared at Ellen intensely during work hours, has made mention of his ability to help her career if she would like to further discuss it privately, and has continued to persistently invite Ellen to additional gatherings at his home, which she has declined. Ellen has become very uncomfortable at work and is concerned about what to do as a new resident.

Case Study Discussion

Dr Hellman's behavior experienced by Ellen constitutes sexual harassment. Residents and fellows are protected against sexual harassment (and harassment based on any protected status) under Title VII. Because Ellen is a new resident, these prohibited behaviors fall under the umbrella of both Title VII and Title IX, federal employment statutes. It is important to note that a medical student in a similar situation would solely be protected by Title IX, because medical students are not considered employees.

Ellen should become familiar with the hospital's employment policies and reporting procedures, and she should report Dr Hellman's actions to Human Resources or another designated supervisor (not Dr Hellman). Patrick should encourage Ellen to make this report. Human Resources should then investigate Ellen's report, and Patrick may need to speak with Human Resources to corroborate Ellen's report through the course of their investigation. Just as Title VII prohibits sexual harassment, it also prohibits retaliation; both Ellen and Patrick will be protected from the hospital taking adverse actions against them for reporting Dr Hellman's conduct to Human Resources. As you read this chapter, reflect on Ellen and Patrick's situation and consider what processes are in place at your institution or program to protect residents and fellows from harassment, discrimination, or other forms of mistreatment based on federally protected attributes.

INTRODUCTION

For the purpose of the educational continuum, residents and fellows (hereafter, residents) are learners. In addition, considerable legal precedent supports that, for legal purposes, residents are also employees. Hence, this chapter focuses on federal employment laws that are applicable to residents and should be understood by residents, faculty members, and leadership of Sponsoring Institutions and GME programs to ensure compliance with legal requirements. We will review foundational knowledge on basic federal employment laws, including Title VII of the Civil Rights Act of 1964, Title IX of the Education Amendments of 1972, the Americans with Disabilities Act, the Pregnancy Workers Fairness Act, and the Family Medical Leave Act. While this list of employment laws is not exhaustive, it covers many common and critical issues that affect residents during their employment for residency and fellowship. In addition to reviewing the content and implications of each of these laws, we will outline good practices for institutions to remain compliant with federal employment laws. These practices benefit residents by protecting their federal rights, and they may also have the added benefit of improving residents' well-being and ability to thrive in the physician workforce, leading to a more positive clinical learning and practice environment and improved patient care.

TITLE VII OF THE CIVIL RIGHTS ACT OF 1964

Title VII is a federal employment law intended to protect equal employment opportunities and protect residents as employees. It prohibits the following:

- Employment decisions based on race, color, religion, sex, national origin. Under Title VII, it is unlawful to discriminate in any aspect of employment, including hiring and termination; compensation or assignment; transfer, promotion, layoff; recruitment; testing; use of employer facilities; and training programs.
- Harassment based on a protected status (race, color, religion, sex, national origin) and requires reasonable accommodations for sincerely held religious beliefs.
- Retaliation for engaging in protected activity, such as reporting discrimination by an employer.

What Remedies Are Available to Residents for an Employer's Violation of Title VII?

As employees, if residents experience a violation of Title VII, they must first file a charge with the Equal Employment Opportunity Commission (EEOC), a federal agency that investigates claims of discrimination. The EEOC may make a finding. When the EEOC closes the file, the EEOC issues a Notice of Rights letter to the employee. The employee may then file a lawsuit in federal court based on the allegations raised in the charge. In rare circumstances, the EEOC may also file a lawsuit against the employer on the employee's behalf.

If an employer is found liable in a lawsuit for a Title VII violation, the employee can receive monetary damages and **injunctive relief**, meaning that the employer is required to do something such as put the employee in a certain job.

What Steps Should Hospitals and Other Employers Take to Comply with and Limit Liability Under Title VII?

There are several steps that Sponsoring Institutions and GME programs can take to position themselves to readily comply with Title VII with regards to non-discrimination and policies around harassment. **Harassment**, as prohibited by Title VII, consists of unwelcome conduct, whether verbal, physical, or visual, that is based on a person's protected status. Sexual harassment is the type of harassment most frequently reported. According to the EEOC, unwelcome sexual advances, requests for sexual favors, and other verbal, visual, or physical conduct based on sex constitute sexual harassment when the following conditions apply: submission to the conduct is made either an express or implied condition of employment or association; submission to, or rejection of, the conduct is used as the basis for an employment decision; or the conduct has the purpose or effect of unreasonably interfering with an individual's work performance or creating an intimidating, hostile, or abusive work environment.[1]

Drawing from guidance from the EEOC,[1] we propose the following key steps, with examples of how each one can be accomplished.

1. Formulate and publicize an Equal Employment Opportunity policy. The authors have drafted the following example that can be reviewed and adapted by others:

    This institution is an equal opportunity employer. We will recruit, hire, train, and promote persons in all job titles without regard to race, color, religion, national origin, sex (including pregnancy, sexual orientation and gender identity or expression), marital status, age, physical or mental disability, veteran status, genetic information, or any legally protected status (hereafter, protected status). All decisions regarding compensation, benefits, transfers, layoffs, sponsored training, education, and social and recreational programs will be administered without regard to any protected status. This institution will also make reasonable accommodation for known physical or mental disabilities unless such actions cause undue hardship. Similarly, we will provide reasonable accommodations related to your sincerely held religious belief unless it would pose an undue hardship. If you need a reasonable accommodation for a disability or religious accommodation, please contact Human Resources.

2. Implement a policy making clear that harassment is prohibited and outlining a reporting procedure for employees, including residents, who feel that they have experienced or witnessed harassment. Such a policy should be specifically publicized among residents to highlight the institution's commitment to a harassment-free environment. The authors have drafted example language that can be reviewed and adapted by others:

> *This institution is committed to maintaining a work environment that is free of unlawful harassment. In keeping with this commitment, we will not tolerate discrimination against or unlawful harassment of employees by anyone, including any lawyer, clinician, staff member, patient, visitor, or outside vendor. We will not tolerate harassment by, or directed toward, any person associated with the institution, and we will investigate and resolve appropriately any complaint received. Anyone who feels they have witnessed or experienced harassment should contact Human Resources.*

3. An institution's policies should also make clear that **retaliation**—adverse actions taken because someone makes a report—is prohibited and will not be tolerated.
4. Provide training for employees at all levels to ensure that everyone is familiar with the employer's policies, reporting procedures, and applicable federal laws.[3]

Title IX of the Education Amendments of 1972

Title IX of the Education Amendments of 1972 is another federal law that prohibits the events described in the above case study in any GME program where the institution receives federal assistance. Title IX sets forth that "[n]o person in the United States shall, on the basis of sex, be excluded from participation in, be denied the benefits of, or be subjected to discrimination under any education program or activity receiving Federal financial assistance…."[2] Separate from the protections of Title VII, Title IX serves to prohibit the use of federal money to support education programs where sex discrimination and sexual harassment in particular have occurred. The law generally applies to educational institutions but also covers "any education program or activity" operated by a recipient of federal financial assistance. Accordingly, this description includes most GME programs, mandating compliance with Title IX.

What Remedies Are Available to Residents for a Title IX Violation?

Individuals who believe they have experienced sexual harassment or sex discrimination and wish to file a Title IX complaint may do so through a Title IX coordinator at their institution. Alternatively, the individual may submit a complaint to the Office of Civil Rights of the Department of Justice.[2] In employment situations, the EEOC may also be tasked with investigating a Title IX complaint.

If a Title IX complaint is made, the primary remedies are for the institution to ensure the complainant's educational opportunities are not limited by the alleged events. In other words, the institution may be required to change the resident's schedule, adjust the supervising physicians with whom the resident is assigned to work, or otherwise make changes to the program to limit interaction with the individuals about whom the resident has complained.

What Steps Should Hospitals and Other Employers Take to Comply with Title IX and Limit Liability?

GME programs should take the following steps to comply with Title IX:

1. Connect with the institution's Title IX office to ensure that the GME program's policies are aligned with the institutional policies and procedures, supportive measures, and possible accommodations necessary to comply with Title IX in the event there is a Title IX violation that requires resolution.
2. Share information with residents and all employees about how to contact the Title IX office to whom related complaints should be reported. Examples for disseminating Title IX information include hosting the Title IX office to speak about their services and resources; providing Title IX contact information on the Human Resource website page; and/or creating an information sheet of Title IX information for all residents and employees.

THE AMERICANS WITH DISABILITIES ACT

The Americans with Disabilities Act (ADA) protects qualified individuals with disabilities from employment discrimination. Under the ADA, persons have a disability if they have a physical or mental impairment that substantially limits a major life activity.[3] The ADA also protects individuals who have a record of a substantially limiting impairment and people who are regarded as having a substantially limiting impairment.[3]

To be protected under the ADA, an individual must have an impairment that is considered substantial rather than minor. A **substantial impairment** is defined as one that significantly limits or restricts a major life activity such as hearing, seeing, speaking, breathing, performing manual tasks, walking, caring for oneself, learning or working.

In order to be protected by the ADA, an individual with a disability must also be qualified to perform the essential functions of the job with or without reasonable accommodation. This means that the job applicant or employee, such as a residency applicant or resident employee, must do the following:

- Satisfy the job requirements for educational background, employment experience, skills, licenses, and any other qualification standards that are job related; and,
- be able to perform those tasks that are essential to the job, with or without reasonable accommodation.

What Remedies Are Available to Residents for an Employer's Violation of the ADA?

As with an alleged violation of Title VII, to bring a claim under the ADA, an employee must also file a charge with the EEOC, which will investigate and ultimately issue a Notice of Rights letter to the employee. The employee may then file a lawsuit in federal court based on the allegations raised in the charge. In rare circumstances, the EEOC may also file a lawsuit against the employer on the employee's behalf. If an employer is found liable in a lawsuit for an ADA violation, the employee can receive monetary damages and **injunctive relief**.

What Steps Should Hospitals and Other Employers Take to Comply with and Limit Liability Under the ADA?

Institutions should take proactive steps to comply with the ADA, including the following:

1. Ensure that the institution's Equal Employment Opportunity policy makes clear that the institution will offer reasonable accommodation for known physical or mental disabilities unless such actions would cause an undue hardship and that the employee, such as a resident, should contact Human Resources to request a reasonable accommodation.
2. If an employee requests an accommodation, the employer must then go through the interactive process (outlined below) with the employee to determine if the requested accommodation is reasonable and warranted.

What Is the ADA Interactive Process?

The interactive process set forth in the ADA is the process of requesting an accommodation and determining whether it is a **reasonable accommodation**:

- Step 1: The employee has to ask for an accommodation. Note that it is not necessary for the employee to mention the ADA. The institution can ask what the disability is but should not get distracted at this stage on whether the stated disability meets the legal definition of disability under the ADA or if the employee actually needs an accommodation.
- Step 2: The institution must talk to the employee about the employee's request. Institutions should not assume what the employee can or cannot do; instead, the employee should provide that information. The institution should not assume that an employee's disability is the same as someone else's who has the same diagnosis. The employee should be ready to provide a doctor's note or other information from a clinician.

- Step 3: The employer must determine if the requested accommodation is reasonable. An accommodation is not reasonable if it (a) eliminates an essential function (but may have to eliminate non-essential functions); (b) poses direct threat of imminent harm; or, (c) poses an undue hardship (eg, it is impossible to implement, it costs more than the job).
- Step 4: If the requested accommodation is determined to not be reasonable, the employer should look at other options for potential accommodations that would be reasonable.

What Are Situations in Which a Resident May Request a Reasonable Accommodation Under the ADA?

Consistent with federal law, the ACGME's Institutional Requirements indicate that "the Sponsoring Institution must have a policy, not necessarily GME-specific, regarding accommodations for disabilities consistent with all applicable laws and regulations" (ACGME Institutional Requirement IV.I.4). The following brief scenarios illustrate the diverse nature of situations in which a resident may request accommodations under the ADA and also showcase some of the potential challenges involved in determining whether accommodations are reasonable.

- Scenario 1: A resident has diabetes and needs to take more frequent breaks than are currently provided to check their glucose and have a snack, as needed, to maintain healthy glucose levels.
- Scenario 2: A resident in a surgical specialty has broken her wrist and is unable to properly hold medical instruments to perform the procedures for which she is training in her program. In this situation, the resident is likely unable to perform the essential functions of her job, which means a reasonable accommodation may not be available for her to perform her job. Instead, the institution may be obligated to give her an unpaid leave of absence for her wrist to heal, depending on her expected recovery time. Other options could include considering whether schedule adjustments are possible such that the resident could complete other required rotations that do not require wrist mobility while she is recovering from her injury.
- Scenario 3: A radiology resident has attention deficit hyperactivity disorder and is unable to concentrate to review scans in the busy hospital setting. He provides documentation of his diagnosis and requests a quiet, separate office where he can review scans and do his other case work.

These scenarios demonstrate that requests for reasonable accommodations, and the conditions underlying those requests, can vary greatly. Other scenarios may arise where the resident is not entitled to accommodation. For example, a resident who is experiencing stress because he is supervised by a "difficult" attending physician is not entitled to switch to a different attending as a reasonable accommodation. The ADA does not offer protections for job-related stress.

Title IX Regulations Governing Student Rights on Pregnancy, Childbirth, and Parenting

The Title IX Regulations of 2024 requires all higher education entities to provide learning environments free from all sex-based discrimination to include individuals that are pregnant and parenting within GME programs that are federally funded.[4-5] Within these programs, the Title IX Coordinator must inform expectant mothers and parents of their rights and will become the designated person to help them access these rights.

"Reasonable modifications" or adjustments must be made so that expectant mothers and parents can continue learning while they are pregnant, recovering from childbirth, lactating, or experiencing any condition related to pregnancy. Unless it is shown that the modifications would "fundamentally alter" the nature of the education program or activity, modifications can include changes in schedule or course sequence, counseling, elevator access, protective gear, ability to sit or stand, excused absences to attend medical appointments, and breaks to take care of pregnancy-related health needs, such as eating, drinking, using the restroom, or expressing milk. Depending on where the GME program is located, additional rights under other federal, state, or local laws may apply such as the Pregnant Workers Fairness Act.

THE PREGNANCY WORKERS FAIRNESS ACT

The Pregnancy Workers Fairness Act is a law enacted in 2023 that requires covered employers to provide "reasonable accommodations" for an employee's known limitations related to pregnancy, childbirth, or related medical conditions, unless the accommodation will cause the employer an "undue hardship."[6]

Such accommodations may include modified schedules, private areas other than a bathroom stall for lactation, and flexibility to attend prenatal appointments. Pregnancy-related conditions do not have to meet the definitions of a disability under the ADA to require a reasonable accommodation under this new law, although some individuals may still qualify for ADA protections based on pregnancy if they have particular complications.

What Remedies Are Available to Residents for Employer Violations of the Pregnancy Workers Fairness Act?

To file a complaint, residents should follow the institution's internal reporting policies and procedures as specified. If after doing so the resident is not satisfied with the outcome, the resident may file a charge with the EEOC.

Of note, in addition to the federal employment laws and regulations described in this chapter are the ACGME's Common Program Requirements and Institutional Requirements that align with them. These requirements include providing accessible lactation spaces and allowing residents to attend medical, dental, and mental health appointments.

What Steps Should an Employer Take to Comply with and Limit Liability Under the Pregnancy Workers Fairness Act?

Institutions should review their existing policies to ensure that they are in compliance with the Pregnancy Workers Fairness Act. Since this is a more recent addition to federal employment laws, a periodic review of institutional and program policies may be needed to ensure ongoing compliance as new modifications arise.

THE FAMILY AND MEDICAL LEAVE ACT

The Family and Medical Leave Act (FMLA) is designed to help employees, including residents, balance their work and family responsibilities by allowing them to take reasonable unpaid leave for certain family and medical reasons. It also seeks to accommodate the legitimate interests of employers and promote equal employment opportunity regardless of gender. The FMLA applies to all public agencies, schools, and companies with 50 or more employees.

Covered employers must provide an eligible employee with up to 12 weeks of unpaid leave each year for any of the following reasons:

- For the birth and care of the newborn child of an employee;
- For placement with the employee of a child for adoption or foster care;
- To care for an immediate family member (ie, spouse, child, or parent) with a serious health condition; or,
- To take medical leave when the employee is unable to work because of a serious health condition.

Employees are eligible for FMLA leave if they have worked for their employer during at least 12 months, for at least 1,250 hours over the past 12 months, and if they work at a location where the company employs 50 or more employees within 75 miles. Employees may be eligible for continuous leave, or days or weeks at a time, or intermittent leave for sporadic appointments (or flare-ups of a condition), which may cover only several hours at a time.

> Residents are employees and, as such, are protected by federal employment laws, which include non-discrimination based on race, color, religion, sex, or national origin under Title VII of the 1964 Civil Rights Act.

> As federal employment laws may be added or modified over time, institutions that employ residents should periodically review their policies to ensure compliance with federal law and limit their liability.

What Remedies Are Available to Residents Who Believe They Have Been Treated Unfairly with Regard to FMLA?

Employees, including residents, can file a complaint with the US Department of Labor or else file suit in federal court on claims of FMLA violations.[7] The available claims are (a) FMLA interference—that the employer interfered with the employee's leave under the FMLA either by not allowing them to take it or by requiring them to work during the leave; or, (b) FMLA retaliation—that the employee suffered an adverse action as a result of exercising their rights under the FMLA. An adverse action may mean termination, demotion, a pay reduction, or other denial of a professional opportunity. If an employer is found liable for an FMLA violation, an employee may be awarded monetary damages and/or injunctive relief, such as job reinstatement.

What Steps Should an Employer Take to Comply with and Limit Liability Under the FMLA?

Covered employers are required to post notices informing employees of their rights under the FMLA and should implement and circulate a policy consistent with those rights. Employers must make clear that a covered employee may request medical leave through Human Resources, and if it is requested, provide a form for a provider to complete in support of the requested leave.

Take Home Points

- Title VII of the 1964 Civil Rights Act protects equal employment opportunities; prohibits discrimination based on protected characteristics; and is overseen by the EEOC.
- Title IX of the Education Amendments of 1972 prohibits the use of federal money to support education programs where sex discrimination and sexual harassment, in particular, have occurred. Residents are protected from sexual harassment by both Title VII and Title IX.
- The ADA protects qualified individuals with disabilities from employment discrimination and establishes that employees, including residents, be able to perform essential job tasks with or without reasonable accommodations.
- The Pregnancy Workers Fairness Act requires employers to provide reasonable accommodations for employees', including residents', known limitations related to pregnancy, childbirth, or related medical conditions.
- The FMLA requires employers to provide employees, including residents, with up to 12 weeks of unpaid leave each year for specific reasons related to parenting, caregiving, and/or personal illness.

? QUESTIONS FOR FURTHER THOUGHT

1. Human Resources departments play an important role for employees, including residents, to help ensure employee rights under federal law are enforced. In your institution, department, or GME program, what avenues exist or may be developed to enhance the accessibility of Human Resources for employees?

2. How is your institution, department, or GME program currently addressing issues involving residents as related to the federal employment laws shared in this chapter?
3. Going back to the case study (sexual harassment) or the scenarios (disability accommodations) presented in the chapter, if such a scenario played out in your current work environment, what steps would be taken to address it? If you are unsure, how can you find out?

REFERENCES

1. U.S. Equal Employment Opportunity Commission. Accessed June 13, 2024. https://www.eeoc.gov
2. U.S. Department of Justice: Civil Rights Division. Title IX. Accessed June 13, 2024. https://www.justice.gov/crt/title-ix
3. U.S. Equal Employment Opportunity Commission. Fact sheet: sexual harassment discrimination. Accessed June 13, 2024. https://www.eeoc.gov/laws/guidance/fact-sheet-sexual-harassment-discrimination
4. U.S. Department of Justice: Civil Rights Division (ADA.gov). Americans with Disabilities Act of 1990, as amended. Accessed June 13, 2024. https://www.ada.gov/law-and-regs/ada/
5. U.S. Department of Education. Fact sheet: U.S. Department of Education's 2024 Title IX final rule overview. Accessed April 25, 2024. https://www2.ed.gov/about/offices/list/ocr/docs/19-unofficial-final-rule-2024.pdf
6. U.S. Equal Employment Opportunity Commission. What you should know about the Pregnant Workers Fairness Act. Accessed June 13, 2024. https://www.eeoc.gov/wysk/what-you-should-know-about-pregnant-workers-fairness-act
7. U.S. Department of Labor. Family and Medical Leave Act. Accessed June 13, 2024. https://www.dol.gov/agencies/whd/fmla

Navigating the ACGME Institutional and Program Requirements for Due Process

Sidney S. Welch, JD, MPH, Partner, Bradley Arant Boult Cummings LLP, Birmingham, AL

CHAPTER SUMMARY

Sponsoring Institutions, residents, and fellows alike invest significant time, effort, and money in the educational success of physicians. As a consequence, stakeholders have a vested interest in making sure that a resident or fellow emerges from a graduate medical education (GME) program with required skillsets from a positive, equitable, and high-quality learning environment. To partner successfully with Sponsoring Institutions, it is essential that residents know and understand their rights and responsibilities, and that Sponsoring Institutions and program directors have a similar understanding of due process procedure when addressing residents' concerns, as well as the consequences of failure to follow those procedures. In this chapter, we outline the GME processes leading to discipline or termination of resident contracts, the role of the ACGME, and practical considerations before and during the process.

Throughout this chapter, we will use the term *residents* when referring to GME learners, but the same due process rights apply to fellows as well.

LEARNING OBJECTIVES

1. Outline the processes within GME leading to discipline or termination of resident contracts.
2. Describe how resident physicians can protect their interests when being disciplined, abused, harassed, or mistreated for discriminatory reasons.
3. Explain the Accreditation Council for Graduate Medical Education's role in program violations.
4. Develop strategies to improve communication, equity, and inclusion in situations related to discipline or termination of resident contracts.

Case Study

Dr Jones is a resident who identifies as an African American male. In his residency application, he disclosed that he has a learning disability that requires additional time and other accommodations in any test-taking environment. He matched to a relatively new surgical residency program located outside a metropolitan area in a health system that consists of multiple hospital locations. The program requires rotations at other academic institutions in the metropolitan region, some of which have their own residency programs. The program's first group of residents had mixed results taking their initial Board certification written examinations.

During his post-graduate year two (PGY-2), Dr Jones receives verbal and written generalized feedback that he needs to "slow down" in performing surgical procedures and that the nursing staff and physician leadership

(continued)

in the program perceive him as arrogant and condescending. Dr Jones is upset by the feedback but has taken significant proactive steps to check-in with attending physicians regularly and to seek real-time feedback for each surgical procedure on technique, patient management, and overall performance. Separated from family and his fiancé in a rural community and recognizing himself to be academically focused and introverted by nature, he independently initiated and spent significant time interacting with and developing positive working relationships with nursing staff members and supervising physicians. His scores on the American Board of Surgery In-Training Examination (ABSITE) in preparation for his initial certification have been on the low-end of passing, consistent with his past written test performances, but not reflective of his high level of knowledge expressed on oral examination. Thus, he has invested significant time preparing for the annual ABSITE.

Now a PGY-4 resident physician, Dr Jones meets with the interim program director, who provides feedback that while his speed of surgical procedures and interpersonal relationships have improved, the Clinical Competency Committee (CCC) has concerns regarding his "attention to detail" in post-surgical care and treatment of patients, as well as his arrogance and unwillingness to receive feedback. He is told that, without sufficient progress, he will not be promoted to PGY-5 and will be required to repeat PGY-4 rotations. He is instructed to meet with the Employee Assistance Program to support his testing skills, as well as perform extra test preparation activities with submissions to the program director, both of which he has already diligently completed. In Dr Jones' opinion, none of Dr Jones' White colleagues have been subjected to the same level of scrutiny.

Dr Jones asks for copies of his evaluations and is provided with five or six and is told that the program has requested, but has not received, all of his evaluations by the faculty. He suggests the program director reach out to the affiliated sites where he received positive feedback and had been told by those faculty members that they had submitted evaluations. The program director replies that those sites generally have a low response rate in returned resident evaluations because many surgeons responsible for supervising residents are not interested in participating in GME. Further, the program does not typically give consideration to evaluations from other rotation sites because "they are easy graders," even though they are premier institutions and academic centers in their own right. He repeatedly asks for specific examples of instances in which he has not shown "attention to detail" and has demonstrated "arrogance and unwillingness to receive feedback," but none are given. Now in the Spring of his PGY-4 year, decisions regarding promotion to PGY-5 are fast approaching, and he fears that without more information or feedback than the generalized statements previously received, the program will require him to repeat his PGY-4 year.

Case Discussion

Dr Jones' case illustrates a substantial disconnect between the resident physician's perceptions and behaviors, and the feedback, perceptions, and procedures undertaken by his residency program. As you review the chapter, consider Dr Jones' options and what the program director can do (and should have done prior to this point) to appropriately address the current situation.

ACGME DUE PROCESS REQUIREMENT FOR RESIDENCY PROGRAMS

The Accreditation Council for Graduate Medical Education (ACGME) sets and monitors voluntary professional educational requirements for graduate medical education (GME) (residency and fellowship) programs in the US.[1] The ACGME requirements for *resident promotion, appointment renewal, and dismissal* are set forth in Section IV.D. of the Institutional Requirements.[2] As described below, Sponsoring Institutions hosting residency programs must be in substantial compliance with ACGME's Requirements to remain accredited. Of note, the ACGME will not adjudicate specific disputes between residents and Sponsoring Institutions or residency/fellowship programs with respect to the promotion, appointment renewal, or dismissal of residents.[3] Its role—and it can be an important one—is to address any non-compliance by a Sponsoring Institution or program with the published ACGME Requirement that states that an institution must have a policy that provides residents with due process relating to the following actions regardless of when the action is taken during the appointment period: suspension, non-renewal, non-promotion, or dismissal. Further, ACGME reviews situations in which a complaint is raised to determine whether that mechanism of due process was executed as written. Consequently, any complaint filed or involvement of the ACGME sought by a resident should be laser-focused on non-compliance with the published ACGME Requirements, which state that an institution must have a due process policy and follow that policy.

The ACGME Institutional Requirements require that each Sponsoring Institution have "a policy" for determining "the criteria for promotion and/or renewal" of a resident's appointment and to provide residents with due process when faced with disciplinary action.[2] If an accredited program chooses not to renew a resident's appointment, not to promote a resident, or to dismiss a resident, the Sponsoring Institution is required to provide the resident a written notice of that intent.[2] The ACGME Common Program Requirements also vest program directors with personal accountability for ensuring due process—naming program directors as ultimately responsible for (1) ensuring the program's compliance with the Sponsoring Institution's procedures for due process; (2) evaluating and promoting residents; and, (3) taking any disciplinary actions.[4]

SPONSORING INSTITUTIONS' IMPLEMENTATION OF THE ACGME'S DUE PROCESS REQUIREMENT

Residency/fellowship programs that are accredited by the ACGME function under the authority and oversight of an ACGME-accredited Sponsoring Institution which must ensure that each ACGME-accredited program under its oversight is in substantial compliance with the its own program requirements and that the institution is in substantial compliance with Institutional Requirements.[2] Failure to do so could result in loss of accreditation for either or both.[4]

Significant latitude is accorded to the Sponsoring Institution in implementing these baseline requirements, and often, the requirements get incorporated into the Sponsoring Institution's GME policies and procedures. Sponsoring Institutions can be held accountable to the ACGME (and can potentially lose accreditation and funding for their programs) and can be named in legal action brought by residents for failure to follow their policies and procedures. For these reasons, Sponsoring Institutions are incentivized to have at least "bare bones" policies and procedures to reduce their legal risk of non-compliance with their own standards and potential litigation.

Typically, ACGME Requirements for due process can be found in a Sponsoring Institution's Resident Due Process Policy. Generally, such policies will require that all residents be provided a fair and reasonable opportunity for due process in the event of certain **disciplinary actions**, including suspension, non-renewal, non-promotion, or dismissal of a resident. A Sponsoring Institution may define those disciplinary actions in alignment with its state's Medical Practice Act (governing discipline of license holders) or the Health Care Quality Improvement Act of 1986 and the National Practitioner Data Bank (NPDB)'s definitions of reportable professional review actions.[5] Of note, the Health Care Quality Improvement Act, which implemented the NPDB, and the NPDB Guidebook, define "physician" to include medical residents.[5] Because of the long-lasting and negative impact on the credentialing of and career of a physician with state license discipline or an NPDB report—and permanency in an academic file, it is critical for a resident to understand, verify, and address the Sponsoring Institution's position on reporting of any proposed or final disciplinary action. The typical step-by-step process taken by a Sponsoring Institution when considering a disciplinary action is outlined as follows:

1. **Initial Action by the Clinical Competency Committee (CCC)**
   Typically, the initial actor in a Sponsoring Institution's due process is the program's CCC. Residents are periodically evaluated by faculty members, under the framework of the ACGME specialty-specific Milestones, and, usually, the CCC then determines whether to recommend promotion of the resident. Next, the CCC reports its recommendation to the program director. The program director is usually responsible for taking disciplinary actions based upon the CCC's recommendation, and must report any disciplinary action to the Sponsoring Institution's designated institutional official (DIO) and the Office of GME within a certain time period after receiving the CCC's recommendation. *Any remedial actions at this phase generally are not considered disciplinary actions and thus do not have the consequence of reportability to a state licensure board or the NPDB*. Consequently, the program and the resident have an opportunity for constructive discussion and remediation, but it can be frustrating if proper discussion and remediation do not occur, since non-reportable actions generally are unappealable under due process policies. Such non-reportable actions may include, but are not limited to remediation, performance-improvement plans, or even probation; although, some medical licensing jurisdictions require instances of probation to be reported to them. Non-reportable actions are typically implemented to elevate the level of performance of a resident/fellow believed to be in need of such additional educational effort.

2. **Notice of Disciplinary Actions and Request for Appeal**
   If a program director decides that disciplinary action is warranted, the next step typically is to notify the resident of the disciplinary action and the resident's right to appeal such action, which the resident must exercise in writing within a certain number of days following the notice. *It is very important that residents pay attention to the deadlines notice. Otherwise, they may be deemed to have waived their right to appeal and to have accepted the disciplinary action*. For a resident to be afforded the required due process, the institution's policies typically require the notice to state the reason for the appeal and to provide any applicable supporting documents. Policies will vary in the degree of specificity required, and if the notice is insufficient, the resident should immediately request greater detail and all supporting documents. Applicable documents may include items as fundamental as the resident's contract, program policies and manuals, evaluations by attending physicians, and the examination results. In many circumstances of dismissal or non-renewal, institutions may restrict access to their information systems to the resident, which prevents access to documentation that had previously been available. It is therefore important for the resident to assemble all necessary supporting documentation before an initial action is taken. Since a reportable disciplinary action is typically not the first notice that the program endorses a performance problem with the resident, the collection of supporting documentation should begin immediately when there is notification of such a concern.

3. **Arranging for an Appeal Hearing**
   If a request for an appeal is submitted in a timely manner, the DIO will arrange and notify the resident of the date, time, and location of the hearing within a certain time period of receiving the resident's request. Typically, this timing will require the resident to prepare quickly. Appeals generally are heard by an appeal panel or some subset of the GME Committee; the Sponsoring Institution's policy will set the number of members and composition of the hearing panel. Any member of the CCC or the body who was initially involved in the disciplinary action or who is part of the resident's program should be disqualified from serving on the panel, and, if not, the resident should consider requesting their recusal.

4. **The Hearing**
   A hearing is conducted within a certain time period from the appointing of the appeal panel. The resident will typically receive notice of the hearing date a certain number of days in advance, as set by the policy. The institution's due process/appeals policy may give the resident the option to attend the

hearing or to submit materials in lieu of an appearance, but residents are advised to review the policy to prevent their absence from being automatically considered a waiver of their right to be heard or any subsequent appeal. The policy will also specify whether attorneys or other advisors may attend the hearing on behalf of either party, which is generally precluded by many institutions even though this approach may benefit the resident and the institution with clear specifications as to the attorney's role. Some institutions may also provide an ombudsperson to assist the resident in the preparation of materials and support during the hearing. The ombudsperson is not to represent the interests of the institution; rather, this individual is provided to ensure the resident is fully informed regarding the process and how an appeal is mounted.

The hearing will proceed in the format of an informal mini-trial, typically with the program representative leading off by providing information regarding the nature of the disciplinary action, the recommendations of the CCC and the program director, and any supporting evidence. Following this presentation, the resident will present any evidence in support of the resident's position, such as the testimony of voluntary witnesses. The appeal panel may request additional information from either party. Ideally, the hearings should be non-adversarial exchanges of information, but often, given the high professional stakes, and possibly a history of unresolved conflict and frustration, the proceedings may take a more adversarial tone. Because the proceedings are generally considered to be peer review and entitled to confidentiality (and potential immunities) under state law, the hearing is not open to outside parties. The hearing may or may not be recorded or a staff person may be assigned responsibility for taking minutes. The resident should have access to both and if minutes are taken in lieu of a recording, an attorney or other advisor attending on behalf of the resident should take notes and immediately correct any discrepancies in the written minutes following the hearing.

After the hearing, most due processes allow for an appeal. The appeal panel must report its recommendations regarding the disciplinary action to the DIO within a specified timeframe. The appeal panel's recommendation is deemed advisory in nature and may be rejected or modified, in whole or in part, by the DIO. The DIO will then communicate a decision, in writing, to the resident, program director, and CCC within a specified time period and inform the resident of the right to any further appeal, which often would be made before the leadership of the Sponsoring Institution (dean, chief executve officer, chief medical officer or other such individual). The resident, again, will have a time-limited appeal right, which will need to be closely observed to avoid waiving this appeal right and being deemed as having accepted the DIO's decision.

5. **Final Appeal**

   A final appeal of the DIO's determination may be made upon timely appeal. Often, the policy will set a standard for the appeal, meaning that to overturn the lower recommendations and decisions, the resident must demonstrate that, by way of example only, the prior recommendation/decision was not supported by the evidence presented. The other grounds for this final level of appeal is that the written institutional due process mechanism was not followed at the earlier levels of disciplinary action. This level of appeal may be by written submission only, oral presentation, or a combination of the two. Typically, this appeal decision is considered final and binding, provided it was done in good faith.

CONSIDERATIONS FOR RESIDENT AND FELLOW PHYSICIANS

In the allotted space, this chapter cannot cover everything a resident should consider if involved in a disciplinary action by a Sponsoring Institution. Below are a few key points for consideration by residents.

1. *Residents should build a trusted support network.* First, any resident, from the start of a program, should have a close, self-selected council of mentors, which includes trusted advisors, generally outside of the Sponsoring Institution (although, with experience and passage of time, the council may be expanded to include close, respected professional relationships and advocates within the Sponsoring Institution). This council should include at least one or more individuals, possibly from the resident's medical school or through associations, who are experienced and excellent communicators, as well as

familiar with the ACGME Requirements and politics of academic medicine. If such individuals are not in a resident's circle, the resident should be deliberate about seeking them out through professional associations and prior academic advisors. Consider regular check-ins with this group to discuss areas for improvement and guidance on how to navigate challenges before they become more significant. Over time, this group of trusted advisors may include an attorney with experience in key areas (eg, employment, contract, academic or medical staff processes).

It is important for the resident to involve legal counsel well before conflicts reach the due process phase, at which point costs, time, delay in education/training, and damages to reputation or negative perceptions may be irreversible. Organizations like the National Medical Association maintain information on legal counsel experienced in these issues. If a resident is experiencing any type of conflict or disciplinary action at the Sponsoring Institution, it will also be critical to have emotional and mental health support systems in place given the significant stressors involved. The ACGME also hosts on its website well-being resources that can be used in conjunction with the resident's own personal support systems.[6]

2. **Residents should be attentive to feedback, particularly when it points to potential areas of conflict, incidents that were misperceived or misunderstood, or negative feedback about performance.** It is recommended that residents be attuned to any conflict or negative feedback, whether conveyed orally or in writing. If it has the potential to impact their success, it needs to be addressed sooner rather than later, and residents may need to document their response and request the response be placed in their academic file. If the feedback is conveyed orally, it may need to be put in writing at the request of the resident. The resident should request any clarification of deficiencies with specific examples so that any corrective measures can be taken and to make sure there is a viable avenue for demonstrating progress.
3. **Residents should be proactive in communicating about their performance.** Neither institutions nor residents should wait until the due process phase in a program to discuss concerns regarding a resident's progress. If that happens, the relationship can become adversarial, and it is often difficult for the clinical leadership of a Sponsoring Institution, the CCC, and the program director to change course or reverse a history of perceptions regarding a resident's performance.
4. **Residents should prioritize effective communication.** Resident physicians should prioritize working on and improving effective communication skills as part of their education and training. They should read books, take courses, and observe people in their sphere who have mastered the art of the difficult conversation or who are respected leaders. Practice with friends, family members, and confidants. Even for the experienced communicator, there is always room for improvement. In the context of GME, this often means doing more listening than responding—at least at first. Listen (*really* listen) to feedback. Take copious notes. Ask for the opportunity to reflect on what was said. Resist the temptation to rebut or respond defensively. Consult that council of trusted advisors. Consider what a response needs to say and how it gets communicated, including whether it needs to be memorialized in writing. It may be helpful to consult with legal counsel, and if they have experience in academic matters, they will be able to advise the resident as to whether their role as counsel should be behind the scenes or directly communicating with the Sponsoring Institution, which has a different set of strategic considerations.
5. **Resident physicians should be mindful not to say, write, post, or text anything they would not want read aloud in front of a group of colleagues or a jury.** In turn, make sure to document anything of potential consequence, particularly if conversations are occurring one-on-one and have the potential to turn into a future difference of opinion issue. Take contemporaneous notes, ask for written follow-up to conversations or, better yet, the resident should follow the conversation with an email or letter that starts with "Thank you for our conversation on [insert date]. I wanted to confirm that we discussed [insert]. If this understanding is incorrect any way, please let me know immediately." If a resident agrees in person to extensions of deadlines or deviations from written processes, that understanding should be confirmed in writing. Residents should consider offloading and saving all texts, pager messages, and email exchanges of importance to a personal device. They should also visit the ACGME resident portal to obtain copies of each Milestone evaluations period that documents their performance as soon as it is made available.

6. ***Do not let time pass you by.*** Resident physicians should be cognizant of potential problems and deal with them proactively before they become more significant. They are advised to pay attention to deadlines made in correspondence. Open all correspondence from the program promptly and respond accordingly. Because, as stated previously, if such dates/deadlines are ignored or missed, the resident may not be able to "unring the bell" and regain important due process rights.
7. ***Residents should consider both short- and long-term consequences of their actions and responses.*** Said another way, pick battles and understand the consequences before selecting an action. A resident will need to balance potential career risks against the need to address mistreatment that has, or that the resident believes has, occurred. It will be critical to consider the different scenarios and options with that group of trusted advisors, and to understand what there is to gain and lose from each.
8. ***Residents should understand the due process at their institution and their current status in the process.*** This includes understanding the standard due process (outlined above), where the resident is in the process, and where the current course could lead. Take any correspondence received and correlate it to the Sponsoring Institution's policy. If unclear on what something means or what to do next, residents should ask their trusted advisors, an experienced attorney, or the Sponsoring Institution's leadership. Equally important, know the ramifications of an action or proposed course of action. Is it possible that the resident's continued participation in the program is in jeopardy? Is there a path to success for the resident within the Sponsoring Institution? Is it possible that a report of disciplinary action could be filed with the state licensure board or the NPDB? Remember, any complaint to or request for involvement of the ACGME should be limited to a Sponsoring Institution's non-compliance with ACGME Requirements.
9. ***Generally, as a matter of state and federal law, a resident would need to exhaust administrative remedies (the Sponsoring Institution's own due process) before filing any sort of legal action in a court of law.*** Often, success of litigation depends on whether there is a legal claim available and the documentation that exists to support it. For this reason, a resident's documentation of concerns and communications of the same—ie, the knowledge of the Sponsoring Institution regarding the concerns—should read like a medical record. Any reader picking up the record of this documentation should have a timeline of exactly what transpired, the current state, any efforts at resolution, and the problems experienced along the way.
10. ***Residents should document actions or behaviors at the time they occur.*** In conjunction with the prior recommendation, if residents have experienced or believe they have experienced discriminatory actions at any point during their GME program, ideally these would be documented at the time they occurred, and the affected resident should consult with trusted advisors and qualified legal counsel about the proper method for reporting the concerns. ACGME Common Program Requirement VI.B.5. specifically sets forth programs' obligations, in partnership with their Sponsoring Institution, to provide a professional, equitable, respectful, and civil environment free from discrimination, sexual and other forms of harassment, mistreatment, abuse or coercion of students, residents, faculty members, and staff members.[4] Avenues exist for residents to report **concerns**, defined as impediments to learning in the GME environment. Concerns may be reported through avenues within residents' GME programs, and to ACGME anonymously through ACGME's Office of the Ombudsperson. Additionally, formal **complaints**, defined as allegations that a Sponsoring Institution or program is non-compliant with ACGME accreditation or recognition requirements, may be reported to the ACGME's Office of Complaints. Formal complaints can be reported confidentially but not necessarily anonymously since a formal complaint may impact the accreditation status of a Sponsoring Institution. Therefore, the identity of the aggrieved individual and the details of the alleged complaint need to be made available to the institution to allow it to internally investigate the claim and prepare its response.[7]

ACGME Institutional Requirement[2] IV.E also states that the Sponsoring Institution must have a policy that outlines the procedures for submitting and processing resident grievances at the program and institutional level and that minimizes conflicts of interest. ACGME Common Program Requirement II.A.4.(a).7 states that a program director's role is to provide a learning and working environment in which residents have the opportunity to raise concerns, report mistreatment, and provide feedback in a confidential manner as appropriate, without fear of intimidation or retaliation.[4] Residents should not wait until they are in a defensive disciplinary posture to raise allegations of discrimination. Rather, such belated elevation of allegations may ring hollow if brought only after a disciplinary decision has been leveled against them. In some cases, residents may be able to benefit from federal whistleblower protections by raising legitimate concerns regarding discrimination or other misconduct that then entitles them to protection against any retaliatory action. It is important to consult qualified counsel on these matters to assist with navigating proper reporting, not only through the ACGME, but also through the Sponsoring Institution's Human Resources, the Sponsoring Institution's own complaint process (which may include its office of equity, diversity, and inclusion, legal counsel, and/or compliance program, among others), and the Equal Employment Opportunity Commission.

CONSIDERATIONS FOR PROGRAM DIRECTORS

Program directors have a vested interest in ensuring residents understand their rights and how to properly communicate and use the ACGME Program Requirements, as they are ultimately accountable for the overall program and promoting a positive learning environment at the Sponsoring Institution.[4] The case study in this chapter highlights a few areas commonly observed. Program directors have a responsibility to improve program operations overall and create and promote a positive learning environment. Two key areas for program directions to consider are (1) feedback and evaluations; and, (2) diversity, equity, and inclusion efforts.

1. *The Critical Role of Effective Feedback and Evaluations.* Actionability is key to constructive feedback and evaluations. The actionability has to be two-sided—both on the part of the resident as well as the assigned attending physician or faculty member. Behaviors that can facilitate such a bidirectional exchange[8] are highlighted in Table 7.1.

    The Sponsoring Institution, the program director, and all faculty members and attending physicians should always be mindful that they are operating in an academic *learning* environment. The period of GME is the most essential time for professional formation and growth of a physician, and recognition of

Table 7.1 Bidirectional Exchange Between Learner and Educator Leading to Effective, Actionable Feedback

	Behaviors that Facilitate Effective Bidirectional Exchange
Learner (eg, resident/fellow physician)	• Exhibits confident humility, resiliency, and patience • Listens for understanding • Open to receiving criticism and is not in search only for appraisals when receiving feedback • Considers how to modify their own performance • Reflects on their own actions
Educator (eg, faculty member)	• Transmits a message effectively • Listens for understanding • Exhibits empathy • Is able to identify and address biases • Prioritizes respectful communication and opportunities for improvement without seeking to humiliate or intimidate when providing feedback • Exemplifies professionalism • Is open to questions from the learner • Reflects on their own actions and seeks to modify their own behavior based on how the feedback was received

Eidt LB. Feedback in medical education: beyond the traditional evaluation, *Rev Assoc Med Bras (1992)*. 2023;69(1):9-12; adapted from Maia et al., Adapted feedback strategy aimed at undergraduate outpatient clinics, 2018.

this awesome responsibility is at the core of postgraduate teaching. As a teacher, it is of utmost importance to elevate fair, professional behavior through evaluation of the learner's observed performance. Residents need to exhibit behaviors consistent with always being in a learning mode, and those with teaching responsibilities need to understand their own responsibilities as educators; both need to accept those roles to obtain the optimal learning conditions. Consequently, faculty members should be required to participate in training on, or demonstrate skills in, providing effective feedback. All faculty members should understand the important role of evaluations. With proper training, they should be able to evaluate and give feedback that concretely identifies performance areas where a resident needs to demonstrate improvement. They should also provide tangible examples of what improvement they seek and, when possible, they should support the rationale for the proposed change with evidence and construct a mutually understood pathway for realizing that improvement from the resident. When giving feedback, educators should reference observable skills and abilities, provide specific information, utilize explicit standard models, establish goals for performance improvement, and make plans for repeat observations and feedback.[9]

Evaluations and feedback can come in a more formal, written form or orally as education and training are occurring. A successful program will provide continuous feedback with routine, periodic written evaluations. If effective education and training is occurring, a resident should not be surprised by any feedback on a written evaluation. In fact, if the system is working properly, any areas of improvement should be well underway in being addressed by the time a written evaluation is shared. If this is not happening, the system requires further examination and retooling by the program director and the members of the faculty. It is only when feedback is given and an opportunity to correct the observed deficiency occurs that a true evaluation of the ability of the resident to learn can be made.

Effective feedback should be accompanied by an effective working process for Sponsoring Institutions to procure timely, complete, and accurate evaluations. Systemic problems are common in the evaluation process. For example, faculty members may not turn in evaluations or may not do so in a timely fashion; relatedly, the Sponsoring Institution and program director may not have a process to ensure return of all evaluations. Another common problem exemplified by the case study is that unilateral, informal decisions may be made internally to discount or disregard certain evaluations, whether from other facilities within the Sponsoring Institution or from certain evaluators. Such deficiencies should not be communicated to the resident by the program to explain why all evaluations are not considered actionable. If a faculty member was considered suitable for the opportunity to teach in the program, then their evaluation of the learner should likewise be accepted, or the decision to permit teaching should be re-evaluated. Program directors should review their evaluation processes to check whether any of these common problems are present. They are low-hanging, but critical opportunities to improve a program rapidly. The ACGME Improving Assessment Using Direct Observation Toolkit provides an invaluable guide to giving learner feedback and address faculty development in assessment that connects teachers with a community of clinician educators to strengthen these essential skills.[10]

> Reporting an incident of bias, discrimination, or other concerns internally at their Sponsoring Institution or program is an important first step that may allow residents to access and mobilize local resources to improve their learning environment. It is essential for institutions and programs to have clear mechanisms for internally reporting concerns and for all parties (residents, faculty members, staff members) to understand these steps.

> If the resident or other individual reporting an incident or behavior fears retaliation at the program, seeking a neutral third party, such as an ombudsperson, with whom the concern can be discussed may be helpful. The resident should bear in mind that retaliation is prohibited by the ACGME when concerns have been documented and formally reported.

> If a resident has exhausted local resources with regards to an incident or behavior, or if the resident considers the situation to be so egregious as to directly impact the program's or Sponsoring Institution's compliance with ACGME Requirements, the resident may report a concern (anonymously) or a complaint (confidentially, but not anonymously) to the ACGME.

Dismissal is an uncommon outcome in GME. Each year, fewer than 0.15% of residents are dismissed. It should be rare for a program to dismiss a resident and multiple dismissals over a 10-year period at a single program is a cause for grave concern. If all of the above are working effectively, due process proceedings involving disciplinary actions should seldom occur because most problems can and should be addressed and corrected early on to the satisfaction of all participants.

2. **Diversity, Equity, and Inclusion Considerations.** At a minimum, program directors should be sure to engage in continuing in-depth education on issues related to bias and equity in evaluation, selection, and promotion. They should also take care to incorporate diverse perspectives in program leadership opportunities and committees, such as the CCC, which may have an impact on resident selection, retention, and promotion. By gaining knowledge, experience, and diverse perspectives in leadership, program directors may enhance their program's ability to support an inclusive environment, as well as examine whether there are biases at play that can ultimately lead to discriminatory acts, which can both permanently damage a resident's education and training, as well as the program's reputation and accreditation status.

Take Home Points

- The ACGME sets and monitors voluntary professional educational standards, including standards for resident promotion, appointment renewal, and dismissal, for GME programs in the US.
- Any complaint filed or involvement of the ACGME sought by a resident should be laser-focused on non-compliance with ACGME Requirements.
- Disciplinary actions include resident suspension, non-renewal, non-promotion, or dismissal, and Sponsoring Institutions must follow due process for implementing any of these actions. Remedial actions (eg, instituting a learning improvement plan) are not considered disciplinary actions.
- Residents have the right to appeal a disciplinary action, but must respond to the disciplinary action notice within the specified deadline in order for an appeal to be considered.
- Program directors are ultimately accountable for making sure that residents understand their rights and for promoting a positive learning environment within the program. This goal can be achieved by focusing on improving faculty evaluations of resident performance and incorporating diversity, equity, and inclusion efforts.
- Ensuring and sustaining effective communication, including processes for providing feedback, between all parties (residents program leadership, Sponsoring Institution leadership, faculty members, staff members) is a key step that may reduce interpersonal misunderstandings, allow for more effective resolution of concerns at the local level, and promote inclusive GME learning environments.

? QUESTIONS FOR FURTHER THOUGHT

1. Reflecting on the Case Study at the start of the chapter, were there any missed opportunities on the part of Dr Jones to protect or position himself more favorably and on part of the program director or residency program for educational improvement?
2. Is Dr Jones' situation reversible at this juncture, and what are the next best steps on the part of Dr Jones, the Sponsoring Institution, and the program director?

3. At your own Sponsoring Institution or program, what internal processes are available for residents to express their concerns or report incidents of bias or discrimination? What strategies presented in this chapter do you plan to incorporate to enhance your current processes?
4. What is your program's process for submitting faculty evaluations? What mechanisms are in place to ensure that all faculty members submit evaluations, that evaluations are submitted in a timely fashion, that feedback from all sites/faculty members is considered appropriately, and that all faculty members are trained in avoiding bias in evaluation?

Acknowledgments
The author would like to acknowledge the contributions of Jack Baath, a second-year law student at Duke University School of Law, and to Garfield Clunie, MD, Dotun Ogunyemi, MD, and the National Medical Association for their continuing commitment to this work and for providing critical expertise.

REFERENCES

1. Accreditation Council of Graduate Medical Education. Overview. Accessed June 12, 2023. https://www.acgme.org/about/overview/
2. Accreditation Council of Graduate Medical Education. Institutional requirements. 2023. Accessed June 12, 2023. https://www.acgme.org/globalassets/pfassets/programrequirements/800_institutionalrequirements2022.pdf
3. Accreditation Council of Graduate Medical Education. Office of complaints. Accessed June 12, 2023. https://www.acgme.org/Residents-and-Fellows/Report-an-Issue/Office-of-Complaints/
4. Accreditation Council of Graduate Medical Education. ACGME common program requirements. Accessed July 1, 2023. www.acgme.org/programs-and-institutions/programs/common-program-requirements/
5. National Practitioner Data Bank Guidebook, Definitions. Accessed January 10, 2025. www.npdb.hrsa.ogv/guidebook/CDefinitions.jsp
6. Accreditation Council for Graduate Medical Education. Well-being in GME. Accessed June 12, 2023. https://dl.acgme.org/pages/well-being
7. Accreditation Council for Graduate Medical Education. FAQs about raising issues with the ACGME. www.acgme.org/residents-and-fellows/report-an-issue/faqs/
8. Eidt LB. Feedback in medical education: beyond the traditional evaluation, *Rev Assoc Med Bras (1992)*. 2023;69(1):9-12. doi:10.1590/1806-9282.20221086; *adapted from Maia et al., Adapted feedback strategy aimed at undergraduate outpatient clinics,* 2019.
9. Van De Ridder JMM, Stokking KM, McGaghie WC, Ten Cate OTJ. What is feedback in clinical education? *Med Educ*. 2008;42(2):189-197.
10. Accreditation Council for Graduate Medical Education. Improving assessment using direct observation toolkit. Accessed January 30, 2025. https://www.acgme.org/education-and-resources/courses-and-workshops/improving-assessment-using-direct-observation-toolkit/

SECTION 2

On Racial and Ethnic Experiences in Graduate Medical Education

William McDade, MD, PhD, Chief Diversity, Equity, and Inclusion Officer, Accreditation Council for Graduate Medical Education, Chicago, IL

Monica Vela, MD, Professor of Medicine, Director, Hispanic Center of Excellence, Departments of Medicine and Medical Education, Division of Academic Internal Medicine and Geriatrics, University of Illinois College of Medicine, Chicago, IL

The second section of *A Guide* addresses the racial and ethnic experiences of residents and fellows in graduate medical education (GME). Under the best circumstances, a diverse learning space should support one's race and identity and allow each learner a glimpse into the world of others who may not share the same origins. Unfortunately, however, racial and ethnic stereotyping and bias often play a role detrimental to the success of physician learners, affecting how they are perceived and subsequently treated in the clinical learning environment.[1] As W.E.B. DuBois wrote over a century ago in *The Souls of Black Folk*: "The problem of the Twentieth Century is the problem of the color-line, the relation of the darker to the lighter races of men of Asia and Africa, in America and the islands of the sea."[2] For many, that color/racial/ethnic line still exists and tempers the experiences of those on either side of it.

Each of the chapters in this section describe and analyze how such negative racial and ethnic experiences in the clinical learning environment affect learners who are American Indians/Alaska Natives (AI/AN), Asians and Pacific Islanders (API), Black, and Latino, Hispanic, or of Spanish Origin (LHS+). The authors juxtapose the power and privilege of Whiteness in the context of US racism to help us better understand the role and responsibilities of the dominant culture and embrace antiracism. Finally, because of societal stereotypes, they reveal how race and ethnicity is unfortunately associated with the justice-involved population. The chapters also look at the harm done to physician learners and how such harm relates to some of them leaving academic medicine or medical practice in general. Many have experienced microaggressions, subtle acts of exclusion, bias in evaluation, and discrimination, such as through overpolicing—supervisors overreacting to learners' minor errors or mislabeling learners' behavior as pathological or problematic when it simply differs from the most common behaviors of the dominant culture. Such experiences, in turn, may lead to discouragement, depression, and trauma that causes learners to avoid similar environments in the future, thus excluding them from the positive contribution they could make as faculty members.

In its 2023 decision in *Students for Fair Admissions v. Harvard* and *Students for Fair Admissions v. the University of North Carolina*, the US Supreme Court held that race-based affirmative action programs in college admissions processes violate the Equal Protection Clause of the Fourteenth Amendment.[3] When studying each chapter in Section Two and throughout the book, readers should recognize that this decision has added to the difficulty to assemble a workforce reflective of the anticipated US population in college and medical school. Diversifying the physician workforce requires attending to the entire pathway to medicine, such that individuals from all racial and ethnic groups in the population have an opportunity to pursue careers in medicine. Engaging minoritized physicians to provide care to underserved and marginalized individuals is impactful to the health care system overall by reducing health disparities and improving access to care for all patients.[4] These physicians most often understand this principle from their own personal experience.

This section also underscores the need for intentional efforts to accelerate progress on building the pathway into medicine for minoritized early learners, and the shared responsibility to do so must come from both the undergraduate medical education and GME communities.

* * *

Chapter 8:   American Indian and Alaska Native Presence in Medicine
Natasha Bray, DO, MSEd; Alec Calac, PhD; Holly Pilson, MD; Siobhan Wescott, MD, MPH

Bray et al describe the role of historical trauma and cultural assimilation that have been the hallmark of the AI/AN experience in American education. As with each of the marginalized groups described throughout this section, their unique history is among the contributing factors as to why AI/AN individuals are easily overlooked in medical education; most years have seen fewer than 50 AI/AN students across all first year medical school classes.[5] In their case in particular, such invisibility means that AI/AN learners are most often excluded from being reported and subsequently discussed in quantitative research. Complicating the effort to understand these marginalized peoples indigenous to the United States is the diversity of tribal affiliations and the rich mixture of AI/AN with individuals from other races and ethnicities. This characteristic makes it difficult to disaggregate data and to interpret satisfying representation or concordance when studying AI/AN self-identification among physicians at all levels of the medical education continuum.[6] In particular, because of the paucity of AI/AN faculty members, the protection and guidance afforded from racially concordant mentors is not typically available to AI/AN learners in GME environments, making it essential that all involved in GME support and mentor these learners without the expectation that they must assimilate to dominant cultural norms. The chapter offers additional solutions to stimulate inclusiveness of AI/AN values and culture into the learning environment.

Chapter 9:   Asian, Pacific Islander, Native Hawaiian and Asian Pacific Islander American Experience
Tonya L. Fancher, MD, MPH; Iris Vuong, MD, MPH; Rosa Lee, MD; Sunny Nakae, PhD, MSW

Far from being a monolithic racial group, Fancher et al help readers to recognize how Asian-identifying individuals represent a diasporic assortment of countries that constitute a collective racial identity. For the past 40 years, colleges and medical schools have found favor with Asian candidates because of their overall success in performance on standardized exams and studious stereotype. In the meritocratic domain of academics, there has been an overemphasis on the valuation of standardized testing that has resulted in the relative overrepresentation of Asians in medicine. Yet, discrimination in academic medicine has also adversely impacted Asian-identifying individuals who are disproportionately underrepresented in leadership roles on medical faculties and who remain the target of racism, misunderstanding, and harassment in society.[7] Lack of understanding of cultural styles, as much as stereotyping and bias, presents difficulties for Asian residents and fellows. For example, often excluded from the conversation regarding Asian persons is the hazard of lumping of all who identify as Asian into the framework of being successful. Many Asian communities associated with particular national identities struggle with health, educational, and income disparities and are in need of support as the pathway of physicians is being built to serve disaffected Asian populations as well.[8] Once in GME, Asians are also often victims of discrimination, bias, and harassment.[9]

Native Hawaiian or Pacific Islander (NHPI) individuals are invisible statistically when aggregated with more numerous Asian individuals; these individuals are invisible as people when a historical health policy ignores the colonialism and structural racism that led to today's social disadvantage and health inequities.[10] The authors examine how disaggregating data for API and breaking down the monolith is critical to understanding the challenges they face in GME.[11]

Chapter 10: Aspects of the Black Experience in Graduate Medical Education
Monica Lypson, MD, MHPE; Maurice Sholas, MD, PhD; Anita Blanchard, MD; Alden Landry, MD, MPH; William McDade, MD, PhD

Being Black across the continuum of medical education engenders feelings of isolation, marginalization, and discrimination in many of our institutions. Lypson et al point to how the paucity of Black physician faculty members gives Black medical students, residents, and fellows few role models to emulate, and a lack of comrades with whom to commiserate, to address challenges, and to share strategies for success. They find themselves excluded from learning communities, a pattern replayed for many in previous educational circumstances, and in many cases, where they had been prejudged and presumed incompetent.[12] These experiences bring about a phenomenon where internalized racism acts in concert with actualized racialism to produce the imposter syndrome and stereotype threat, both of which undermine confidence and imperil success. Finally, Black learners suffer mistreatment in an assortment of ways that places undue strain on their well-being and creates significant barriers to their success.[13] The authors describe the urgent need to support Black learners and to actively engage in antiracist practices that allow them to develop into the physicians needed to provide access to culturally sensitive and trusted care for communities estranged from the medical establishment.

Chapter 11: The Graduate Medical Education Experience of Individuals Who Identify as Latino, Hispanic, or of Spanish Origin
Maria J. Ruiz, MD, MPH; Santiago Avila, MD; Monica Vela, MD

For learners who identify as Latino, Latina, Latinx, Hispanic, or of Spanish origin (LHS+), racial and ethnic issues compound with those of culture and language. The historical discrimination and dispossession driven by the dominant culture have contributed to loss of agency by Brown populations. The history and impact of colonialism on current LHS+ learners underscores the need for physicians who understand the culture to better serve communities where language concordance can make significant strides toward improving health care outcomes.[14] However, the very thing that makes physicians who can deliver care in Spanish or languages indigenous to Central and South America valuable to linguistically diverse populations, also marginalizes them; may frequently relegate them to a predetermined expectation of a career that is not borne by members of the dominant culture. Like that for the other minoritized populations described by the Ruiz et al in this chapter, the pathway into medicine is fraught for LHS+ young learners with educational disparities driving low rates of high school completion, college preparation, and college enrollment. They may not be encouraged to pursue academic careers or certain specialties because their roles are in primary care and giving back to the underserved. As the LHS+ population continues to increase, medical education has an even greater mission to inculcate institutional cultural humility by ensuring there is a culturally fluent lineage of physicians who possess the requisite skills to provide linguistically and culturally appropriate care.

Chapter 12: Reimagining Graduate Medical Education by Contextualizing "Whiteness"
David F. McIntosh, PhD, MA; Camara Phyllis Jones, MD, PhD, MPH;
Jessica Elizabeth Isom, MD, MPH

Most learning environments in the United States are racialized. In this dominant culture, students are "actors" for whom race plays a favorable role. McIntosh et al help the reader to understand the historical roots of racialized learning and how it underplays the importance of identity, emphasizing its impact on all physician learners, faculty members, and staff in the clinical learning environment.[15] Using Frankenberg's framework for Whiteness and Jones' definitions for the various forms of racism, they illustrate how clinicians, administrators, and educators create and maintain White institutional spaces in GME programs through their feeling, thinking, and doing. They encourage readers to ask questions regarding their institutional and program structures, policies, practices, norms, and values to determine how these core elements undermine provide a strategy for applying antiracism to dismantle White institutional spaces and build equitable spaces for the benefit of all.

Within *A Guide,* Chapter 12 stands as an important primer in how race has been constructed and how antiracism is essential for its dismantling.

Chapter 13: Health Disparities in Correctional Medicine and the Justice-Involved Population: Impact on Physician Education and Training
Dionne Hart, MD, DFAPA, FASAM; Jill Strachan-Batson, MD, AAFP; Monica Taylor-Desir, MD, MPH

Hart, Strachan-Baton, and Taylor-Desir focus on health inequities in the justice-involved population as a function of lifespan. They describe how the Black and Brown populations are disproportionately represented in incarcerated populations. Aging, chronic health problems, and chronic mental illness are among the most prevalent conditions characterizing the justice-involved population. However, even when these individuals leave the correctional system, they often return to unstable homes or to underserved communities, which often results in recidivism, continuing the cycle of disparities and health care challenges.

The authors demonstrate how dealing with such challenges impacts physician learners as well as patients. They challenge GME institutions to interact with correctional institutions as places wherein medical education can occur. They also recommend other strategies for assisting residents and fellows to understand the challenges in caring for the justice-involved population.

By emphasizing the relationship between race, the persons incarcerated in the United States, and the provision of adequate, culturally appropriate health care, authors describe how the correctional institution can be a living laboratory to help GME educate physician learners in the delivery of humanistic, culturally humble care.

REFERENCES

1. Osseo-Asare A, Balasuriya L, Huot SJ, et al. Minority resident physicians' views on the role of race/ethnicity in their training experiences in the workplace. *JAMA Netw Open.* 2018;1(5):e182723. doi:10.1001/jamanetworkopen.2018.2723
2. DuBois WE. *The Souls of Black Folk.* A.C. McClurg & Co. 1903.
3. Rubin R. How the SCOTUS affirmative action ruling could affect medical schools and health care. *JAMA.* 2023;330(6):492-494. doi:10.1001/jama.2023.13603
4. Pfeffinger A, Fernández A, Tapia M, Rios-Fetchko F, Coffman J. *Recovery with limited progress: impact of California proposition 209 on racial/ethnic diversity of California medical school matriculants, 1990 to 2019.* University of California, San Francisco, Healthforce Center and University of California Latinx Center of Excellence; 2020. Accessed August 20, 2024. https://healthforce.ucsf.edu/publications/recovery-limited-progress-impact-california-proposition-209-racialethnic-diversity
5. Association of American Medical Colleges. Race/ethnicity responses (alone and in combination) of acceptees to U.S. MD-granting medical schools, 2019-2020 through 2023-2024. Accessed August 19, 2024. https://www.aamc.org/media/9406/download?attachment

6. Connolly M, Jacobs B. Counting indigenous American Indians and Alaska Natives in the US census. *Stat IAOS*. 2020;36(1): 201-210. Accessed August 20, 2024. https://content.iospress.com/articles/statistical-journal-of-the-iaos/sji200615
7. Choi AMK, Rustgi AK. Diversity in leadership at academic medical centers: addressing underrepresentation among Asian American faculty. *JAMA*. 2021;326(7): 605-606. doi:10.1001/jama.2021.12028
8. Weng SS, Wolfe WW. Asian American health inequities: an exploration of cultural and language incongruity and discrimination in accessing and utilizing the healthcare system. *Int Public Health J*. 2016;8(2):155-167. Accessed August 20, 2024. https://research.ebsco.com/linkprocessor/plink?id=954501fc-0ab5-389b-a4e1-22a557f4865d
9. Dill M, Hu X, Conrad S. *Asian physicians' reports of bias, harm and discrimination*. Association of American Medical Colleges. Accessed August 19, 2024. https://www.aamc.org/media/52346/download
10. Muramatsu N, Chin MH. Asian, Native Hawaiian, and Pacific Islander populations in the US—moving from invisibility to health equity. *JAMA Netw Open*. 2024;7(5):e2411617. doi:10.1001/jamanetworkopen.2024.11617
11. Kauh TJ, Read JG, Scheitler AJ. The critical role of racial/ethnic data disaggregation for health equity. *Popul Res Policy Rev*. 2021;40(1):1-7. doi:10.1007/s11113-020-09631-6
12. Boatright D, Nguyen M, Hill K, et al. Development of a tool to measure student perceptions of equity and inclusion in medical schools. *JAMA Netw Open*. 2024;7(2):e240001. doi:10.1001/jamanetworkopen.2024.0001
13. Ode GE, Williams RJ, Harrington MA, Bennett CH, Hogan MV, Porter S. Achieving a diverse, equitable, and inclusive environment for the black orthopaedic surgeon: part 2: obstacles faced in inclusion and retention of black orthopaedic residents. *J Bone Joint Surg Am*. 2021;103(11):1040-1045. doi: 10.2106/JBJS.21.00037
14. Diamond L, Izquierdo K, Canfield D, Matsoukas K, Gany F. A systematic review of the impact of patient–physician non-English language concordance on quality of care and outcomes. *J Gen Intern Med*. 2019;34(8)1591-1606. doi:10.1007/s11606-019-04847-5
15. National Academies of Sciences, Engineering, and Medicine; Health and Medicine Division; Policy and Global Affairs; Roundtable on Black Men and Black Women in Science, Engineering, and Medicine. *The Impacts of Racism and Bias on Black People Pursuing Careers in Science, Engineering, and Medicine: Proceedings of a Workshop*. In: Jones CP, Bright CM, Laurencin CT, eds. National Academies Press (US); 2020. doi:10.17226/25849

American Indian and Alaska Native Presence in Medicine

Natasha Bray, DO, MSEd, Clinical Professor Rural Health, Associate Dean of Accreditation, Oklahoma State University College of Osteopathic Medicine, Tahlequah, OK

Alec Calac, PhD, Adjunct Scientist, J. Craig Venter Institute, UC San Diego School of Medicine, San Diego, CA

Holly Pilson, MD, Associate Professor, Orthopaedic Trauma; Vice Chair, Social Impact; Co-Director of Diversity and Inclusion, Department of Orthopaedic Surgery and Rehabilitation, Wake Forest University School of Medicine, Winston-Salem, NC

Siobhan Wescott, MD, MPH, Associate Professor, Department of Health Promotion; Director, American Indian Health Program, University of Nebraska Medical Center, Omaha, NE

CHAPTER SUMMARY

In this chapter, we explore American Indian and Alaska Native (AI/AN) identity from a cultural and historical perspective, as well as the complexities it creates for the ways in which we support AI/AN physician learners today. We summarize the representation of AI/AN members in the medical workforce from the medical student level through to the practicing physician, including academic faculty members. We also describe several barriers that impede the successful matriculation of AI/AN along the pathway from medical school to clinical practice, including historical trauma, lack of mentorship, and other financial and cultural barriers. Lastly, we work toward developing a shared understanding of the recommended opportunities to enhance AI/AN advancement along the medical education continuum.

LEARNING OBJECTIVES

1. Describe the factors that shape AI/AN identity through a sociopolitical lens.
2. Evaluate the representation of AI/AN within residents, fellows, faculty members, and academic leadership.
3. Identify the key challenges and barriers to recruitment, selection, and advancement of AI/AN physician learners in graduate medical education (GME).
4. Discuss recommended opportunities and solutions for inclusion and equity of AI/AN populations in the physician workforce.

Case Study

Joseph is a fourth-year medical student applying to an internal medicine residency program. His father is an enrolled member of a Tribe in California and has a blood quantum of 50%. Because Joseph's mother is not AI/AN, Joseph's blood quantum is 25%, so he does not meet his Tribe's criteria for enrollment and is not an

(continued)

enrolled tribal member. While this situation causes internal strife for Joseph, he is an active member of the community, participates in tribal ceremonies and outreach programs, and is enrolled in language classes offered by the tribe. During Joseph's residency interview, the program director took an interest in his application and experiences. The program director asks curiously, "how Native are you?" Confused, Joseph asks for clarification with and receives the response, "are you full blood?" He answers, "My father is Native American, but my mother is not." The program director responds, "Oh, so you aren't really Native American." Joseph does not immediately answer, and the interview ends shortly thereafter. He thanks the program director for the opportunity and completes his interview. Joseph does not report the incident because he knows there are so few AI/AN applicants and he fears retaliation in the form of a rejection.

Case Discussion

AI/AN physician learners come from a variety of backgrounds and experiences. With hundreds of federally recognized AI/AN tribes and many more seeking recognition, one should not assume cultural homogeneity among them. Furthermore, other factors add complexity, such as **blood quantum** and tribal membership. Blood quantum is a product of federal assimilationist policy that assigns various degrees of "pure Indian blood" to AI/AN individuals enrolled in or descended from enrolled members of federally recognized AI/AN Tribes. In the case study, Joseph was asked an inappropriate question that has no bearing on his skills and competencies as a future physician. Interview questions should be structured as to be free from bias and to avoid presenting opportunities for stereotyping. In this case, how might Joseph's interview have gone differently if the program director asked how the applicant's upbringing had influenced the desire to become a physician, if at all?

Members of the Association of Native American Medical Students (ANAMS) and Association of American Indian Physicians (AAIP) have described incidents wherein medical school, residency, and fellowship program interviewers ask AI/AN applicants to disclose their blood quantum to "verify" claims about their identity and minimize the possibility of ethnic fraud. Not all AI/AN tribes use blood quantum as a criterion for membership, so neither of these constructs have any bearing on an individual's cultural connectedness with and belonging to a specific AI/AN community. Importantly, AI/AN individuals do not see themselves as a sum of fractions or parts. Each aspect of their identity is important and valued and cannot be parsed out as individual fractions.[1] In response to these incidents, the American Medical Association (AMA) worked with the ACGME, National Residency Matching Program (NRMP), Association of American Medical Colleges (AAMC), and other interested parties to eliminate questioning about or discrimination based on AI/AN blood quantum during the medical school, residency, and fellowship application process (see AMA Policy H-295.852).[2] As you review the chapter, consider what strategies programs, institutions, and individuals can use to eliminate identity-based discrimination and enhance the AI/AN experience in GME.

AMERICAN INDIAN AND ALASKA NATIVE TERMINOLOGY AND IDENTITY

Native, **Native American**, Indian, **American Indian (AI)**, **Alaska Native (AN)**, and **Indigenous** are among the terms that have been used to describe people indigenous to the United States. We will start by providing clarity around these terms; what they mean, and to whom they refer. AI and AN both denote the cultural and historical distinctions between people belonging to the Indigenous communities of the continental United States (AI) and the Indigenous villages of Alaska (AN). The term Native American came into broad usage in the 1970s as an alternative to AI and AN. Since then, the term Native American has gradually expanded to include *all* peoples native or indigenous to the United States and its territories. This expansion can include Native Hawaiians, Chamorros, and American Samoans, as well as persons from Indigenous communities in Mexico and Central and South America who are US residents.

Indigenous is an international term that has become increasingly used over the past decade in the United States and refers more broadly to first or aboriginal people who have pre-colonial ties and cultural origins to a place which has been colonized and settled by another ethnic group. It is important to note that there are personal, tribal, and regional preferences to these terms and ways in which individuals prefer to be identified.[3] For the purposes of this chapter, we will focus on the American Indian and Alaska Native (AI/AN) population, especially AI/AN Tribes who maintain a government-to-government relationship with the United States, based on treaties.

Understandably, AI/AN identity has become increasingly complex. It is important, therefore, to lay the groundwork for the ways in which identity and terminology have shaped how Native people live, work, and provide health care today to this population. AI/AN communities, tribes, and societies were historically known to be kinship or relationship-oriented; colonial identity politics and motives have externally redefined AI/AN identities. Early concepts of racial formation in the United States were centered around ideas that advanced colonialism, land, and resource acquisition at the expense of Indigenous humanity. As such, non-scientific and flawed concepts such as blood quantum were introduced as ways of identifying and tracking with pre-colonial origins in the Americas.[4]

There is no other racial or ethnic group in our country whose identity is often queried for quantity, proof of existence, or legitimacy as frequently as those belonging to an AI/AN community. Through request for "proof" of AI/AN identity, such as with a Certificate Degree of Indian Blood (US issued document) or a tribal membership card (issued by a tribal government), one's "Indian-ness," both in authenticity and quantity, may be questioned. This reductive mechanism has ensured that AI/AN political identity will gradually diminish, as blood quantum inevitably shrinks from generation to generation. Some posit that this process is essentially a racialization of AI/AN political identity, justifying continued AI/AN diaspora, hardship, and marginalization within the greater US populace.

Expansive identity concepts such as the "one drop rule," similarly adopted from colonial cultural appropriations of people of African ancestry for the benefit of slave labor, teach us to assume African ancestry based on the flawed and unscientific idea that one single "drop" of African ancestry qualifies someone for being Black, and therefore identifiable with that racial group.[5]

Thus, we must consider the way history has strategically marginalized Indigenous concepts of belonging and identity, and how to re-engage these values into shaping and influencing our ideas, biases, and strategies to improve the health and well-being of all AI/AN and Indigenous Peoples in health care.

REPRESENTATION AMONG MEDICAL STUDENTS, RESIDENTS/FELLOWS, FACULTY MEMBERS, AND LEADERSHIP

No single dataset exists to track the progression of students from their application and matriculation to medical school through to becoming a practicing physician. Multiple databases have utilized varying methods of collecting demographic data for race and ethnicity between these systems *and* over time. This lack of a single dataset is problematic in general, but especially when considering AI/AN populations. Data on single-race, non-Hispanic AI/AN individuals is often utilized in workforce analysis to represent the entire population of AI/AN students and physicians which can be extremely misleading, considering that the majority of AI/AN persons identify as belonging to more than one race.[6] For small populations, like AI/AN students, with over 70% reporting they belong to more than one racial/ethnic group, the data becomes difficult to disaggregate and interpret. In the joint publication by AAMC and the AAIP, *Reshaping the Journey*,[7] only 9% of US Liaison Committee on Medical Education (LCME) accredited medical schools had an enrollment of four or more solely identified AI/AN students in 2016-2017 and a remarkable 43% of schools did not have any solely identified enrolled AI/AN students. Of the 31,377 individuals who matriculated into a medical school accredited by the LCME or Commission on Osteopathic College Accreditation (COCA)

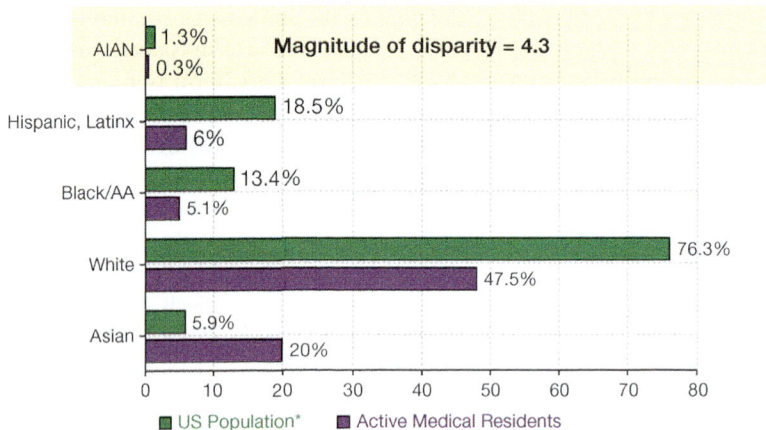

FIGURE 8.1 Active medical residents compared to US population.
* Based on US Census estimate for 2020. (**Source:** Accreditation Council for Graduate Medical Education. 2020-2021 GME data resource book. https://www.acgme.org/globalassets/pfassets/publicationsbooks/2020-2021_acgme__databook_document)

in the fall of 2020, 51 (0.16%) of students identified as AI/AN alone.[8,9] This number jumps to 319 (1.02%) students when AI/AN alone or in combination is utilized.

When we look at the number of AI/AN physicians enrolled in GME programs, data from 2019-2020 ACGME *GME Data Resource Book* demonstrates that AI/AN comprise only 0.3% of active residents in the United States (Figure 8.1).[10] Primary care fields including family medicine, internal medicine, and pediatrics have among the highest enrollment of AI/AN (Table 8.1).[10] The high participation in primary care training programs is likely tied to the number of AI/AN physicians who participate in the Indian Health Services (IHS) scholarship program. IHS scholarships are contingent on the recipient pursuing an approved residency program in the following specialties: emergency medicine, family medicine, internal medicine, pediatrics, anesthesiology, psychiatry, obstetrics/gynecology, and general surgery. IHS scholarship recipients

Table 8.1 AI/AN Physicians Enrolled in ACGME Accredited Residency Programs by Specialty from 2015-2016 Through 2021-2022

Specialty	2020-2021	2019-2020	2018-2019	2017-2018	2016-2017
Family medicine*	29	59	42	44	64
Internal medicine*	25	54	27	23	28
Surgery	10	36	23	20	25
Psychiatry	11	25	23	22	19
Emergency medicine	12	29	19	16	16
Anesthesiology	9	25	20	18	17
Pediatrics*	11	35	14	15	13
Obstetrics and gynecology	6	20	15	14	13
Radiology-diagnostic	4	14	14	11	11
Orthopedic surgery	2	11	9	10	11

*Designates primary care specialty.

Note: 2020-2021 is the first year that it allows for "multiple race/ethnicity."

Source: Accreditation Council for Graduate Medical Education. 2020-2021 GME data resource book. https://www.acgme.org/globalassets/pfassets/publicationsbooks/2020-2021_acgme__databook_document

are not allowed to defer their service obligations to pursue other specialties or fellowship programs, limiting their opportunities for advanced training.

Comparing the percentages of active US resident physicians by race/ethnicity to their representation in the 2019 US population, we can see that not only do AI/AN comprise the most underrepresented group in medicine, but they also represent the greatest workforce disparity. AI/AN comprise 1.9% of the US population[11] but only 0.3% of active US resident physicians, a magnitude of disparity of 4.3 (Figure 8.1).

AI/AN are further underrepresented in the US practicing physician workforce. Of the nearly 920,000 active US physicians in 2019, only 2,570 (0.3%) were AI/AN; a decrease from 0.57% in 2016.[12] Most of these physicians are working in areas with a high concentration of AI/AN people.[7,13,14] Additionally, there is a lack of AI/AN serving as medical school faculty. According to 2018 AAMC data, AI/AN made up only 0.2% of full-time medical school faculty, a decrease from 0.48% in 2016.[15] To fully understand the lack of representation by AI/AN physicians in the medical school faculty is beyond the scope of this chapter but needs further research, especially when considering workforce development.

KEY CHALLENGES TO RECRUITMENT, SELECTION, AND RETENTION

The consistently low level of AI/AN representation in medicine has prompted national coordination among key stakeholders to determine the underlying factors preventing AI/AN students from matriculating into medical school.[7] Partners in these national efforts include, but are not limited to, AAIP, AAMC, AMA, and medical schools with a significant number of AI/AN students who participate and become members in ANAMS and AAIP. To date, these collaborations have produced multiple reports and meetings to delve into the challenges and potential solutions.

While a full examination of the reasons for AI/AN underrepresentation in medicine is beyond the scope of this chapter, we will discuss three key factors: (1) the role of historical trauma and cultural assimilation; (2) lack of mentorship; and, (3) financial barriers.

ROLE OF HISTORICAL TRAUMA AND CULTURAL ASSIMILATION

The extensive historical trauma experienced by AI/AN populations has caused a high degree of disruption, harm, and death. The lack of understanding by the general public about these additional challenges faced by AI/AN populations creates ongoing problems within their communities. Evans-Campbell (2008) provides a succinct overview of AI/AN historical trauma and the long shadow it has cast on current AI/AN communities:

> Over successive generations, American Indian and Alaska Native (AI/AN) people have experienced a series of traumatic assaults that have had enduring consequences for families and communities. An extensive literature documents these assaults, which have included community massacres, genocidal policies, pandemics from the introduction of new diseases, forced relocation, forced removal of children though Indian boarding school policies, and prohibition of spiritual and cultural practices.[16, 17] Together, these events amount to a history of ethnic and cultural genocide.[18] In addition, contemporary AI/AN communities suffer from some of the highest rates of lifetime traumatic events, including interpersonal violence,[19] child abuse and neglect,[20] poor health,[21] and an ongoing barrage of negative stereotypes and microaggressions that disparage and undermine AI/AN society and identity.[22]

Not unlike many marginalized communities, AI/AN people often walk in two distinct worlds–one of deep cultural purpose and enrichment and the other of palpable erasure, exclusion and invisibility. When knowledge and consideration of the historical factors which still affect AI/AN people can be removed, the resulting "space" can be held for healing and reconciliation, thereby promoting greater inclusion of AI/AN health care professionals.

LACK OF MENTORSHIP

A second barrier to achieving AI/AN representation in medicine is lack of mentorship. The documented low number of AI/AN physicians limits the number of race-concordant role models and mentors available to prospective AI/AN pre-med students, and especially in medical faculty positions, by definition, limits the number of race-concordant mentors available to medical students, residents, and fellows. While race-concordant mentorship has been shown to be effective for many groups underrepresented in medicine, mentorship from non-native allies is critical to encourage, support, and sponsor the AI/AN student or the resident or fellow for whom race-concordant mentorship is difficult to obtain.

FINANCIAL BARRIERS

The last barrier we highlight is finances. In a recent survey, AI/AN medical students, reported that being first generation and low income impedes their progress in medical school.[23] Extensive literature exists on the challenges facing medical students with significant financial concerns,[24] many of whom are first generation medical students. Further examples of AI/AN experiences with these and other barriers, including cultural obstacles, are highlighted in *Reshaping the Journey*, the landmark report created by the AAMC and AAIP cited previously.[7]

RECOMMENDED OPPORTUNITIES AND SOLUTIONS

Any member of the GME community interested in improving the learning environment for AI/AN individuals must first be introspective, first identifying functional barriers to the equitable representation of this demographic, and then considering ways to create an environment and culture that promotes the retention and advancement of AI/AN physician learners. In this section, we outline strategies that individuals and, especially, institutional leaders, can use to enhance recruitment, inclusion, and belonging of AI/AN persons in GME.

1. Become familiar with terminology and historical complexities of AI/AN identity.

    We should familiarize ourselves with terminology regarding identification and categorization, as well as understanding historical complexities of AI/AN identity politics and how these complexities are intrinsically intertwined into our lives and work today. We must eliminate exclusionary, and sometimes traumatizing concepts such as blood quantum, and avoid questioning the "degree of Indianness or Nativeness" of a person. Alternatively, we can think more creatively about ways to allow AI/AN people to demonstrate and promote their culture and identity. For example, we should consider asking A/I or A/N persons how they prefer to be identified or recognized.

> Identity can be a complex subject for Indigenous residents and fellows. Rather than asking these physician learners solely about their culture, it is important to work with them to foster an environment that is responsive to their traditions and values.

2. Include AI/AN numbers when reporting data and avoid dehumanizing data collection and reporting practices.

    The medical community and society should avoid the "othering" of AI/AN people in our research and statistics by *not* assuming that the numbers are so low they do not deserve mentioning, or that their absence in the data will not be noticed or missed. Invisibility is a common reality for AI/AN people; it can be demoralizing and dehumanizing to be referred to as "other" or "something else." While 99% of allopathic medical schools reported specific programs or policies to recruit a diverse student body in

> Person-first language is important in the clinical setting. Be mindful to avoid using language that is demeaning and stereotypical of minoritized AI/AN residents and fellows such as "let's have a powwow" (meeting) or that's "low on the totem pole" (not a priority).

2017, only 11% of those schools reported having AI/AN content in their curricula.[7] We can work more collaboratively with our AI/AN colleagues, communities, and organizations to incorporate culturally appropriate and relevant content into medical education.

Some institutions and organizations have adopted a mindset that because the numbers of AI/AN are so small, the ability to show outcomes compared to efforts in recruiting this population for enrollment, or employment has a limited return on investment. We recommend that accrediting bodies such as the ACGME, LCME, and COCA can be agents of change in this area by working towards eliminating and avoiding narrow metrics regarding outcomes for groups as it relates to strategic diversity focus areas.

3. Consider developing a land acknowledgement statement paired with meaningful Indigenous community partnerships

Land acknowledgements can be included in our institutional and organizational diversity statements and programs, to acknowledge both the original Indigenous inhabitants of the land and the traumatic and complex ways in which those groups came to be removed and disinhibited from these places. A necessary component of this process is the intentional fostering of relationships with the Indigenous communities around us. A guide to land acknowledgments can be found at the Native Governance Center.[25]

Lastly, there are organizations we can partner with such as the AAIP, ANAMS, IHS, and even tribal governments, to continue deepening of our understanding and support on AI/AN medical students, residents/fellows, colleagues, and patients.

Take Home Points

- American Indian and Alaska Native (AI/AN) people are not a monolith; they represent a diverse group of over 600 communities including federally recognized Tribes, state recognized Tribes, and urban Indigenous communities throughout the United States.
- We must all consider the way history has strategically marginalized Indigenous concepts of belonging and identity, and how we can re-engage these values into shaping and influencing our ideas, biases, and strategies with the aim of improving the health and well-being of all AI/AN people.
- Low numbers of practicing AI/AN physicians make race-concordant mentorship difficult; AI/AN students, residents, and fellows rely on and benefit immensely from the mentorship of non-AI/AN allies in medicine.
- Invisibility is a commonly held feeling amongst AI/AN people. Seeking opportunities to acknowledge, affirm, and uplift AI/AN history, culture, and other contributions and provide ongoing support and sponsorship to AI/AN residents and fellows is critical to fostering inclusivity in GME.

QUESTIONS FOR FURTHER THOUGHT

1. More than 70% of AI/AN people identify as more than one race. How do your recruitment, research, and data-tracking practices account for demographic information in a way that accounts for individuals who identify as more than one race? Are there changes that may be needed to identify AI/AN individuals in your residents and fellows, faculty members, or patient population?
2. Do you know the Indigenous history of the land on which your institutions now occupy? How can you strategically work towards a broader commitment to honor and steward the land, its history, and ancestors both past and present?

REFERENCES

1. Hilleary C. Some Native Americans fear blood quantum is formula for 'paper genocide.' Accessed April 9, 2024. https://www.voanews.com/a/usa_some-native-americans-fear-blood-quantum-formula-paper-genocide/6208615.html
2. American Medical Association: Policy Finder. Strengthening interview guidelines for American Indian and Alaska native medical school, residency, and fellowship applicants H-295.852. Published 2022. Accessed May 16, 2023.

https://policysearch.ama-assn.org/policyfinder/detail/blood%20quantum?uri=%2FAMADoc%2FHOD.xml-H-295.852.xml
3. Bird MY. What we want to be called: indigenous peoples' perspectives on racial and ethnic identity labels. *Am Indian Q.* 1999;23(2):1–21. doi:10.2307/1185964
4. Gampa V, Bernard K, Oldani MJ. Racialization as a barrier to achieving health equity for Native Americans. *JAMA J Ethics*. 2020;22(10):E874-E881. https://journalofethics.ama-assn.org/article/racialization-barrier-achieving-health-equity-native-americans/2020-10
5. American Association of Colleges of Osteopathic Medicine. Osteopathic Medical College First-Year Enrollment by Race/Ethnicity 2000-2003. Accessed January 13, 2024. https:www.aacom.org/searches/reports/report/2000-23-FYEbyCOMandRE
6. Becker TL, Babey SH, Shimkhada R, Scheitler AJ, Ponce NA. Limited access to health data on American Indian and Alaska natives impedes population health insights. *Health Policy Brief.* UCLA Center for Health Policy Research; 2020. Accessed April 15, 2024. https://healthpolicy.ucla.edu/publications/Documents/PDF/2020/AIAN-policybrief-nov2020.pdf
7. Association of American Medical Colleges and Association of American Indian Physicians. *Reshaping the Journey: American Indians and Alaska Natives in Medicine*. Association of American Medical Colleges; 2018.
8. Association of American Medical Colleges. Table A-14.2: Race/ethnicity responses (alone and in combination) of acceptees to U.S. MD-granting medical schools, 2018-2019 through 2022-2023. Published 2023. Accessed April 15, 2024. https://www.aamc.org/media/9406/download?attachment
9. American Association of Colleges of Osteopathic Medicine. Applicants & matriculants by race and ethnicity 2009-2021. Accessed December 19, 2022. https://www.aacom.org/searches/reports/report/applicants-matriculants-by-race-ethnicity-2009-2021
10. Accreditation Council for Graduate Medical Education. 2020-2021 GME data resource book. https://www.acgme.org/globalassets/pfassets/publicationsbooks/2020-2021_acgme__databook_document.pdf
11. United States Census Bureau. Accessed April 15, 2024. https://www.census.gov/search-results.html?searchType=web&cssp=SERP&q=American%20Indian%20and%20Alaska%20Native
12. Association of American Medical Colleges. Figure 18: Percentage of all active physicians by race/ethnicity, 2018. Accessed April 15, 2024. https://www.aamc.org/data-reports/workforce/data/figure-18-percentage-all-active-physicians-race/ethnicity-2018
13. Xierali IM, Nivet MA, Fair MA. Analyzing physician workforce racial and ethnic composition associations: physician specialties (Part I). *Analysis: In Brief.* Association of American Medical Colleges. 2014;14(8). Accessed July 6, 2018. https://www.aamc.org/media/29866/download
14. Xierali IM, Castillo-Page L, Conrad S, Nivet MA. Analyzing physician workforce racial and ethnic composition associations: geographic distribution (Part II). In. *Analysis: in Brief.* Association of American Medical Colleges. 2014;14(9). Accessed July 6, 2018. https://www.aamc.org/media/29866/download
15. Association of American Medical Colleges. Figure 15: Percentage of full-time U.S. medical school faculty by race/ethnicity, 2018. Accessed April 14, 2024. https://www.aamc.org/data-reports/workforce/data/figure-15-percentage-full-time-us-medical-school-faculty-race/ethnicity-2018
16. Stannard DE. *American Holocaust: The Conquest of the New World*. Oxford University Press; 1993.
17. Thornton R. *American Indian Holocaust and Survival: A Population History Since 1492*. Vol. 186. The Civilization of the American Indian Series. University of Oklahoma Press; 1987.
18. Smith A. *Soul wound: the legacy of Native American schools*. The National Native American Boarding School Healing Coalition. Published October 9, 2015. Accessed April 14, 2024. https://laratracehentz.wordpress.com/2015/10/09/soul-wound-the-legacy-of-native-american-schools
19. Greenfeld LA, Smith SK. American Indians and crime. US Department of Justice; Bureau of Justic Statistics. Published 1999. Accessed April 14, 2024. https://bjs.ojp.gov/library/publications/american-indians-and-crime
20. Cross TA, Earle KA, Simmons D. Child abuse and neglect in Indian country: policy issues. *Fam Soc.* 2000;81(1):49-58. doi:10.1606/1044-3894.1092
21. Walters KL, Simoni JM, Evans-Campbell T. Substance use among American Indians and Alaska natives: incorporating culture in an "indigenist" stress-coping paradigm. *Public Health Rep.* 2002;117(suppl 1):104-117. PMID: 12435834
22. Evans-Campbell T. Historical trauma in American Indian/Native Alaska communities: a multilevel framework for exploring impacts on individuals, families, and communities. *J Interpers Violence.* 2008;23(3):316-338. doi:10.1177/0886260507312290

23. Swain W, Calac AJ, Neimeko CJ, Gasca L, Dodge Francis C. Understanding the experiences of American Indian and Alaska native students enrolled in allopathic and osteopathic medical degree programs. *J Racial Ethn Health Disparities*. 2023;10(5):2145-2154. doi:10.1007/s40615-022-01394-4
24. Salinas KE, Nguyen HB, Kamran SC. The invisible minority: a call to address the persistent socioeconomic diversity gap in U.S. medical schools and the physician workforce. *Front Public Health*. 2022;10:924746. doi:10.3389/fpubh.2022.924746
25. Native Governance Center. A guide to indigenous land acknowledgment. Accessed April 9, 2024. https://nativegov.org/news/a-guide-to-indigenous-land-acknowledgment/

Asian, Pacific Islander, Native Hawaiian and Asian Pacific Islander American Experience

Tonya L Fancher, MD, MPH, Associate Dean for Workforce Innovation and Education Quality Improvement, Professor of Medicine, UC Davis School of Medicine, Sacramento, CA

Iris Vuong, MD, MPH, Chief Medical Resident, Internal Medicine, UC Davis School of Medicine, Sacramento, CA

Rosa Lee, MD, Senior Associate Dean for Curricular Affairs, Columbia University Vagelos College of Physicians and Surgeons, New York, NY

Sunny Nakae, PhD, MSW, Senior Associate Dean for Diversity, Equity, Inclusion, and Partnership, Associate Professor of Medical Education, California University of Science and Medicine, Colton, CA

CHAPTER SUMMARY

The terms Asian, Pacific Islander (API) and Native Hawaiian or Pacific Islander (NHPI) represent a myriad of distinct ethnicities, languages, and cultures brought together as a unifying Asian American voice during the civil rights movement. However, lack of disaggregated data hides the diversity within these communities and perpetuates misunderstandings about representation, challenges, and intersections. In this chapter, we aim to help graduate medical education (GME) programs improve their efforts to recruit, retain, and support residents and fellows with API, NHPI, and API American identities. We will highlight key challenges and opportunities for GME programs and institutions to embrace the wisdom within these communities and provides suggestions to improve inclusion and equity.

LEARNING OBJECTIVES

1. Review current Asian, API, NHPI, and API American representation in GME and academic leadership.
2. Identify challenges and intersectional identities that influence inclusion of API, NHPI, and API American-identifying individuals in GME.
3. Develop strategies to improve inclusion and equity of API, NHPI, and API American-identifying individuals in GME.

Case Study

Quynh is an intern who identifies as Vietnamese American. She is a first-generation resident whose parents emigrated to the United States after the fall of Saigon. She worked throughout high school and college and was a re-applicant to medical school. She matched at her number one residency program. Previously, she received feedback that she speaks too softly when presenting patients, and she is determined to act on that feedback.

Quynh stops to examine Mr X, a patient who was admitted overnight. He asks when the doctor will arrive. When she informs him that she is his new primary doctor in the hospital, he seems surprised. He tells her about his time serving in the military during the Vietnam War and how she reminds him of that very difficult time. He again asks about when his doctor will arrive and declines Quynh's request to exam him.

When Quynh arrives at rounds, her senior resident greets her and says, "Good morning, Michelle! I didn't know you would be back on service so soon!"

"Oh, I'm Quynh. I just started this rotation today."

"Oh my goodness, I'm so sorry. You both look so alike. I know you're Quynh. I'm so sorry."

As the team walks toward the first patient's room ("Quynh, I'm so sorry again. I didn't mean to mix you up with Michelle."), the other intern reports that this patient requested a Vietnamese interpreter overnight. As the team walks in, the attending, Dr G, turns to Quynh and says, "Quynh, do you mind interpreting as we talk?"

"I don't speak Vietnamese."

When the team reaches Mr X, she lets them know that the patient declined the exam from Quynh on her pre-rounds.

After rounds, Dr G meets with each of the residents.

"Quynh, tell me about your goals for the week."

"I'm trying to be more assertive and speak louder on rounds. I've gotten feedback that I talk too quietly."

"Well, you were assertive on rounds today but it came across as overly confident. You also seemed uninterested in rounds. And you must examine all of your patients, even if that means coming in earlier. Try to seem more like part of the team."

Case Discussion

Quynh's experience presents opportunities for enhancing the clinical learning environment. Several moments in this short episode describe a time when someone makes an incorrect assumption about Quynh. These assumptions, at times, come from a patient, and at other times from a supervisor, such as the more senior resident and the attending physician. Quynh's identity as a Vietnamese American is used as a reason why she is rejected in her role as physician (by the patient) and as a reason why she is asked to serve as an untrained interpreter (by the attending). Additionally, stereotyping comments are made about Quynh's physical appearance, comparing her appearance to that of a colleague (by the resident). Quynh is interested in enhancing her clinical performance, and is juggling disparate feedback from different supervisors. The incident illustrated in this case demonstrates how incorrect assumptions about identity, or perceived identity, may affect clinical performance. As you review the chapter, consider what could have gone differently in this scenario and what systems are in place at your institution for physician learners to report concerns about the learning environment.

REPRESENTATION IN GME AND ACADEMIC LEADERSHIP

The terms **Asian, Pacific Islander (API)**, **Native Hawaiian or Pacific Islander (NHPI)**, and **API American** represent a myriad of distinct ethnicities, languages, and cultures brought together under these umbrella terms as a unifying voice during the civil rights era. However, lack of disaggregation masks unique experiences and histories among API, NHPI, and API American identity groups. Asian identities are described as over-represented in medicine. In 2021, 29% of active residents in GME self-identified as Asian (alone or in combination), compared to 7% of the US population.[1,2] In contrast, when using the relatively disaggregated term NHPI, 0.02% of active residents in GME and 0.4% of US residents, respectively, self-identify as NHPI, highlighting their under-representation in the workforce. Further, Asian men and NHPI have higher rates of unsuccessful placement into GME programs compared with White men (Figure 9.1).[3] API, NHPI, and API Americans live throughout the United States (Figure 9.2) with significant representational variability between states (Figure 9.2).

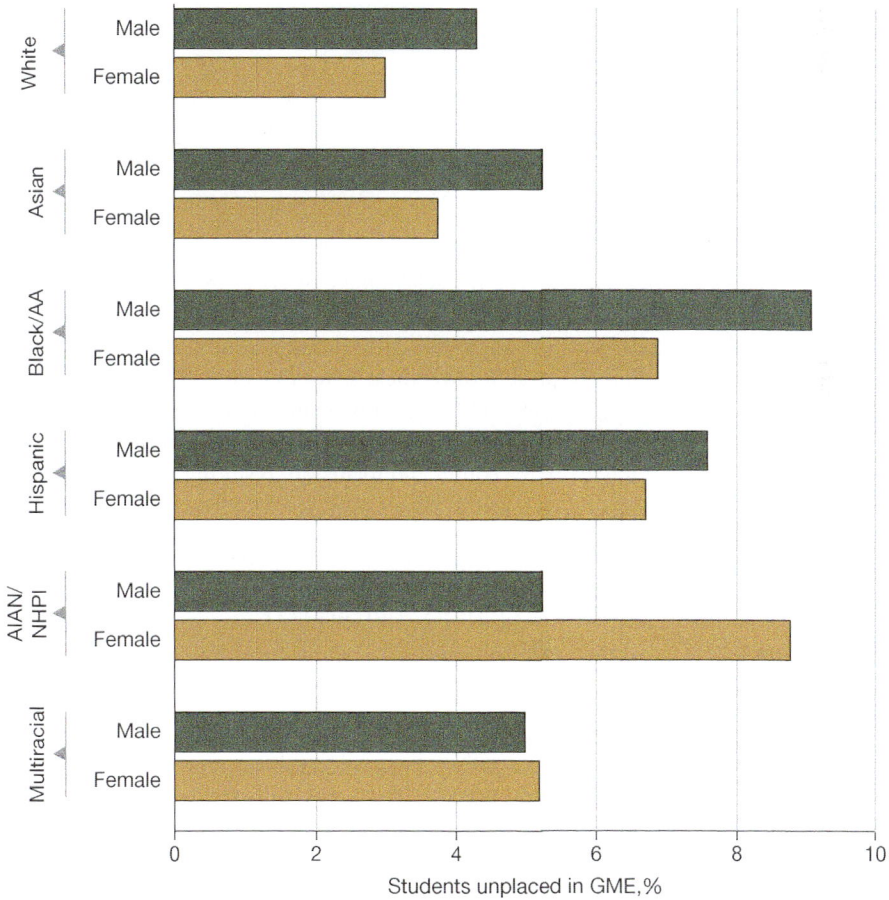

FIGURE 9.1 Unadjusted rate of being unplaced in GME by sex and racial/ethnic groups highlighting importance of disaggregating data for individuals who identify as API, NHPI, or API American. AIAN, American Indian/Alaska Native; NHPI, Native Hawaiian/Pacific Islander. (**Source:** Nguyen M, Chaudhry SI, Desai MM, et al. Rates of medical student placement into graduate medical education by sex, race and ethnicity, and socioeconomic status, 2018-2021. *JAMA Netw Open.* 2022;5(8):e2229243)

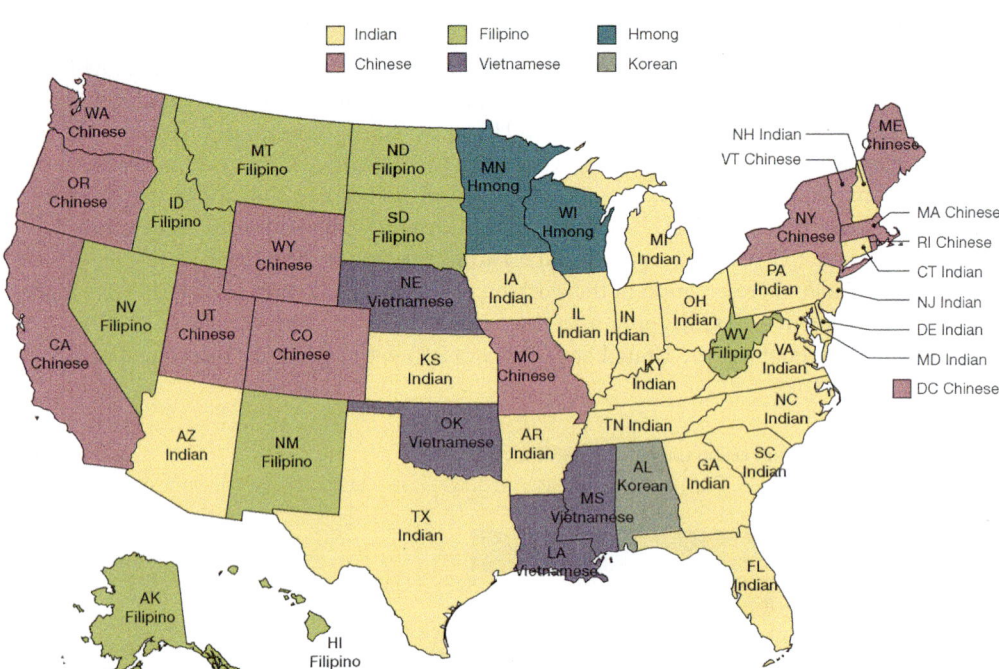

FIGURE 9.2 Largest Asian origin groups by state, 2019. (PEW Research Center Analysis of 2017–2019 American Community Survey [IPUMS])

Leadership in academic medicine is extremely exclusionary of API and NHPI American physicians and professionals. Although the number of medical school deans, student affairs deans, or designated institutional officials (DIOs) positions filled by API and NHPI Americans across US medical schools have decreased over time, Asians make up about 20% of medical school faculty.[4] This underrepresentation in leadership is likely due to stereotyping, racism, and the bamboo ceiling effect.[5] Lack of inclusion in leadership and administration perpetuates the notion that API and NHPI American individuals are not relevant to programming and spaces involving diversity, equity and inclusion, resulting in persistent feelings of exclusion from conversations on racism and, as a result, permitting physician learners to continue to struggle to share their experiences with harassment and discrimination.[6]

CHALLENGES AND INTERSECTIONAL IDENTITIES THAT INFLUENCE INCLUSION

The most challenging intersections faced by NHPI and API American residents and fellows are racism and misattribution as model minorities. API and NHPI American communities face health inequities, lack of access to affordable, language-appropriate, culturally appropriate health care, and many of the same structural vulnerabilities faced by other minoritized groups. NHPI and API American physician learners face microaggressions, discrimination, mistreatment, racism, etc, and yet are often expected to avoid "making waves" due to comparative suffering or negative stereotypes. Yet within academic medicine, these NHPI and API American physician learners are often positioned as "White adjacent" or "middle caste" and therefore not provided with resources or advocacy from leadership.

A broad focus on race may overlook critical aspects of diversity in relation to educational, financial, or social barriers that many NHPI and API American residents may have navigated on their career journeys. For example, the average 2023-2024 Medical College Admission Test (*MCAT*®) score for Asian students was

509.1, the highest of all reported groups. Yet, the average for NHPI test takers was 501.1.[7] Although widely accepted that Asian households in the US have above average annual income, only two Asian origin groups (Indians and Filipinos) had household incomes that exceeded the median for Asian Americans.[8] Most of the other origin groups, including the Southeast Asian Vietnamese, Hmong and Laotian identities, were well below the national median for Asian Americans. Similarly, Mongolian and Burmese had the highest poverty rates among all Asian origin groups, at 25%—more than twice the national average. This translates directly to medical school: *MCAT*® scores are positively associated with income.[9] Further, fewer than one-in-five Laotians (18%) and Bhutanese (15%) have at least a bachelor's degree compared with roughly one-third of all Americans. Medical school applicants who were non-Hispanic API were less likely to be accepted into medical school.[10] In a study of over 9,000 residents from 305 internal medicine residency programs in the United States, Asian residents were rated lower in all ACGME competency milestones, starting in the initial midyear Milestones report, compared with White residents. This racial disparity peaked in the post-graduate-two year and narrowed in the final post-graduate year.[11]

The Deferred Action for Childhood Arrivals (DACA) initiative provides for the temporary deferral of enforcement of immigration laws for certain undocumented individuals brought to the United States before age 16. The cultural and social acumen that many NHPI and API American residents bring via their lived experiences is also subject to exclusion and attrition in medicine due to crude selection models that ignore intersectionality.[12-14]

STRATEGIES TO IMPROVE INCLUSION AND EQUITY FOR API, NHPI, AND API AMERICANS

1. Disaggregate Data.

Supporting NHPI and API American residents and fellows in GME begins with a frank awareness and acknowledgment of the backgrounds, experiences, and challenges faced by this diverse community. Rather than perpetuating perceptions of this population as "not under-represented" minorities within GME and academic medicine, we suggest that programs collect and report disaggregated data that reflects the richness of identities. We suggest that programs use the same Asian-identifying options as used by the American Medical College Application Service (*AMCAS*®) and Electronic Residency Application Service (*ERAS*®) and allow residents to identify with more than one race. We further advocate for programs to collect data on country of origin and languages spoken and use a free text option to allow residents to use additional specificity as they wish. At the national level, the ACGME actively collects disaggregated API and NHPI data.

2. Reconsider the Institutional Approach to Recruitment and Selection.

Medical schools are the gatekeepers to physician careers. Programs can take steps to address structural barriers to entry to medical schools for NHPI and API Americans. GME programs can help bolster the pathway to medicine by partnering with pre-medical schools and organizations that support low-income and first-generation students and with medical schools that have a strong social mission of educational equity. GME programs should examine their recruitment processes and disaggregated data to ensure alignment with program goals and aim to address any misalignment through holistic review for admissions and inclusive recruitment strategies such as blinding application metrics, diversifying interview and recruitment committees, and ensuring implicit bias training for everyone involved in recruitment.

3. Review Institutional Policies and Practices for Exclusionary Practices.

Education and outreach are needed to achieve institutional policies conducive to the inclusion and success of those undocumented in medicine. Exclusionary policies related to residents, fellows, and employee citizenship and immigration status may be in place at the institutional or at the clinical affiliate level, impacting educational and recruitment opportunities. Exclusionary practices might also emerge in the way systems acknowledge and accommodate holidays and religious practices.

> The history of anti-Asian racism in the United States and the alarming rise in bias attacks targeting the API and NHPI American communities must be addressed at all levels within the institution.

> API and NHPI American are the second largest group of Deferred Action for Childhood Arrivals (DACA) beneficiary-students.[15]

4. Analyze Departmental and Institutional Data.

The underrepresentation of API, NHPI, and API Americans in leadership is likely due to stereotyping, racism, and the bamboo ceiling effect. Programs and institutions can review data on faculty promotion and leadership roles (eg, center directors, division and department chairs, associate deans and deans, and in the C-suite) and lead the development of mitigation strategies for any identified inequities.

5. Adopt Name-Affirming Practices.

Taking the time to learn a person's name affirms a commitment to them as a person. Programs could adopt strategies that acknowledge the importance and significance of learning to pronounce names that are unfamiliar. Programs could ask residents and fellows to teach them to say their names at day one of orientation, ask them to record their names so the program can learn them before orientation, and use online tools that attach an audio-file of names to individuals' email signatures.

6. Be Responsive to Reports of Bias and Discrimination.

The history of anti-Asian racism in the United States and the alarming rise in bias attacks targeting the API community must not remain hidden and must also be addressed. We suggest that institutions and programs take steps to deter discrimination, create reporting pathways that are easily accessible, act quickly and be responsive to all reports, support physician learners who experience or witness discrimination, ensure safe reporting, be accountable for resident and fellow safety, and be ready to improve policies and practices.

7. Include NHPI and API Americans in Antiracism Efforts.

API and NHPI American communities should be included in institutional diversity, equity, inclusion, and antiracism efforts. Anti-Asian racism should be recognized among the many forms of oppression in medicine. Programs and institutions can enhance belonging for API and NHPI learners by affirming community practices around culture, language, and outreach. As with other diverse communities, programs and institutions should accommodate observance of API and NHPI holidays and religious practices and support institution-wide affirming name practices such as the use of phonetic and audio-recorded name pronunciation tools for electronic communications, in the Electronic Health Record, and in academic registries. Programs and institutions should ensure that API and NHPI American physician learners and faculty members are equitably considered for awards and advancements.

Take Home Points

- Household income, educational attainment, undocumented and immigration status, language, and health disparities vary by API and NHPI American populations.
- Collecting and reporting disaggregated data is required to improve the recruitment, experience, and promotion of API and NHPI American residents, fellows, and faculty members.
- API and NHPI Americans are markedly underrepresented among academic leadership and dean positions in US academic medical centers.

? QUESTIONS FOR FURTHER THOUGHT

1. What steps could you take to improve the climate for API and NHPI Americans at your institution?
2. Why might the model minority myth and/or White adjacency bias feel more benign than other forms of prejudice? How is the model minority myth and/or White adjacency bias uniquely harmful both to Asian Americans and other minoritized ethnic groups?

REFERENCES

1. US Department of Health and Human Services: Office of Minority Health. Minority population profiles. Accessed June 4, 2024. https://minorityhealth.hhs.gov/omh/browse.aspx?lvl=2&lvlid=26
2. Accreditation Council for Graduate Medical Education. *2021-2022 GME Data Resource Book*. Accessed June 4, 2024. https://www.acgme.org/globalassets/pfassets/publicationsbooks/2021-2022_acgme__databook_document.pdf
3. Nguyen M, Chaudhry SI, Desai MM, et al. Rates of medical student placement into graduate medical education by sex, race and ethnicity, and socioeconomic status, 2018-2021. *JAMA Netw Open*. 2022;5(8):e2229243. doi:10.1001/jamanetworkopen.2022.29243
4. Kamran SC, Winkfield KM, Reede JY, Vapiwala N. Intersectional analysis of U.S. medical faculty diversity over four decades. *N Engl J Med*. 2022;386(14):1363-1371. doi:10.1056/nejmsr2114909
5. Hyun J. *Breaking the Bamboo Ceiling: Career Strategies for Asians*. HarperCollins; 2005.
6. Weng J, Zhu A, Chen CYY. Call to Action: Disaggregating the Asian American medical student experience. *Acad Med* 2022;97(12):1728-1728. doi:10.1097/acm.0000000000004965
7. Association of American Medical Colleges. MCAT® scores and GPAs for applicants and matriculants to U.S. MD-granting medical schools by race/ethnicity, 2023–2024. Accessed June 4, 2024. https://www.aamc.org/media/6066/download
8. Budiman A, Ruiz NG. Key facts about Asian origin groups in the U.S. Pew Research Center. Published April 29, 2021. Accessed June 4, 2024. https://www.pewresearch.org/fact-tank/2021/04/29/key-facts-about-asian-origin-groups-in-the-u-s
9. Lucey CR, Saguil A. The consequences of structural racism on MCAT® scores and medical school admissions. *Acad Med*. 2020;95(3):351-356. doi:10.1097/acm.0000000000002939
10. Mason HRC, Ata A, Nguyen M, et al. First-generation and continuing-generation college graduates' application, acceptance, and matriculation to U.S. medical schools: a national cohort study. *Med Educ Online*. 2022;27(1):2010291. doi:10.1080/10872981.2021.2010291
11. Boatright E, Anderson N, Kim JG, et al. Racial and ethnic differences in internal medicine residency assignments. *JAMA Netw Open*. 2022;5(12):e2247649. doi: 10.1001/jamanetworkopen.2022.47649
12. Nakae S, Rojas Marquez D, Di Bartolo IM, Rodriguez R. Considerations for residency programs regarding accepting undocumented students who are DACA recipients. *Acad Med*. 2017;92(11):1549-1554. doi:10.1097/acm.0000000000001731
13. Nguyen M, Chaudhry SI, Desai MM, et al. Association of sociodemographic characteristics with US medical student attrition. *JAMA Intern Med*. 2022;182(9): 917-924. doi:10.1001/jamainternmed.2022.2194
14. Nguyen M, Fancher T, Boatright D. Attrition of indigenous medical students requires swift institutional response—reply. *JAMA Intern Med*. 2022;182(12):1330-1331. doi:10.1001/jamainternmed.2022.4936
15. Garcia A, Lapidus A, De Witt ML, et al. Deferred Action for Childhood Arrivals (DACA): maximizing impacts in medical education and health care. *MedEdPORTAL*. 2022;18:11279. doi:10.15766/mep_2374-8265.11279

10

Aspects of the Black Experience in Graduate Medical Education

Monica Lypson, MD, MHPE, Vice Dean for Education, Columbia University Vagelos College of Physicians and Surgeons, New York, NY

Maurice Sholas, MD, PhD, Principal & Pediatric Physiatrist, Sholas Medical Consulting, LLC, New Orleans, LA

Anita Blanchard, MD, Retired Professor, Former Designated Institutional Official and Associate Dean for Graduate Medical Education, Pritzker School of Medicine, University of Chicago, Chicago, IL

Alden Landry, MD, MPH, Assistant Dean, Office for Diversity Inclusion and Community Partnership, Associate Director and Advisor, Castle Society Harvard Medical School, Boston, MA

William McDade, MD, PhD, Chief Diversity, Equity, and Inclusion Officer, Accreditation Council for Graduate Medical Education, Chicago, IL

CHAPTER SUMMARY

This chapter offers an overview of many of the issues that Black-identifying residents and fellows might experience in their graduate medical education (GME) programs. Their experience in GME is not monolithic; it offers key lessons to be learned that could apply not only to Black-identifying physician learners, but also to others as well. We provide the perspective of Black-identifying learners through a case study with a series of vignettes, reviewing current demographics in medicine as it relates to Black learners and faculty members, providing evidence to support the need for diversification of the physician workforce. We discuss challenging day-to-day experiences that residents and fellows face navigating in learning environments, including interactions with their patients, peer learners, faculty members, and other health care workers. Ultimately, we aim to promote an asset-based approach to further support the inclusion and belonging of Black residents and fellows, as well as other marginalized groups in GME. These goals can be accomplished by understanding societal stressors, identifying financial pressures, improving assessment systems, focusing on mentorship, and building affinity groups and communities.

LEARNING OBJECTIVES

1. Recognize the varied experiences of physician learners who identify and are seen as Black in the GME learning environment.
2. Apply skills and tools that enhance the appreciation of diversity and improve belonging in GME programs.
3. Develop strategies to support physician diverse learners, in particular, those who are Black-identifying.

Case Study

Dr Brown was excited to begin his residency in Big City, USA, after attending the smaller Historically Black College and University (HBCU). The welcome packet identified several neighborhoods in the nearby suburbs as desirable and convenient to the medical center. Dr Brown followed the suggestions and sought housing in the neighborhoods identified by the residency program. He and his partner submitted applications to a medium-sized apartment complex and got a prompt response and a tour was scheduled. When Dr Brown and his partner arrived for the tour, the leasing agent seemed surprised and uncomfortable. The office staff and tenants seen during the tour were homogeneously White-presenting. Dr Brown remained interested in the property, but none of the complex's managers returned subsequent phone calls or emails. As Dr Brown reviewed other potential options, an incident in that neighborhood trended on social media. A young, African American (AA) male visiting friends in the neighborhood was profiled and arrested by the police, sustaining injuries that required hospitalization.

Dr Brown was concerned that the neighborhoods identified as desirable and implicitly safe did not feel welcoming to them as a non-White-presenting individuals. He was also confused why other neighborhoods in the core area of the city, close to the medical center, were not identified as desirable. Those areas also appeared to have more diverse demographics. As Dr Brown sought to identify a place to live in Big City, USA, the criteria his program and classmates used to identify desirable areas were not criteria that would convey safety to him. Ultimately, Dr Brown sought input from diverse residents and a Black realtor to find housing. He and his partner ultimately ended up in a welcoming, comfortable, convenient, and safe location.[1,2]

Case Discussion

The program intended to provide quality recommendations that helped new residents attend to their fundamental needs, shelter and safety. Unfortunately, the more maternalistic approach of defining appropriate and safe, rather than eliciting the needs of the individual resident to guide its suggestions, led to a disconnect. Rather than assuming that what is considered high quality to the majority of program matriculants who may not share the same racial identity and values as that majority, the program failed to consider the better approach of developing recommendations based on what applicants would identify as important for shelter and safety. For example, some applicants may feel that suburban, gated, multi-family housing with a higher socio-economic status represents a curated living experience of like-minded persons. However, others may see this type of living, physically distant from where they need to report to work, disconnected from the populations with whom they feel most comfortable and centered in values dissonant with a minoritized individual. Residents and fellows are not immune from societal constructs of discrimination, regardless of their career as physicians.

As you review the chapter, consider how Dr Brown's experience in seeking housing may impact his experience as a physician learner and what your program or Sponsoring Institution is doing to address housing, resources, and other support systems for diverse applicants. We will use the experiences of Dr Brown and his fellow Black-presenting residents to increase awareness of realities facing minoritized physicians and offer solutions to create inclusive environments where all can flourish.

DEMOGRAPHIC DATA AND BLACK-IDENTIFYING LEARNERS IN MEDICINE

Many structures along the continuum of medical education perpetuate racism.[3] One measure of such discrimination is the persistent under-representation of Blacks in medical school, in GME, and in clinical and academic practice. The Association of American Medical Colleges (AAMC) in the 2021-2022 academic year, noted that 11% of applicants to medical school identified as Black or AA, either alone or as multiple race/ethnicity including Black/AA. Of these Black/AA-identifying MD-applicants, 11% matriculated into medical school.[4] More disturbingly, only 0.1% of those matriculants to MD-granting medical schools identified as Black/AA/multiple race AA males. In 2021, of the 27,227 applicants to DO-granting schools, 8% were Black or AA applicants and only 4% of those who matriculated were Black or AA. Data on those identifying as Black or AA, either alone or in combination with another race/ethnicity, were not available for DO-granting schools.[5]

Also in 2021-2022, the number of active residents and fellows enrolled in GME programs was noted to be 153,843. Of those residents, 6% identified as Black or AA and 4% reported multiple races/ethnicities of unspecified makeup. Comparing undergraduate medical education (UME) data to GME data, attrition is noted in the transition from UME to GME. Further decreased numbers are noted when tracking the number of practicing physicians.[6] In 2018, 5% of active physicians were Black or AA, and 1% were mixed-race non-Hispanic. A significant percentage of both residents and fellows, and those ultimately becoming practicing physicians, are graduates of international medical schools.[7] These statistics and the dwindling number of Black candidates who complete their transition through the medical continuum highlight the continuing challenges of achieving diverse representation in medical education.

Throughout this chapter, we will use vignettes to review a few of the pertinent issues confronting Blacks in GME and provide insights into some of the possible lived experiences of Black learners. These vignettes are meant to be representative of challenges, and ideally, are designed to provide tools and insights to enhance inclusivity. The examples are illustrative and are not meant to be all encompassing of the Black experience. We intend these stories to highlight common experiences of Black-identifying residents and fellows. It is noteworthy that the majority of those who identify as Black or AA from US medical schools identify as women.[4] Gender identity, race and ethnicity are important considerations as we develop inclusive mentoring and sponsorship programs.[8,9] There is also the reality that Black-presenting residents and fellows may also identify with additional minoritized groups based on gender identity and ethnicity. Intersectionality is defined as the connections and influences of various social categorizations of an individual or group with overlapping identities, a critical concept for effective mentorship and sponsorship. Finally, we recommend strategies to improve recruitment, retention, and belonging of Black-identifying physician learners and faculty members in GME programs.

Key Issues in the Experience of Black-Identifying Physicians

In her autobiography, *The Long Loneliness*, Dorothy Day, American journalist and social activist, describes well the value of community: "We have all known the long loneliness and we have learned that the only solution is love and that love comes with community." The isolation of being Black in spaces where that group (ie, the community) is underrepresented, is profound. Curating with a peer group of individuals having similar life experiences is important and protective; it is the process of creating such a group with intentionality of purpose. The Summer Health Professions Education Program (SHPEP) is one national program funded by the Robert Wood Johnson Foundation and the AAMC which provides such peer support. SHPEP is a six-week summer program focused on academic enrichment, at no cost to enrollees, whose goal is to enrich and support aspiring health professionals. The "magic" of this program is not simply that it provides exposure to science and health concepts; rather, it succeeds in creating peer groups for Black students who would otherwise be geographically isolated. The cure for isolation, and the ills that come from it, is being intentional with creating communities that provide career-long peer support. Social cohesion and interpersonal support are just as vital to Black students as the science and medical knowledge they gain on their journey.

In addition to residents and fellows having a sense of community within the practice of medicine, GME programs can recognize and focus on the following additional key actions to provide support to Black-presenting learners:

- Bystander versus upstander support
- Recognizing micro and macroaggressions
- Inclusive professionalism
- Timely and constructive evaluation
- Imposter syndrome to pioneer syndrome
- Community building beyond medicine

In the case study at the start of the chapter, Dr Brown had a group of six Black peers who met in SHPEP during college. This experience was critical to developing their sense of community and, ultimately, why they chose to highly rank the program into which they matched for matriculation.

Each of the concepts described above will be related through the following vignettes featuring Dr Brown and his six peers.

Bystander Versus Upstander Support

Dr Smith is a first-year resident and colleague of Dr Brown. She was performing well on the cardiology service. Patient Lee was admitted overnight to the unit. Dr Smith received sign-out from the admission team, reviewed test results that came in overnight, and went to pre-round on the patient. Patient Lee was visibly upset when Dr Smith visited them before rounds and asked not to be touched or examined. Dr Smith complied and gathered the information needed for rounds as best as possible. The team, consisting of the cardiology attending, the cardiology fellow, the senior resident, the team co-first-year resident and Dr Smith, returned as a group to Patient Lee's room. Once Patient Lee saw Intern Smith, they exclaimed: "I thought I was clear earlier that I did not want to be seen by that monkey!" The team was silent for a few minutes; then the senior resident stepped forward and led the interaction with the patient and reviewed the clinical information, developing an appropriate treatment plan. The team left Patient Lee's room and continued with rounding on the rest of the service. As the team went to the next patient room, the fellow said quietly to Dr Smith, "Sometimes patients can be tough to deal with." Later, Dr Smith sought advice on how best to handle incidents like this from the program director.

It is personally hurtful for anyone to be rejected in this manner when trying to do their job. Although the fellow in this story seemed sympathetic, the lack of public support left the minoritized Dr Smith feeling isolated, not only disheartened. Often, bystanders who witness such interactions say and do nothing because they are not certain what is most effective or appropriate under the circumstances. The bystanders that witnessed this event need training to know how to stand up for their colleague in a way that diminishes the shame and eliminates the isolation felt by Dr Smith. Programs that diminish stigma and isolation through pro-active instruction around how to support someone who is abused or mistreated are critical to sharing the burden only with the individual directly affected. Persons who move from being only a bystander to racism and subsequently to being an upstander, demonstrate allyship. **Allyship** is critical to share the burden of creating inclusive and welcoming environments for minoritized residents and fellows.

Micro and Macroaggression

Dr Brown is the first person from the SHPEP cohort to matriculate to their GME program from HBCU. When he completed a particularly grueling rotation in the intensive care unit, the attending at the end of rotation said to Dr Brown: "You are so smart I almost forgot you did not go to Big City School of Medicine." Dr Brown was glad he performed well in the eyes of his supervisor, but troubled by what felt like a criticism hidden within a compliment. The attending was shocked and became angry when Dr Brown directly expressed concern about the comment. Ultimately, the attending said: "I see there is no way to be nice to people like you. That seems ungrateful and that kind of attitude gets residents put out of GME programs."

Dr Brown experienced a microaggression that escalated to a macroaggression. **Micro- and macroaggressions** are statements and behaviors that communicate disregard, insensitivity, isolation and otherness.

These aggressions are often directed to those within marginalized groups. As role models and educational leaders, all involved with educating physician learners must work to ensure safe environments that promote belonging for Black-identifying residents. Failing to correct instances of discrimination communicates to learners, particularly those from marginalized groups, that they do not belong. Programs must cultivate skills for learners, faculty members, staff, and to eliminate such incidents. It can be a challenge to eliminate all micro aggressions occurring in the learning environment. To counter the presence of those negative interactions, programs should promote "micro-affirmations' to counterbalance their effects and to strengthen the resilience of those who have had these negative experiences.[10]

Inclusive Professionalism

Most health care institutions have established a code of conduct and principles of professionalism. An aspect often included in these codes is the expectation of professional attire and appearance. We must, however, be aware of the need for inclusivity when considering our definitions of professionalism and expectations. Cross-cultural approaches to hair and other aspects of appearance can often lead to miscommunications at the least and discrimination at the worst.

Dr Thomas is another colleague of Dr Brown from the Case Study that went from Big City, USA on completion of her residency to Mid City, USA, for fellowship. She had a strong and supportive community–including other Ghanaians and her natural hair stylist (**loctician**) as she has been wearing a natural hairstyle for over 4 years. As she reviewed the professionalism codes for her program, she realized that she needed key information to make her transition to fellowship successful. In addition, during her orientation one of the nurses questioned her hairstyle and if it would fit in with the professional code in the operating room. Since there were no other attendings or house officers with natural hairstyles in her program, it was not clear who might be able to help with this key issue essential to Dr Thomas and how she would be evaluated in her new environment.

The CROWN Act (Creating a Respectful and Open World for Natural Hair) is law in 18 states (CA, CO, CN, DE, IL, LA, MA, ME, MD, NE, NV, NJ, NM, NY, OR, TN, VA, WA) and the District of Columbia and over 40 municipalities. CROWN was passed by the US House in 2022 but could not overcome a filibuster in the US Senate. This legislation "…prohibits discrimination based on an individual's style or texture of hair…. by including styles of hair commonly associated with race or national origin in the definition of racial discrimination."[11] Testimony supporting this legislation notes that Black women are 50% more likely to be sent home from work because of their hair, and Black women are 30% more likely to be told of workforce appearance policies as a step toward disciplinary action. Programs can provide information regarding community resources and access to appropriate specialized hair care as a mechanism to demonstrate support of residents, faculty members, and staff, and to avoid biased actions against all Black colleagues who have natural hairstyles. In addition to overt bias, programs should eliminate more covert bias such as a lack of surgical hair coverings which can accommodate natural hairstyles.[12] Acknowledgment of differences in cultural practices and appearance should be reflected in policies and conversations around professionalism and professional dress/appearance in GME programs. Knowledgeable and appropriate personnel should participate in orientation of new learners and help develop policies and practices.

Timely and Constructive Evaluation

The senior resident meets with Dr Brown, his mentee, regularly. Dr Brown is a very competent resident, although introverted and quiet. Six months into his second year, Dr Brown received an evaluation unlike any he previously received. The attending wrote that Dr Brown seemed disinterested in the subject matter discussed on rounds and did not consistently contribute to the conversation around patient care planning. Dr Brown was very surprised because the attending had not given his any feedback prior to this written evaluation. The senior resident, who was also present during the evaluation, listened empathetically and recalled the same attending had evaluated them harshly years ago on that same rotation. In supporting Dr Brown, the senior resident validated his feelings, identified other evaluations that were positive, and gave suggestions on a path forward. After that conversation the senior resident considered a discussion with the residency program director around potentially disparate treatment. They wanted to drive awareness around equity but not cause negative repercussions for them or their mentee.

The assessment of the ACGME competencies and further understanding of the learner's progress in terms of specialty milestones has become a hallmark of the competency based medical education (CBME) movement in the United States and ACGME accreditation. Such assessment offers promise in further understanding the educational paradigms needed to create a physician workforce for the future. Despite the progress in the field to move to CBME, however, there remains concern that inequity in assessment persists. It is not clear that our current processes for resident and fellow evaluations mitigate bias and stereotyping in assessment. Attending faculty may have **unconscious, unrecognized or conscious biases and stereotypes** that influence their assessment of learner performance. These biases may lead to grading disparities based on race, ethnicity, gender, or other social capital issues such as socioeconomic status. In addition, the development and implementation of performance-based assessments may also lead to disparities based on identity, especially if those criteria are inconsistently applied or unclear. More work is needed to ensure Black learners, as well as those from other marginalized groups, have opportunities for equitable feedback based on their actual skill and not personality traits such as introversion.[13-15]

Imposter Syndrome to Pioneer Syndrome

Dr Thomas graduated with honors from college but has never performed well on standardized exams. While she performed well in medical school in the pre-clinical courses and clinical rotations, her *United States Medical Licensing Examination® (USMLE®)* scores were low for the competitive residency program to which she applied. She matched in the specialty of her choice but in the lowest quartile of her rank list through the *Supplemental Offer and Acceptance® (SOAP®)* program. She became the only Black resident accepted in her program and felt as though she had to work much harder than her peers to dispel self-doubt, earn peer respect and achieve career success. She ultimately was voted to be the administrative chief resident after years of hard work and clinical success.

It is hard to believe that someone as outwardly successful as Dr Thomas harbored any internal doubt. **Imposter Syndrome** is an internalized perception of persistent self-doubt, characterized by questioning one 's skills and abilities. It can be summarized as fear of being discovered as a fraud.[16] Tutti Taygerly in *Medium* (2020), identifies four beliefs essential to Imposter Syndrome: (1) I lack the skills to be in this space; (2) I do not belong in this space; (3) my performance is most important; and, (4) I cannot make any mistakes. To pivot from this crippling self-doubt, these beliefs are re-imagined into a **Pioneer Syndrome** approach. Thus, the beliefs pivot from: (1) I lack the skill to be in this space, to no one has done this before and we are figuring it out as a team; (2) I do not belong in this space, to this is a brand new space where few people historically belonged; (3) my performance is most important, to how I show up and the relationships I form will make me stronger; and, (4) I cannot make any mistakes, to we are going to make mistakes and learn quickly from them.[17]

Taygerly's framework is particularly useful to those that have modest or humble beginnings, like using the *SOAP* process to secure a residency slot, then ascend to rare heights of success, such as becoming the first Black woman to be chief resident in the in the case of Dr Thomas. The value in diverse paths to success may be atypical paths; however, these paths also need to be nourished and supported to yield leadership and success opportunities for a wider swatch of persons. Many Black physician learners have atypical stories, atypical paths, and diverse markers of achievement. These realities should not be mistaken for a lack of quality, aptitude or capacity for exceptionalism.

All residents and fellows can become overtaken by Imposter Syndrome from time to time given the nature of medical careers and the precision needed to participate within the profession.[17] Nevertheless, Imposter Syndrome may be particularly disabling for Black learners. Assisting residents and fellows, especially those who identify as Black, to develop a self-actualized professional identity allows them to step into the space they occupy with pride and satisfaction. Such growth can best be nurtured through micro-affirmations and through celebrations of accomplishments by those on the road less traveled.[10, 18]

Community Building Beyond Medicine

Dr Obeh is the last of the SHPEP program alumni in our case study. She was very excited to be living her dream of matriculating in a neurosurgery program. Although she was the first Black woman in the 50-plus year history of the program, her interview and recruitment process reassured her that faculty members and staff were interested in making her experience informative and supportive. The White male attendings were patient and interactive as she worked to master very difficult techniques. However, she was most impacted by the warm and consistent support of the hospital environmental services staff. They made certain her preferences were communicated and supported by the nursing staff and attended to details like making certain she had a stepping stool to match heights with her taller attendings during cases. They also left notes of affirmation and encouragement in her locker in the operating room dressing area.[10,19] This experience showed Dr Obeh that attendings and program staff are important, but the larger village of hospital employees can also add positively to a situation.[19]

> The CROWN Act (Creating a Respectful and Open World for Natural Hair) is law in 18 states (CA, CO, CN, DE, IL, LA, MA, ME, MD, NE, NV, NJ, NM, NY, OR, TN, VA, WA) and the District of Columbia and over 40 municipalities

> Historically Black College or University (HBCUs) are institutions that were established prior to 1964, whose principal mission was the education of Black Americans.

SUMMARY RECOMMENDATIONS FOR GME PROGRAMS

Physician learners need to have the time, space and emotional bandwidth to focus on the knowledge requirements of GME. Their efforts are made more difficult by a sense of isolation endemic in many programs. Combating that isolation, and the reality that Black residents and fellows are targeted by systems and processes that cater to majority learners, is an important step. Those actions are more prescient than the simple sentiment of empathy. Staff, as well as program faculty members, are key to Black resident/fellow well-being and belonging. They are central to improving the retention and promotion of Black physicians in GME. To achieve these goals, we recommend that GME programs adopt the following strategies:

1. Be intentional when facilitating creation of communities for Black learners at the institution and in the GME programs.
2. Empower faculty members and the learner cohort to be not merely bystanders but upstanders when incidents of bias and racism occur affecting Black residents and fellows.
3. Be intentional in tapping into community resources outside of medicine to provide an environment personally and emotionally supportive to Black learners.
4. Eliminate criteria and requirements that disadvantage Black learners in the evaluation process by problematizing immutable elements of Blackness.

Take Home Points

- Intentionally create a space that works for minoritized residents and fellows rather than expect them to make the best of the default environment on their own.
- The program environment is not managed only from top-down; it is enhanced by the action and accountability of persons at various levels within the organization.
- The village contributing to a supportive environment extends beyond the physician staff and includes staff employees and community members outside of the health care environment.

❓ QUESTIONS FOR FURTHER THOUGHT

1. How can your faculty members and other learners use an empathetic approach to consider opinions from an alternate point of view?
2. At your institution, who makes and reviews GME policies; how are diverse perspectives incorporated into that process?
3. What mechanisms in your GME evaluation process monitor for unintentional bias, microaggressions, macroaggressions and inclusivity?
4. How can institutions address impostor syndrome and ensure that residents and fellows feel welcomed and belong at their institutions?

REFERENCES

1. Sun S, Lee H, Hudson DL. Racial/ethnic differences in the relationship between wealth and health across young adulthood. *SSM Popul Health*. 2022;20(21):101313. doi:10.1016/j.ssmph.2022.101313
2. Williams DR, Collins C. Racial residential segregation: a fundamental cause of racial disparities in health. *Public Health Rep*. 2001;116(5):404-416. doi:10.1093/phr/116.5.404
3. Ross PT, Lypson ML, Byington CL, Sánchez JP, Wong BM, Kumagai AK. Learning from the past and working in the present to create an antiracist future for academic medicine. *Acad Med*. 2020;95(12):1781-1786. doi:10.1097/ACM.0000000000003756
4. Association of American Medical Colleges. 2022 facts: matriculants to U.S. medical schools by selected combinations of race/ethnicity and gender, 2019–2020 through 2022–2023. Accessed March 1, 2023. https://www.aamc.org/data-reports/data/2022-facts
5. American Association of Colleges of Osteopathic Medicine. Applicants & matriculants by race/ethnicity, gender and COM 2009-2022. Accessed January 19, 2025. https://www.aacom.org/searches/reports/report/applicants-matriculants-by-race-ethnicity-gender-and-com-2009-2022
6. Accreditation Council for Graduate Medical Education. *2021-2022 GME Data Resource Book*. https://www.acgme.org/globalassets/pfassets/publicationsbooks/2021-2022_acgme__databook_document.pdf
7. Association of American Medical Colleges. Diversity in medicine: facts and figures 2019: figure 18. percentage of all active physicians by race/ethnicity, 2018. Accessed March 1, 2023. https://www.aamc.org/data-reports/workforce/data/figure-18-percentage-all-active-physicians-race/ethnicity-2018
8. Oliver KB Jr, Nadamuni MV, Ahn C, Nivet M, Cryer B, Okorodudu DO. Mentoring black men in medicine. *Acad Med*. 2020;95(12S):S77-S81. doi:10.1097/ACM.0000000000003685
9. Ulloa JG, Viramontes O, Ryan G, Wells K, Maggard-Gibbons M, Moreno G. Perceptual and structural facilitators and barriers to becoming a surgeon: a qualitative study of African American and Latino surgeons. *Acad Med*. 2018;93(9):1326-1334. doi:10.1097/ACM.0000000000002282
10. Solórzano D, Huber LP, Huber-Verjan, L. Theorizing racial microaffirmations as a response to racial microaggressions: counterstories across three generations of critical race scholars. *Seattle J Soc Justice*. 2020;18(2): 185-215. https://digitalcommons.law.seattleu.edu/cgi/viewcontent.cgi?article=1979&context=sjsj
11. US House of Representatives. House letter supporting the Crown act. Published online December 15, 2022. Accessed March 1, 2023. https://watsoncoleman.house.gov/imo/media/doc/crown_act_letter_to_senate_majority_leader.pdf
12. Harvard T.H. Chan School of Public Health. Crown act: ban natural hair style discrimination. Striped. Accessed March 1, 2023. https://www.hsph.harvard.edu/striped/crown-act-ban-natural-hair-style-discrimination/
13. Cohen ME, Kalotra A, Orr AR. Twelve tips for excelling as an introvert in academic medicine (at all levels). *Med Teach*. 2023;45(1):1118-1122. doi:10.1080/01421599X.2023.2216357
14. Borman-Shoap E, Li ST, St. Clair NE, et al. Knowing your personal brand: what academics can learn from marketing 101. *Acad Med*. 2019;94(9):1293-1298. doi:10.1097/ACM.0000000000002737
15. Boatright D, Anderson N, Kim JG, et al. Racial and ethnic differences in internal medicine residency assessments. *JAMA Netw Open*. 2022;5(12):e2247649. doi:10.1001/jamanetworkopen.2022.47649

16. Rivera N, Feldman EA, Augustin DA, Caceres W, Gans HA, Blankenburg R. Do I belong here? confronting imposter syndrome at an individual, peer, and institutional level in health professionals. *MedEdPORTAL*. 2021;17:11166. https://doi.org/10.15766/mep_2374-8265.11166
17. Taygerly T. From imposter syndrome to pioneer syndrome. Medium. October 29, 2020. Accessed March 1, 2023. https://medium.com/swlh/from-imposter-syndrome-to-pioneer-syndrome-fddda8e37e2f
18. Michalak C, Jackson M. Supporting the well-being of your underrepresented employees. *Harvard Business Review*. March 04, 2022. Accessed March 1, 2023. https://store.hbr.org/product/supporting-the-well-being-of-your-underrepresented-employees/H06WAN
19. Ortega CA, Keah NM, Dorismond C, et al. Leveraging the virtual landscape to promote diversity, equity, and inclusion in otolaryngology-head & neck Surgery. *Am J Otolaryngol*. 2023;44(1):103673. doi:10.1016/j.amjoto.2022.103673

The Graduate Medical Education Experience of Individuals Who Identify as Latino, Hispanic, or of Spanish Origin

Maria J. Ruiz, MD, MPH, Resident Physician, Department of Internal Medicine, University of California San Francisco, San Francisco, CA

Santiago Avila, MD, Resident Physician, Department of Medicine, University of California San Francisco, San Francisco, CA

Monica Vela, MD, Professor of Medicine, Director, Hispanic Center of Excellence, Departments of Medicine and Medical Education, Division of Academic Internal Medicine and Geriatrics, University of Illinois College of Medicine, Chicago, IL

CHAPTER SUMMARY

Individuals who identify as Latino, Latina, Latinx, Latine, Hispanic, or of Spanish origin (LHS+) may be of any race and can originate from various countries or regions, including areas where Spanish is or is not spoken. Individuals who identify as LHS+ have faced a long history of oppression, racism, discrimination, and colonization leading to poverty and health inequities. These structural forces limit educational attainment for many in the LHS+ population and hinder advancement in the medical profession. Individuals who identify as LHS+ are poorly represented at all levels of the medical education continuum, academic leadership, upper levels of faculty promotion, and research funding—especially compared to the growing and aging LHS+ population in the United States. It is imperative to increase the representation of LHS+ individuals in academic medicine and address the health inequities of LHS+ populations. In this chapter, *we use LHS+, except when citing figures with other terminology.*

LEARNING OBJECTIVES

1. Understand the complexities of racial and ethnic categorization of Latino, Latina, Latinx, Latine, Hispanic, or Spanish (LHS+) populations in the United States.
2. Review LHS+ representation across the medical education continuum and academic leadership.
3. Describe the historic racism and discrimination faced by LHS+ populations in the United States and outline how this history impacts the experience of trainees in graduate medical education (GME).
4. Identify strategies to improve the learning and working climate for LHS+ residents, fellows, and faculty members in academic medicine.

Case Study

Natalia is a first-generation immigrant from Guatemala who moved to Washington, DC, with her family at a young age. She identifies as Latinx. She speaks English, Spanish, and Tz'utujil. An internal medicine resident, Natalia is applying for a nephrology fellowship. She wants to help ameliorate the high burden of kidney disease and diabetes in LHS+ communities.

Natalia feels empowered and excited about her upcoming interview at her top program. In preparation, she listens to a podcast episode with a prominent researcher in nephrology who will interview her. Near the episode's close, the researcher states he is involved in "diversity programs" for trainees. The researcher explains, "These programs are nice because they're funded externally, and so maybe…you don't have to give up salary support for someone who isn't *trained as well*. Since someone else is paying, you're less…" he chuckles, "impatient."

Natalia sags in her chair. A familiar feeling of invalidation falls back onto her shoulders. *You were only accepted because you are Latinx. People with lower STEP scores are taking the spots of more qualified candidates.* Natalia shakes her head, recognizing the importance of snapping out of this. She recenters, puts away her headphones, and reminds herself that her achievements were not handed to her.

The following day, Natalia sits in the interview suite. A man enters the interview suite and says, "¡Hola! Natalia?" "Hi, I'm Natalia," she responds. They walk into his office. He asks, "Natalia, where are you from?" "Well," she starts, "I grew up in DC and have been in Chicago for the last 7 years for training." With a soft smile, he insists, "Sure, but where in Mexico are you from?"

Taken aback, Natalia responds, "My family is from Guatemala–that heritage is important to me."

"Great–we need more Spanish-speaking physicians here." Natalia pauses and says, "I am fluent in Spanish, but we speak Tz'utujil at home."

They go on to discuss her professional goals and research interests. "In your application, you wrote about your interests in language-concordant care. Could you tell me more about that? In my experience, working with an interpreter makes every visit twice as long. So frustrating."

Natalia's throat feels like it's closing. She thinks of her mom, whose health care benefits from using an interpreter. Natalia wants to speak a truth so strong it makes her voice shake: "Many people face unsafe conditions in their home countries, making them come to the United States. Once here, they face barriers to learning English. Sometimes they may prefer medical care in their native language." Natalia wants to cite the numerous studies demonstrating that language-concordant care improves outcomes. Yet, she can only answer the question briefly and change the topic.

Natalia's responses are terse throughout the rest of the interview–very unusual for her. Her mind keeps running back to the earlier interactions. Natalia leaves feeling deflated. She wonders if she will ever experience a true sense of belonging or find a space where she is seen and valued for who she is, what she has experienced, and the skills and talents she brings to the table.

Case Discussion

Natalia's experience exemplifies many, but not all the negative experiences that keep LHS+ trainees from developing a sense of belonging during GME. The interview Natalia listened to on the podcast alluded to "diversity hires," not truly having earned their position and not being as qualified as other candidates. Natalia internalized this narrative and was consumed by stereotype threat—a cognitive load rooted in the situational risk of validating identity-based stereotypes. Natalia spirals into negative self-talk that requires extra effort and energy to overcome. This is not an uncommon experience. Trainees historically **underrepresented in medicine** often express feeling exhausted at the end of each day due to the amount of energy that goes into warding off the feelings that come from fielding multiple microaggressions.

Natalia's interviewer immediately assumes she can speak Spanish, addresses her in Spanish, and asks if she is Mexican. These are common, incorrect assumptions made about people with Latinx names. First, clustering all LHS+ individuals as Spanish speakers belies the cultural richness of Latinx populations. Spanish was a language brought to Latin America by Spanish colonizers. While thousands of Indigenous languages have been lost, many are spoken daily by Indigenous, Afro-Latinx, and other LHS+ communities. Second, many LHS+ communities in the United States have been pressured to relinquish their language in response to an anti-immigrant push for assimilation or to avoid discrimination.[1] Third, while nearly 60% of Latinos in the United States are of Mexican heritage, Puerto Ricans, Salvadorans, Cubans, and Dominicans also have large groups (Table 11.1).[2] These percentages are also shifting, with Venezuelans, Paraguayans, Hondurans, and Guatemalans growing more than 6-fold in the last 10 years. Additionally, people can and do identify as more than one racial or ethnic category. In Natalia's case, although she identifies as a Latinx woman, others in her family may identify as Latina and Indigenous—or more specifically, Maya Tz'utujil.

Finally, Natalia faces a phenomenon growing among the newest generation of physicians who often have a more nuanced understanding of the structural violence that drives health inequities than past generations of physicians. For example, providing language-concordant care should easily be recognized as a patient's legally protected right and an ethical obligation for all clinicians, yet the interviewer in this case study questions the use of an interpreter. Finding a way to share that knowledge in the current hierarchy of academic medicine is difficult for individuals in racial and ethnic minoritized groups. As you review the chapter, consider what the interviewer or the interviewee could have done differently. Imagine that this interview experience happened at your institution and consider what steps you would want to take to ensure an environment where trainees like Natalia can belong and thrive.

Table 11.1 Five Largest Detailed Hispanic or Latino Origin Groups: 2020

Rank	Hispanic or Latino Detailed Group	Number
1	Mexican	35,850,702
2	Puerto Rican	5,601,863
3	Salvadoran	2,342,001
4	Cuban	2,245,686
5	Dominican	2,196,076

Note: The top five excludes residual categories, such as "All other Hispanic or Latino, not specified." Information on suppression, confidentiality protection, nonsampling error, definitions and guidance on using the data are available at https://www2.census.gov/programs-surveys/ decennial/2020/technical-documentation/complete-tech-docs/detailed-demographic-and-housing-charactenstics-file-a/2020census-detailed-dhc-a-techdoc.pdf

Source: U.S. Census Bureau, 2020 Census Detailed Demographic and Housing Characteristics File A.

UNDERSTANDING RACE AND ETHNICITY AS RELATED TO LHS+ POPULATIONS

The confusion over appropriate terminology related to the race and ethnicity of the LHS+ population and the multiple views on the categorizations of these individuals demonstrate the social construction of these terms. It has proven difficult to construct terminology that is inclusive of culturally heterogeneous people in the United States with origin in or ethnic heritage from the Caribbean, Mexico, Central and South America, and other Spanish-speaking countries worldwide. The different endonyms across history show that these labels are not innocuous but nested in socio-political contexts.

The term Hispanic first appeared in the US Census in 1970s to refer to individuals of any race who have origins in Mexico, Puerto Rico, and Central and South America. This term was used as a self-reported identification of ethnicity but was ultimately deemed inadequate as it referred only to Spanish speakers and excluded Indigenous and Brazilian people. Civil rights activists rallied around terms that better described their national origins, opting for Chicano (Mexican American) and Boricua (Puerto Rican), among others. In the 1990s, the term Latino was introduced to remove any Spanish colonial contextualization. This term was created as a categorization of ethnicity to include all persons who trace their origins to Latin America, irrespective of race, language, or culture. More recently, some have advocated for the gender-neutral terms *Latinx* or *Latine*, but these terms have not yet gained universal appeal.

In an effort to be as inclusive as possible, the Latino Medical Student Association has begun to use the shortened term LHS+ to designate Latino/Hispanic/of Spanish origin plus others. For this chapter, *we use LHS+ in most instances, except when citing specific figures that use other terminology*. We recognize that these terms are evolving, and many, especially those not 'of Spanish origin' (eg, Haitian people or Maya Tz'utujil people), may prefer other endonyms. We also recognize that individuals' social identity (as seen by others) and self-identity can differ according to geography. Indeed, while light-skinned individuals in many Latin American countries may be considered White, the same individuals may not be considered White in the United States.

Many population surveys do not allow LHS+ individuals to appropriately identify their national origins or self-described race. For example, in the 2020 Census, 93.9% of all respondents classified as "Some Other Race" were of Hispanic or Latino origin.[2] This struggle to conform to the race and ethnicity options presented in the survey tool demonstrates how socially constructed categories inadequately reflect individuals' self-identity. In addition, until 2003, the Association of American Medical Colleges (AAMC) recognized only Mexican American and Mainland Puerto Ricans as under-represented in medicine, excluding all other LHS+ identifying individuals from this group. Despite these data challenges, it is imperative to continue collecting data and tracking the health and well-being of the LHS+ population. Disaggregation of LHS+ groups will be essential to understanding representation in the medical profession.

LHS+ REPRESENTATION WITHIN ACADEMIC MEDICINE

In 2020, those who identified as Latino comprised 19% (62 million) of the US population and are projected to make up 29% of the US population by 2050.[3] In a 2021 AAMC report, The Complexities of Physician Supply and Demand: Projections from 2019 to 2034, analysts project that if current utilization patterns continue over the next 15 years, the need for physicians will increase by 136,000 Full Time Effort physicians (FTE). Furthermore, "more than two-thirds of this growth is associated with the projected growth in demand for physician services by racial and ethnic minority populations, including a 45,720 FTE growth to provide care to the growing and aging Hispanic population."[4]

Unfortunately, LHS+ representation has not increased at the same rate within the medical profession. In 2023, LHS+ students represented only 12% of matriculants, up from 8% in 2020. As of 2023, LHS+ identifying individuals comprise 8.3% of active residents in GME. Representation continues to drop in the upper faculty ranks and among leadership positions. In 2018, less than 6% of full-time allopathic faculty members identified as LHS+. Only 5% of NIH research grants were awarded to LHS+ principal investigators between 2016 and 2020. Only 2% of LHS+ faculty are tenured professors, and as of 2022, only one LCME-accredited medical school has an LHS+ dean (Herbert Wertheim College of Medicine).[5-7]

OBSTACLES TO LHS+ ADVANCEMENT

Examining the historical and present-day racism, discrimination, and **coloniality** that affects LHS+ populations is necessary to understand the obstacles to their advancement. LHS+ populations have been subjected to race-based residential and school segregation, state-sanctioned mob attacks and lynchings in the 1920s, and deportations of those with US citizenship in the 1930s.[8,9] Forced sterilization of

Mexican-American women occurred under California's Eugenics Sterilization Program from 1920-1945; one-third of Puerto Rican women were subjected to surgical sterilization in the 1950s, and forced sterilization of LHS+ women is still occurring in present-day deportation centers.[10,11] Dire work conditions continue to plague migrant farm workers, most of whom identify as LHS+. LHS+ individuals also bear a "pollution burden" of 63% excess exposure relative to the exposure caused by their consumption.[12] In a national 2019 survey of the LHS+ population in the United States, 20% reported discrimination in clinical encounters, 33% in employment, 31% in seeking housing, and 27% in police interactions.[13] One study shows that two-thirds of healthcare professionals hold implicit bias against LHS+ patients.[14] These health inequities, rooted in anti-immigrant sentiment, harm the health of both United States and foreign-born LHS+ individuals.[15]

Unfortunately, the evidence of disparities in the health and healthcare of the LHS+ population in the United States is abundant. LHS+ adults have an 80% higher diabetes rate than non-Hispanic White (NHW) adults; LHS+ children have a 5-fold higher diabetes rate than NHW children.[16] Puerto Ricans have the highest asthma mortality of any racial or ethnic subgroup, nearly 3 times the rate for NHW people. COVID-19 was the third leading cause of death in 2020, and the highest death rate was among Hispanic people.[17] Hispanic individuals also have the highest uninsured rates of any racial or ethnic group in the United States. In 2020, the Census Bureau reported that 50% of Hispanic individuals had private insurance, compared to 75% of NHW individuals. Language can also impact access to healthcare. Census data shows that 71% of Hispanic people speak a language other than English at home.[18] This linguistic discordance between clinicians and patients highlights the importance for healthcare facilities to have language access plans (eg, interpreters).

Disparities in educational attainment continue to challenge LHS+ advancement. The 2023 U.S. Census Bureau report notes that 75.2% of Hispanic individuals completed high school, compared to 95.2% of NHW. Just over 20% of Hispanic individuals, compared to nearly 42% of NHW, had a bachelor's degree or higher.[19] Data from 2019 shows that less than 6% of Hispanic individuals held a graduate or advanced professional degree, compared to more than 14% of NHW.[18]

OPPORTUNITIES TO IMPROVE THE LEARNING AND WORKING ENVIRONMENT FOR LHS+ TRAINEES

1. *Support affinity groups.*

    Affinity groups can be a powerful mechanism to increase belonging by diminishing social isolation and stereotype threat that can impact LHS+ residents and fellows. LHS+ physician learners should be able to access a list of LHS+ faculty members who can mentor, advise, and sponsor them. Because many institutions have very low numbers of LHS+ faculty, institutions must also provide residents and fellows with financial sponsorship and time to attend regional and national meetings of organizations such as the National Hispanic Medical Association, the Latino Medical Student Association, Building the Next Generation of Academic Physicians, the Medical Organization for Latino Advancement, and the National Association of Medical Spanish. These personal connections will foster meaningful relationships across the national academic medicine collective, promote role modeling, and support identity development as LHS+ faculty in academic medicine. These connections can also lead to opportunities for residents and fellows to transform their community engagement and scholarly work into academic credit for their career progression.

2. *Promote pathway programs.*

    Universities, GME programs, funding bodies, and professional societies should create, support, and invest in **pathway programs** to promote the advancement of residents and fellows underrepresented in medicine. Pathway programs are a direct redress of structural violence and have successfully improved measures such as grade point average, standardized test scores, graduation rates, and graduate program admissions.[20] Pathway programming can be expanded to encourage LHS+ medical students to matriculate to GME programs and encourage them to enter the fellowship programs or faculty rungs. In return, faculty members, residents, and fellows may gain a sense of empowerment,

> Residency program selection does little to promote the recruitment of bilingual medical trainees who can promote the language-concordant care of patients with non-English language preference. Recruiting trainees who can offer competent language-concordant care and designing robust language access plans can improve patient safety in the GME clinical learning environment by reducing the risk of communication errors with clinical consequences.

> US legal and policy-sanctioned violence and racism against LHS+ individuals have had long-standing consequences on the economic status, educational attainment, housing status, incarceration, and health inequities experienced by LHS+ communities. Supporting affinity groups, pathway programs, and creating inclusive environments can directly redress structural violence and provide opportunities for LHS+ advancement.

connectedness to their patients' communities, and a greater sense of belonging to the institution supporting them. LHS+ physicians along with residents and fellows should have protected time and support to engage in pathway programs and these contributions must be recognized in academic promotion processes.

3. *Inculcate institutional cultural humility.*

    It is incumbent on institutional leaders to promote **cultural humility** among their faculty members, staff, and students and an eagerness to learn about, respect, and appreciate cultures unlike their own. LHS+ individuals hold **intersectional identities**. Thus, they face discrimination not only for their race and ethnicity but also for their skin color, language, accents, socio-economic status, citizenship status, first-generation status, surname, religion, gender, and sexual orientation, among others. The promotion of cultural humility must be paired with **implicit bias** training, a review of the historic complicity of the medical profession in health inequities, and **critical consciousness** around institutionalized racism and discrimination. Additionally, a well-structured **bias reporting mechanism** that protects reporters is crucial. Residents and fellows must be instructed to report transgressions, including **microaggressions**, which plague their daily life since being from racially and ethnically minoritized groups can deteriorate mental health and hinder attainment. The data generated drive institutions to take decisive action to create inclusive environments.

4. *Value and invest in language-concordant care.*

    While over one-third of resident and fellows in GME programs speak at least one non-English language, the languages they speak are not those in greatest need by the US population with non-English language preference.[21] Indeed, Spanish had the lowest national language-concordant resident physician-to-patient ratio.[21,22] Bilingual or multilingual LHS+ medical students enhance the quality of patient care and patient safety. Providing language-concordant care should be readily recognized by faculty members, residents, and fellows: (1) supported by the Civil Rights Act and numerous other legal precedents; (2) a quality and safety measure that reduces medical errors and negative clinical consequences for patients with non-English language preference; (3) a measure that reduces hospital costs and readmissions; and, (4) an ethical obligation for all clinicians seeking to do no harm. Recognizing the value of **language concordance** is one way to promote the recruitment and advancement of bilingual LHS+ residents and fellows. One note of caution—we do not want to invalidate or belittle those LHS+ physician learners who are not bilingual. Spanish is a language imposed through colonization to many Latin American communities, obliterating many Indigenous languages. There are many valid reasons—chief among them historic discrimination, racism, and acculturative pressures—for individuals to not acquire particular language skills.

Take Home Points

- Individuals who identify as Latino, Hispanic, or of Spanish origin (LHS+) may be of any race or multiple races and can originate from various countries or regions, including areas where Spanish is or is not spoken.
- Individuals who identify as LHS+ have faced a long history of oppression, racism, discrimination, and coloniality leading to poverty, reduced educational attainment and advancement in the medical profession, and health and healthcare inequities.
- LHS+ individuals are poorly represented at all levels of the medical education continuum, as well as academic leadership, upper levels of faculty promotion, and research grants—especially when compared to the growing and aging LHS+ population in the United States.
- GME has the power and responsibility to support LHS+ residents and fellows and ensure their successful advancement by supporting affinity groups, promoting pathway programs, inculcating institutional cultural humility, and valuing and investing in language concordant care.

QUESTIONS FOR FURTHER THOUGHT

1. How do the complexities and evolving terminologies of racial and ethnic categorizations among LHS+ populations in the United States impact their representation and identity in medical education and beyond?
2. In what ways have historical racism and discrimination against LHS+ populations in the United States shaped the current challenges and opportunities faced by LHS+ trainees in graduate medical education?
3. What specific strategies can academic institutions implement to improve the learning and working environment for LHS+ residents, fellows, and faculty members, and how can these strategies address both institutional and individual barriers?

REFERENCES

1. Lopez MH, Krogstad JM, Flores A. *Most Hispanic Parents Speak Spanish to Their Children, but This Is Less the Case in Later Immigrant Generations*. Pew Research Center; 2018.
2. Census Bureau. Census Bureau releases 2020 census data for nearly 1,500 detailed race and ethnicity groups, tribes and villages. Press Release Number CB23-CN.156.
3. Lopez MH, Krogstad JM, Passel JS. *Who Is Hispanic?* Pew Research Center. Accessed May 22, 2023. https://www.pewresearch.org/short-reads/2024/09/12/who-is-hispanic/
4. IHS Markit Ltd. *The Complexities of Physician Supply and Demand: Projections from 2019 to 2034*. AAMC; 2021.
5. Association of American Medical Colleges. *2023 Fall Applicant, Matriculant, and Enrollment Data Tables*. AAMC; 2023.
6. Association of American Medical Colleges. Diversity facts & figures. Accessed May 22, 2023. https://www.aamc.org/data-reports/workforce/report/diversity-facts-figures
7. National Institutes of Health. *Number of Principal Investigators Funded by the National Institutes of Health by Grand Mechanism and Gender, Race, Ethnicity, and Disability*. National Institutes of Health; 2021.
8. Balderrama FE, Rodriguez R. *Decade of Betrayal: Mexican Repatriation in the 1930s*. Rev. ed. University of New Mexico Press; 2006.
9. Martinez MM. *The Injustice Never Leaves You: Anti-Mexican Violence in Texas*. Harvard University Press; 2018.
10. Presser HB. The role of sterilization in controlling Puerto Rican fertility. *Popul Stud*. 1969;23(3):343. doi:10.2307/2172875
11. Novak NL, Lira N, O'Connor KE, Harlow SD, Kardia SLR, Stern AM. Disproportionate Sterilization of Latinos Under California's Eugenic Sterilization Program, 1920-1945. *Am J Public Health*. 2018;108(5):611-613. doi:10.2105/AJPH.2018.304369

12. Tessum CW, Apte JS, Goodkind AL, et al. Inequity in consumption of goods and services adds to racial–ethnic disparities in air pollution exposure. *Proc Natl Acad Sci USA*. 2019;116(13):6001-6006. doi:10.1073/pnas.1818859116
13. Findling MG, Bleich SN, Casey LS, et al. Discrimination in the United States: experiences of Latinos. *Health Serv Res*. 2019;54(S2):1409-1418. doi:10.1111/1475-6773.13216
14. Blair IV, Havranek EP, Price DW, et al. Assessment of biases against Latinos and African Americans among primary care providers and community members. *Am J Public Health*. 2013;103(1):92-98. doi:10.2105/AJPH.2012.300812
15. Novak N, Geronimus A, Maritnez-Cardoso A. Change in birth outcomes among infants born to Latina mothers after a major immigration raid. *Int J Epidemiol*. 2017;46(3):839-849. doi:10.1093/ije/dyw346
16. Aguayo-Mazzucato C, Diaque P, Hernandez S, Rosas S, Kostic A, Caballero AE. Understanding the growing epidemic of type 2 diabetes in the Hispanic population living in the United States. *Diabetes Metab Res Rev*. 2019;35(2):e3097. doi:10.1002/dmrr.3097
17. Ahmad FB, Cisewski JA, Miniño A, Anderson RN. Provisional mortality data—United States, 2020. *Morb Mortal Wkly Rep*. 2021;70(14):519-522. doi:10.15585/mmwr.mm7014e1
18. U.S. Department of Health and Human Services, Office of Minority Health. *Hispanic/Latino Health*. Office of Minority Health. Published October 12, 2021. https://minorityhealth.hhs.gov/hispaniclatino-health
19. Census Bureau. Census Bureau releases new educational attainment data. Press Release Number CB23-TPS.21.
20. Strayhorn G. A Pre-admission program for underrepresented minority and disadvantaged students: application, acceptance, graduation rates, and timeliness of graduating from medical school. *Acad Med*. 2000;75(4):355-361. doi:10.1097/00001888-200004000-00015
21. Diamond LC, Mujawar I, Vickstrom E, Garzon MG, Gany F. Supply and Demand: Association between non-English language-speaking first year resident physicians and areas of need in the USA. *J Gen Intern Med*. 2020;35(8):2289-2295. doi:10.1007/s11606-020-05935-7
22. Ortega P, Felida N, Avila S, Conrad S, Dill M. Language profile of the US physician workforce: a descriptive study from a National Physician Survey. *J Gen Intern Med*. 2023;38(4):1098-1101. doi:10.1007/s11606-022-07938-y

12

Reimagining Graduate Medical Education by Contextualizing "Whiteness"

David F. McIntosh, PhD, MA, Adjunct Associate Professor, David Geffen School of Medicine, University of California, Los Angeles, Los Angeles, CA

Camara Phyllis Jones, MD, PhD, MPH, Commissioner, O'Neill-Lancet Commission on Racism, Structural Discrimination, and Global Health, New Jersey Ave NW, Washington, DC; Adjunct Professor, Rollins School of Public Health; Senior Fellow and Adjunct Associate Professor, Morehouse School of Medicine, Atlanta, GA; Visiting Professor, King's College London, London, UK

Jessica Elizabeth Isom, MD, MPH, Clinical Instructor; Co-Director, Yale Psychiatry Social Justice and Health Equity Curriculum; Yale University, New Haven, CT; Attending Psychiatrist, Codman Square Health Center, Boston, MA

CHAPTER SUMMARY

We describe the operation of Whiteness as a paradigm that creates and maintains inequity. We illustrate how clinicians, administrators, and educators create and maintain White institutional spaces in graduate medical education (GME) programs through their feeling, thinking, and doing. We provide a strategy for applying antiracism to dismantle these White institutional spaces and build equitable spaces for the benefit of all.

LEARNING OBJECTIVES

1. Articulate what is meant when Whiteness is described as a system of oppression.
2. Describe how Whiteness operates within institutional spaces to create differences in access, experiences, and outcomes for physician learners.
3. Identify some of the mechanisms of Whiteness in GME programs.
4. Describe how racism, as manifest in Whiteness' values and practices, saps the strength of GME programs.

Case Study

Carolyn, an Afro-Latina resident in her second year, speaks Spanish and English proficiently. She enjoys strong relationships with her patients, resident colleagues, and faculty members. As one of the first to bring ethno-racial diversity to a predominantly White department, she feels out of place. A champion for diversity, equity, and inclusion, Carolyn is driven to serve marginalized communities. Carolyn feels a strong sense of responsibility to serve those whose health and health care needs have been chronically neglected.

Her dedication extends beyond her medical duties, involving mentoring, community service, and committee participation. This additional work is often uncredited. While her White counterparts find time for relaxation, Carolyn feels burdened by unacknowledged extra tasks. Though she enjoys some aspects of the program, it has never felt like a welcoming place where she would choose to stay long-term.

(continued)

Recently, the Associate Program Director shared with her that faculty members were concerned by feedback about her professionalism and her lengthy interactions with patients and warned her that she might have to repeat a year of her residency program. This news came as a complete surprise to Carolyn, who had been led to believe that her academic and clinical work were quite strong, having often received positive comments from colleagues. She had previously received no formal negative feedback about her performance. While she does not want to repeat a year, she also does not want to push back against this faculty member because she will need strong recommendations for fellowships and her own faculty appointment.

Carolyn doubles down on the amount of time she spends studying while continuing her commitments to the department and to the community. She also completely cuts herself off from family, friends, and any other "distractions" so that she can prove herself.

One day, when discussing a required article with one of her resident peers, her colleague off-handedly mentions that they and several of the other residents were part of a study group, one to which Carolyn had never been invited. Furthermore, she learns that many of the department's faculty members routinely helped this study group by coming to the meetings to share advice and insights. When Carolyn asks why she had not been invited, her peers say they thought she had been. This situation made Carolyn feel even more invisible.

Further experiences of invisibility continue to happen to Carolyn. When helping with resident interviewing and ranking, Carolyn invests a great deal of time and energy reading about the candidates and writing complete notes to honor the program's reported holistic review process. However, when it comes to the ranking meeting, it becomes clear to Carolyn that holistic review is not being fully honored. For example, on several occasions, faculty members make comments like "this young man reminds me of myself, of course he's a great fit" or "this candidate is someone with whom I'd love to have a beer" or "they ski, so they'll fit right in with the department." Carolyn does not self-identify with any of these informal criteria of "fit." She finds it difficult to share her own notes about the candidates with the other committee members because they are such a departure from the tone of the conversation. She also fears commenting about the tone of the conversation itself because she does not want to make herself a target. Nonetheless, on a few occasions, she perseveres and takes the risk to speak up to more accurately portray several excellent candidates who were about to be overlooked.

When she learns that the new residency class joining the program in just a few months includes two ethno-racially diverse residents (the highest number in any one class in the program's history), Carolyn envisions what this might mean for her as a source of validation and support, even as she also anticipates devoting extra time and effort to serve as validation and support for the new residents.

Carolyn also wonders how the existing program, residents, and patients will respond to a "different" type of resident, colleague, and clinician. She spends some time reading about diversity resistance and its manifestations at the individual and organizational levels to understand her own experiences and anticipate how some of the incoming residents may be mistreated within a program newly "adjusting" to a growing number of ethno-racially minoritized residents.

Case Discussion

Carolyn is facing multiple challenges due to racism supported by White institutional space[1] in her residency program. She is hypervisible as an ethno-racially minoritized resident, meaning that she is constantly being scrutinized and feels like she must work harder than her White peers to prove herself. She is also, in many ways, invisible to her peers and the faculty members, who often forget to invite her to meetings or events, or socially distance themselves from her when she is present. She is excluded from the social life of the program and feels like she does not belong, which has detrimental effects on her ability to create a formal and informal network of mentors and sponsors for her professional development and career goals. Her concerns about racism in the program are often dismissed by her peers and the faculty members, even though they claim that the program is committed to diversity, equity, and inclusion. These claims are a manifestation of racism denial,[2] a product of White racial socialization into the White Racial Frame,[3] which stymies discussions on how Whiteness within institutional cultures and structures perpetuates racism and, at the same time, minimizes recognition of the consequences of racism.

Carolyn also feels that she is being avoided by her peers and the faculty members and is being pushed out of the program through a combination of actions and inactions around her exclusionary and discriminatory experiences. She feels like her White peers and the faculty members have low expectations of her and that she is not being taken seriously, which likely results in a lack of timely offers of feedback on her performance and the additional burden of Carolyn managing their racial stereotype threat. Furthermore, she feels like she must carry the burden of educating her peers and faculty about racism, just one example of a harmful minority tax in the program. Finally, she feels like she is forced conform to the dominant cultural norms in the program, even though they do not reflect her values or experiences.

While Carolyn is facing a lot of challenges, she is not alone. Many other ethno-racially minoritized residents and fellows face similar challenges in predominantly White institutions. It is important to talk about these challenges and to confront racism and its manifestations in White dominant culture.

WHITENESS AS A PARADIGM THAT CREATES AND MAINTAINS INEQUITY

In her seminal work, Ruth Frankenberg (1993) describes **Whiteness** as (1) a system that maintains a structural advantage over people of color; (2) a perspective though which White people see society, other people, and themselves; and, (3) practices that are unmarked, unnamed, and are seen as "normal."[4] This paradigm of Whiteness succinctly describes the realities that are seen in academic medicine.

White supremacist ideology is the false idea that there is a hierarchy of human valuation by "race" (there is not), and the false notion that would put White people at the top of this fictional hierarchy as the ideal or the norm.[5] Academic medicine has been infused with White supremacist ideology and structures from the beginning, including the maintenance of segregated hospital systems and the restriction of Black students from academics and medicine (redoubled through the Flexner Report).[6] Whiteness has also been reinforced in clinical practice: the US Public Health Service Study of Untreated Syphilis in the Negro Male at Tuskegee[7]; the experimentation on Black bodies by J. Marion Sims[8]; and the exploitation of Henrietta Lacks' genetic information.[9] In fact, the day-to-day institutionalization of White supremacist ideology is so common, it often hardly registers with those who are not oppressed by the interactions or systems.

As described by Wendy Leo Moore,[1] White institutional space describes how the norms, values, and standards of Whiteness become imbued within structures, so much so that it is often just viewed as normal. When Whiteness is the uninterrogated norm, it becomes nearly impossible to change, because it is simply unobservable to the uncritical observer. As Moore described, most people "forget to make the connection between historical racist exclusion and contemporary institutional norms, [where] much of the White frame remains tacit, thereby reifying Whiteness within the space without need for the intentional action to do so" (p.28).[1] In this way, the systematic exclusion of those who are ethno-racially minoritized is the normal state of the institution, and any disparate experiences can be explained under the myth of meritocracy, instead of considering the longstanding advantages that the system of White supremacy has afforded those who reinforce White institutional space. Further, developing antiracism actions and ways of being are seen as unnecessary, extra work: a burden. This is particularly true in academic medicine where our educational model is largely an apprenticeship model. This situation facilitates unexamined lessons such as Black patients receiving worse treatment and outcomes, which are passed down for generations and justified as "the ways things have always been."[10]

Whiteness is a force that creates and perpetuates hostile environments, oppressive opportunity structures, and dehumanizing value systems.

THE NECESSITY OF CONFRONTING WHITENESS: HEALTH EQUITY, RACISM, ANTIRACISM

There are three core principles for achieving health equity: (1) value all individuals and populations equally; (2) recognize and rectify historical injustices; and, (3) provide resources according to need.[11]

Racism, the "system of structuring opportunity and assigning value based on the social interpretation of how one looks, which is what we call 'race,'"[12-14] is a principal roadblock to achieving **health equity** in the United States. "Racism unfairly disadvantages some individuals and communities, unfairly advantages other individuals and communities, and saps the strength of the whole society through the waste of human resources."[12-14] Depending on varying contextual elements, racism may be defined in different ways. For example, **institutionalized/structural racism** is defined as "the differential access to goods, services, and opportunities of society by race. Institutionalized racism is normative, sometimes legalized, and often manifests an inherited disadvantage. It is structural, having been codified in our institutions of custom, practice, and law, so there need not be an identifiable perpetrator."[15] **Personally mediated racism** is "prejudice and discrimination where prejudice means differential assumptions about the abilities, motives, and intentions of others according to their race, and discrimination means differential actions toward others according to their race. Personally mediated racism can be intentional as well as unintentional and it includes acts of commission as well as acts of omission."[15] Finally, "**internalized racism** is identified as "acceptance by members of the stigmatized races of negative messages about their own abilities and intrinsic worth. It is characterized by their not believing in others who look like them, and not believing in themselves."[15]

Antiracism is necessary to achieve health equity. Antiracism is a process with three essential tasks:

1. *Name racism.* A problem must be named in order to get started on the solution. And if you do not say the whole word "racism" in our national context of widespread and staunchly held racism denial, then you are complicit with that denial.
2. *Ask the question,* "How is racism operating here?" to identify promising levers for intervention and early targets for action. We provide an application of this question to our case study in the section below, "How Is Racism Operating Here?"
3. *Organize and strategize to act.* We each have individual power to confront racism, and collective action greatly amplifies our power. "Collective action informs us, inspires us, propels us, and protects us."[16]

Antiracism is a sequential, iterative process and may well span generations. The goals are to dismantle oppressive opportunity structures and nullify dehumanizing value systems. But that work will be unsuccessful if we also do not confront racism denial and anticipate and prepare for pushback. That is, confronting the hegemony of Whiteness is an important aspect of antiracism.

We must be clear that antiracism is not anti-White people. Antiracism is a powerful and necessary tool to interrogate and combat the normative, controlling aspects of the paradigm of Whiteness. And because racism saps the strength of the whole society, antiracism and confronting Whiteness will benefit us all.

"HOW IS RACISM OPERATING HERE?" IN WHITE INSTITUTIONAL SPACE

The question "How is racism operating here?" is an extremely useful tool for identifying promising levers for antiracism intervention and early targets for antiracism action.[2,17]

Racism is not a cloud or miasma. "Racism is a system with identifiable and addressable mechanisms"[18] in our structures, policies, practices, norms, and values.[2,12,17] It is liberating to recognize that these are simply the elements of decision-making:

- *Structures* are the "who?," "what?," "when?," and "where?" of decision-making, especially "who is at the table?" and "who is not?," and "what is on the agenda?" and "what is not?"

- *Policies* are the written "how?" of decision-making, the formal rule book.
- *Practices* are the unwritten "how?" of decision-making that are visible here and now, our *ad hoc* patterns of conduct.
- *Norms* are the unwritten "how?" of decision-making that are deeply rules of appropriate conduct which expected and protected.
- *Values* are the "why?" of decision-making, including group prioritization and sense of urgency.

The persistence and promotion of White institutional space is a manifestation of racism. Applying the question "How is racism operating here?" to the case study above of a resident in a GME learning environment, we see the following:

- *Structures* (the who, what, when, and where of decision-making)
  - Limited presence of ethno-racially minoritized persons among the faculty and leadership of the residency program and
  - Limited presence of ethno-racially minoritized persons on the resident ranking committee.
- *Policies* (the written how of decision-making)
  - Lack of a clear policy (or lack of communication of a clear policy) about criteria for asking a resident to repeat a year and
  - Holistic review policy that supports "practices that focus on mission-driven, ongoing, systematic recruitment and retention of a diverse and inclusive workforce…" (ACGME Institutional Requirement, III.B.8.[19]; Common Program Requirement, I.C.[20]) but with limited follow-through by the institution.
- *Practices* (the unwritten how of decision-making, here and now)
  - Study group not advertised to all residents;
  - Indifference to Carolyn's absence from the study group; and
  - Minority tax: disproportionate expectations to fulfill community service, mentoring of medical students, and participating in departmental committees to interview and rank prospective residents.
- *Norms* (the unwritten how of decision-making, embedded and expected)
  - Measures of "fit" in discussing residency applicants and
  - Low expectations as reflected in a lack of full investment in Carolyn's career trajectory.
- *Values* (the why of decision-making)
  - Limited acknowledgement and reward for the kinds of additional service that Carolyn provides;
  - Lack of prioritizing diversity as a good that enhances the residency experience and improves patient care for all;
  - Seeming indifference to Carolyn's full participation in academic activities within the department; and
  - Disconnect about Carolyn's career goals, with seeming indifference to the negative impacts of multiple requests for her service and the request for her to repeat a year.

ANTIRACISM STRATEGIES TO DISMANTLE WHITE INSTITUTIONAL SPACE AND BUILD EQUITABLE SPACES FOR ALL

Embracing strategies that seek to create an antiracism space is a critical step that occasionally gets skipped by institutional leaders. To build an authentic equitable space, the efforts undertaken must be intentional, accountable, and transparent. However, doing justice work requires a change in paradigm, which can be uncomfortable for many people within an organization. This discomfort can lead to intransigence that shows up as resistance, notably when aspects of White institutional space are challenged. To effectively create equitable spaces, leaders should remain steadfast in pursuit of justice, despite the manifold tactics and strategies of Whiteness to interrupt or stall progress in racial justice. The following

> Antiracism is a necessary commitment to dismantle White institutional space, as it recognizes the exclusionary consequences of tacit norms that have been woven into our society and into academic medicine. However, no amount of discrete antiracism training experiences or static checklists will make someone antiracist. Antiracism is a process embraced because of a conscious decision to resist exclusionary structures.

list of strategies provides institutional leaders with guidance as they begin considering how to build antiracist space:

1. *Audit outcomes*. The design of processes and procedures are almost always equitable in conception, but need continual auditing to ensure that they are working in equitable ways.
2. *Interrogate the unwritten rules*. Whiteness can be built into structures through practices, which are often unwritten, unexamined, and operate in clandestine ways. Consistent with tenets of shared governance, all the structures of the institution should be connected to formal, vetted systems and structures.[21]
3. *Adopt a race-conscious approach to building structures*. The systems of White supremacy that have undergirded an institution were built with explicit race consciousness. Any effort to dismantle structures of racism will have to focus on the impact of racist policies, practices, and procedures to remediate the racialized environment. Valuing all learners, faculty members, staff members, and candidates' life distances traveled by understanding their life stories and experiences with oppression throughout their journeys will create the openness that allows for an understanding of the impact of structures such as racism.
4. *Utilize holistic review*. This is essential in many aspects of institutional life, including faculty/staff member recruitment, along with medical student, resident, and fellow recruitment. Most institutions purport to utilize holistic review, so it is critical to interrogate the mechanisms being utilized and instill accountability measures in place.
5. *Use strong active bystander/upstander approaches*. Ensure that these proactive and supportive cultural skills are adopted and utilized at the highest levels of the organization, so that everyone has the tools to identify and interrupt racial harm.[22]

> Although White skin will not protect a person from poverty or homophobia, Whiteness in this country continues to confer high expectations, benefit of the doubt, relative safety in police encounters, full humanity, and many other benefits. The system of racism continues to unfairly disadvantage racially and minoritized individuals and communities, unfairly advantage White individuals and communities, and sap the strength of the whole society through the waste of human resources. The sense of White grievance that raises the specter of "reverse racism" is based in racism denial, which in turn is based on the narrow focus on the individual, an ahistorical stance, the myth of meritocracy,[26] and White supremacist ideology.[5,14]

6. *Create a culture of accountability, transparency, and justice*. Creating and monitoring change toward justice will only be successful to the extent that it is broadly communicated, roundly embraced, and transparently monitored. This effort includes monitoring and publishing racial presence (headcount data), ensuring meaningful consequences for racist interactions, and insisting on professional development.[23]
7. *Ensure a recognition of and proactive response to resistance to health equity and antiracism efforts*. Strategies for managing resistance must include subverting its obvious (open opposition, refusal to participate) and subtle forms (silent non-compliance, sabotage). These strategies must also focus on managing the emotionality present in diverse experiences of these efforts from racial battle fatigue[24] to **White emotionality**.[25] Advocates being prepared to confront the White Racial Frame[3] will also increase their likelihood of successful championing. Initiatives such as restorative justice and crucial conversations are both heavily studied and cited and have a track record of efficacy.

Take Home Points

- The path to challenging the system of Whiteness necessitates processes such antiracism, which requires honest self-reflection about how racism is operating in a particular context.
- Institutional leaders should audit their outcomes as well as the throughput of systems to understand the ways that Whiteness and White institutional spaces are implemented, functioning, and reified over time.
- All individuals within a larger system have a role to play and should be bravely self-reflective about their own roles in the maintenance of White supremacist ideology and White institutional spaces.
- Auditing outcomes, interrogating the unwritten rules, adopting a race-conscious approach to building structures, using holistic review, developing strong active bystander/upstander approaches, and creating a proactive response to the resistance to health equity and antiracism efforts are recommended strategies to reinforce justice and antiracism.

QUESTIONS FOR FURTHER THOUGHT

1. How is racism operating at your institution? What are the spaces/structures within your organization that explicitly or tacitly maintain White institutional space? Who maintains those systems and how do you interact with those spaces?
2. To effectively create antiracism space at your institution, who needs to be part of the project? How will this work be communicated, transparent, and accountable? What resources do you have to navigate barriers and resistance? How will you manage the people within the process? How might you obtain information about prior efforts or processes that have been successful and/or unsuccessful?

REFERENCES

1. Moore WL. *Reproducing Racism: White Space, Elite Law Schools, and Racial Inequality.* Rowman and Littlefield; 2008.
2. Jones CP, Jones CY, Jones CA. Anti-racism primer: naming racism and moving to action. In: Holden KB, Jones CP, eds. *Black Women and Resilience: Power, Perseverance, and Public Health.* State University of New York Press; 2024.
3. Feagin JR. *The White Racial Frame.* Routledge; 2013.
4. Frankenberg R. *The Social Construction of Whiteness: White Women, Race Matters.* University of Minnesota Press; 1993.
5. Jones CP. *Seeing the Water: Seven Values Targets for Anti-Racism Action.* Harvard Primary Care blog. Accessed June 19, 2024. http://info.primarycare.hms.harvard.edu/blog/seven-values-targets-anti-racism-action
6. Laws T. How should we respond to racist legacies in health professionals education originating in the Flexner report? *AMA J Ethics.* 2021;23(3);e271-275. doi: 10.1001/amajethics.2021.271
7. Washington HA. *Medical Apartheid: The Dark History of Medical Experimentation on Black Americans from Colonial Times to Present.* Doubleday; 2006.
8. Wailoo K. Historical aspects of race and medicine: the case of J. Marion Sims. *JAMA.* 2018;320(15):1529-1530. doi: 10.1001/jama.2018.11944
9. Skloot R. *The Immortal Life of Henrietta Lacks.* Crown Publishing Group; 2011.
10. Hoffman KM, Trawalter S, Axt JR, Oliver MN. Racial bias in pain assessment and treatment recommendations, and false beliefs about biological differences between Blacks and Whites. *Proc Natl Acad Sci USA.* 2016;113(16): 4296-4301. doi: 10.1073/pnas.1516047113
11. Jones CP. Systems of power, axes of inequity: parallels, intersections, braiding the strands. *Medl Care.* 2014;52 (10 suppl 3):S71-S75. doi:10.1097/MLR.0000000000000216
12. Jones CP. Confronting institutionalized racism. *Phylon.* 2002;50(1/2):7-22. doi:10.2307/4149999
13. Jones CP, Truman BI, Elam-Evans, LD, et al. Using "socially-assigned race" to probe white advantages in health status. *Ethn Dis.* 2008;18(4):496-504. PMID: 19157256

14. Jones CP. Addressing violence against children through anti-racism action. *Pediatr Clin North Am.* 2021;68(2):449-453. doi: 10.1016/j.pcl.2021.01.002
15. Jones CP. Levels of racism: a theoretic framework and a gardener's tale. *Am J Public Health.* 2000;90(8):1212-1215. doi: 10.2105/ajph.90.8.1217
16. Jones CP. Recognizing and addressing disparities in health care. *AMA Update Video/AMA.* Accessed January 23, 2025. https://www.ama-assn.org/delivering-care/health-equity/recognizing-and-addressing-disparities-health-care-camara-phyllis
17. Jones CP. Toward the science and practice of anti-racism: launching a national campaign against racism. *Ethn Dis.* 2018;28(suppl 1):231-234. doi:10.18865/ed.28.S1.239
18. Public Affairs. Fighting racism: how to restructure society so it's open to all. *UC Berkley News.* Accessed January 23, 2025. https://news.berkeley.edu/2020/06/26/berkeley-talks-transcript-amani-allen-and-camara-jones
19. Accreditation Council for Graduate Medical Education. Institutional requirements. Accessed June 19, 2024. https://www.acgme.org/globalassets/pfassets/programrequirements/800_institutionalrequirements2022.pdf
20. Accreditation Council for Graduate Medical Education. Common program requirements (residency). Accessed June 19, 2024. https://www.acgme.org/programs-and-institutions/programs/common-program-requirements/
21. Legha RK, Martinek NN. White supremacy culture and the assimilation trauma of medical training: ungaslighting the physician burnout discourse. *Med Humanit.* 2023;49(1):142-146. doi: 10.1136/medhum-2022-012398
22. Sue DW, Alsaidi S, Awad MN, Glaeser E, Calle CZ, Mendez N. Disarming racial microaggressions: microintervention strategies for targets, white allies, and bystanders. *Am Psychol.* 2019;74(1)128-142. doi: 10.1037/amp0000296
23. Stanley CA, Watson KL, Reyes JM, Varela KS. Organizational change and the chief diversity officer: a case study of institutionalizing a diversity plan. *J Divers High Educ.* 2019;12(3):255-265. Accessed June 24, 2024. https://psycnet.apa.org/doi/10.1037/dhe0000099
24. Fasching-Varner KJ, Albert KA, Mitchell RW, Allen CM, eds. *Racial Battle Fatigue in Higher Education: Exposing the Myth of Post-Racial America.* Rowman & Littlefield; 2014.
25. Matias CE, Leonardo Z. *Feeling White: Whiteness Emotionality and Education.* Sense; 2016.
26. Zoey Sky. CDC Training Course on Critical Race Theory Canceled After Whistleblower Steps Forward. Accessed January 23, 2025. https://www.liberalmob.com/2020-10-03-cdc-training-course-canceled-after-whistleblower.html

ADDITIONAL RESOURCES

Mentor M, Sealey-Ruiz Y. Doing the deep work of antiracist pedagogy: toward self-excavation for equitable classroom teaching. *Lang Arts.* 2021;99(1):19-24.

Akram A. Challenging anti-Black racism. *Horizons.* 2020;34(3):26.

Wainwright C. Building Narrative Power for Racial Justice and Health Equity. Accessed January 23, 2025. https://core.ac.uk/download/480182737.pdf

Kendi IX. *How to Be an Antiracist.* One World, 2019.

Smith WA, Yosso TJ, Solorzano DG. Challenging racial battle fatigue on historically white campuses: a critical race examination of race-related stress. In: Coates RD, ed. *Covert Racism: Theories, Institutions, and Experiences.* Brill Publishers; 2011:211-237.

Badenhorst P. Raced encounter on a Hilltop: a call for soulful justice alongside social justice work. *Engl Educ.* 2019; 51(2):200-208.

Cepeda R. Why do I have to prove my credentials to you?: Women of color community college faculty and intersectional aggressions. *J Appl Res Community Coll.* 2024;31(1):3-17.

Health Disparities in Correctional Medicine and the Justice-Involved Population: Impact on Physician Education and Training

Dionne Hart, MD, DFAPA, FASAM, Medical Doctor, Care From the Hart, Rochester, MN

Jill Strachan-Batson, MD, AAFP, Attending Physician, Community Medicine, Dallas, TX

Monica Taylor-Desir, MD, MPH, Assistant Professor, Mayo Clinic Department of Psychiatry and Psychology, Rochester, MN

CHAPTER SUMMARY

A limited amount of graduate medical education (GME) takes place in correctional facilities in comparison to the substantial need and opportunities for learning that can be found there. This chapter provides an overview of the disparities and health care challenges faced by those involved with the correctional system across the lifespan and how these challenges impact learners. We review the risk factors for incarceration of youth and the challenges in providing care for this population in a correctional setting. In addition, we examine the multiple health care transitions experienced by persons involved in the correctional system. Finally, because the aging incarcerated population is often overlooked, we highlight the effects of the correctional system on this population. We also discuss the health care risks faced by residents, fellows, physicians, and other clinicians while working in this system and conclude by providing action steps for GME programs, health care leaders, and advocates to improve care to this marginalized population.

LEARNING OBJECTIVES

1. Describe the challenges residents and fellows face when caring for justice involved youth.
2. Recognize health disparities in the adult population under correctional supervision, including the emerging crisis of people older than age 65 designated to correctional facilities.
3. Propose action steps for residents, fellows, practicing physicians, and care teams to decrease health disparities for the justice-involved patient population

Case Study

A 25-year-old Black male presented to the jail infirmary with a complaint of severe joint pain. He meets with a resident physician. His medical chart notes a diagnosis of cannabis use disorder. The patient says, "Doc, I'm having a sickle crisis. I need some real pain killers." He endorses a painful erection. He begins to pull down his pants but the resident stops him. A correctional officer is asked to stand by.

(continued)

The resident informs the patient that his medical history does not include information prior to his incarceration including "sickle disease." The patient requests that the resident contact his mother or family physician. Without any further interaction with the patient, the resident places a request for the unit team to contact family, then directs the patient to purchase an over-the-counter analgesic at the commissary. The patient raises his voice and says, "That ain't gonna cut it. I'm not leaving here until I get my meds." The correctional officer escorts the patient to restricted housing for causing a disturbance. The patient receives an incident report for insolence. His medical record is updated to include differential diagnoses of possible malingering and drug-seeking behaviors.

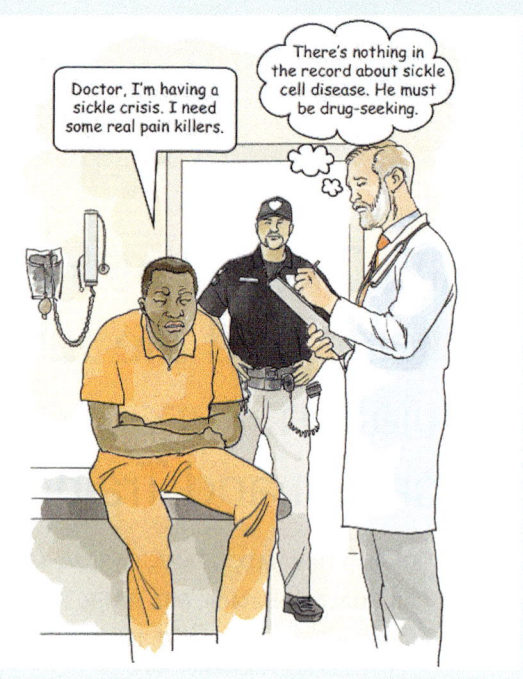

In restricted housing, the patient refuses meals and minimally interacts with staff. Three days later, under the hunger strike protocol, the patient is examined. The examination shows dry mucous membranes, swollen hands and feet, and jaundice. He has a fever, hypotension, and tachycardia.

He is transferred to the infirmary where he receives intravenous fluids. A case manager unsuccessfully attempts to contact his mother but is finally able to reach his sister who confirms the patient has sickle cell anemia. The staff also learn the patient was charged with trafficking opioids after a plastic bag containing oxycodone was found in his car and he could not produce the prescription bottle or recall the name of the physician who prescribed the medications.

At a community hospital, the patient is given intravenous meperidine, supplemental oxygen by nasal cannula, and treated for priapism. He is prescribed hydroxyurea. His jail medical record is updated to include sickle cell anemia but the notations about drug-seeking behaviors and suspected malingering are not retracted. At the next clinic, the resident apologizes to the patient and requests his full community medical record.

Case Discussion

In correctional settings, patients may be mislabeled as drug-seeking or malingering when advocating for their appropriate medical treatment, particularly if they are members of a minority group or diagnosed with rare medical conditions and/or pain syndromes. Additionally, minority physicians and other health care providers who have prior experience taking care of underserved populations and are most familiar with these rare disorders are underrepresented in medicine and among other health care professions and correctional staff.

Sickle cell anemia is an inherited disorder that affects the shape of red blood cells that carry oxygen to all parts of the body. In the United States, sickle cell anemia most commonly affects people of African, Mediterranean, and Middle Eastern descent. According to the Centers for Disease Control, sickle cell disease affects 1 in 13 Black or African American babies born with the sickle cell trait. Life-threatening medical complications of this disorder include stroke, acute chest syndrome, priapism, pulmonary hypertension, and deep vein thrombosis. Patients experiencing a sickle cell crisis have moderate to severe pain. There is no objective measure to determine the quality and severity of pain. Black Americans are systematically undertreated for pain relative to White Americans; a study found that physician learners who believed that Black people are not as sensitive to pain as White people were less likely to appropriately treat Black people's pain.[1] In this case, the resident faced the challenge of having a limited medical record and was influenced by unconscious biases based upon personal experience or the biases of the correctional staff. It is, therefore, important for residents and fellows to be aware of their own biases and how societal views of justice-involved populations may impact their health care outcomes. In addition, administrative barriers exist in correctional settings that are not present in other communities. For example, policies may prevent a physician from directly contacting family or obtaining community medical records. While communication restrictions may be unique to correctional facilities, a resident or fellow will acquire experience in addressing administrative barriers present in all settings. And most importantly, the Office of Justice Programs estimates 3,745,000 adults or an estimated 7 out of 10 persons under correctional supervision are in the community. Graduate medical education (GME) provided in correctional facilities can provide residents/fellows with opportunities to increase their understanding of the impact of the social determinants of health; learn to provide evidence-based health care in settings where resources are limited or the medical record is fragmented; understand the limits of health care privacy laws; and develop skill in the art of bedside advocacy outside of traditional health care settings. Currently, few psychiatry programs provide residents/fellows with exposure to adults in custody, despite correctional facilities being the largest mental health providers in the country. It is imperative that residents and fellows have increased opportunities to rotate in these facilities and receive active supervision when treating adults in custody in community hospital settings. These opportunities will prepare physicians to positively impact patient outcomes for justice-involved populations who may have limited health literacy, previous negative health experiences, and under-diagnosed or misdiagnosed mental health disorders. As you review the chapter, consider how training in your GME program or Sponsoring Institution prepares learners to address the needs of justice-involved patients.

INTRODUCTION TO JUSTICE-INVOLVED POPULATIONS

Justice-involved populations are defined as individuals who are convicted, have been convicted, or have been incarcerated. The United States has the highest incarceration rate in the world with 1.9 million people incarcerated nationwide. Justice-involved populations typically have high rates of mental illness including substance use disorders, chronic illness, and sexually transmitted infections. These individuals have a constitutional right to health care (Figure 13.1).

FIGURE 13.1 Health care transitions experienced by justice-Involved individuals. (Reprinted by permission from Springer Nature. Binswanger IA, Redmond N, Steiner JF, Hicks LRS. Health disparities and the criminal justice system: an agenda for further action and research. *J Urban Health*. 2012;89(1):98-107. doi: 10.1007/s11524-011-9614-1)

Physicians and other health care professionals receive limited, dedicated education and training in the care of justice-involved populations; are unaware of guidelines for the treatment of patients in custody; and, face unique medical, legal, and ethical issues in doing so. While GME may take place in correctional facilities, the number of physician learners who receive direct training in these facilities is unknown even though there are opportunities to establish clinical rotations since most GME programs are within 3 to 4 miles of correctional facilities.[2] Furthermore, while correctional facilities are the largest providers of mental health care in the United States, the level of exposure by physician learners does not reflect the need and disease burden represented in this population. For these reasons, it is critical to ensure that GME programs and Sponsoring Institutions actively seek opportunities for residents and fellows to rotate in these environments so they can understand the justice-involved population and are adequately prepared to treat their needs as well as to reduce health disparities in these marginalized groups.

Justice-Involved Youth

On average, almost 30,000 youth are incarcerated over a 12-month period in United States. These individuals are disproportionately male and persons of color. "The placement rate for minority youth in 2019 was more than twice the rate for White youth."[3] There are many factors that place youth at risk for contact with the justice system. Shader states that these risks include socioeconomic disparities as well as the lack of community-based resources.[4] As a result, at-risk youth may face mental and physical health challenges prior to incarceration. "Youth in the juvenile correctional system are a high-risk population who, in many cases, have unmet physical, developmental, and mental health needs. Multiple studies have found that some of these health issues occur at higher rates than in the general adolescent population."[5]

The correctional facility has the unique opportunity to address some of these needs. Health professionals who practice in correctional facilities, including residents and fellows, must be skilled in the management of common pediatric diagnoses and should follow clinical guidelines by the American Academy of Pediatrics and American Academy of Family Physicians. Allergies, asthma, eczema, and diabetes are frequently encountered diagnoses, but clinicians may also be faced with less-commonly seen chronic illnesses such as sickle cell disease, hemophilia, and cystic fibrosis. Management of rarer conditions may require a partnership with specialists off-site. Adolescent care providers can also be faced with the postoperative follow up of trauma from gunshot wounds, lacerations, or fractures. Psychiatric and behavioral health care is also a critical need that has often not been addressed prior to the incarceration of the youth.

Resources for mental health services are not consistently available at every correctional facility nationwide. A review of mental health services in juvenile centers found "[f]acilities that provided mental health treatment on-site were more likely to also have a mental health professional evaluate all the youth. Larger facilities were more likely than smaller ones to screen all youth for suicide risk and to evaluate all youth for mental health needs. Privately operated facilities (62 percent) were more likely to evaluate all youth than were public facilities (41 percent)".[5] Additionally with the increasing prevalence of opioid abuse, there can be a need for the treatment of drug dependent individuals. In 2021, the National Institutes of Drug Abuse reported that "Opioid-involved overdose deaths rose from 21,089 in 2010 to 47,600 in 2017 and remained steady through 2019. This was followed by a significant increase in 2020 with 68,630 reported deaths and again in 2021 with 80,411 reported overdose deaths."[6] The prevalence of opioid misuse suggests that this finding will remain an emerging concern for many correctional care providers caring for youth as well as adults.

Smaller populations of justice-involved individuals include females and lesbian, gay, transgender, queer and intersex (LGBTQIA+) youth who may have additional special care needs including pregnancy management and treatment after sexual abuse or trafficking. The correctional care provider should be prepared to provide high quality care to a diverse population of youth that reflect the diversity of our nation.

For the physician, a jail is a unique setting to provide medical care. There are many factors to consider while providing care to adolescents. Local educational requirements, correctional facility staffing at any one time, and available medical resources are elements that the physician may have to consider when designing a care plan. It is important to recognize potential long-term consequences that can follow youth into adulthood. While an individual is incarcerated, opportunities exist to improve their health status by preventing the sequelae of chronic illness and helping them to build trust with the medical establishment. Social workers and mental health providers give a critical element of care by forming a linkage to community-based medical care. Youth with mental health problems in juvenile justice who experiences integrated and individualized wraparound planning within a system of care is less likely to recidivate at all.[7] These resources can help establish the connection to needed support services when returning home to an unstable or underserved community and reduce the risk of return to correctional facilities. The juvenile correctional health team is critical in helping to establish the relationships that can help youth thrive once released and reduce the risk of future incarceration.

HEALTH DISPARITIES IN JUSTICE-INVOLVED ADULTS

Black and Brown populations are disproportionately represented in incarcerated populations. One in 40 adults in the United States are under some form of correctional supervision. Black Americans are incarcerated at nearly 5 times the rate of White Americans. Hispanic/Latinx individuals are incarcerated in state prisons at nearly 1.3 times the incarceration of White Americans. Native American males are incarcerated 4 times the rate of White men and American Indian women are imprisoned at 6 times the rate of White women.[8] The majority of adults under correctional supervision are probationers or parolees who have inadequate access to health care and risk deterioration in health status and death. Even though the majority of prisoners rely on emergency departments as their primary health care provider, the use of emergency departments for primary health care often predates an individual's entry into the correctional system.

Incarcerated individuals experience many transitions that also include health care settings when moving from the community to jail to prison to other facilities within the system, to half-way houses, and eventually returning to the community (Figure 13.1).[9] Within these settings, asthma, cancer, infectious diseases, high blood pressure, mental health conditions, and substance use disorders must be managed along with medications, and treatments must be monitored and continued. When a person enters the health care system, physicians, including residents and fellows, can provide evidence-based health screening based on both standard recommendations on for specific issues of high prevalence and concern in minoritized or incarcerated populations. In order to improve health care upon release from the correctional system, physicians can lead the charge in coordinating correctional and community health services, improving access to care, and advocating for timely reinstatement of insurance.[9] Community physicians could also target community supervision sites such as **probation** offices and half-way houses as a place to implement health care screenings for health issues identified during incarceration in addition to advocating for patient privacy when receiving health care.

Aging Incarcerated Population

The US correctional system was developed to detain mentally and physically healthy young males who would re-enter the community at the completion of their sentence. Ninety-five percent of prisoners return to their community; however, changes in sentencing guidelines cut mandatory minimum sentences, disparities in drug sentencing, and life sentences without **parole** have resulted in inmates aging and dying in correctional settings. Most correctional facilities are not equipped to address the special health needs of these individuals. Older inmates have difficulty navigating distances to pick up meals and medications, face a shortage of upper bunks, or cannot enter narrow doorways with their wheelchairs or walkers, or safely walk on steep, uneven pathways.

Within the general US population, geriatric age is usually defined as 65 years or older. The federal government defines 50 as the cutoff for geriatric patients, while the states' definition ranges from 50 to 65 years of age. The number of older adults (age 50 and above) in US prisons is growing.[10] Eleven percent of federal prisoners age 51 or older are serving sentences ranging from 30 years to life. Those incarcerated and 50 years or older have a physiological age that is 10 to 15 years older than their non-incarcerated counterparts, a phenomenon known as accelerated aging. In 2004, there were more than 120,000 inmates aged 50 and older. Older individuals who make up 16% of the US prison population are the fastest growing demographic in the US prison system.

People in jails and prisons are more likely to have chronic health problems, such as diabetes, hypertension, sexually transmitted infections, and chronic mental illness. They have an average of three chronic health conditions and at least 15% to 20% of those incarcerated have a chronic mental illness. Older prisoners require more intensive medical attention due to having a greater burden of health care needs compared to their younger counterparts.

Despite an aging prison population with greater than three or more chronic illnesses, many state and local jurisdictions have a health care budget based upon the number of inmates in the facility—not the population's disease burden—resulting in correctional facilities having insufficient funding to manage the health care costs of their wards. In state-operated correctional facilities, annual medical expenditures are 3 to 9 times greater for geriatric patients compared to others. Seventy-two percent of all **correctional health care** budgets are spent on geriatric prisoners.

IMPROVING GME TO REDUCE HEALTH DISPARITIES FOR JUSTICE-INVOLVED PATIENTS

Engagement of GME programs and Sponsoring Institutions represents a key opportunity to improve health, health care access, and quality of care for justice-involved individuals. In order to prepare physician learners to care for these marginalized populations, we propose the following strategies:

1. We recommend GME programs include correctional medicine topics as part of the curriculum.
2. Correctional facilities are the largest mental health providers in the United States. The prevalence of mental health disorders is 5 times greater in correctional facilities than compared to the general population. There is a shortage of psychiatrists in correctional facilities. One article using the National Health Provider Scarcity Area database identified 457 correctional facilities in the United States with greater than 250 minutes travel time and an inmates per year to full time psychiatrist ratio greater than 2,000:1. However, despite the need for mental health treatment and the proximity of teaching hospitals, residents and fellows do not receive an opportunity to enhance their medical education by rotating in these facilities. Faculty members should support those learners interested in correctional medicine by exposing them to opportunities to complete a correctional medicine rotation. One of the authors developed a clinical rotation through which residents and medical students receive a complete understanding of the experience of justice involved patients living with mental health disorders. Their rotation includes a ride-along with local enforcement, evaluating and treating adults in custody, and exposure to community organizations focusing on successful reentry. The feedback has been positive.

   Correction facilities have inherent, often impenetrable barriers to serving as rotation sites for residents and fellows; however, the unmet mental health needs and chronic medical disorder burden necessitates the critical inclusion of internal medicine, family medicine, and psychiatry GME programs. These experiences may be virtual or in-person.

3. GME faculty members should encourage residents and fellows to inquire about a person's incarceration history given the high risk of co-occurring social determinants of health and high prevalence of trauma related disorders.

   The justice-involved population has a high medical illness burden, history of severe mental illness, and high risk of death post incarceration.[11] It is imperative for residents and fellows to further develop their medical history-taking skills to develop a full picture of the social determinants impacting patients' health presentation and prognosis. A full history should be gathered in a nonjudgmental, caring manner using a structural competence approach that is sensitive to mental health screening and chronic medical conditions. In particular, screening questions to consider with an incarcerated population should include:

   - Many of my patients and their family members have experienced incarceration in the past and this can affect how healthy people and their families are. Has this ever happened to you or a loved one?[12]
   - Are you currently dealing with any legal issues, such as pending charges or court dates?
   - Are you currently under court supervision?

4. Correctional medical staff have unique skill sets and clinical experiences. GME programs should perform outreach to correctional medical staff to consider adjunct teaching positions.
5. GME programs can provide opportunities to teach residents and fellows about the local jail/prison population and the demographics and co-morbidities of the **re-entry** population including psychiatric, substance use and physical diagnoses. Correctional staff

> Persons affected by incarceration include thousands of US youth under the age of 18. The medical care provided to these individuals as they cycle through the correctional system can impact their future mental and physical well-being as adults.

> Interprofessional collaboration between nurses, social workers, and residents/fellows and practicing physicians are key to ensure appropriate follow-up for justice-involved patients.

can delineate the treatments available to persons that are incarcerated and what can and cannot be managed in a specific correctional facility. Working with correctional staff and learning about systems affecting the justice-involved population provide opportunities to examine and improve equity in program, material, and services designed to serve this population. In addition, building on relationships formed with correctional staff, residents and fellows may have the opportunity to facilitate warm handoffs to community behavioral health and medical services that provide chronic health treatment. In these situations, physician learners will need to develop their skills in working with multidisciplinary staff including case managers, peer navigators, social workers and their patients' social support network.

Take Home Points

- Justice-involved individuals experience multiple health care transitions throughout the correctional system, which can result in loss of follow-up and missed opportunities to enhance health and well-being.
- Physicians, including residents and fellows, who provide care at correctional facilities, are instrumental in providing evidence-based care to reduce health disparities in the justice-involved population.
- By enhancing GME that addresses care at correctional facilities, institutions can help improve health for justice-involved individuals.

QUESTIONS FOR FURTHER THOUGHT

1. How does your GME program or health care Institution interact with correctional facilities? Are there opportunities to enhance these connections with the goal of improving the GME experience for learners and care for justice-involved patients? If onsite training is not available, have you reached out to a correctional physician to present at a grand rounds or GME program didactics?
2. What education could be implemented for residents and fellows to improve their understanding of the limited health literacy prevalent within populations of individuals connected to the community justice system?

REFERENCES

1. Hoffman KM, Trawalter S, Axt JR, Oliver MN. Racial bias in pain assessment and treatment recommendations, and false beliefs about biological differences between blacks and whites. *Proc Natl Acad Sci USA*. 2016; 113(16): 4296-4301. doi:10.1073/pnas.1516047113
2. Jha MK, Fuehrlein BS, North CS, Brenner AM. Training psychiatry residents at correctional facilities. *Acad Psychiatry*. 2014;39(1):123-124. doi:10.1007/s40596-014-0238-0
3. Jones C. OJJDP is taking action to achieve an equitable juvenile justice system. Office of Juvenile Justice and Delinquency Prevention. Published October 26, 2021. Accessed December 10, 2023. https://ojjdp.ojp.gov/blog/ojjdp-taking-action-achieve-equitable-juvenile-justice-system
4. Shader M, Risk factors for delinquency: an overview. U.S. Department of Justice Office of Justice Programs. Published 2003. Accessed December 10, 2023. https://www.ojp.gov/ncjrs/virtual-library/abstracts/risk-factors-delinquency-overview
5. Braverman PK, Murray PJ, Adelman WP, et al. Health care for youth in the Juvenile Justice System. *Pediatrics*. 2011;128(6):1219-1235. doi:10.1542/peds.2011-1757
6. National Institute on Drug Abuse. Drug overdose deaths: facts and figures. National Institutes of Health. Published 2023. Accessed December 10, 2023. https://nida.nih.gov/research-topics/trends-statistics/overdose-death-rates
7. Pullmann MD, Kerbs J, Koroloff N, et al. Juvenile offenders with mental health needs: Reducing recidivism using wraparound. *Crime Delinq*. 2006;52(3):375-397. Accessed December 10, 2023. https://www.ojp.gov/ncjrs/virtual-library/abstracts/juvenile-offenders-mental-health-needs-reducing-recidivism-using

8. Nellis, Ashley. *The Color of Justice: Racial and Ethnic Disparity in State Prisons*. The Sentencing Project; 2021. https://www.sentencingproject.org/reports/the-color-of-justice-racial-and-ethnic-disparity-in-state-prisons-the-sentencing-project/
9. Binswanger IA, Redmond N, Steiner JF, Hicks LRS. Health disparities and the criminal justice system: an agenda for further action and research. *J Urban Health*. 2012;89(1):98-107. doi:10.1007/s11524-011-9614-1
10. Loeb SJ, AbuDagga A. Health-related research on older inmates: an integrative review. *Res Nurs Health*. 2006;29(6):556-565. doi:10.1002/nur.20177
11. Walsh-Felz D, Westergaard R, Waclawik G, Pandhi N. "Service with open arms": enhancing community health care experiences for individuals with a history of incarceration. *Health Justice*. 2019;7(1):20. doi:10.1186/s40352-019-0101-1
12. Sue K. How to talk with patients about incarceration and health. *AMA J Ethics*. 2017;19(9):885-893. doi:10.1001/journalofethics.2017.19.9.ecas2-1709

SECTION 3

Ethnocultural, Immigrant, Multilingual, and Religious Experiences in Graduate Medical Education

Pilar Ortega, MD, MGM, Vice President, Diversity, Equity, and Inclusion, Accreditation Council for Graduate Medical Education; Clinical Associate Professor, Emergency Medicine and Medical Education, University of Illinois College of Medicine, Chicago, IL

William McDade, MD, PhD, Chief, Diversity, Equity, and Inclusion Officer, Accreditation Council for Graduate Medical Education Officer, Chicago, IL

In Section Three, *A Guide* focuses on the ethnocultural, religious, and linguistic backgrounds as well as the immigrant and socioeconomic experiences that residents and fellows bring to graduate medical education (GME). These various identities, affiliations, and experiences often intersect and may influence learners' selection of a GME program, their sense of belonging in the GME community, and even their choice of the location where they will eventually practice. These experiences may also influence how they are evaluated by supervisors or perceived and treated by peers and patients.

Of most concern to the authors in Section Three, when these same varying backgrounds and experiences differ from what is considered normative or dominant in society, residents and fellows may feel "othered" or singled-out by individual, structural, and systemic perspectives, which fail to consider or value their differences. Although religion, ethnicity, culture, language, and immigration status are core to individuals' identity and values, these attributes are often invisible. However, the traumatic impact they may experience in the GME environment is just as real as the impact experienced by those who have visible identity differences. When individuals feel that some invisible aspect of their identity is excluded, unwelcome, or considered "unprofessional," they may choose to separate that aspect from their professional identity.[1] The practice of separating professional from personal identity can be used as a survival strategy but may also cause considerable short- and long-term stress, curtailing the ability of physician learners to thrive fully in GME and throughout their careers.[2]

The medical profession largely perceives itself as a "culture of no culture" wherein decisions are evidence-based and two physicians given the same set of findings would arrive at the same conclusion.[3] Such an image promotes a shared world-view or mindset, which can minimize differences instead of acknowledging and celebrating them. It can undermine the cultural humility necessary for the development of physician learners who care for the individuality of each patient and appreciate colleagues who may not share a common identity.[4] The concept of acculturation or assimilation implies that formative identities must be subordinated or suppressed in favor of the dominant culture's identity. When residents and fellows receive an implicit message that they should acculturate to dominant practices, they are not able to bring their full, authentic selves to the GME setting. In such circumstances, physician learners from marginalized and minoritized backgrounds experience a lack of inclusion.

The chapters in Section Three challenge the perception of "no culture" in medicine by describing experiences of physician learners who are first generation and low-income, international medical graduates (IMGs) and those having Deferred Action for Childhood Arrivals (DACA) status, those who have diverse linguistic skills, and who practice the Muslim and Orthodox Jewish religions. In each instance, the authors demonstrate how these attributes can contribute directly or indirectly to both immediate and long-term potentially adverse effects on the self-image of residents and fellows and carry with them that same self-image as practicing physicians and leaders in medicine. Importantly, the authors also highlight ways in which these attributes can be conversely viewed as assets that can contribute to physicians' skill sets in enhancing population health.

* * *

Chapter 14: Building an Inclusive Environment for Residents and Fellows from First-Generation College Graduate and Low-Income Backgrounds
Jamieson O'Marr, MS; Mytien Nguyen, MSc; Catherine Havemann, MD; Roselande Marcellon, MD, MPH, MA

First-generation college graduates and low-income (FGLI) physician learners are unique among minoritized populations because they represent a heterogenous mix of ethnocultural, religious, and linguistic backgrounds. O'Marr et al use data to demonstrate that these individuals are underrepresented in medical education. This fact explains why FGLI learners are not simply a minority, but often are not identified as a minoritized group—or even as minoritized individuals within a given GME program. As a result, the unique contributions of FGLI residents and fellows are often undervalued in GME settings. Unfortunately, the disparity that exists between FGLI residents and fellows and their colleagues can often hinder their ability to succeed and flourish.

Chapter 15: Pathways to Graduate Medical Education for Foreign National Physicians and DACA Recipients
Mario Lorenzana De Witt, MD; Sunny Nakae, PhD, MSW; Tracy Wallowicz, MLS

De Witt et al focus on how immigration status is frequently an added complication for IMGs and DACA individuals that can adversely affect their inclusion and acceptance into the GME community. Such status already differentiates these individuals within the dominant homogeneous culture in the United States and in medicine. Even before they begin GME, the complexities of an application to residency for these groups are often exacerbated by immigration obstacles and other challenges to receiving equitable consideration and treatment. The authors clarify terminology associated with immigration status and the meaning of DACA, describe the structural barriers faced by both these minoritized populations, and the strengths they bring to their GME settings.

SECTION 3 • Ethnocultural, Immigrant, Multilingual, and Religious Experiences

Chapter 16: Creating an Inclusive Environment for Multilingual Learners and Faculty Members
Pilar Ortega, MD, MGM; Itzel López-Hinojosa, MD

Ortega and López-Hinojosa explore the impact of stereotyping that results from linguistic diversity and multilingualism, both which frequently marginalize physician learners. For example, such stereotyping often puts linguistically diverse residents and fellows at an immediate disadvantage when they are expected to interpret for a patient in a language with which they are assumed to be familiar. Considerable data show the negative impacts of language discordance to the care, satisfaction, and outcomes of patients with non-English language preference, yet fewer scholars have focused on the impacts this has on learners. This chapter sheds light on how multilingual learners are disproportionately affected by factors such as accent bias, the minority tax, and the lack of language proficiency assessment and data collection in GME and health care settings. The authors discuss how GME learning environments can empower these individuals, protect them from mistreatment related to linguistic stereotypes, and recognize the positive contributions that can be made to learning and patient care by the communication skills of multilingual, multicultural residents and fellows.

Chapter 17: Creating Inclusive Environments for Muslim Residents and Fellows
Deena Kishawi, MD

Accommodations for religious expression are required by labor law; institutions and programs must take these requirements into account as residents and fellows train in clinical learning environments. In this context, Kishawi explain that Muslims are a diverse and heterogenous population in which no racial or ethnic group constitutes a majority of Muslim American adults. They describe experiences of Muslim and Sikh physician learners and how leaders and faculty members can support them in meeting the challenges they face. Obvious differences in appearance and religious practices that are not considered "mainstream" in the dominant culture, may subject Muslim residents and fellows to harassment or mistreatment in Islamophobic settings. The authors explain the meaning and significance of some of these more notable religious customs to help dispel misunderstandings that may result in discrimination and other hardships often faced by this minoritized population. The authors thus endeavor to encourage respect for deeply held Muslim beliefs that will result in their sense of well-being and inclusion in the GME community. They demonstrate that Muslim residents and fellows can play an important role in the education of the health care team and in supporting diversity of the patient population by allowing all Muslim community members to be true to their ethnocultural and religious backgrounds.

Chapter 18: Creating Inclusive Environments for Orthodox Jewish Learners in Graduate Medical Education
Chana Weinstock, MD; Daniel Eisenberg, MD

Along with other minoritized groups discussed throughout this section, observant Orthodox Jewish residents and fellows frequently face discrimination and disrespect because of their ethnocultural and religious background. GME leadership may be unaware of these physician learners' legally protected rights as they strive to adhere to the tenets of Jewish law that govern their customs and religious norms. As a result, Orthodox Jewish physician learners may suffer, often in silence, the effects of a lack of inclusivity due to misunderstanding. Weinstock and Eisenberg examine the challenges faced by these individuals. They provide useful information that explains how adherence to Jewish law by observant Orthodox Jewish residents and fellows requires GME leaders to understand the need for accommodations for scheduling for celebration of the Sabbath and for specific holidays, recognition of how clinical and ethical situations may be viewed through the lens of Jewish law, and attention to dietary restrictions when food is provided either on call or at social events. They offer recommendations for creating inclusive environments and suggest resources to assist with developing strategies that address special needs for observant Orthodox Jewish physician learners within GME programs.

REFERENCES

1. Gallegos A, Gordon LK, Moreno G, et al. Visibility and support for first generation college graduates in medicine. *Med Educ Online*. 2022;27(1):2011605. doi:10.1080/10872981.2021.2011605
2. Symes HA, Boulet J, Yaghmour NA, Wallowicz T, McKinley DW. International medical graduate resident wellness: examining qualitative data from J-1 visa physician recipients. *Acad Med*. 2022;97(3):420-425. PMID: 34524136
3. Cerdeña JP, Asabor EN, Rendell S, Okolo T, Lett E. Resculpting professionalism for equity and accountability. *Ann Fam Med*. 2022;20(6):573-577. doi:10.1370/afm.2892
4. David YN, Issaka RB. Advancing diversity: the role of international medical graduates. *Lancet Gastroenterol Hepatol*. 2021;6(12):980-981. PMID: 34774151

14

Building an Inclusive Environment for Residents and Fellows from First-Generation College Graduate and Low-Income Backgrounds

Jamieson O'Marr, MS, Medical Student, Yale School of Medicine, New Haven, CT
Mytien Nguyen, MSc, Medical Student, PhD Candidate, Yale School of Medicine, New Haven, CT
Catherine Havemann, MD, Emergency Medicine Resident, University of Chicago, Chicago, IL
Roselande Marcellon, MD, MPH, MA, Internal Medicine Resident, University of Miami/Jackson Memorial Hospital, Miami, FL

CHAPTER SUMMARY

Residents and fellows who are first-generation college graduates and/or from low-income (FGLI) backgrounds are a demographically diverse and unique cohort who embody many necessary strengths and perspectives in the pursuit of patient-centered, culturally responsive health care. However, the expectations, norms, and structure of the current medical education and training environment can create disproportionate barriers for these individuals. The support of residents and fellows from FGLI backgrounds requires a flexible, innovative, and multifaceted approach to address the challenges they face in the sociocultural, financial, and educational domains.

LEARNING OBJECTIVES

1. Define the first-generation college graduate and low-income identity and contextualize it within the graduate medical education (GME).
2. Review existing literature surrounding FGLI residents and fellows in medicine.
3. Identify the key strengths, challenges, and structural barriers for FGLI residents and fellows.
4. Propose opportunities and solutions for inclusion of and equity for FGLI residents and fellows in GME.

Case Study

Layla, a first-generation college graduate from a low-income background is now an internal medicine intern starting a new block on the cardiology service. This is a typical day for Layla.

6:00 AM: While pre-rounding in the team room, the senior resident gets to know the interns by asking "are you a skiing or a snowboarding person?" While her co-interns have strong opinions, she has never done either of these prohibitively expensive hobbies and cannot fully participate.

(continued)

7:00 AM: While pre-rounding, Layla spends 10 extra minutes helping their patient who newly requires community dialysis but reads at a third grade level and is facing multiple barriers to care as he is food insecure and cannot afford a cell phone. In addition to explaining renal disease and dialysis basics, they discuss food stamps, local food pantries, and a hospital program that helps patients afford a cell phone to facilitate their medical care. She is 2 minutes late to rounds but gives strong presentations. Her attending later writes feedback that says, "Very empathetic, but inefficient clinically. Focus on the medicine."

9:00 AM: During rounds, Layla is the only resident wearing hospital-issued scrubs rather than an expensive custom pair and is mistaken for a non-clinical staff member by the nurse whom she spoke to earlier regarding the patient's care.

12:00 PM: Over a virtual lunch conference, Layla sends a few emails in an attempt to identify a faculty mentor for her community engagement program. Though

she attended medical school at the same institution where she is now a resident, she has struggled to find a faculty mentor for her program. Her co-intern suggests the Chair of the Department of Medicine, with whom he is already working on a systematic review.

3:00 PM: Layla admits a patient presents in acute decompensated heart failure with many similar admissions over the last year. Her attending remarks, "Funny how the patient can get here for this but not for her regular appointments." Layla, who sometimes struggles to get to other clinical sites herself, quietly ascertains that the patient lives in a poor urban area with famously fragmented public transportation and contacts the social worker for help setting up more reliable alternatives.

7:00 PM: Her co-interns plan to grab drinks after work. Layla, who has to pay her family's $120 electric bill each month and lives paycheck to paycheck, stresses over joining them. Not wanting to be left out, she attends and gets by on meal card swipes in the hospital cafeteria over the following few days.

Case Discussion

First-generation and low-income (FGLI) identity can permeate every aspect of a resident's or fellow's experience within GME. To build an inclusive culture and learning environment, we must work to mitigate the challenges and uplift the assets of this population. Layla's case study includes examples of how she, like many FGLI learners, brings a wealth of experience that makes her an insightful, culturally responsive clinician. Unfortunately, this is not always valued despite its demonstrated value to the health care system. As is seen in Layla's story, some of these strengths may not only go unrecognized, but may even be actively discouraged by supervisors through problematic or biased feedback. Moreover, FGLI residents and fellows often identify deeply with their patients from similar backgrounds. When inappropriate remarks are made about these patients, it can negatively impact the resident or fellow whose family or community may face similar circumstances. Layla's example also shows how having limited financial resources can affect the ability of FGLI residents and fellows to participate in social events and crucial bonding activities within their programs—activities that can create a sense of belonging. It also impacts the ability to purchase visible markers of belonging, such as custom scrubs and monogrammed jackets, which are common among continuing generation residents and fellows. In reviewing this chapter, consider how your program currently creates an inclusive environment for FGLI learners, and what changes could lead to improvement.

INTRODUCTION

FGLI residents and fellows are a heterogenous group of individuals who represent a variety of distinct racial, ethnic, and cultural backgrounds. While the challenges and disparities faced by FGLI students have been documented to some extent for several decades, recognition of the FGLI identity is relatively new, only becoming more broadly accepted in the mid-to-late 2000s.[1] The Association of American Medical Colleges (AAMC) defines first-generation status as individuals "whose parents have not earned an associate's degree or higher."[2] Residents and fellows who come from this background are also more likely to both identify as **underrepresented in medicine** and hail from low-income backgrounds.[3,4] The impact of the intersectional identities held by FGLI residents and fellows cannot be understated; however, given that other chapters in this book focus more directly on race, ethnicity, gender, sexuality, and other intersectional identities, this chapter will look specifically at FGLI identity.

The current literature surrounding FGLI physician learners is sparse given that applicant data related to socioeconomic status and parental education have only recently begun being collected. The AAMC did not include first-generation status on medical school applications until 2017, which was followed shortly thereafter by the addition of the socioeconomic status indicator.[2,5] Recent research has highlighted a substantial underrepresentation of FGLI students in medical education. Despite FGLI students accounting for 42% of college graduates, their representation among medical school matriculants is less than 20%.[4] According to the AAMC, in the 2021-2022 cycle, only 12.4% of matriculants to MD-granting medical schools identified as first-generation.[6] Mason et al found that, even after controlling for potential confounders, first-generation students were less likely to apply and be accepted into medical education programs than their continuing-generation peers.[6] This disparity would then propagate into the resident and faculty levels, leading to even lower representation.

First-generation residents and fellows encounter additional obstacles stemming from socioeconomic challenges, and AAMC data reveal that individuals from low-income backgrounds are similarly underrepresented. One study revealed that residents and fellows originating from families in the top 40% of US household incomes (earning over $75,000) comprise nearly 80% of the total resident/fellow population.[3] There is an even larger concentration at the top, with those from the top 5% of US household incomes (earning more than $225,000) exceeding the number of residents and fellows from the bottom 60% of US households.[3] Even after matriculation into medical school, learners from low-income backgrounds face unique challenges that can lead to higher rates of attrition. A study by Brewer et al found that, even after controlling for MCAT [Medical College Admission Test] scores, low-income medical students were nearly twice as likely to face attrition compared to their peers.[7] Finally, another study by Nguyen et al found that, even after controlling for multiple potential confounding factors, students from lower income backgrounds were less likely to be Alpha Omega Alpha Honor Medical Society members compared to their peers from higher-income settings, and thus faced greater difficulties in ultimately matching into residency programs.[8] These studies emphasize the significant loss of FGLI learners within the existing training pathways. Not only is there a lack of initial representation of FGLI learners, but they are also disproportionately lost during medical school and in the transition to GME compared to their peers. This loss is particularly concerning because FGLI physician learners play a crucial role as essential members of diverse clinical teams, which have been shown to provide higher quality patient care.[9]

BARRIERS FACED BY FGLI LEARNERS DURING THEIR EDUCATION AND TRAINING

FGLI learners encounter numerous challenges, which can impose significant burdens, such as the presence of hidden costs associated with medical education and training. These include expenses for essential equipment, examination fees, relocation expenses, and other financial obligations. These expenses can be substantial and, in many cases, arise before learners receive any form of payment from their programs. See Figure 14.1.

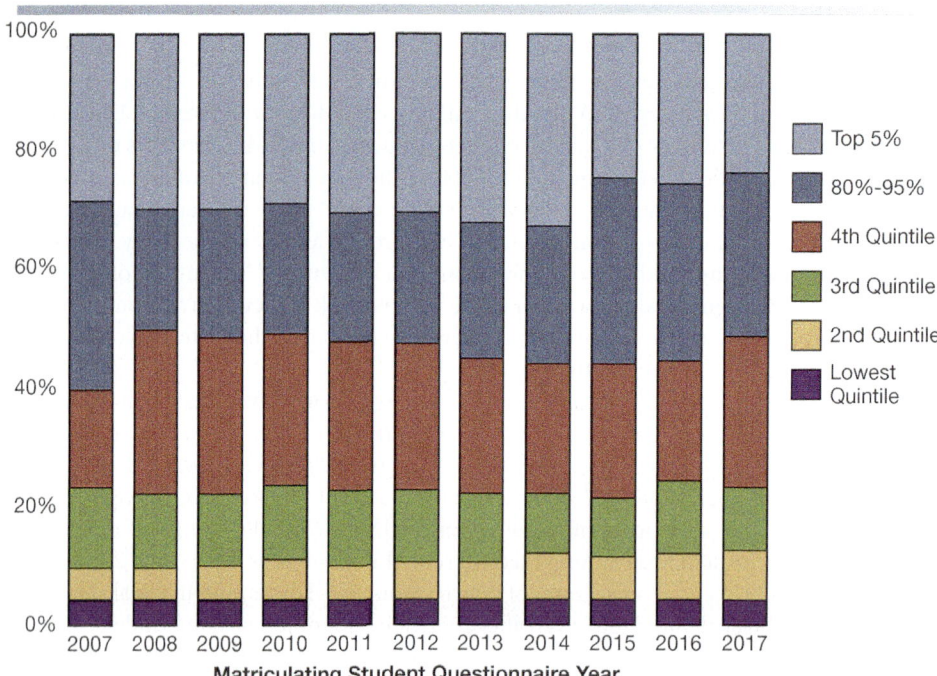

FIGURE 14.1 Parental income of first-year US medical students by quintiles of US household income obtained from the AAMC Medical School Questionnaire, years 2007-2017. (Figure Attribution: Youngclaus J, Roskovensky L. An updated look at the economic diversity of U.S. medical students. *AAMC Anal Brief.* 2018;18(5).)

Hidden costs place additional stress on FGLI learners as they are less likely than their peers to have access to financial support from family. In many cases, FGLI learners themselves may actually be providing some financial support to their families. Thus, added financial burdens may drive them to make difficult financial decisions, such as having to rely on additional loans from private lenders. These financial pressures compound the stressors within a medical education process that is already demanding, leaving these learners with added stressors and few options for earning additional income.

Another barrier faced by many FGLI learners is the lack of access to adequate career mentorship. The medical education pathway is complex and filled with "hidden knowledge." Some examples of this are navigation of the fellowship application process following residency and the job search process upon the completion of education. There is limited publicly available information about either of these processes. Given the exclusive nature, both are notoriously susceptible to bias, and success can be determined by "who you know." This hidden knowledge is often passed down informally through family or career networks to which FGLI learners often may not have equal access. Without the proper guidance, or mentors who are willing to practice **sponsorship**, FGLI learners can face difficulties in navigating and advancing in their careers in medicine.

STRENGTHS OF FGLI LEARNERS AND ACTIONABLE STRATEGIES FOR IMPROVING THEIR INCLUSION

FGLI learners are often acknowledged for the obstacles they overcome, but it is important to recognize that they can harness their experiences and adversity as catalysts for transformative leadership. Their unique perspectives as newcomers to the field of medicine, shaped by their encounters with a flawed health care system, have the potential to cultivate insight, advocacy, and leadership that propel the advancement of health equity.

In residency, FGLI learners' backgrounds afford them unique skills that allow them to excel as clinicians. For example, their often first-hand experience allows them to understand the context of patient populations with limited resources. Family support is also an important predictor for a student's educational success as it promotes well-being and facilitates student engagement. FGLI students often come from families that operate as a team, providing them with the foundational support to pursue challenging academic medicine positions. Furthermore, FGLI students are typically insightful and reflective, characteristics built from their lived experiences. Their self-awareness is critical for success during career changes into academic medicine positions.

Despite possessing admirable qualities that make them exemplary physicians, FGLI learners have historically faced significant underrepresentation in physician education programs. This marginalization begins at the door to medical school, where, in recent years, the proportion of medical school applicants and matriculants from low-income households (household annual income <$75,000) has significantly decreased. Even after adjusting for academic credentials, students from households with annual income <$50,000 were half as likely as students from households with annual income >$200,000 to be admitted into medical school. This disparity suggests that traditional definitions of merit utilized in medical school admissions are likely indicators of privilege.[10] Furthermore, once in medical school, FGLI learners can be marginalized and may encounter an unwelcoming and exclusive education and training environment that hinders their ability to succeed and flourish. Although limited research exists on how negative education and training environments in residency affect FGLI residents specifically, studies have shown that adverse learning environments during medical school contribute to higher rates of leaves of absence and a greater likelihood of FGLI students leaving medical school altogether, compared to their peers from more privileged backgrounds.[11-13]

In a 2023 study of diversity, equity, and inclusion practices across ACGME programs, no programmatic practices were identified that focused on FGLI identity.[14] FGLI identity is not often visible, which further sidelines the struggles and challenges that FGLI learners face. Program directors should utilize information available in the application process and investigations during orientation to be better aware of their own residency's socio-economic make-up and make efforts to alleviate such feelings of invisibility among FGLI students by providing resources. To address this gap, it is imperative that GME programs move toward implementation of FGLI-informed practices to begin to repair the broken pathway. The authors propose a series of recommendations focusing on multiple aspects of learner support for program and Sponsoring Institution leadership to ensure an inclusive environment for FGLI learners (summarized in Table 14.1). These recommendations take many forms and include novel ideas such as the inclusion of FGLI learners' diverse communities and families through multilingual/multimedia communications. In general, each aspect aims to make the "hidden" knowledge of how to succeed in academic medicine visible to all while embracing the inherent diversity that exists among FGLI learners. This can help to ensure FGLI learners are entering workplaces where they will receive appropriate, class-conscious support from their programs, and will eliminate the invisibility factor that is faced by so many.

> Learners who come from households with incomes in the bottom 40% in the United States make up less than 10% of all medical learners. Meanwhile, learners from households with incomes in the top 20% make up over half of all medical learners (with 25% coming from households with incomes in the top 5%).

> FGLI learners are a demographically diverse, uniquely qualified group, and addressing their unique needs holds benefits for learners of many other marginalized identities, as well as patients and colleagues.

Table 14.1	Recommendations to Create an Inclusive GME Environment for FGLI Learners
Focus Area Within GME	**Recommendation for Program or Sponsoring Institution Leadership**
Academic Development	• Prioritize progress-informed and holistic evaluation of learners, accounting for non-traditional strengths. • Develop policies for destigmatized flexibility in meeting deadlines for learners facing adversity to account for additional familial responsibilities. • Provide funding for learning resources and opportunities. • Make class-consciousness an integrated component of the curriculum by ensuring learners understand how financial status affects their patients ability to receive care. • Include topics of class and income inequity in microaggression and bystander trainings. • Restructure awards and resident/fellow achievement opportunities in a class-conscious manner, moving away from traditional metrics of merit, such as test scores, to more holistic metrics.
Career Development	• Facilitate mentorship among FGLI faculty members, residents/fellows, and medical students. • Organize workshops on topics such as professional identity, financial management, mental health, and stress resilience. • Design education modules for medical educators on specific strategies to overcome the FGLI invisibility factor and acknowledge intersectionality. • Redesign and evaluate curricular workshops throughout medical school to address less explicit aspects of medical education culture (eg, what 'professionalism' means, reconciling FGLI and professional identities, balancing learners' ability to relate to patients with medical practice norms, and managing family and community of origin interactions during GME).
Financial Well-Being	• Consider non-loan options for supplemental funding and emergency funds. • Perform basic needs assessments to assess insecurity (housing, food, transportation) among FGLI house staff. • Subsidize or fully cover the cost of basic house staff materials, including orientation/board fees, any required equipment, and adequate relocation costs. • Provide relocation stipends for FGLI house staff.
Social and Cultural Aspects	• Ensure learners have ready access to free and accessible mental health services. • Designate a faculty or staff member with cultural experience among first-generation and low-income learners as the point person to receive, triage, and troubleshoot learners' questions and concerns. • Develop multilingual and multimedia communications to FGLI learners and their families. • Support FGLI house staff organizations and diversity/inclusion offices with appropriate funding and staff support. • Subsidize or fully fund entrance fees, apparel costs, and dues related to student/resident/fellow organizations and social events for all students/residents/fellows with significant financial need.

Take Home Points

- It is important to consider the FGLI identity among a program's own learners in order to recognize and alleviate challenges common to this group of learners and support their ability to thrive as physicians.
- GME programs and their Sponsoring Institutions should recognize both the strengths of the FGLI identity and the barriers that exist in the current educational and health care systems and make active efforts to improve inclusion of FGLI individuals in medicine.
- All stakeholders in medical education should recognize that classism exists at all levels of medical education and training and patient care. FGLI applicants to residency programs are less likely to match due to differences in evaluation and cost-prohibitive opportunities they are unable to pursue due to circumstances beyond their control.
- Medicine has a significant amount of "up-front" costs at all levels of education and training. It is important to put into place systems that can help defray these costs throughout the program in order to increase accessibility of careers in medicine to candidates from lower income backgrounds.

QUESTIONS FOR FURTHER THOUGHT

1. Do you know who the FGLI learners in your program or institution are? What are ways in which you can support them without singling them out? How will you incorporate more of these ideas into your program or institution to be more inclusive of FGLI learners?
2. How will your program formalize mentorship or sponsorship opportunities for FGLI learners?

Acknowledgments

We would like to acknowledge everyone who has supported FGLI residents and fellows, and in particular Drs Hyacinth Mason and Dowin Boatright for their critical input, expertise, and unwavering commitment to this field and our endeavors.

REFERENCES

1. Bettencourt GM, Mansour KE, Hedayet M, et al. Is first-gen an identity? How first-generation college students make meaning of institutional and familial constructions of self. *J Coll Stud Retent Res Theory Pract*. 2022 Aug;24(2): 271-289. doi: 10.1177/1521025120913302
2. Romero R, Miotto K, Casillas A, Sanford J. Understanding the experiences of first-generation medical students: implications for a diverse physician workforce. *Acad Psychiatry*. 2020 Aug;44(4):467-470. doi: 10.1007/s40596-020-01235-8
3. Youngclaus J, Roskovensky L. An updated look at the economic diversity of U.S. medical students. *AAMC Anal Breif*. 2018 Oct;18(5).
4. Grbic D, Garrison G, Jolly P. Diversity of U.S. medical school students by parental education. *AAMC Anal Brief*. 2010 Aug;9(10).
5. Sawyer DL, Gratreak BD. Medical schools must do more to open the door to first generation and low income students. *BMJ*. 2022 May 18;o1246.
6. Mason HRC, Ata A, Nguyen M, et al. First-generation and continuing-generation college graduates' application, acceptance, and matriculation to U.S. medical schools: a national cohort study. *Med Educ Online*. 2022 Dec 31;27(1):2010291. doi: 10.1080/10872981.2021.2010291
7. Brewer L, Grbic D. Medical students' socioeconomic background and their completion of the first two years of medical school. *AAMC Anal Brief*. 2010 Dec;9(11).

8. Nguyen M, Mason HRC, O'Connor PG, et al. Association of socioeconomic status with Alpha Omega Alpha honor society membership among medical students. *JAMA Netw Open*. 2021 Jun 2;4(6):e2110730. doi:10.1001/jamanetworkopen.2021.10730
9. Gomez LE, Bernet P. Diversity improves performance and outcomes. *J Natl Med Assoc*. 2019 Aug;111(4):383-392. doi: 10.1016/j.jnma.2019.01.006
10. Nguyen M, Desai MM, Fancher TL, Chaudhry SI, Mason HRC, Boatright D. Temporal trends in childhood household income among applicants and matriculants to medical school and the likelihood of acceptance by income, 2014-2019. *JAMA*. 2023;329(21):1882-1884. doi:10.1001/jama.2023.5654
11. Nguyen M, Song SH, Ferritto A, Ata A, Mason HRC. Demographic factors and academic outcomes associated with taking a leave of absence from medical school. *JAMA Netw Open*. 2021 Jan 22;4(1):e2033570. doi: 10.1001/jamanetworkopen.2020.33570
12. O'Marr JM, Chan SM, Crawford L, Wong AH, Samuels E, Boatright D. Perceptions on burnout and the medical school learning environment of medical students who are underrepresented in medicine. *JAMA Netw Open*. 2022 Feb 23;5(2):e220115. doi: 10.1001/jamanetworkopen.2022.0115
13. Nguyen M, Chaudhry SI, Desai MM, et al. Association of sociodemographic characteristics with US medical student attrition. *JAMA Intern Med*. 2022 Sep 1;182(9):917-924. doi: 10.1001/jamainternmed.2022.2194
14. Boatright D, London M, Soriano AJ, Westervelt M, Sanchez S, Gonzalo JD, et al. Strategies and best practices to improve diversity, equity, and inclusion among US graduate medical education programs. *JAMA Netw Open*. 2023 Feb 8;6(2):e2255110. doi: 10.1001/jamanetworkopen.2022.55110

Pathways to Graduate Medical Education for Foreign National Physicians and DACA Recipients

Mario Lorenzana De Witt, MD, PGY-1—Jacobi/Montefiore Emergency Medicine, Bronx, NY

Sunny Nakae, PhD, MSW, Senior Associate Dean for Diversity, Equity, Inclusion, and Partnership, Associate Professor of Medical Education, California University of Science and Medicine, Colton, CA

Tracy Wallowicz, MLS, Senior Vice President of External Relations and Chief of Staff, Intealth, Philadelphia, PA

CHAPTER SUMMARY

Many physicians in the United States are non-US citizens and make significant contributions to US health care. Some of these non-US citizen physicians include graduates of medical schools outside the United States and recipients of Deferred Action for Childhood Arrivals (DACA). Physicians with temporary statuses are engaged in US graduate medical education (GME) programs while facing unique challenges. Physicians from other countries add diversity to their GME programs, enhance language and cultural concordance with patients, and bring valuable diversity of thought and critical perspectives to their GME environments. However, their US experiences often include difficult immigration obstacles and other challenges in receiving equitable consideration and treatment. This chapter will provide insight into the experiences and contributions of DACA recipients and foreign national physicians in US GME and propose strategies to create more inclusive educational and clinical environments.

LEARNING OBJECTIVES

1. Review terminology associated with foreign national physicians and DACA recipients participating in US GME programs, as well as the challenges they face.
2. Examine the diversity of ethnicity, culture, lived experiences, and perspectives that foreign national and DACA physicians bring to GME in the United States.
3. Identify and mitigate regulatory and structural barriers that prevent foreign national and DACA physicians from thriving in US GME and in practice.

Case Study

Benito is a DACA recipient who seeks to study medicine in the United States. He faces unique challenges that other prospective students do not encounter in his application and matriculation to medical school because of his DACA status. For example, when applying to medical schools, he must specifically look only for schools that accept DACA recipients. In April 2024, only 74 schools accredited by the Liaison Committee for Medical Education

(continued)

accepted DACA recipients according to a list maintained by the Association of American Medical Colleges (AAMC).[1] No central list exists for osteopathic medical schools. His home state of Tennessee has no public state medical schools that accept DACA recipients, which means he will be required to apply to out-of-state schools, which is generally a more costly endeavor. Once accepted, finding financial aid will be more challenging than for his non-DACA peers since DACA recipients are not eligible for federal loans. Obtaining private loans is also challenging since these loans require US citizen cosigners; he has few members of his immediate family or social network who are US citizens and therefore he is unable to identify a willing or financially capable cosigner. Private loans also have higher interest rates and no deferment clauses, making them more costly. Benito is not eligible for a broad array of scholarships due to eligibility being limited to US citizens or permanent residents. He goes to his state newspaper in hopes of finding a donor or sponsor to lend him funds for 4 years of medical school. Eventually, Benito successfully gains admission to All-State Medical University, but faces challenges with matriculation due to lack of financial aid. Approximately 2 weeks before his start date, he finds a private sponsor and moves to his new state. The Dean of Admissions and financial aid staff at All-State Medical University are helpful and encouraging during this process; however, it is still a chaotic and stressful experience for Benito.

As matriculation approaches, he realizes there is a lack of awareness about DACA both among his peers and among those school administrators not involved in the admissions process. He worries about how this situation will affect his future and how he will encounter many such biases and misconceptions about his place in medicine. He encounters people who do not comprehend how he lacks legal status in the United States and why he cannot simply "fix it." Other biases he experiences include the perception that he is a drain on resources even though he and his family worked in the United States for many years, attended school, and paid taxes. His classmates are generally unaware of the challenges faced by undocumented immigrants, such as obtaining government identification or accessing health care. Administrators at Benito's medical school are not sure how to categorize him in the registration system because none of the limited categories of citizen, permanent resident, or international student visa holder are accurate for Benito's situation. Support staff cannot answer questions about background checks and security clearances for him, which are routinely required for preceptorships, clerkships, and the typical onboarding processes for students in the health care professions.

Residency will present similar challenges for Benito as he navigates the application process in a competitive, vast landscape of programs that generally lack transparency about their selection criteria and for whom they will consider for admission to their programs. The admissions staff at All-State Medical University were knowledgeable about DACA because they had students with similar statuses to Benito who matriculated before him. However, GME programs appear far less likely to have experience with DACA recipients. Benito will therefore face challenges around lack of awareness and bias about his status when seeking to match into a GME program of his choice. The private loans he secured to fund his medical degree may present additional challenges for Benito's GME journey, as they may lack deferment, hardship, or forgiveness contingencies like federal loans. This situation might impact his overall quality of life during residency as he is faced with comparatively more financial stress than his US-born peers.

Case Discussion

Benito's experience demonstrates both the struggles that DACA recipients face in applying and in receiving funding to attend medical school in the United States, as well as the lack of institutional awareness about DACA and the barriers that its recipients often face. There are many ways the process of applying to medical school and residency, as well as financing both, could have been improved for Benito and for other DACA recipients. As you read the chapter, consider what systems are (or are not) in place at your institution and what changes might be needed to provide opportunities and create more inclusive learning environments for DACA physician learners.

INTRODUCTION

This chapter addresses non-US citizen physicians and foreign national **international medical graduates (IMGs)**. Physicians in the United States who are non-US citizens include graduates of medical schools outside the United States and recipients of **DACA**, among others. Physicians with temporary statuses are engaged in US GME programs and provide critical contributions to US health care while facing unique challenges. Temporary statuses may include various types of employment or training visas, deferred action of deportation (via DACA or situationally granted), refugee, asylee, U-visa, or Temporary Protected Status. The breadth of experiences among non-citizen physician learners varies greatly by country of origin, impetus for temporary status, and the medical education structure of country or school of origin. This chapter does not address US citizen IMGs who are US citizens that attend medical school outside the United States. While these individuals still must have their foreign medical education credentials certified by the **Educational Commission for Foreign Medical Graduates (ECFMG)** to practice medicine in the United States, they generally do not face the same challenges as non-US citizen physicians.

This chapter will first describe and provide insight into the experiences and contributions of two main groups of non-US citizens on the medical education pathway, namely, international medical graduates on J-1 visas and DACA recipients. We will then describe recommendations for creating inclusive GME environments for foreign national physicians and DACA recipients.

J-1 PHYSICIANS IN GME

IMGs account for nearly 25% of the active US physician workforce, including those in GME programs and in practice.[2] Non-US citizen IMGs bring much-needed diversity to US medicine and provide quality patient care. While in their education programs, most non-US citizen IMGs migrate to the United States on **J-1 visas** sponsored by ECFMG. In 2022, ECFMG sponsored more than 13,000 foreign national physicians for training at more than 700 teaching hospitals across the United States. They came from about 150 different countries. Examining this cohort provides insight into the challenges faced by and distinct contributions of US physicians from other countries.

Beginning in 2017, the US government initiated a series of immigration measures that had the potential to significantly impact the ability of foreign national physicians to secure visas to enter the United States for training. With the onset of the COVID-19 pandemic in 2020, additional immigration challenges were introduced. Fortunately, the US Department of State, which administers the J-1 **BridgeUSA** program, proved to be instrumental in mitigating barriers to US immigration for these physicians. As a result, more than 98% of foreign national physicians who matched to US residencies were able to join their GME programs in 2020. This number is consistent with arrival percentages seen before 2017. However, the possibility of political threats impacting access for foreign national physicians remains present, as we saw in January of 2017 via Executive Order 13769 banning entry to the United States for individuals from Muslim-majority countries.

KEY CHALLENGES FOR IMGS SEEKING ENTRY INTO US GME PROGRAMS

The challenges faced by IMGs in applying to US GME programs start before they apply for residency, continue as they transition into their residency programs, and remain as they begin their education and training.[3] IMGs are less likely to be chosen to interview for a position in a residency program, and subsequently are less likely to secure a position than US medical graduates; higher US Medical Licensing Examination (*USMLE*®) scores for IMGs do not increase their likelihood of being chosen for an interview.[3] Additionally, there is evidence that some program directors categorically reject IMGs from consideration for positions in their programs.[2] Even after IMGs manage to secure a position in a residency program, they are likely to encounter linguistic, cultural, and ethnic barriers as they begin their education and training. Racial discrimination, which can be perpetrated by patients, peers, nurses, attending faculty members, or other individuals with whom the IMG will interact during their residency, is a significant issue; 23% of participants in a 1994 study on the issue reported at least one incident of ethnic harassment.[2]

IMGs may have limited access to financial capital from their families and countries of origin, as well as restrictions on financial resources in the United States, a situation that can negatively impact their overall experience and quality of life during training. They may also face challenges when applying for research funding since the majority of federal and state sources require applicants to be US citizens or permanent residents.

CONTRIBUTIONS OF FOREIGN NATIONAL PHYSICIANS

Physicians from other countries fill important gaps in both access to care and quality of care in US medicine. These include ethnic and cultural gaps in representation, as well as gaps experienced across specialties and geographic distribution. For instance, upon completion of training, many IMGs go on to work in underserved areas of the United States.[4] Additionally, a majority of J-1 physicians participate in primary care residencies.[5] By sharing ethnic, racial, or cultural backgrounds with diverse patient populations in underserved areas, many foreign national physician learners may positively affect health outcomes through language and/or cultural concordance. IMGs may be willing to participate in GME programs located in areas of the United States that experience physician shortages which expands access to medical care for patients in these areas.

IMGs are a cohort with great demographic diversity. According to 2022 data from ECFMG on J-1 physicians, the more than 13,000 IMGs sponsored by the ECFMG came from 150 different countries across the world.[6] The 10 countries with the highest number of J-1 physicians (the first being Canada with 2,783 J-1 physicians and the last being Colombia with 221 J-1 physicians) span four continents, from North and South America to Asia and Africa.[6] Combining data from ECFMG, the American Medical Association, and the Association of American Medical Colleges (AAMC), a 2008 study of diversity in the US physician workforce determined that the IMG population has more Asians and Latinos, fewer Blacks and American Indian/Pacific Islanders, and far fewer Whites than the US medical graduate population. Both groups had similar gender representation.[7]

A 2017 study of more than 1.2 million hospitalizations at US hospitals found that patients were slightly less likely to die within 30 days after admission if their physician completed medical school in another country, although this figure also includes US citizens who graduated from foreign medical schools.[8] However, the findings of this study underline the importance of ensuring that physicians from other countries are provided with opportunities to train and work in the United States.

DACA RECIPIENTS

In 2012, President Obama issued an executive order offering temporary immigration relief for thousands of young people who had been brought into the United States as children and resided in the country without lawful status. The policy, which is called **DACA**, offered work authorization and a temporary stay of deportation. Thousands of young people who had accessed higher education through state-specific policies

CHAPTER 15 • Pathways to GME for Foreign National Physicians and DACA Recipients

(ie, Development, Relief, and Education for Alien Minors [DREAM] Acts) were now able to formally enter the workforce. This work authorization opened doors for access to medical education, as completion of graduate education (including medical school and residency training) and full licensure, became possible. US medical schools welcomed the first cohort of **undocumented immigrant** students with DACA status in 2013. Since then, DACA recipients have continued to enter medicine, contributing critical perspectives, cultural capital, and language skills to health care. Although many structural and interpersonal barriers remain, DACA recipients continue to pursue careers in medicine. It is worth noting that prior to DACA there were a small number of undocumented students who graduated from medical school that were unable to continue their education. Some pursued other avenues, others were able to finally adjust their status after years of attempts, and some who had stepped out were granted DACA and were able to complete their GME after receiving their MD degree.

Starting in the 2014-2015 cycle, the AAMC formally recognized DACA recipients on the common application to medical school (*AMCAS*®) by adding a specific designation under the citizenship/immigration status section. (See Table 15.1.) In 2017, a designation for DACA was added to the Electronic Residency Application Service (*ERAS*®) application. DACA recipients differ from IMGs in that they do not require sponsorship of a visa to enter GME programs. Their work authorization is completed through a regular I-9 employment eligibility verification with a social security number issued every 2 years by the US Citizenship and Immigration Services, which administers the DACA program. Having a specific designation in

Table 15.1 Applicants, Acceptees, and Matriculants with Deferred Action Childhood Arrivals (DACA) Status to US MD_Granting Medical Schools, Academic Years 2018-2019 Through 2022-2023

The table below displays the number of applicants, acceptees, and matriculants with DACA status to US MD-granting medical schools from 2018-2019 through 2022-2023. Please email datarequest@aamc.org if you need further assistance or have additional inquiries.

Applicants, Acceptees, and Matriculants	Academic Year	DACA		Total
		Number	Percent of Total	
Applicants	2018-2019	150	0.3	52,777
	2019-2020	134	0.3	53,370
	2020-2021	148	0.3	53,030
	2021-2022	208	0.3	62,443
	2022-2023	159	0.3	55,188
Acceptees	2018-2019	43	0.2	22,483
	2019-2020	38	0.2	22,687
	2020-2021	50	0.2	23,105
	2021-2022	71	0.3	23,711
	2022-2023	55	0.2	23,810
Matriculants	2018-2019	42	0.2	21,622
	2019-2020	35	0.2	21,869
	2020-2021	46	0.2	22,239
	2021-2022	65	0.3	22,666
	2022-2023	53	0.2	22,712

Each academic year includes applicants, acceptees, and matriculants that applied to enter medical school in the fall of the given year. For example, academic year 2022-2023 represents the applicants, acceptees, and matriculants that applied to enter medical school during the 2022 application cycle.

> An IMG physician's cultural background can allow for greater understanding of diverse patient needs and contribute to improved health outcomes. For example, an IMG physician may speak a non-US born patient's language and be able to provide language-concordant care, which has been shown to improve health outcomes.

> DACA allows for undocumented immigrants who came to the United States as children to receive authorization to work. Although there are some provisions in place for DACA recipients to attend medical school, their status can make the process more challenging.

ERAS® was a step forward, but certainly did not mitigate all barriers to GME for DACA graduates applying for residency. Many programs were unaware of DACA or routinely screened only for US citizens and permanent residents. Nakae et al raised awareness about the issue in support of DACA learners.

Key Challenges Faced by DACA Students in the Medical Education Pathway

The largest barrier for DACA recipients seeking careers in medicine is lack of financial aid. As non-citizens, DACA recipients are ineligible for federal aid. Although many manage to self-fund through private loans and scholarships, the financial factor remains one of the most important obstacles for many. In addition, not all medical schools consider applications from DACA recipients, largely due to lack of awareness, restrictive state policies, or anticipated challenges with funding. DACA recipients may also experience increased stress related to the stability and well-being of their family members with vulnerable statuses. Many students and residents live with constant worry of deportation of family members, financial hardships, and mistreatment by employers or law enforcement agents. DACA recipients have similar restrictions to eligibility for research funding as IMGs, since they are not US citizens or permanent residents which can negatively impact those seeking a career in academia after residency.

Contributions of DACA Students and Physicians

According to a study by Pre-Health Dreamers, a national organization that provides resources for undocumented young people in the United States on the path to becoming physicians, 98% of DACA recipients are bilingual, speaking at least one language additional to English.[9] Because they are members of undocumented communities who commonly experience difficulties in accessing health care, DACA recipients bring critical perspectives to GME programs in serving patients who are uninsured and have limited or no access to health care. Thus, it is critically important to recognize and champion the rights of these physicians as they pursue their medical education and training.

STRATEGIES TO MITIGATE BARRIERS TO IMG AND DACA PHYSICIANS THRIVING IN GME AND BEYOND

We propose several recommendations that GME programs and Sponsoring Institutions should consider in order to create an inclusive learning environment for IMGs and DACA physician learners.

1. *Utilize and implement holistic principles in selection processes that recognize and value the skills and backgrounds of IMG and DACA applicants.* These principles can include more recognition for language skills, experiences working with underserved communities, exposure to immigration challenges, and understanding of the structural determinants of health, etc.
2. *Avoid systemic discrimination and use of filters that select only for US citizens.* Commit to reviewing the pool of applicants without prejudice for immigration status.
3. *Provide an accessible list of scholarships, research funding opportunities, grants, and other forms of financial assistance that DACA recipients and IMGs are eligible to access nationally and at your institution.*

4. ***Increase institutional awareness about DACA policies and the challenges that DACA recipients face throughout their medical education.*** Educate stakeholders and review process data to ensure that IMGs and DACA recipients have equitable access to your GME programs. Institutional awareness is especially critical in helping DACA-recipient students matriculate and achieve success in their medical careers. A better understanding of barriers can help faculty and selection committees create better solutions for DACA-recipient students, and thus make the process more equitable. For example, the AAMC has a list of medical schools and their respective DACA policies.[1] No such centralized list exists for residency programs to help DACA recipients select programs to apply. The ACGME and the AAMC have distributed a guide for programs directors for consideration of DACA recipients each year since 2015. More resources are needed to help allopathic and osteopathic graduates who are DACA recipients connect with GME programs that would welcome and value their talent. This list needs to grow as programs increasingly realize the importance of including these physicians as trainees.
5. ***Provide resources to reduce economic hardship and disparities among all residents in your program so every learner can thrive.*** These resources might include robust coaching and mental well-being services, board examination preparation, tutoring, housing assistance, etc.

Take Home Points

- IMGs constitute nearly 25% of the active US physician workforce. In 2022, over 13,000 foreign national physicians were training at more than 700 US teaching hospitals, coming from approximately 150 different countries. This diversity enriches the US medical field, with many IMGs contributing significantly to primary care and working in underserved areas, providing much-needed healthcare service
- IMGs often face significant barriers, including difficulties in securing interviews and positions in residency programs. These challenges persist even for those with high USMLE scores. Upon entering residency, IMGs may encounter linguistic, cultural, and ethnic discrimination, as well as financial constraints due to limited access to financial resources from their home countries and restrictions on funding in the United States.
- One of the most significant challenges for DACA recipients is the lack of access to federal financial aid. Many medical schools do not consider applications from DACA recipients due to restrictive state policies or institutional unawareness, further complicating their pathway to medical education

QUESTIONS FOR FURTHER THOUGHT

1. How can we collectively work to better create equitable and inclusive training environments for physicians with non-US citizenship status?
2. Who are the key stakeholders involved in facilitating pathways to GME for international medical graduates and DACA recipients?
3. Which patient populations in your program's service area might be better served by including international medical graduates and DACA recipients in the physician workforce pathway?

Acknowledgments

We would like to thank the students and residents who have shared their journeys with us over the years. Their stories have made our advocacy possible. Their trust has empowered us to make change. Their excellence continues to inspire us.

REFERENCES

1. Association of American Medical Colleges. Medical School Admission Requirements™ (MSAR®) report for applicants and advisors. 2023 Deferred Action for Childhood Arrivals (DACA). https://students-residents.aamc.org/media/7031/download
2. Association of American Medical Colleges. Active physicians who are international medical graduates (IMGs) by specialty, 2021. Published December 31, 2021. Accessed June 1, 2023. https://www.aamc.org/data-reports/workforce/data/active-physicians-international-medical-graduates-imgs-specialty-2021
3. Murillo Zepeda C, Alcalá Aguirre FO, Luna Landa EM, et al. Challenges for international medical graduates in the US graduate medical education and health care system environment: a narrative review. *Cureus*. 2022;14(7):e27351. doi:10.7759/cureus.27351
4. American Immigration Council. Foreign-trained doctors are critical to serving many U.S. communities. Published January 17, 2018. Accessed June 1, 2023. https://www.americanimmigrationcouncil.org/sites/default/files/research/foreign-trained_doctors_are_critical_to_serving_many_us_communities.pdf
5. Intealth. ECFMG J-1 visa sponsorship: specialties pursued by exchange visitor Physicians, 2021. Published November 2, 2022. Accessed June 1, 2023. ecfmg.org. https://www.intealth.org/data/#j1
6. Intealth. ECFMG J-1 Visa sponsorship: top 10 nations of origin, 2021. Published November 3, 2022. Accessed June 1, 2023. ecfmg.org. https://www.intealth.org/data/#j1
7. Norcini JJ, van Zanten M, Boulet JR. The contribution of international medical graduates to diversity in the U.S. physician workforce: graduate medical education. *J Health Care Poor Underserved*. 2008;19(2):493-499. doi:10.1353/hpu.0.0015
8. Tsugawa Y, Jena AB, Orav EJ, Jha AK. Quality of care delivered by general internists in US hospitals who graduated from foreign versus US medical schools: observational study. *BMJ*. 2017;356:j273. doi:10.1136/bmj.j273
9. Pre-Health Dreamers. Institutional guidance: medicine. phdreamers.org. Accessed February 23, 2023. https://www.phdreamers.org/resource-medicine

ADDITIONAL RESOURCES

Nakae S, Rojas Marquez D, Di Bartolo IM, Rodriguez R. Considerations for residency programs regarding accepting undocumented students who are DACA recipients. *Acad Med*. 2017;92(11):1549-1554. doi:10.1097/ACM.0000000000001731

Garcia A, Lapidus A, De Witt ML, et al. Deferred action for childhood arrivals (DACA): maximizing impacts in medical education and health care. *MedEdPORTAL*. 2022;18:11279. https://doi.org/10.15766/mep_2374-8265.11279

Kuczewski M, Nakae S. Universities seek DACA recipient strategies. *Health Progress*. 2017:98(4):15-21. Accessed February 23, 2023. https://www.chausa.org/publications/health-progress/archives/issues/july-august-2017/universities-seek-daca-recipient-strategies

Kaushal N, Kaestner R, Rigzin T. Foreign-trained physicians in the United States: a descriptive profile. *Med Care Res Rev*. 2022;79(5):717-730. doi:10.1177/10775587211066994

Mick SS, Comfort ME. The quality of care of international medical graduates: how does it compare to that of U.S. medical graduates? *Med Care Res Rev*. 1997;54(4):379-413. doi:10.1177/107755879705400401

Pinsky WW. The importance of international medical graduates in the United States. *Ann Intern Med*. 2017;166(11):840-841. doi:10.7326/M17-0505

Butt A, Mankbadi M, Erikson C, et al. Bias against international medical graduates in the hematology/oncology fellowship recruitment process: findings from a nationwide survey of fellowship program directors. *JCO Oncol Pract*. 2022;18(12):783-787. doi:10.1200/OP.22.00219

Woofter R, Sudhinaraset M. Differences in barriers to healthcare and discrimination in healthcare settings among undocumented immigrants by Deferred Action for Childhood Arrivals (DACA) status. *J Immigr Minor Health*. 2022;24(4):937-944. doi:10.1007/s10903-022-01346-4

Arias FD. The barriers to medical school for DACA students continue. *Acad Med*. 2017;92(8):1072. PMID: 28742567

Kuczewksi MG. Addressing systemic health inequities involving undocumented youth in the United States. *AMA J Ethics*. 2021;23(2):E146-E155. doi:10.1001/amajethics.2021.146

Sudhinaraset M, To TM, Ling I, Melo J, Chavarin J. The influence of Deferred Action for Childhood Arrivals on undocumented Asian and Pacific Islander young adults: through a social determinants of health lens. *J Adolesc Health*. 2017;60(6):741-746. doi:10.1016/j.jadohealth.2017.01.008

Carranco S, Carrasquillo O, Young B, Kenya S. Is medicine just a DREAM for DACA students? DACA practices and policies among U.S. medical schools. *J Immigr Minor Health*. 2022;24(1):300-303. doi:10.1007/s10903-021-01211-w

Svaljenka NP. A demographic profile of DACA recipients on the frontlines of the coronavirus response. Center for American Progress. Published April 6, 2020. Accessed February 23, 2023. https://www.americanprogress.org/article/demographic-profile-daca-recipients-frontlines-coronavirus-response/

16

Creating an Inclusive Environment for Multilingual Learners and Faculty Members

Pilar Ortega, MD, MGM, Vice President, Diversity, Equity and Inclusion, ACGME; Clinical Associate Professor, Departments of Medical Education and Emergency Medicine, University of Illinois College of Medicine, Chicago, IL

Itzel López-Hinojosa, MD, Resident Physician, Department of Anesthesiology, University of Michigan, Ann Arbor, MI

CHAPTER SUMMARY

Language is a fundamental aspect of identity and a critical tool that physicians use in patient care. In the health care setting, language concordance is achieved when the clinician and patient communicate directly in the same language, either between themselves or with the help of a professional medical interpreter. Language-appropriate health care, achieved through language concordance has been shown to improve health outcomes. Despite the growing number of patients in the United States with non-English language preferences, the language skills of resident physicians and faculty members have remained largely unexplored. Additionally, learners and faculty members from linguistically diverse backgrounds often report being burdened, discriminated against, or mistreated based on their perceived language abilities. In this chapter, we aim to share strategies that can enhance programs' efforts to recruit, retain, and support residents and faculty members with diverse linguistic backgrounds who can uniquely address the language needs of their patient populations. We will examine key challenges faced by multilingual physicians in graduate medical education (GME) programs and propose strategies for improving the recognition, incentivization, and sense of belonging of residents and faculty members with multilingual skills in the GME setting.

LEARNING OBJECTIVES

1. Describe the linguistic profile of residents, faculty members, and leadership in GME.
2. Explore the intersectionality of language with other identities, such as culture, race, ethnicity, and ancestry.
3. Identify the challenges encountered by multilingual residents and faculty members in GME programs.
4. Create strategies for enhancing the recognition, incentivization, and sense of belonging of residents, fellows, and faculty members with multilingual skills in the GME setting.

Case Study

Clara, a second-year resident who is proficient in Spanish and English, is caring for Ms K, a 78-year-old Arabic-speaking woman from Iraq admitted for sepsis and altered mental status. Ms K is accompanied by her four adult English-speaking children. Ms K's past medical history is complex, including severe aortic regurgitation, end stage renal disease, a remote history of female circumcision due to tribal customs, and multiple

(continued)

recent admissions for urinary tract infections. Clara observes that medical decisions for Ms K are made as a family and community, but sometimes the plans of care change depending on what family member is at the bedside. Each child communicates differently with Clara and the health care team. For example, the youngest son tends to use medical terminology and answer Clara's questions without consulting other family members. In contrast, the oldest daughter is less communicative with Clara and frequently calls a sibling for support when Clara updates or asks questions, causing Clara to use simpler language to explain things. Siblings share information with each other in Arabic, raising Clara's concerns about potential information gaps. Clara also notices differences in how each family member communicates (eg, the types of questions they ask, the facial expressions they make, and body language used) leading her to question if they all understand her equally well.

Clara decides to bring up the language concerns during rounds and suggests holding a family meeting with a professional Arabic-English medical interpreter. The attending physician at first expresses disbelief, "Really? They all speak English. I never had a problem communicating with them." Another team member adds, "If you offer an interpreter, they will probably refuse. I'm pretty sure one of the nurses on the floor speaks Arabic, though. Do you want me to call them?"

Clara is able to advocate for the patient and her family by describing some of the reasons why differences in language skills may be contributing to confusion and differing perceptions about Ms K's care among her children. Even though Clara's non-English skills are not concordant with the language preferences of Ms K and her family, Clara's own identity as part of a linguistically minoritized group allows her to identify subtle signs of language-related miscommunication in a highly complex medical situation. Additionally, having been asked to serve as an ad hoc interpreter many times herself, Clara is able to articulate the reasons why it would not be ideal to call upon the Arabic-speaking nurse for this meeting. The attending physician ultimately agrees with coordinating a professional interpreter-mediated family meeting.

Case Discussion

Clara noticed communication differences among Ms K's family members that were overlooked by the health care team. Reflecting on this case, consider how Clara's multilingual identity and prior lived experiences informed her ability to care for this patient and her family. In addition, contemplate how the family's stated and perceived communication preferences affected the clinical learning environment for Clara. Patients and families with non-English language preferences may be perceived as more likely to refuse care, interpersonally difficult or unengaged, or having low health literacy. These inaccurate and harmful stereotypes may have played a role in whether Ms K's family was offered a professional medical interpreter. These stereotypes may also harm learners from linguistically diverse backgrounds who may have experienced similar situations during their own family members' interactions with the health care system. As you review the chapter, consider what could have gone differently in this scenario and what systems are in place at your institution for learners, faculty members, and staff to gain skills in effective communication for linguistically diverse encounters and to advocate for language-appropriate communication.

INTRODUCTION

Language is a core aspect of identity and the principal tool that physicians use in caring for patients. Achieving language-appropriate health care through **language concordance**[1] or professional medical interpreters[2] have been shown to improve health outcomes. Language concordance occurs when a clinician and patient directly and effectively communicate in the same language; for example, a physician is said to be language-concordant with a patient if she is able to perform her usual medical duties with the patient in the patient's preferred language. By contrast, professional medical interpreters are individuals who are trained and qualified to facilitate communication by orally changing words from one language to another, and vice versa, during language-discordant health care encounters. Both language-concordant and interpreter-mediated communication are evidence-based strategies to achieve language-appropriate health care responsive to patient needs. However, implementing such health care requires a multifaceted approach involving health policy, research, education, and collaboration across various disciplines.[3]

Medical education plays a crucial role in ensuring language-appropriate health care by teaching and assessing communication skills with linguistically diverse populations. During their education and training, physician learners establish practice habits that will follow them for their entire career. When shortcuts that result in linguistic discrimination through substandard care of patients are permitted and modeled in the clinical learning environment, these practices may create or normalize career-long habits that can impact a learner's care of patients longitudinally. In addition to their academic contributions to medical education, practicing physicians, residents, and fellows with **multilingual** skills are in a unique position to address the health care needs of linguistically marginalized populations and advance health equity for all.

Representation of Linguistically Diverse Physicians in GME

Despite the increasing number of patients in the United States with **non-English language preferences**, the language skills of physician learners and faculty members have not been thoroughly studied and no detailed description of the linguistic profile of these GME learners and faculty members has been published.[4] This knowledge gap presents a critical challenge in equitably addressing the language needs of the public. Without a basic understanding of the languages spoken by physician learners and faculty members, it becomes difficult to teach effective communication with diverse patient populations or determine the resources needed to comply with federal requirements for language assistance services.

According to the data from the *Electronic Residency Application Service® (ERAS®)* in 2013, 84% of applicants reported some skills in a non-English language, with Spanish being the most commonly reported language (53%), followed by Hindi, French, Urdu, and Arabic.[5] These data debunk the misconception that multilingualism is only relevant to a small group of medical students or residents and fellows, or that it pertains only to individuals from specific cultural or ethnic backgrounds. Rather, non-English language skills are common but understudied and underrecognized in GME. When exploring the representation of linguistic diversity among physicians it is important to consider certain nuances. For example, not all individuals who report having *some* skills in a language are ready to use those skills in patient care. Proficiency level in a language can vary greatly among individuals depending on their prior exposure, education, and the context in which the language is being used.[5] Someone may feel comfortable using a language to order food at a restaurant but not be competent to explain the risks and benefits of a medical procedure in that language. In a study of *ERAS®* data, while 84% of applicants reported some language skills, only 50% reported that their skills were at an advanced level or higher.[5] Another study of practicing physicians found that while 40% of respondents were multilingual, only 10% of them (25% of multilingual physicians, on average) reported using non-English languages with patients.[6]

Population language characteristics reveal that residents and fellows with particular non-English language skills are not equally distributed across metropolitan areas, resulting in significant mismatches between physician learners' language skills and the language needs of the local population.[7] Nationally, while Spanish is the most commonly reported language skill among physicians, it also has the lowest ratio of Spanish-speaking resident physicians to Spanish-speaking patients with only 14 resident physicians per 100,000 Spanish speakers. Moreover, the languages with the greatest deficit in language-proficient physicians vary by local population with Tagalog, a Philippine language, having the greatest discrepancy in local misalignment depending on the city. For instance, the Tagalog-speaking resident-to-patient ratio is 70/100,000 in New York City and is as low as 0/100,000 in San Diego, San José, and Seattle.[7]

Understanding the language profile of physicians requires a nuanced understanding of language as deeply contextualized and intersectional with other aspects of identity, such as race, ethnicity, educational background, and culture.[8] Multilingual physician learners and faculty members frequently report overburdening, discrimination, and mistreatment related to the languages they speak or are perceived to speak. Therefore, it is critical to address the key challenges faced by multilingual physicians and propose strategies for programs to improve the recruitment, retention, and support of residents, fellows, and faculty members with linguistically diverse backgrounds. In what follows, we will explore these challenges and propose strategies for promoting equity and inclusion in medical education and practice.

KEY CHALLENGES FACED BY MULTILINGUAL PHYSICIANS IN GME PROGRAMS

Overburdening Learners Who Have Non-English Language Skills

Perhaps the most common challenge reported by physicians with multilingual skills is related to overburdening, sometimes known as the "minority tax." This refers to situations where multilingual physicians, or those perceived to speak a certain language, are asked to serve as a **medical interpreter**, placing additional demands on their time and expertise.[9] It is difficult to estimate the burden of ad hoc medical interpreting on multilingual physicians, as physician language skills are not consistently documented, and **ad hoc medical interpreting** is unofficial and may never be tracked by the health care system. This can lead to underestimation of the need for language assistance services, such as professional medical interpreters, and result in a vicious cycle where insufficient resources are allocated for the care of linguistically diverse groups. The gap is often filled by untrained multilingual students, physician learners, and staff, who are often unpaid and not properly prepared for the task. This situation is representative of the argument that "something is better than nothing," but ultimately fails to address the need for quality language-appropriate care.

There are several unintended negative consequences of using physician learners as medical interpreters. First, ad hoc interpreting is substandard patient care that increases the risk of medical error.[2,10] Residents and fellows who have some multilingual skills may not have sufficiently advanced **medical language proficiency** to effectively communicate in a health care context. Despite federal regulations that require professional services for language-appropriate communication, studies evaluating health systems' practices consistently identify ad hoc interpreting as the most common communication technique used for linguistically minoritized groups.[10] This reliance on untrained interpreters not only puts patients at risk, but it also places an undue burden on physician learners, staff, and faculty members who are expected to fulfill the role of a professional medical interpreter without adequate training, compensation, or recognition. Moreover, this practice perpetuates the notion that multilingual residents and fellows are solely or primarily valued for their language skills, rather than for their clinical competence, contributions to patient care, or scholarly merits.

Secondly, asking a physician learner to serve as an interpreter when this is not their role sets up a psychologically unsafe clinical learning environment. Psychological safety includes being able to speak up and be oneself without fear of negative retribution. Yet, when a faculty physician asks a resident or fellow to interpret, the power dynamics of the situation may prevent a learner from admitting their discomfort with the task of serving as an interpreter. Additionally, physician learners may feel a personal obligation to help the patient and community, even when it involves ad hoc interpreting rather than providing language-concordant care as a physician. This is particularly true when the situation is perceived as urgent or if they do not believe there are any better alternatives. In fact, the role of ad hoc interpreter may be one that the physician has internalized since childhood from serving as an ad hoc child interpreter and health care navigator for their own family.[11] A third unintended consequence of physician learners serving as ad hoc interpreters is that they may not have enough time to complete other essential tasks for their medical training. Some report concerns that they are not gaining sufficient experience caring for other populations or that their clinical load is higher than that of their monolingual English-speaking peers. As a result, ad hoc interpreting may negatively impact resident or fellow performance on milestones, case logs, standardized testing (eg, board examinations), and other educational outcomes. No research to date has examined these potential associations; at present, these are theoretical risks.

Discrimination, Bias, and Mistreatment

Multilingual learners may also face mistreatment related to their linguistic identity. Accent-based discrimination is a type of **linguistic discrimination** prevalent in health care,[12] with some patients refusing treatment from doctors who have perceived "foreign" accents. Physician learners with perceived foreign accents may be assumed to have less medical knowledge and inferior clinical skills by faculty members or peers. International medical graduates (IMGs) commonly experience bias, mistreatment, and stereotyping related to their accent. Interestingly, certain accents and linguistic features are associated with prestige, while others may be associated with a lower social class.[8] Learners from linguistically diverse backgrounds may choose not to disclose their language skills for fear of mistreatment, similar to patients who fear receiving substandard care if they report a non-English language preference.

Mispronouncing the names of individuals from linguistically diverse backgrounds or incorrect attribution of names to language skill is a common issue that can lead to stereotyping. For example, not all persons with a non-English name speak a non-English language, and the opposite may be true as well; individuals with an English name may be multilingual. Assuming language skills and background based on name may further disadvantage physicians and applicants throughout their educational and professional trajectories. Micro- and macroaggressions related to such assumptions include congratulating learners on their English skills, refusing to say someone's name out loud because it is considered difficult to pronounce, and suggesting alternative names for physician learners that are easier to pronounce or remember for monolingual English speakers. Names can be a source of bias in the application and interview process for medical school, residency, fellowship, and faculty positions. For example, some names may lead selection committee members to make unfounded assumptions about the candidate's English proficiency, immigration status, degree of acculturation, and overall "fit" within the institution. Additionally, advisors may discourage or passively not encourage learners from linguistically diverse backgrounds from pursuing subspecialty or academic careers.

INTERSECTIONALITY

Each individual from a linguistically diverse background is unique in how their language skills and identity intersect with other aspects of their personal and professional identity. These various elements collectively interact with the GME learning and clinical practice environments. Commonly, physician learners experience marginalization due to aspects of their identity that are interrelated with but also extend beyond language itself. One such instance is the intersection of language with race and ethnicity.

Medical students, residents, fellows, and practicing physicians who identify with certain racial and ethnic groups are more likely to report multilingual skills, according to *ERAS*® data. For example, 91% of Hispanic/Latinx (LHS+)applicants reported advanced or greater skills in Spanish, compared to 21% of the overall applicant pool.[5] The prevalence of advanced skills varied by nationality within the LHS+ community. Similarly, Asian *ERAS*® applicants reported higher-than-average rates of advanced proficiency in non-English languages, with the prevalence of advanced multilingualism ranging between 60% and 90% depending on linguistic group. For example, 90% of applicants identifying as Pakistani or Bangladeshi, 80% of Indian applicants, and 78% of Japanese respondents reported advanced or greater non-English language skills.[4] These findings underscore the importance of disaggregating data to gain a more nuanced understanding of the diverse attributes and skills represented within heterogeneous racial/ethnic categorizations. Practicing physician data show similar trends with multilingual physicians being significantly more likely than monolingual English-speaking physicians to identify as LHS+, Asian, or "other" race/ethnicity.[6] Multilingual physicians also were more likely to identify as women, practice in urban settings, and be IMGs, highlighting other areas of intersectionality. Factors such as family educational attainment, socioeconomic status, sexual orientation, religious preferences, and disability are areas of potential intersectionality that should be explored in future research.

Another example of how language intersects with other aspects of identity is seen in the experiences of IMG learners and faculty members. IMGs make up a significant portion of the US physician workforce, with 25% of practicing physicians being IMGs. These physicians disproportionately serve patients in underserved rural areas; many bring valuable expertise in non-English languages and an understanding of immigrant struggles based on their own lived experiences. In fact, 43% of US physicians who reported multilingual skills in a 2019 national survey were IMGs, accounting for nearly half of the linguistic diversity among practicing physicians in the United States.[6] Given that IMGs were actually underrepresented in that survey by 6%, the 43% number is likely a substantial underestimate of the linguistic contributions of IMGs in the United States. A study of patient outcomes showed decreased mortality for patients whose physician was an IMG, demonstrating that the skills that IMGs bring to US health care result in excellent quality care.[13] However, IMGs face discrimination when applying for residency and faculty positions and encounter structural barriers to academic success. Examples include restrictions on research grants for non-US citizens and unfamiliarity with and reluctance to undertake compliance with visa requirements by institutional/program leadership.

STRATEGIES TO IMPROVE LINGUISTIC DIVERSITY, EQUITY, AND INCLUSION IN GME

We recommend implementing the following five strategies to improve the recognition, incentivization, and sense of belonging of residents and faculty with multilingual skills in the GME setting:

1. ***Collect data about resident, fellow, faculty member, and leadership language skills.***
   Medical schools and GME programs should consider formally asking students, residents, and fellows about their language skills and assess their proficiency levels. The way language information is collected matters. Publicly available clinician directories often include the "languages" of practicing physicians as a field, but this information is typically collected in an informal binary fashion in which physicians may enter a list of any non-English languages they wish to report,[4] while few hospitals actually confirm or assess language proficiency.[14] Some clinicians may list languages that are spoken by staff in their medical practice but not necessarily by the physician themselves. Others may report a language even if they are not fully proficient and would still need a medical interpreter to provide language-appropriate care. While some institutions have no standardized protocol to determine when a physician or learner is deemed proficient enough to use a language in patient care, others place inappropriate demands on doctors who report non-English language skills, such as asking them to complete interpreter certification examinations not intended to assess nor credential direct, language-concordant care.

   We recommend that institutions collect data on the languages spoken by their physician learners, faculty members, and leadership, and ensure that the collected data accurately reflects the proficiency level of each individual, which may change over time. Clinician directories should be updated to include language proficiency levels, and hospitals should confirm and assess language proficiency levels before listing them publicly. By formalizing this process, institutions can better collect data on the language proficiencies of their physician learners, faculty members, and leadership. Moreover, previously collected language data about physician candidates may be available to institutions (eg, through the American Medical College Application Service® [*AMCAS*®] or *ERAS*® applications); medical schools and GME programs should consider ways to appropriately use such data to inform their policies and plan for the appropriate resources learners may need to enhance their skills in communicating with patients as they advance in their medical training.

   Institutions should also ensure that any demands or expectations related to language use by clinicians are appropriate and do not place undue burden on individuals who report non-English language skills. Collecting data about the language skills of learners, faculty members, and staff will help institutions understand the linguistic diversity of their staff. This important step will help to ensure that language-appropriate care is provided to patients. Ultimately, enhancing language data collection at the institutional level can further serve to drive resource allocation towards the goal of implementing language equity practices within GME, the institution, and/or health system.

To appropriately collect physician language data, programs can use a rapid, validated self-reporting tool, the Interagency Language Roundtable for health care scale (ILR-H).[15] The ILR-H has five levels that clinicians can choose from to describe their health care communication skills in a particular language. It is important to note that language self-assessment has limitations and should not replace formal proficiency testing. In particular, physicians who self-report skills in the intermediate range of the scale need objective assessment to more clearly delineate when they are able to competently provide language-concordant care. Using a validated self-assessment scale like the ILR-H can help institutions and programs collect accurate and useful data about the language skills of their learners and faculty members.[16] The ILR-H can be easily used as part of periodic surveys of residents, fellows, faculty members, and leadership to identify the language skills and proficiency levels of individuals in a GME program. The ILR-H has also been proposed as a tool to help identify individuals who are eligible for and interested in additional training, assessment, or certification for using a particular language in patient care.

In addition to institutional-level evaluations of linguistic diversity, there is a need to periodically update the national language trends of residency applicants, matriculants, and graduates to track the success of strategies that aim to recruit and retain linguistically diverse individuals. Simultaneously, institutions should be attentive to creating systems that are linguistically diverse at all levels, including faculty members and leadership. Collecting language skills information normalizes multilingualism and sends a message about language equity: non-English language skills are valued, and patients with non-English language preferences are as deserving of high-quality communication with their physician as any other patient.

2. **Intentionally recruit residents with multilingual skills, particularly those that match the patient population you serve.**

   Many learners with multilingual skills have a desire to provide language-concordant care for the linguistically marginalized populations with whom they identify. Therefore, programs should evaluate what opportunities they can offer for physician learners to develop their language-concordant communication skills and clinical experiences while ensuring that they are not pulled away from their responsibilities as physicians to provide ad hoc interpreting for faculty members, peers, or other health care staff members. This also involves ensuring that faculty members and staff are knowledgeable about language-appropriate health care, including how to access to language assistance services and how to apply communication strategies to work effectively with professional interpreters. Residency and fellowship applicants with multilingual skills may be seeking programs that offer opportunities for them to use their non-English language skills to contribute to their professional development as a multilingual physician and enhance their ability to provide high quality care to linguistically diverse communities.

   To recruit multilingual learners, GME programs should consider actively and publicly communicating information about the linguistic diversity of their patient population, faculty members, and physician learners. This signals to applicants that the program values multilingualism as an important factor in providing quality health care. Additionally, programs could share information about the types of curricular opportunities and educational resources available for language skills training. Many physician learners who report non-English languages may be attracted to programs that offer **medical language courses** as well as **medical language proficiency testing/certification** opportunities.[17] In terms of medical language proficiency testing/certification options, pilot validity evidence has been published for the Kaiser Permanente Clinician Cultural Language Assessment, and reliability and validity evidence have been published for the Physician Oral Language Observation Matrix.[17]

3. **Include language-appropriate health care as an educational objective for all learners.**

   Language-appropriate health care should be a learning and performance objective for all residents and fellows, regardless of the individual languages they speak. All physician learners must gain the skills to communicate effectively with patients from linguistically diverse backgrounds and partner effectively with professional interpreters to provide equitable care when language discordance occurs. Given the diverse US population, it is impossible for any individual physician to speak all the potential languages of the patients they serve. It is important to avoid placing the burden of providing language-concordant care solely on physicians with non-English language skills, as this can lead to burnout and decreased quality of care.

Linguistically diverse learners bring unique perspectives and experiences to the table. Learners who have themselves had to navigate health care systems in unfamiliar languages, or who watched their family doing so, may be able to relate to patients who are experiencing similar challenges. In some situations, such as our Case Study, these experiences may enable physicians to relate to patients, identify and problem-solve communication challenges, and provide high quality, personalized care even when they themselves do not share a common language with a particular patient or family. Programs can recognize the value of non-English language skills by providing linguistically diverse learners and faculty members with opportunities for educational, clinical, and scholarly leadership, as well as supporting educational innovations. For instance, programs can offer medical language courses to learners with intermediate language skills or higher to enhance their communication with patients. Medical Spanish is the most commonly offered **medical language course** in the United States,[18] and programs in medical Portuguese and medical Mandarin have also been reported.[19]

4. *Critically review the clinical learning environment for policies regarding language-appropriate care.*

GME leaders should familiarize themselves with the language-related policies in the clinical learning environments which physician learners rotate. These policies and their practical applications may vary between clinical sites. For example, some sites may have onsite professional medical interpreters for high frequency languages, whereas others may only have access to remote professional interpreting through a language line. Be mindful that all federally funded health care facilities are required by law to provide professional health care services in a patient's preferred language at no additional cost to the patient. When reviewing language policies, it is important to ensure that they protect patients and multilingual clinical staff from inappropriate use of ad hoc, untrained interpreters. Policies should explicitly state that family members (including children), untrained staff, and students should not be used as interpreters due to the risk of medical error. It is important to ensure that all leadership, faculty members, and residents are all aware of these policies.

As a next step, GME leaders should consider collaborating with language services departments and other interested parties to improve existing policies and practices to better serve linguistically diverse patients, learners, faculty members, and staff members. This may involve working together on initiatives to increase access to language assistance services, such as onsite or remote professional interpreting. Language services departments can also provide education and training for staff on how to access and effectively utilize these services. In addition, partnerships between programs and professional interpreters can include **language coaching**, whereby professional interpreters and faculty members work with physician learners having partial skills in a language to advance language-concordant care longitudinally throughout their education and training.[20] By working together, GME leaders and

> Physician learners who are perceived to speak a non-English language are frequently asked to serve as ad hoc interpreters, yet this practice can constitute mistreatment and result in substandard care for patients with non-English language preferences.

> As the country with the largest number of immigrants in the world, the United States is home to over 350 languages and over 67 million people who preferentially speak a non-English language. To ensure health equity for this growing population, it is essential to collect and track data about physician language skills and to teach residents and fellows best practices in communicating effectively with linguistically diverse populations through language-concordant care and by partnering with professional interpreters.

language services departments can create a more equitable and inclusive health care environment for all patients and clinicians.

If your institution offers training related to unconscious bias, anti-racism, and/or other aspects of diversity, equity, and inclusion, it is crucial to include linguistic diversity as an intersectional factor that is often overlooked in health care spaces. Everyone in the system, including leadership, faculty members, staff, physician learners, and members of selection and promotions committees should understand the common sources of inaccurate stereotyping and bias related to names, accents, and other characteristics of linguistically diverse groups in GME.

5. ***Respond appropriately to reports of mistreatment.***

As the value of linguistic diversity becomes increasingly recognized at your institution, you may find that learners become more attuned to identifying language-related mistreatment events that were previously underrecognized. As a result, GME leaders should be prepared to listen to learner concerns and respond appropriately. Asking residents and fellows to serve as ad hoc interpreters constitutes mistreatment (in addition to presenting a high risk of medical error and poor patient outcomes), yet it is a pervasive problem in clinical learning environments. A multifaceted approach is needed to address anticipated increases in reporting of this problem, and should include training faculty members, residents, fellows, and staff in appropriate use of language services, and teaching and incentivizing language-concordant care among learners and faculty members with confirmed language proficiencies.

Take Home Points

- Collecting data about the language profile of residents and fellows, faculty members, and leadership is an important step toward normalizing multilingualism and ensuring that individuals from linguistically diverse backgrounds feel supported and have a sense of belonging in GME programs.
- Language skills are dynamic, and persons who share ethnic or racial identities may vary greatly in their linguistic profile; hence, assumptions regarding language abilities should be avoided.
- Physician learners from linguistically diverse backgrounds often experience challenges such as being assumed to have medical language skills, being asked to serve as untrained interpreters, being criticized or stereotyped based on linguistic features (eg, accent), and other forms of bias and discrimination.
- Having non-English language skills is highly intersectional with other marginalized characteristics, such as ethnicity, race, national origin, and immigration status.
- GME programs can use multiple strategies to create a welcoming environment in which linguistically diverse physician learners can belong and thrive, such as normalizing multilingualism through thoughtful language data collection, teaching all residents, fellows, and faculty members to provide language-appropriate care, and responding appropriately to reports of mistreatment.

QUESTIONS FOR FURTHER THOUGHT

1. Physician learners who have skills in a language besides English may be able to use their skills for language-concordant care, improving care for your patient population. What additional benefits does multilingualism provide, and how can those benefits be highlighted and supported for linguistically diverse learners in your program?

2. What resources are available in your hospital, university, city, or local community that could be leveraged to enhance your GME program's support of multilingualism for physician learners and faculty members interested in pursuing additional language education or formal language proficiency testing?

Acknowledgments

We would like to acknowledge the directors and members of National Association of Medical Spanish for their scholarly contributions to the curricular development, program evaluation, and skills assessment pertaining to language-appropriate health care.

REFERENCES

1. Diamond L, Izquierdo K, Canfield D, Matsoukas K, Gany F. A systematic review of the impact of patient-physician non-English language concordance on quality of care and outcomes. *J Gen Intern Med*. 2019;34(8):1591-1606. doi:10.1007/s11606-019-04847-5
2. Karliner LS, Jacobs EA, Chen AH, Mutha S. Do professional interpreters improve clinical care for patients with limited English proficiency? A systematic review of the literature. *Health Serv Res*. 2007;42(2):727-754. doi:10.1111/j.1475-6773.2006.00629.x
3. Ortega P. Spanish language concordance in U.S. medical care: a multifaceted challenge and call to action. *Acad Med*. 2018;93(9):1276-1280. doi:10.1097/ACM.0000000000002307
4. Ortega P, Shin T. Language is not a barrier—it is an opportunity to improve health equity through education. Health Affairs Blog, July 30, 2021. https://www.healthaffairs.org/do/10.1377/forefront.20210726.579549/full/
5. Diamond L, Grbic D, Genoff M, et al. Non-English-language proficiency of applicants to US residency programs. *JAMA*. 2014;312(22):2405-2407. doi:10.1001/jama.2014.15444
6. Ortega P, Felida N, Avila S, Conrad S, Dill M. Language profile of the US physician workforce: a descriptive study from a national physician survey. *J Gen Intern Med*. 2022;38:1098-1101. doi:10.1007/s11606-022-07938-y
7. Diamond LC, Mujawar I, Vickstrom E, Garzon MG, Gany F. Supply and demand: association between non-English language-speaking first year resident physicians and areas of need in the USA. *J Gen Intern Med*. 2020;35(8):2289-2295. doi:10.1007/s11606-020-05935-7
8. Ortega P, Martínez G, Alemán MA, Zapién-Hidalgo A, Shin TM. Recognizing and dismantling raciolinguistic hierarchies in Latinx health. *AMA J Ethics*. 2022;24(4):E296-E304. Published April 1, 2022. doi:10.1001/amajethics.2022.296
9. Vela MB, Fritz C, Press VG, Girotti J. Medical students' experiences and perspectives on interpreting for LEP patients at two US medical schools. *J Racial Ethn Health Disparities*. 2016;3(2):245-249. doi:10.1007/s40615-015-0134-7
10. Flores G, Abreu M, Barone CP, Bachur R, Lin H. Errors of medical interpretation and their potential clinical consequences: a comparison of professional versus ad hoc versus no interpreters. *Ann Emerg Med*. 2012;60(5):545-553. doi:10.1016/j.annemergmed.2012.01.025
11. Rodriguez JA. My son, my interpreter. *J Gen Intern Med*. 2021;36(10):3232-3233. doi:10.1007/s11606-021-06867-6
12. Iheduru-Anderson K. Accent bias: a barrier to Black African-born nurses seeking managerial and faculty positions in the United States. *Nurs Inq*. 2020;27(4):e12355. doi:10.1111/nin.12355
13. Tsugawa Y, Jena AB, Orav EJ, Jha AK. Quality of care delivered by general internists in US hospitals who graduated from foreign versus US medical schools: observational study. *BMJ*. 2017;356:j273. Published February 2, 2017. doi:10.1136/bmj.j273
14. Diamond LC, Wilson-Stronks A, Jacobs EA. Do hospitals measure up to the national culturally and linguistically appropriate services standards? *Med Care*. 2010;48(12):1080-1087. doi:10.1097/MLR.0b013e3181f380bc
15. Diamond LC, Luft HS, Chung S, Jacobs EA. "Does this doctor speak my language?" Improving the characterization of physician non-English language skills. *Health Serv Res*. 2012;47(1 Pt 2):556-569. doi:10.1111/j.1475-6773.2011.01338.x
16. Diamond L, Chung S, Ferguson W, Gonzalez J, Jacobs EA, Gany F. Relationship between self-assessed and tested non-English-language proficiency among primary care providers. *Med Care*. 2014;52(5):435-438. doi:10.1097/MLR.0000000000000102
17. Diamond LC, Gregorich SE, Karliner L, et al. Development of a tool to assess medical oral language proficiency. *Acad Med*. 2023;98(4):480-490. doi:10.1097/ACM.0000000000004942
18. Ortega P, Diamond L, Alemán MA, et al. Medical Spanish standardization in U.S. medical schools: consensus statement from a multidisciplinary expert panel. *Acad Med*. 2020;95(1):22-31. doi:10.1097/ACM.0000000000002917
19. Pereira JA, Hannibal K, Stecker J, Kasper J, Katz JN, Molina RL. Professional language use by alumni of the Harvard Medical School Medical Language Program. *BMC Med Educ*. 2020;20(1):407. Published November 6, 2020. doi:10.1186/s12909-020-02323-x
20. Cowden JD, Martinez FJ, Dickmeyer JJ, Bratcher D. Culture and language coaching for bilingual residents: the first 10 years of the CHiCoS model [published online ahead of print, June 30, 2022]. *Teach Learn Med*. 2022;1-12. doi:10.1080/10401334.2022.2092113

Creating Inclusive Environments for Muslim Residents and Fellows

Deena Kishawi, MD, Case New England Medical Group, Women & Infants Hospital, Brown University, Providence, RI

CHAPTER SUMMARY

Muslim physician scientists have made significant contributions throughout history to the field of medicine, including advancements in anatomy, surgery, pharmacology, and medical ethics.[1] However, many Muslim American physicians report encountering non-inclusive work environments during their careers, and feel this contributes negatively to their sense of well-being.[2]

Such discrimination, prejudice, and Islamophobia may meaningfully and negatively affect Muslim physician learners' medical education since they face a unique set of challenges and barriers. For example, Muslim physician learners may require religious accommodations, such as for prayer areas, fasting during Ramadan, access to halal foods, modest clothing requirements (eg, *hijab*), and exemptions for religious holidays that are not readily offered and/or available in the learning environment.

Islam is the fastest growing religion worldwide and the third largest religion in the United States.[3] As the Muslim American population grows, there will be an increasing number of Muslim physician learners.[4] It is imperative, therefore, to create an inclusive environment that will have a positive effect on these learners, their patients, and the entirety of the health care system. This chapter intends to provide an overview of the basic tenets of Islam and identify discrimination, hardship, and other obstacles that Muslim Americans, and especially Muslim physician learners, may face. This chapter will also offer suggestions and recommendations regarding opportunities and solutions for inclusion, especially in a medical education environment.

LEARNING OBJECTIVES

1. Become familiar with the demographic landscape for Muslim Americans in medicine.
2. Describe the basic components of Islam and the challenges experienced by Muslim residents and fellows in graduate medical education (GME).
3. Develop strategies and solutions for inclusion of Muslim residents and fellows in GME.

Case Study

A general surgery resident, Farah Muhammad, who observes *hijab*, enters the operating room on the first day of her residency. Upon entering, Farah is reprimanded for wearing her white coat and *hijab*. Unsure of what to do, she quickly rushes out of the operating room and returns to the locker room. She remains in the locker room for a significant portion of the day, hoping to find a *hijab*-wearing woman who can guide her as she is new at this hospital and unsure what accommodations are in place for *hijab*. Eventually, after not encountering

(*continued*)

someone wearing a *hijab*, she reaches out to her surgery director and her program director. The surgery director informs Farah that she has never worked with a resident who wore *hijab*. Her program director is also unable to assist her, so Farah feels disheartened. She feels uncomfortable not wearing her white coat, as it is the only thing she felt was appropriate to wear in the operating room to keep her arms covered. She also feels uncomfortable removing her *hijab* or tying it in a turban, as she feels doing so takes away from her Muslim identity. Unsure of what to do and not wanting to appear "difficult" or "uninterested" on her first day of residency, she decides to come in the next day wearing a short-sleeve scrub shirt and bouffant cap. She makes this decision knowing that she will be very uncomfortable doing so.

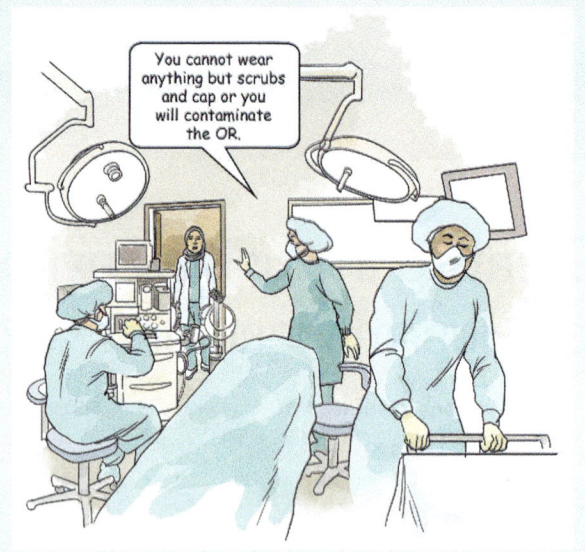

Case Discussion

This general surgery resident is faced with an identity conflict. She wants to be a compliant resident and attend to her duties while also being an observant Muslim. This case presents multiple barriers to the resident obtaining a meaningful educational experience in the operating room, including: an operating room staff member reprimanding the resident rather than presenting alternatives that would accommodate her religious beliefs; her own perception that she can only be in the operating room with a scrub bouffant cap or short sleeves; and, a lack of understanding and awareness of available accommodations by the surgery coordinator and the program director. Potential solutions involve:

- building an overall culture of inclusivity that incorporates educating the operating room staff members, the surgery coordinator, and the program director about accommodations for attire in the operating room for Muslims and other learners with modesty and/or other clothing preferences;
- educating operating room staff members, the surgery coordinator, and the program director about necessary accommodations for Muslim residents and fellows and/or other learners who wish to dress modestly;
- empowering learners with information about their right to accommodations; and,
- ensuring the availability of alternate attire in operating rooms.

In this case, the hospital does not have accommodations in place to allow the resident to wear *hijab* while simultaneously complying with substerile procedures. She is also uncomfortable advocating for herself. Therefore, she is limited in her ability to obtain a complete operating room learning experience. She is under the impression that she can only enter the operating room wearing a scrub bouffant cap or short sleeves. This lack of understanding likely causes a strain on her educational experience and a misperception that impacts the kind of clinical experiences in which she believes she will be able to participate. The surgery coordinator, Farah's program director, and Farah are all unaware that an accommodation exists, further exacerbating the situation. It is, however, possible to provide accommodation to allow for a *hijab*-wearing learner to participate in the operating room. This accommodation is made by providing a long sleeve scrub jacket that can be worn atop her short sleeve scrub shirt as well as a surgical hood that covers her *hijab*, or providing her with a light-colored, lint-free *hijab* that she can wear in the hospital.

As you review the chapter, consider how a similar situation would be approached at your institution, and what steps you might take to address accommodations related to a Muslim physician learner's religious practices.

DEMOGRAPHIC LANDSCAPE OF MUSLIM AMERICANS

Muslims account for approximately 3.5 million people in the United States; however, that number may be underestimated since some Muslims choose not to religiously identify due to fear of persecution, prejudice, and discrimination.[5-9] Muslims are a diverse and heterogenous group of people within which no racial or ethnic group makes up a majority of Muslim American adults. The vast majority of US Muslims are immigrants or children of immigrants from various ethnic and cultural backgrounds. Forty-one percent are White, a category that includes those who describe their race as Arab, Middle Eastern, or Persian/Iranian, or in a variety of other ways. About one-third are Asian and one-fifth are Black. Fewer are Hispanic (8%), and an additional 3% identify with another race or with multiple races.[10] Given the diversity of the US Muslim population, Muslim practices may vary based on personal beliefs and other factors. There are different sects of Islam–Sunni and Shia being the most common. But even within sects, there are different levels of personal observance. Some Muslims may practice at a stricter level in compliance with more traditional interpretations of the religion and associated religious text, while others may practice with more personal interpretation and modern context. Although US Muslims represent only about 1% of the total US population, they comprise 5% of the US health care workforce.[4,11]

Muslim contributions to the medical field began as far back as Ibn Sina (Avicenna) (AD 980-1037) whose book, *The Canon of Medicine*, was a comprehensive medical encyclopedia that remained a standard medical textbook in Europe and the Islamic world for centuries. The history of medicine is rich with discoveries of Muslim physicians, including Ibn al Nafis (AD 1213-1288) who discovered pulmonary circulation and Al-Zahwawi (AD 936-1013), often referred to as "the father of modern surgery," whose books featured surgical techniques that greatly influenced surgical practices at that time. More recently, Ayub Ommaya, MD, ScD, FRCS, FACS (AD 1930-2008) was a neurological surgeon known for his pioneering work in the development of the Ommaya reservoir, a device used to deliver drugs directly to the brain to treat brain tumors and neurological disorders. Dr Huda Zoghbi, MD (AD 1954-) is a neurologist and geneticist who discovered the genetic basis of several neurological disorders, including Rett syndrome.

Recent surveys have reported that nearly half of US Muslim physicians feel their work environment is unwelcoming and not inclusive. US Muslim physicians felt greater scrutiny at work, feel they have been passed over for career advancement due to their religion, and believe that religious discrimination has taken place often during their careers.[2,12,13] Follow-up qualitative surveys reveal participants feel that organizational structures do not allow them to engage in their religious practices and observances and that religious discrimination has impacted their personal well-being and may have impacted their career trajectory. Interestingly, participants also believe that institutions could implement specific educational and policy interventions to advance the religious accommodation of Muslims in health care.[2,12,14]

Despite efforts to increase minority populations in the workforce, US Muslims face obstacles in negotiating their professional and personal identities that can lead to adverse effects on their individual well-being, negatively impact their career advancement, and affect patient care and health care equity. It is incumbent upon medical education to provide an environment that fosters a culture of inclusivity so that learners' education, well-being, and ability to provide quality health care to patients is not adversely affected.

KEY CHALLENGES

The need for accommodations that are not always readily accessible to them may create challenges for Muslim residents and fellows as they strive to feel integrated in the learning environment. When they ask for such accommodations, they may feel as though they are a burden or that they are excluded from full acceptance in their GME setting. Challenges resulting from discrimination and Islamophobia that Muslim residents and fellows could commonly face in GME can emerge from others' perceptions of their modesty and dress requirements, dietary restrictions, religious holidays and observance, and conduct of regular daily and weekly prayers. The next section of the chapter will review examples of Muslim religious practices in greater detail, along with proposed strategies for creating inclusive GME environments.

Creating an inclusive environment for Muslims in GME may result in an increased sense of belonging, increased recruitment and retention of religiously and culturally diverse candidates, increased well-being and mental health, and, ultimately, improved patient care.[2,5,11,12,14-16] For example, by increasing their sense of belonging, Muslim physician learners may experience reduced feelings of isolation, increased feelings of acceptance in their learning environment, and improved attitudes toward medical education overall. Such positive effects may, in turn, impact their mental health by improving their sense of well-being. Because Muslim residents and fellows are vulnerable to microaggressions and additional stressors as a result of Islamophobia and discrimination; inclusive learning environments may alleviate such experiences so they can better focus on patient care rather than on how to deal with unnecessary stress.[5,12,13] Similarly, when a learning environment is inclusive and religious practices are respected and accommodated, the result may be increased recruitment and retention of Muslim learners, since they will not find it necessary to compromise their religious values as a result of the demands of their education. Accommodations that enable Muslim physicians to continue to learn and practice may even have a trickle-down effect on patient care with improved health outcomes, reduced health care disparities, and increased patient satisfaction.[12-14]

STRATEGIES TO IMPROVE INCLUSION

Muslim residents and fellows may experience unique challenges in GME related to their religious practices. In this section, we will review common practices of Muslims and how these practices may intersect with the learning environment. On occasion, these practices may appear to conflict with systemic, institutional, programmatic, or supervisory expectations of medical students, residents and fellows, and faculty members. We will review each practice and propose strategies and solutions to assist with efforts to provide inclusive GME learning environments that will allow Muslim and, indeed, all physician learners to thrive.

As stated at the beginning of this chapter, Muslims follow their religion along a spectrum of observance. Some Muslims participate in many outward-appearing practices to make it known they are Muslim, while others practice in a more personal, private manner, without outwardly identifying as Muslim. With this fact in mind, it is imperative for GME environments to be welcoming and safe for Muslims, regardless of how individuals observe their religion.

Prayers

Muslims are instructed to pray five times a day, with the timing of the prayers shifting daily in accordance with the sunrise and sunset. The first prayer, *Fajr*, is recited at dawn, before sunrise and lasts until the sunrise. For many residents and fellows, this prayer can be said before coming into the hospital. However, instances might arise in the winter months when this prayer can be conducted at work. The second prayer, *Dhuhr*, is usually said during the middle of the day and ends right before the sun hits its peak, and therefore would happen during traditional work hours. The third prayer, *Asr*, occurs in the late afternoon and ends at sunset. The fourth prayer, *Maghrib*, occurs at sunset and ends just before the night begins. The fifth and final prayer, *Isha*, occurs at night and continues until the end of the night. Thus, there will be times during the year when, due to longer workdays and shorter days in the winter season, Muslims will pray all five prayers at the hospital. To address this expectation, programs and institutions should provide a safe, quiet, and easily accessible space for physician learners to pray, and allow them to step away from clinical duties or lectures and hand off their pager to be allowed 5-to-10 minutes to pray.

On a weekly basis, Friday prayers occur in congregation, usually in a large group setting in which a short sermon is given prior to a communal prayer. These prayers take approximately 30 minutes in total, usually in a larger prayer room or mosque to accommodate the number of people praying. Programs should allow practicing physician learners to step away on a weekly basis to participate in and attend this prayer, since it is considered an obligation.

Some residents and fellows are hesitant to ask for prayer-related accommodations, as they might feel they are a burden to others in their program. In these circumstances, since they typically must ask someone to "hold the pager" or cover their clinical duties on the floor for a short amount of time, they might refrain from praying at work to avoid asking for accommodations. Allowing residents and fellows the opportunity to ask for some undisrupted quiet time to observe prayers may greatly increase well-being.

Fasting and the Holy Month of *Ramadan*

Ramadan is a holy month for Muslims, marked as a sacred time in which they increase their devotion to God. Activities specific to Ramadan include fasting and increased communal prayers. Fasting entails abstaining from food, drink, water, coffee, and ingestion of any kind from dawn until sunset. This practice occurs continuously for 30 days during the month of Ramadan and culminates with ***Eid*** Al-Fitr, the first significant Muslim holiday of the lunar calendar. Since Muslims follow the lunar calendar as opposed to the Gregorian calendar, the timing of *Ramadan* changes annually.

Recommended opportunities for programs to provide accommodations for *Ramadan* would include allowing physician learners to assume lighter responsibilities during the daytime, scheduling them for less intense rotations during this time, or allowing them to create their schedule in accordance with their abilities. If none of these accommodations are feasible, then programs may consider, at minimum, allowing residents and fellows to step away at sunset to break their fast and eat a small meal. To accomplish this routine, they should avoid assignments for clinical duties, clinic appointments, or surgeries scheduled at sunset. Some Muslim residents and fellows will frequently request night float rotations during *Ramadan* so they can be alert, more energized, and eat during their working hours.

Religious Holidays: *Eid Al-Fitr* and *Eid Al-Adha*

As previously mentioned, *Eid Al-Fitr* marks the culmination of *Ramadan*, one of two major holidays in Islam; the second is *Eid Al-Adha*, approximately 2 months and 10 days after *Eid Al-Fitr*. Muslim physician learners might not request this time off in fear of repercussions for missing work. As the Islamic calendar and Muslim holidays follow the lunar calendar, and, therefore, many communities determine the holidays based on the moonsighting, a resident or fellow may not know what day *Eid* is scheduled until the prior night. To address this challenge, a resident or fellow might request 2 or 3 days off, ensuring that one of those requested days off will include the holiday. Programs might also allow physician learners to request more flexible rotations during their holiday season. Lastly, programs can accommodate the needs of Muslim learners by not scheduling them for clinical assignments or exams on the potential dates of the holiday. Once the exact date of the holiday is determined by the moonsighting, learners should immediately inform their program so that schedules can be set or adjusted accordingly.

Hijab

Hijab is an Islamic religious practice of modesty in which a Muslim woman covers her hair, neck, and body up to her wrists and ankles. In doing so, only her hands, face, and feet can be exposed. *Hijab* is expected to be practiced in front of males and forms a large part of a Muslim woman's identity. Typically, observant Muslim women will also wear loose opaque clothing. Several strategies can be implemented in GME programs and clinical settings to ensure that *hijab*-wearing Muslim residents and fellows feel comfortable with their religious identity and do not feel the need to compromise their education or their religious practices. For example, hospitals should provide surgical hoods or sub-sterile *hijabs* in the operating room so Muslim women can don them prior to entering any surgical areas. Long-sleeve scrub jackets should be made readily available to residents and fellows so they can wear them prior to scrubbing and donning a sterile surgical gown. Lastly, private scrub sinks should be considered so that *hijab*-wearing Muslim women can comfortably scrub without feeling exposed.[17] Additional opportunities for accommodations in the operating room can be found at HijabInTheOR.com. We recommend, hospitals and medical schools consider preparing for these circumstances in advance of having Muslim learners and staff as well; and have accommodations in place in the event that a practicing Muslim must enter the operating room unexpectedly (See Figure 17.1.)

FIGURE 17.1 Different styles of *hijab* that are commonly practiced. (Original artwork by Zarin Rahman.)

Beard

Many Muslim men are observant, maintaining a beard for religious purposes. In such cases, beard covers should be made readily accessible for the operating room so that Muslim men can enter without difficulty. Similarly, proper personal protective equipment (PPE) should be readily available so that all men who keep a fully grown beard do not need to shave in order to fit a respirator or a mask. When physician learners participate in annual fit tests for proper PPE, GME programs should include different options, like N95, N99, and N100 respirator masks. Fittings should also include additional information about facial hair and how to properly wear a mask that provides adequate coverage and protection. Such practice is not specific for Muslim men keeping a beard for a religious purpose; this practice can be generally applied for all men with beards.

Gender Interactions and Physical Exams

Muslims are strongly encouraged to avoid physical touch by individuals of a different gender as a means to maintain modesty unless deemed a necessity. This practice may affect personal interactions while learners are conducing basic physical exam maneuvers or ultrasounds on one another, such as during physical diagnosis courses or simulation. To address this, GME programs can consider making accommodations by pairing residents and fellows with people of the same gender when it is reasonable and does not interfere with the educational objective of the session.

Dietary Accommodations

Muslims are prohibited from eating pork or pork products and consuming alcohol. Furthermore, some observant Muslims also abstain from eating meat or poultry that has not been slaughtered in the religious practice called ***Zabiha Halal***. Program leaders should ask residents and fellows about their dietary preferences and provide *Halal* options when possible. If there is no vendor for *Halal* meat, vegetarian and pescatarian options can be reasonable alternatives. Similarly, if residents or fellows will be in the hospital during *Ramadan* when they break their fast at sunset, adequate and accessible food options should be available for them.

Social Gatherings

Islam prohibits alcohol consumption, and observant learners may feel uncomfortable at bars or in settings in which alcohol is the sole focus. However, if they do not attend these optional social gatherings, they may miss an opportunity to get to know their fellow physician learners, as well as faculty members, and staff members. This missed opportunity, in turn, threatens their sense of belonging to the overall learning community.

GME programs should endeavor to conduct at least some social gatherings in spaces that are not surrounded by alcohol and conduct events in which the focus is not on drinking alcohol. This effort allows for a more inclusive environment for anyone who chooses not to drink for personal or religious reasons.

Support Groups and Other Efforts to Address Bias

Although Muslim physician learners might not feel comfortable discussing the need for accommodations with their non-Muslim counterparts, it would be beneficial to have structured support groups in which they can earnestly express themselves. This experience would also allow them to have comfort and security knowing there are people like them, and would be helpful in preventing feelings of isolation. Muslim learners may also commonly experience mistreatment and discrimination related to their religious practices, and the sources of mistreatment may vary, including peers, faculty and staff members, and patients.[3,5,7,8,12,15,16,18]

In a 2021 study, more than one-third of participants reported experiencing workplace discrimination and 57% of participants reported that they have been passed over for professional advancements and promotions because of their religion.[15,18] Physicians reported feeling marginalized because their requests for inclusivity, such as dietary accommodations or refraining from alcohol, were not catered to. One-third of physicians reported having experiences in which patients refused to be cared for by them due to their religious identity.[15] In instances like this, GME programs should create a reporting system to allow the individual to feel supported and to address workplace discrimination. A policy report comparing a 2013 and a 2021 study found that negative experiences that Muslim physicians in the United States are facing due to religious discrimination may be increasing. To prevent physician burnout and feelings of exclusion or institutionalized discrimination, programs should strive to provide accommodations, access to hospital-wide learning opportunities and peer support groups to address discrimination, determine the root cause of institutionalized discrimination, and to work toward creating standardized policies that include religious accommodations.[15,18]

At the same time, it would be useful to offer educational opportunities for all residents, fellows, faculty and staff members that address cultural and religious bias against Muslims and other marginalized groups. Small group sessions where non-Muslim learners can hear about religious accommodations and how to create inclusive environments for Muslim colleagues may also be helpful educational interventions in GME programs and institutions.

> The largest Muslim population in the United States is in Wayne County, Michigan. However, the largest Muslim population per capita is in Cook County, Illinois.

Diverse Representation in Leadership

Muslim physicians working in the United States report that they feel Muslims are not in positions of leadership and are often overlooked due to their religion.[18] The absence of research studies demonstrating Muslim physicians in leadership reinforces this point, but also represents a lack of interest in such representation. It is necessary to have diverse representation with Muslim physicians in positions of leadership, when possible, so that Muslim physician learners feel and believe they can succeed in GME environments.

> There is a *hadith*, a saying, by the Prophet Mohammed (*peace be upon him*) that states, "For every disease, Allah has created a cure." This thinking has motivated Islamic advancements in medicine, as well as current research and development.

Take Home Points

- Islam is the fastest growing religion in the world, and the third largest religion in the United States. Although Muslims make up 1% of the US population, they make up greater than 5% of the health care workforce.
- Muslim physicians working in the United States face discrimination in the workplace, either from peers, leadership, or patients. Reporting systems should be in place so physician learners can safely disclose instances of discrimination. GME programs and institutions should take extensive measures to ensure discrimination is not tolerated and that residents and fellows feel supported. Peer support groups can be offered to allow for a more inclusive and encouraging environment.
- Programs and Sponsoring Institutions should provide reasonable accommodations for Muslim physician learners, faculty and staff members; such as: enabling time and safe space to pray; planning social gatherings that do not always involve alcohol; accommodating schedules for fasting during *Ramadan* religious holidays, such as *Eid Al-Fitr* and *Eid Al-Adha*; providing dietary alternatives, such as *Zabiha Halal*; and, educating staff members on dress and modesty-related accommodations.

QUESTIONS FOR FURTHER THOUGHT

- Who are the key stakeholders involved in facilitating religious accommodations for Muslim residents and fellows, and how can they collaborate to promote an inclusive learning environment in GME?
- Which patient populations in your program's service area might benefit from the inclusion of culturally and religiously diverse physicians, such as Muslim residents and fellows in the healthcare workforce?

REFERENCES

1. Majeed A. How Islam changed medicine. *BMJ*. 2005;331(7531):1486-1487. doi:10.1136/bmj.331.7531.1486
2. Baqai B, Azam L, Davila O, Murrar S, Padela AI. Religious identity discrimination in the physician workforce: insights from two national studies of Muslim clinicians in the US. *J Gen Intern Med*. 2023;38:1167-1174. doi:10.1007/s11606-022-07923-5
3. Pew Foundation. *The Future of World Religions: Population Growth Projections, 2010-2050*. Pew Research Center; 2015.
4. Boulet JR, Duvivier RJ, Pinsky WW. Prevalence of international medical graduates from Muslim-majority nations in the US physician workforce from 2009 to 2019. *JAMA Network Open*. 2020;3(7):e209418. doi:10.1001/jamanetworkopen.2020.9418
5. Kathawalla UK, Syed M. Discrimination, life stress, and mental health among Muslims: a preregistered systematic review and meta-analysis. *Collabra Psychol*. 2021;7(1):28248. doi:10.1525/collabra.28248
6. Samari G. Islamophobia and public health in the United States. *Am J Public Health*. 2016;106(11):1920-1925. [published correction appears in *Am J Public Health*. 2016;106(12):e13]. doi:10.2105/ajph.2016.303374
7. Ahmed N, Quinn SC, Limaye RJ, Khan S. From interpersonal violence to institutionalized discrimination: documenting and assessing the impact of Islamophobia on Muslim Americans. *J Muslim Ment Health*. 2021;15(2). doi:10.3998/jmmh.119
8. Rehman I, Hanley T. Muslim minorities' experiences of Islamophobia in the West: a systematic review. *Cult Psychol*. 2023;29(1):139-156. https://journals.sagepub.com/doi/epub/10.1177/1354067X221103996
9. Abderrazzaq M. Attitudes of Muslim Americans regarding prejudice and discrimination displayed by non-Muslims. *J Soc Work Glob Commun*. 2023;7(1). doi:10.5590/jswgc.2023.8.1.02
10. Mohamed B. *New estimates show U.S. Muslim population continues to grow*. Pew Research Center. January 3, 2018. https://www.pewresearch.org/short-reads/2018/01/03/new-estimates-show-u-s-muslim-population-continues-to-grow/
11. Al Sad S, Padela AI. Career satisfaction and burnout among American Muslim physicians. *Avicenna J Med*. 2023;13(2):117-129. doi:10.1055/s-0043-1770701

12. Padela AI, Azam L, Murrar S, Baqai B. Muslim American physicians' experiences with, and views on, religious discrimination and accommodation in academic medicine. *Health Services Res.* 2023;58(3):733-743. doi:10.1111/1475-6773.14146
13. Murrar S, Azam L, Baqai B, Davila O, Padela AI. Relationships between religious commitment, workplace experiences, and professional and psychological outcomes among US Muslim physicians. *Acad Med.* Published online ahead of print: March 5, 2024. doi:10.1097/ACM.0000000000005686
14. Padela AI., Munzareen P, Saadi A. Muslim resident cases. In: *Diversity and Inclusion in Quality Patient Care: Your Story/Our Story–A Case-Based Compendium.* Martin M, Heron S, Moreno-Walton L, eds. Springer; 2019.
15. Padela AI, Adam H, Ahmad M, Hosseinian Z, Curlin F. Religious identity and workplace discrimination: A national survey of American Muslim physicians. *AJOB Empirical Bioethics.* 2015;7(3):149-159. doi:10.1080/23294515.2015.1111271
16. Hopkins AF, Kooken WC, Winger EN. Inclusive clinical practice and policy for Muslim nursing students. *J Transcult Nurs.* 2020;31(1):100-106. doi:10.1177/1043659619832079
17. Malik A, Qureshi H, Abdul-Razakq H, et al. 'I decided not to go into surgery due to dress code': a cross-sectional study within the UK investigating experiences of female Muslim medical health professionals on bare below the elbows (BBE) policy and wearing headscarves (hijabs) in theatre. *BMJ Open.* 2019;9(3):e019954. doi:10.1136/bmjopen-2017-019954
18. Padela AI, Azam L, Quryshi A. Advancing equity for Muslim physicians in the healthcare workforce. Medical College of Wisconsin; Initiative on Islam and Medicine; Tanenbaum; American Muslim Health Professionals. 2022. https://www.medicineandislam.org/wp-content/uploads/2022/12/Final-Policy-Report_18-10-2022.pdf

Creating Inclusive Environments for Orthodox Jewish Learners in Graduate Medical Education

Chana Weinstock, MD, Medical Oncologist, Baltimore, MD

Daniel Eisenberg, MD, Staff Radiologist, Department of Radiology, Einstein Healthcare Network—Jefferson Health; Clinical Assistant Professor of Radiology, Sidney Kimmel Medical College, Philadelphia, PA

CHAPTER SUMMARY

In this chapter, we introduce the unique challenges potentially faced by Orthodox Jewish residents and fellows during their graduate medical education (GME). Orthodox Jews, by definition, are adherents of *halacha*, a traditional system of Jewish law. *Halacha* has many tenets that may be relevant in a medical setting, encompassing everything from the requirement to eat kosher food to the requirement to follow a code of ethics pertaining to medicine. Observance of both the Sabbath (also referred to as *"Shabbos"* or *"Shabbat"*)—a 25-hour period beginning each Friday evening—and of several Jewish holidays, is an important consideration for Orthodox Jews that precludes them from doing work-related activities. Programs should respect the rights and preferences of Orthodox Jews and act to reasonably accommodate requests not to work on the Sabbath and Jewish holidays. Additionally, each program should decide *a priori* whether scheduling and program size allow for the feasibility of accommodating a Sabbath-observant learner; interviewees should feel safe broaching the topic of Sabbath observance without fear of being overlooked in The Match®. In this chapter, we review unique challenges faced by Orthodox Jewish physician learners and strategies that programs can use to feasibly accommodate religious requests and to equitably consider these Sabbath-observant residents and fellows in the application, interview, and selection processes, and throughout their education.

LEARNING OBJECTIVES

1. Identify challenges facing Orthodox Jewish residents and fellows during their graduate medical education (GME) application process and subsequent education.
2. Describe the concept of Jewish law/*halacha* and its potential impact on Orthodox Jewish residents and fellows.
3. Describe how observance of the Sabbath and Jewish holidays factors into GME for Orthodox Jewish residents and fellows.
4. Develop strategies to enable GME programs to reasonably accommodate the needs of the Orthodox Jewish residents and fellows related to Sabbath observance.

Case Study

Risa is a fourth-year medical student applying for a residency in neurology. She is projected to graduate with top honors from her class and is well-recommended by mentors, having published original research in neurology journals and engaging in relevant clinical and laboratory experience. She has won a young investigator award highlighting new talent in neurology and is considered an outstanding applicant entering the application cycle.

Risa receives an email with the offer of an interview from her first-choice residency program. However, the interviews are only offered on three dates, each of which is a Saturday. Risa is a Sabbath-observant Orthodox Jew and, for religious reasons, cannot perform activities related to work on the Sabbath, which extends from sundown on Friday to nightfall on Saturday. She requests an alternate date but is told that only the Saturday dates are available and that she will need to "make one of the dates work." In the absence of flexibility by the program, Risa is forced to decline the opportunity to interview and potentially match at her dream program.

Risa is able to attend other neurology residency program interviews held on Sundays or during the week. At each interview, she assesses whether the program is a good fit based on many factors, such as reputation, quality of faculty, and resident satisfaction. In addition to these common criteria, she also assesses the program's potential to accommodate her need to not work on Saturdays. She does so at each interview by asking about the call schedule and weekend coverage during lunch with a group of current residents. Some programs are small, with only two or three residents available for weekend coverage. However, Risa identifies four programs with a large potential pool of covering residents and a flexible weekend coverage schedule that seems to be a good fit. She broaches the topic of Sabbath observance when interviewing at each program, and offers to cover Saturday nights, Sunday nights, and secular holidays as needed in lieu of being placed on call during the Sabbath. Two residency program directors realize that Risa is offering a workable alternative within their existing call schedules, and state that, should she match into their program, they would ensure a fair and equal weekend call coverage schedule to simultaneously honor her religious requirements and ensure an equitable division of coverage for other residents.

On Match Day, Risa is thrilled to match into one of the programs that has signaled willingness to work with her Sabbath requirements. However, she also regrets that her top-choice program did not provide her with a chance to interview by arranging a non-Saturday date. She has discovered that Sabbath coverage would actually have been easy to arrange at her top-choice program, since weekend coverage at that program is primarily provided by physician assistants, with residents identifying a weekend day of their choice to round on patients. While pleased with her Match® results overall, Risa is left wondering whether, by failing to provide her with a non-Saturday interview, the "program of her dreams" disregarded her religious rights. She also wonders if other residency programs that were large enough to offer the possibility of alternative weekend coverage schedules, but chose not to consider doing so, had infringed on her religious rights.

Case Discussion
Risa is an excellent candidate for a neurology program; however, additional considerations related to her religious requirements complicate the process for her. These considerations are also likely to factor into her functioning as a resident. Risa attempted accommodations on her end, that is, by offering alternate non-Saturday dates for a residency interview and finding programs with large enough residency classes to accommodate a Sabbath-observant schedule. However, in the case of the inflexible Saturday interview date, her residency program of first choice failed to accommodate her religious requirements. As you review the chapter, consider what processes are in place in your Sponsoring Institution or program to support residents and fellows with specific religious observances.

INTRODUCTION

Individuals of Jewish descent are currently well-represented in medicine, with a survey in 2005 showing that 14% of US physicians were Jewish, compared with an approximately 2% representation in the general population.[1] There are various denominations within Judaism, primarily defined by religious affiliation. There are also many Jewish individuals who do not affiliate with a particular denomination and who are secular in terms of religiosity but who identify culturally as Jewish. This chapter will primarily focus on issues of religious discrimination as they apply to Orthodox Jews, whose religious observances are consistent with a strict interpretation of Jewish law, thus putting these individuals at risk for issues related to religious discrimination. We acknowledge that many considerations around religious discrimination may also apply to other denominations of Judaism, as well as to other religions, and similar mitigation strategies would also apply to their religious needs.

Religious discrimination refers to the practice of treating individuals differently because of religious beliefs and practices, and/or their request for accommodations of their religious beliefs and practices. This definition also applies to moral or ethical beliefs sincerely held with the strength of traditional religious views.[2] Religious discrimination in the workplace is not unique to medicine and is certainly not unique to adherents of Orthodox Judaism. Issues related to religious discrimination in general are addressed directly in Title VII of the Civil Rights Act of 1964, which protects employees and job applicants from discrimination based on religion. Title VII also requires employers to reasonably accommodate the religious practices of an employee/prospective employee unless doing this would create an "undue hardship" on the employer.[3]

Orthodox Judaism
Orthodox Jews are defined by strict adherence to a system of traditional Jewish law known as **halacha**. *Halacha* is sourced in the Bible and in the ***Talmud*** with subsequent codification by rabbis over the centuries. Adherence is not voluntary, and an individual rabbi cannot provide religious exemptions on a case-by-case basis. However, rabbis are often consulted for guidance when it comes to applying *halacha* to real-life situations, such as those faced by physician learners during their medical education.

Halacha places a premium on the value of human life and considers the pursuit of healing as an exalted calling. Many facets of *halacha* relating to aspects of patient care and daily activities are potentially relevant to the Orthodox Jewish physician learner. Examples include the requirements to eat **kosher** food, to pray at certain hours, and to adhere to principles of Jewish medical ethics. In many cases, Orthodox Jews are accustomed to caring for these concerns, for example, by setting aside personal time for prayer prior to the workday and packing a kosher lunch if not available in the hospital cafeteria. These issues are generally dealt with easily and will be discussed in the next section.

CHALLENGES, NOT MAJOR BARRIERS

Several daily activities and interactions may pose challenges that impact everyday aspects of medical education for Orthodox Jewish learners. Some issues are of minor significance, constituting challenges only, and do not play a substantial role in medical education or in a learner's interactions with peers. These issues are discussed here to raise the awareness of anyone unfamiliar with *halachic* practices.

For instance, Orthodox Jewish residents and fellows adhere to dietary regulations (**kashrus** or **kashrut**) that preclude them from eating food provided at most department activities, for example, department luncheons and retirement parties. While providing kosher food is not a necessity since learners can arrange for their own food, greater inclusiveness would result if a kosher option were available at department events. Nevertheless, this restriction does not pose a significant impediment to education overall.

Other issues demonstrate how a lack of familiarity with the cultural and religious norms of Orthodox Judaism might lead to misunderstandings. For example, Jewish law generally prohibits a man from physical contact with a woman or a woman from physical contact with a man in most situations, other than with the individual's spouse or immediate family members. This prohibition does not apply to contact that is part of providing medical care and does not affect the ability of a learner to participate fully in all areas of patient care; however, it might prevent an Orthodox Jewish learner from contact such as shaking hands with coworkers or visitors of the opposite sex. This religious norm should not be interpreted as aloofness or indifference to others; it is simply a religious requirement related to modesty and residents and fellows are free to interact with coworkers in a professional manner that does not involve physical contact.

Additional modesty requirements may affect the dress of Orthodox Jewish physician learners. For example, a female resident or fellow might request to wear a scrub skirt instead of traditional scrub pants due to interpretations around requirements of modesty in dress. It would be appropriate for a department to provide access to such an option in situations where wearing scrubs would be expected, if a learner so desires.

The requirement of the male Orthodox physician learner to pray 3 times a day is unlikely to be an important practical issue for any program since the time required is minimal on a normal workday; both morning and evening prayers occur before and after work, and afternoon prayers, which require only a few minutes, can be said after work during many months of the year. Nevertheless, it is important for the GME program to respect the need of a learner to take a few minutes when necessary.

The issues raised above do not represent obstacles to medical education itself. However, recognition of and respect for the religious needs of residents and fellows is an important component of a robust graduate medical education (GME) program; it builds a healthy social environment within the program. Recognizing and accommodating the religious needs of all learners fosters inclusivity and creates an inclusive learning and working environment.

POSSIBLE BARRIERS

There are some cases in which *halacha* may dictate that participation in certain activities in a medical setting is problematic. This situation may arise particularly, but not exclusively, in end-of-life care. In such occurrences, Jewish law limits many actions perceived as "life-shortening," such as extubating a ventilator-dependent patient with the intention to cause death, regardless of medical or family perception that further intensive care would be "futile." An Orthodox Jewish resident or fellow would generally not be permitted to assist a patient in committing suicide or assist in organ-harvesting surgery when acceptable criteria for declaring death per *halacha* are not met, regardless of whether such activities are legal. Other potential challenges arise when Orthodox Jewish physician learners are asked to participate in surgeries involving the male or female reproductive organs where the outcome is sterility, such as vasectomies, tubal ligations, or gender-affirming surgeries. Generally, if an Orthodox Jewish learner expresses discomfort with participating in these activities, it is not a dereliction of duty but rather a *halachic* or ethical conflict. The topic of Jewish medical ethics and how these issues may impact specific scenarios in medicine is beyond the scope of this chapter.

A major topic confronting an Orthodox Jewish learner is the requirement to rest on the Sabbath (also known as **Shabbos**, or **Shabbat**). During this time, Orthodox Jews are forbidden from performing routine work-related activities. Additionally, there are several Jewish holidays when work is forbidden (Table 18.1).

Table 18.1	Major Jewish Holidays with Similar Restrictions as the Sabbath

Rosh Hashana (2 days)
Yom Kippur (1 day)
Sukkot (first 2 days and last 2 days)
Passover (first 2 days and last 2 days)
Shavuot (2 days)

All dates on the Jewish calendar begin in the evening at sundown and end approximately 1 hour after sundown the next evening.

The requirement to not work on these days is a major obstacle facing Orthodox Jews hoping to pursue careers in medicine, as almost every GME program requires Saturday coverage.[4-6] The remainder of this chapter will, therefore, focus on issues related to Sabbath observance as they pertain to Orthodox Jewish residents, fellows and faculty members.

SABBATH OBSERVANCE AND ORTHODOX JEWISH LEARNERS

All Orthodox Jews, by definition, observe the Sabbath as a day of rest, and are known as Sabbath-observant, or *"Shomer Shabbos."* The required rest on the Sabbath is to abstain from specific areas of normal daily work/actions specified by *halacha* as forbidden. Due to these limitations, normal functioning in the hospital for a Sabbath-observant Orthodox Jewish learner may become difficult or impossible. For example, writing and using electricity, such as turning on lights and using a computer are prohibited work-related activities. While these prohibitions might be set aside in some rare instances of life-threatening situations, many activities that occur in an inpatient setting relate to more routine matters of inpatient care and thus are considered forbidden work/actions per *halacha*.

Additionally, there is a distinction between a life-threatening situation that a person may face in an *unplanned* fashion versus voluntarily placing oneself into a position where one knows in advance that one will be routinely performing otherwise forbidden activities due to medical emergencies. Thus, if one unexpectedly encounters a patient with an acute myocardial infarction on the street, using a phone to call emergency services is permitted due to the emergent and life-threatening nature of the event. However, choosing to match into a non-Shomer Shabbos residency, even where life-threatening medical emergencies will almost certainly be occurring, particularly where much of the expected work does not entail life-threatening medical emergencies, is problematic. Therefore, although some Orthodox Jewish residents and fellows have agreed to work on the Sabbath if not doing so would involve forfeiture of their career in medicine, many others have simply given up on medicine as a field altogether because of this consideration.[7]

There are many ways to work with Orthodox Jewish residents and fellows in an attempt to offer education and training compatible with Sabbath observance; indeed, many programs have successfully done so and have thereby prevented religious discrimination towards Sabbath-observant learners. A successful strategy includes ensuring equitable division of weekends between Sabbath observers and others, for example, with the former taking coverage from Saturday nights through Sunday nights and the latter covering Friday nights through Saturday nights. Similar considerations apply to the observance of Jewish holidays. However, as the precise dates for Jewish holidays differ each year but are known well in advance and often do not involve weekends, one suggestion involves booking vacation or leave time to coincide with those days so the learner can arrange coverage akin to any other (ie, non-religious) leave. Such flexibility in coverage is especially feasible in larger programs when coverage pools are extensive; these programs are generally well-positioned to accommodate the needs of all learners who require some amount of flexibility for personal considerations in terms of weekend coverage or other scenarios.

Table 18.2 Suggestions for Creating Match Opportunities for Sabbath-observant Learners

Programs can determine the number of Sabbath-observant learners their schedule can realistically accommodate.
Programs can designate this number of match spots with a different number or letter (S) within the total number of their allotted spots.
Programs can create match list independent of Sabbath-observant status of applicants.

A suggested approach to ensure that the needs of Sabbath observers are met is for each program to assess the realistic feasibility of accommodating Sabbath observers, with an eye towards maximizing equitable education and training opportunities when possible.[8-10] From their perspective, applicants should accurately convey their religious needs before The Match® to allow for maximal accommodation with minimal disruption of scheduling, especially if Sabbath observance is a key consideration. Programs should provide a safe environment to discuss Sabbath accommodation needs without fear of discrimination, either during an interview or at some other time. A fair match would offer accommodation for learners' religious requirements (Table 18.2). In this way, the religious rights of residents and fellows can be met in as equitable a manner as possible.

SUGGESTED STRATEGIES FOR ACCOMMODATION

A Program Approach

First, each program can individually assess its own ability to realistically accommodate a Sabbath-observant physician learner. This effort would include examining the departmental workflow to determine what changes, if any, would be required to accommodate Sabbath observance. Such an examination would particularly work well in large programs with many residents and fellows to help with patient coverage so that Sabbath-observant physician learners have a pool of others to help divide weekend coverage equitably.

The program could then create a schedule conducive to Sabbath observance for a potential applicant who is interested in a Sabbath-compatible schedule. This schedule would not include a Sabbath-observant resident or fellow from Friday night through Saturday evening (although Saturday night call beginning after nightfall can often be easily arranged) and would allow the learner to leave the hospital at an adequate (but reasonably short) time before sundown on Fridays. Such a schedule could also apply to a few specific Jewish holidays as well. Sabbath-observant residents and fellows *may* take call on Sundays, secular holidays, and Saturday nights after nightfall, depending on the time of year. This arrangement might mean, for example, that a Sabbath-observant physician learner is scheduled for two Sundays in a given month rather than on one Saturday and one Sunday as would be the case in a standard schedule. Additionally, Sunday coverage by this individual could begin on Saturday nights if allowed by work hour regulations.

An additional approach to enable this accommodation is to schedule Sabbath-observant learners for rotations likely to finish earlier in the day for winter months. Such an arrangement allows them to leave in time for the start of the Sabbath on Friday afternoon, thereby saving those rotations with long days for summer months when the Sabbath does not begin until much later in the day due to longer daylight hours. This approach might also require some flexibility in clinic scheduling. For example, more patients could be scheduled on other afternoons to allow for a Sabbath-observant learner to have fewer patients on Friday afternoon and to end clinic in time for Sabbath on winter Fridays when sundown occurs early. By scheduling more patients on other days, overall patient numbers and workload equity can be maintained.

Accommodations by Residents and Fellows

Sabbath-observant learners can be expected to make reasonable accommodations themselves, including, for example, living close enough to the hospital to require only a modest amount of time to travel home before the beginning of the Sabbath. Other accommodations for ancillary religious and family obligations are the learner's responsibility, such as arranging for discretionary travel around Jewish holidays.

Considerations to Achieve Clarity

To ensure overall fairness, the program should clarify to all residents and fellows (Sabbath-observant and others) that a Sabbath-observant learner's schedule will entail an equivalent time commitment and equivalent division of responsibility. Additionally, the program might approach creating the schedule that accommodates Sabbath-observant learners with the recognition that Saturday might be a particularly undesired day for assigned call; equivalently undesirable days would be assigned to make up for that fact (eg, secular holidays).

Generally, the program should also make clear that like all other educational commitments, it is ultimately the program's responsibility to create a fair schedule that encompasses the needs of all learners and meets the expectations of the ACGME Common and specialty-specific Program Requirements. While input and cooperation of all residents and fellows are crucial for the smooth functioning of the department and educational components of the program, ultimately it would not be in the hands of a Sabbath-observant resident and fellow, or the other learners to ensure that the commitments made to accommodation are effectively implemented. There should be no requirement for Sabbath-observant learners (or anyone) to "find" someone to "trade with" to allow for Sabbath observance, although developing a workable schedule certainly may benefit from the input and active participation of all residents and fellows. In the spirit of accommodation and helpfulness that all learners should display, Sabbath-observant learners should also be expected to be as accommodating as possible to their fellow learners for other scheduling issues in which they can be helpful, to allow priorities of other learners to be similarly accommodated.

Many resources are available to assist with scheduling. For instance, scheduling software can be programmed in advance to schedule Sabbath observant residents/fellows appropriately; and many programs have done so successfully.

Sabbath Observance and The Match®

While it may not be feasible for some programs to accommodate a Sabbath-observant resident or fellow, or to set up a "*Shomer Shabbos*" program, each program should realistically assess the extent to which Sabbath accommodation is possible and set up mechanisms to allow for it to occur, if feasible.

During the application process, the program should offer at least some non-Saturday interview dates; applicants should not be penalized for interviewing on one of these non-Saturday dates. The program should allow for open dialogue in the interview regarding how accommodation for Sabbath observance would work for the applicant within the program and what expectations are held by both the program and the applicant regarding work schedules. This dialogue includes discussion of specifics for accommodations and how these accommodations would practically be implemented in light of any issues that might require resolution. Such a conversation could alleviate future misunderstandings and may lead to solutions that had not been previously considered. Such an approach would enable applicants to make an informed choice and to discuss pertinent details of the particular program during or following the interview. As much as possible, this information should be made available to applicants in an easily accessible way such as on the program website, so that such expectations could be taken into consideration when the applicant is early in the matching process.

> As an Orthodox Jewish resident, Risa will be observing the Sabbath, which encompasses a 25-hour period beginning at sundown on Friday and extending until nightfall on Saturday. There are also several Jewish holidays per year. During these times, Risa is forbidden from performing routine work activities.

> Risa, an Orthodox Jewish resident, has asked her program director if weekends could be divided equitably between her as a Sabbath observer and others in the program. She has offered coverage from Saturday nights through Sunday night, with other residents covering Friday nights through Saturday nights.

Additional Suggestions and References to Facilitate Accommodation

We offer several additional suggestions useful to Sponsoring Institutions and programs interested in further information:

1. *Consider replicating strategies from other programs that have successfully accommodated Sabbath-observant residents and fellows.*

    Examples of programs that have formally allowed for Sabbath accommodation, and that have had success with this approach, can be reviewed and implemented according to local need.[10] In some cases, programs have created a specific slot in The Match® to allow for a Sabbath-observant learner to match into the program with the understanding that the schedule would be Sabbath-observant for that individual, according to the suggestions described in this chapter. If no qualified Sabbath-observant learner applied and/or if the spot remained unfilled, the schedule could then default to that used for a standard applicant. Sabbath-observant candidates would only be ranked if they would otherwise have been ranked by the program in terms of qualifications and other criteria taken into account when the program formulates its match ranking. Generating a slot through The Match® would allow for the formalization of the process and require less guesswork or unspoken agreements on the part of the program and is a strategy we recommend. Gathering information from programs that have successfully implemented Sabbath-observant schedules should be pursued.

2. *Review available online resources that can enhance foundational knowledge regarding how their Orthodox Judaism affects physician learners; these resources may also serve to provide networking and community-building opportunities for Orthodox Jewish physician learners.*

    Some examples include:
    - The Jewish Physician Network (JPN)[11] is an organization that assists Jewish health care professionals in navigating the intricacies of the medical profession and Jewish ethical and cultural values. JPN aims to ease potential conflicts by creating valuable educational resources for clinicians and patients, facilitating open conversations, and acting as a liaison between medical professionals, rabbinical, and community leaders.
    - The Shomer Shabbos website[12] by Daniel Eisenberg, MD, is a resource for applicants seeking practical advice on how to find and interview at a program that may accommodate Sabbath observance. Program directors and any other interested parties can use this site as a reference and resource.
    - The Shomer Shabbos Residency website[13] provides a database of programs that have offered Sabbath accommodations for residents and fellows.
    - The Shomer Shabbos Medicine Network[14] maintains a national database of testimonials by current and former students, residents, and fellows who have worked with their respective programs to make their years in medical education as "Sabbath-friendly" as possible, ranging from fully Sabbath-observant residencies to various accommodations around Sabbath observance. The database, with more than 300 entries and counting, has already been invaluable for scores of medical students, residents, and fellows researching their options for Sabbath-observant and Sabbath-friendly medical education. For privacy purposes, the database is a closed community, and only those who have joined the database have access to its contents.

Take Home Points

- *Halacha*, a system of traditional Jewish law, is relevant to Orthodox Jewish residents'/fellows' medical education in many ways, including guiding their conduct through a code of medical ethics.
- Sabbath observance is critical to Orthodox Jews and precludes performance of work-related activities during a 25-hour period from Friday at sundown through Saturday night, in addition to Jewish holidays.
- Arranging coverage for weekends so that the Sabbath-observant resident or fellow does not need to work on the Sabbath is feasible and represents a reasonable accommodation that programs should seek to accomplish in an effort to provide equitable educational opportunities.
- Each program should decide *a priori* whether scheduling and program size allows for feasibility of accommodating Sabbath-observant applicants; interviewees should feel safe broaching the topic of Sabbath observance without fear of being overlooked in The Match®.

QUESTIONS FOR FURTHER THOUGHT

1. What systems are in place in your program to provide accommodations to an Orthodox Jewish applicant in the interview process or regarding working hours during the Sabbath? What steps could your program take to review or change its current system to allow for such accommodations?
2. How is accommodating the Sabbath-observing needs of Orthodox Jewish residents and fellows similar to accommodating the needs of a parent requiring parental leave to care for a newborn child or maternity leave, which is an accepted and required accommodation for post-partum learners or individuals from other religious backgrounds? How are these types of situations similar and how are they different?
3. Is a program that fails to provide a non-Saturday interview date to an Orthodox Jewish applicant practicing religious discrimination? Why or why not?[15]

REFERENCES

1. Curlin FA, Lantos JD, Roach CJ, Sellergren SA, Chin MH. Religious characteristics of U.S. physicians: a national survey. *J Gen Intern Med*. 2005;20(7):629-634. doi:10.1111/j.1525-1497.2005.0119.x
2. Howard B. Making space for spirituality. *AAMC News*. Published June 25, 2019. Accessed June 19, 2024. https://www.aamc.org/news-insights/making-space-spirituality
3. Office of Civil Rights. Religious discrimination. US Department of Commerce. Accessed June 19, 2024. https://www.commerce.gov/cr/reports-and-resources/discrimination-quick-facts/religious-discrimination
4. Schachter RH. Shemiras Shabbos for doctors and medical students. *TorahWeb*. Published 2007. Accessed June 19, 2024. https://torahweb.org/torah/special/2007/rsch_shabbos1.html
5. Sulton R, Sulton S. Shomer-Shabbat residency. *J Halacha Contemporary Society*. 2009;(58):45-59.
6. Karp J, Schaikewitz M. Residency and Shabbat. In: *Sacred Training: A Halakhic Guidebook for Medical Students and Residents*. Ammud Press; 2018.
7. Appel E. Still a doctor in the house? *Mishpacha*. 2020;84. https://mishpacha.com/still-a-doctor-in-the-house/
8. University of Connecticut. Religious accommodations. Published March 2021. Accessed June 19, 2024. https://health.uconn.edu/graduate-medical-education/wp-content/uploads/sites/20/2021/03/132.pdf
9. Jacobs School of Medicine and Biomedical Sciences; University at Buffalo. Religious accommodation policy. Published October 19. 2021. https://medicine.buffalo.edu/offices/gme/policies/religious-accommodation-policy.html
10. Howard A. Can a Shabbat-observant Jew get through medical residency at Baylor? *Jewish Herald-Voice*. Published March 8, 2012. Accessed June 19, 2024. https://jhvonline.com/can-a-shabbatobservant-jew-get-through-medical-residency-at-baylor-p12688-89.htm

11. The Jewish Physician Network. Accessed June 26, 2024. https://jewishphysiciansnetwork.squarespace.com
12. Eisenberg D. Jewish medical ethics. Shomer Shabbos Residency. Accessed June 19, 2024. https://www.jewishmedicalethics.com/shomer-shabbos-residency.html
13. Shomer Shabbos Residency. Published December 25, 2023. Accessed June 26, 2024. https://sites.google.com/site/shomershabbosresidency
14. Shomer Shabbos Medicine. Published August 13, 2020. Accessed June 26, 2024. http://www.shomershabbosmedicine.com/
15. U.S. Equal Employment Opportunity Commission. Religious discrimination. Accessed June 19, 2024. https://www.eeoc.gov/religious-discrimination

SECTION 4

Gender and Sexual Identity, Disability, and Age in Graduate Medical Education

Allison Cox-Simpson, MA, Diversity, Equity, Inclusion Communications Liaison, Accreditation Council for Graduate Medical Education

Various facets of a person's identity, such as gender and sexual orientation, disability, and age, intersect to determine how that person experiences the world around them. For residents and fellows in graduate medical education (GME), that reality includes the clinical learning environment. Each chapter in Section Four aligns with the principles and findings outlined throughout *A Guide* by describing how each of these facets can contribute to marginalizing and minoritizing residents, fellows, faculty members, and patients whose identities differ from the dominant culture in GME.

Transgender, non-binary, or otherwise gender-diverse physician learners and their patients have experienced bias and mistreatment because of their gender identities.[1] The term sexual minority refers to individuals who do not identify as straight or heterosexual. Like inclusive language in general, the preferred terminology for inclusive representation of the LGBTQIA+ community constantly evolves.[2] While in one case, a particular term may be preferred by an individual, in other instances individuals may self-describe their gender or sexual identity differently. To provide space for a nuanced discussion of distinct preferences and identities, several of the following chapters discuss gender identity and sexual orientation separately.

Gender and sexual minority learners often face challenges from discrimination, bias, and lack of representation. GME programs must recognize and address these disparities as they can influence mental health, career advancement, and overall sense of belonging. Many in these identity groups face microaggressions and may also identify with other attributes or marginalized characteristics that can impact their day-to-day experience in health care environments and their long-term career success. For example, although the number of women entering medical education has surpassed that of men, there are still many areas, such as specific specialties, leadership roles, and tenured faculty positions, that remain highly underrepresented with respect to women. Additionally, women in academic medicine continue to face numerous challenges such as navigating the complexities of balancing their work and home life while programs may provide inadequate parental leave or resources for working parents.[3] Although parental and caregiver leave considerations apply to any parent regardless of gender, women in medicine have been and continue to be disproportionately affected.

Disability and non-traditional age are crucial factors that merit careful consideration when creating inclusive clinical and educational environments. Individuals with disabilities are an essential and valuable part of the health care workforce, with the potential to improve health care for all and reduce disparities for patients with disabilities through informed experiences. Individuals of non-traditional age have significant life experiences that can positively add to their medical teams' efficacy and help improve their rapport with patients and patient outcomes. Both demographic groups experience barriers, such as bias in evaluation, that can hinder their participation and success. Providing the necessary accommodations and support may foster an environment where all can thrive.

By addressing the challenges faced by women, transgender and gender-diverse individuals, sexual minorities, individuals with disabilities, and non-traditionally aged learners, GME programs can create a more inclusive and equitable environment for all residents, fellows, and faculty members. In each chapter, the authors also propose strategies for how gender and sexual identities, disability, and age differences can be included and celebrated in the clinical learning environment.

* * *

Chapter 19: Women in Academic Medicine: Optimizing Equity, Inclusion, and Belonging
Vidhya Prakash, MD, FACP, FIDSA, FAMWA; Susan M. Pollart, MD, MS; Wendi El-Amin, MD; Julie K. Silver, MD

Women face significant barriers in medicine at all stages of their education and careers despite the fact they have made great strides in eradicating the gender gap in medical school admissions. As a result, women in medicine warrant particular consideration in discussions of equity and inclusion in *A Guide*. Prakash et al provide ample evidence of these challenges, which are magnified for women whose identity intersects with being racially or ethnically minoritized.

The cumulative effect of numerous microaggressions against women, particularly in medicine, often results in a negative impact on wellness and academic performance, including anxiety, depression, and hypertension. Unconscious bias demonstrated in recruiting and hiring processes, such as in the language and graphic design of recruiting literature, can send an implicit message that certain individuals belong, while others do not. The authors suggest strategies to help GME programs identify and overcome gender and racial bias against women-identifying learners and professionals and suggest methods to provide optimal support for women as integral to the health care workforce.

Chapter 20: Transgender and Gender-Diverse Patients, Physician Learners, Clinicians, and Staff: Improving Inclusion, Equity, and Belonging
Keisha Bell, MD, FAAP, FCCM; Monique Gary, DO, MSc, FACS, FSSO

Recognizing that health care for gender-diverse patients has been historically poor, Bell and Gary focus specifically on physician learners in GME programs who are transgender, non-binary, or otherwise gender-diverse and may have experienced mistreatment and bias because of their gender identities. They guide readers through a review of basic terminology and demographics, along with the historical context and current state of health care of transgender individuals. The authors explore unique cultural and societal considerations that place this community at risk and provide strategies that promote equity in the patient encounter and in the clinical work environment.

Chapter 21: Inclusion and Health Equity for Sexual Minorities
Nelson Sánchez, MD; Tyree M.S. Winters, DO

Sánchez and Winters help to extend discussion of the importance of inclusive learning environments for sexual minorities, ie, those who do not identify as straight or heterosexual, in GME. They point to the US Supreme Court ruling that prohibits workplace discrimination based on sexual orientation or gender identity (*Bostock v. Clayton County*) wherein institutions and programs can find judicial justification for their efforts to advance LGBTQIA+ inclusion. The authors provide resources and practical strategies that can be used by GME programs and institutions when aiming to recruit, retain, and support residents and fellows with sexual minority identities.

Chapter 22: Creating Inclusive Working and Learning Climates for Residents and Fellows with Disabilities in Graduate Medical Education
Michael S. Argenyi, MD, MPH, MSW; Jasmine R. Marcelin, MD; Nichole Taylor, DO; Christopher J. Moreland, MD, MPH; Lisa M. Meeks, PhD, MA

Argenyi et al remind readers that discussions related to diversity, equity, and inclusion in medicine often overlook disability, even though individuals with disabilities represent a diverse, marginalized group in GME. Despite a demonstrated commitment through various levels of guidance by accreditors and medical associations, and with regulatory support from national and state agencies, these physician learners continue to experience the challenges associated with misunderstanding, lack of support, and stereotyping that result in discrimination and inequitable treatment. Based on their own experience and input from disabled physician learners who shared their stories and experiences, the authors offer ways to challenge stereotypes and increase disability consciousness, stressing education of resident and fellow colleagues and faculty members alike. The chapter stresses, as has been noted throughout *A Guide,* that such efforts to understand a new way of thinking require cultural humility to recognize the need for changing attitudes. The chapter discusses guidance from professional associations, the challenges associated with a lack of funding structure to support accommodations, and other specific strategies to improve inclusion of physician learners with disabilities in GME.

Chapter 23: Remaining Inclusive of and Supporting Non-traditionally Aged Residents
Ngozi F. Anachebe, PharmD, MD; Leila E. Harrison (née Diaz), PhD, MA, MEd

Non-traditionally aged physician learners bring unique and diverse life experiences and perspectives to their GME experience. Anachebe and Harrison demonstrate how the concept of intersectionality once again plays a critical role in understanding the contributions of these residents and fellows, whose age is only one aspect of their identity that can positively contribute to patient care and the GME learning environment. They propose strategies to improve the educational experience of residents and fellows of non-traditional age, enhance faculty development to equip educators with the skills needed to support these learners, and build an inclusive learning environment that recognizes and values the experience of all physician learners, including those of non-traditional age.

REFERENCES

1. Egelko A, Agarwal S, Erkmen C. Confronting the scope of LGBT inequity in surgery. *J Am Coll Surg.* 2022;234(5):959-963. doi:10.1097/XCS.0000000000000101
2. Ortega P, Osman-Krinsky M, Silva D. Slow and steady: using inclusive language to enhance academic medicine's social accountability. *Acad Med.* 2024;99(12):1323-1327. doi.org/10.1097/ACM.0000000000005792
3. Finch SJ. Pregnancy during residency: a literature review. *Acad Med.* 2003;78(4):418-428. doi:10.1097/00001888-200304000-00021

Women in Academic Medicine: Optimizing Equity, Inclusion, and Belonging

Vidhya Prakash, MD, FACP, FIDSA, FAMWA, Chief Medical Officer, Associate Dean of Clinical Affairs and Population Health, Professor of Internal Medicine, Infectious Diseases Faculty, Southern Illinois University School of Medicine, Springfield, IL

Susan M. Pollart, MD, MS, Senior Associate Dean for Faculty Affairs and Faculty Development, Ruth E. Murdaugh Professor of Family Medicine, University of Virginia School of Medicine, UVA Health, Charlottesville, VA

Wendi El-Amin, MD, Associate Dean of Equity, Diversity, and Inclusion, Professor of Family and Community Medicine, Southern Illinois University School of Medicine, Springfield, IL

Julie K. Silver, MD, Associate Professor, Associate Chair, Department of Physical Medicine and Rehabilitation, Harvard Medical School, Spaulding Rehabilitation Hospital, Massachusetts General Hospital, and Brigham and Women's Hospital, Boston, MA

CHAPTER SUMMARY

Individuals who identify as women in academic medicine face numerous challenges and serve as important role models as they navigate the complexities of balancing their work and home spheres. Women physicians lag behind their male counterparts in promotion and tenure and are not sufficiently represented in leadership. Furthermore, women are paid less for the same amount of work and experience many forms of harassment from colleagues, supervisors, and patients both in and outside of academic medicine. These issues are amplified for women whose identity intersects with other marginalized characteristics, leading to feelings of isolation and lack of support for minoritized learners and faculty members. Inadequate parental leave policies coupled with a dearth of resources for working parents only intensify the struggle for women in medicine. This chapter provides data and strategies to help graduate medical education (GME) programs overcome gender and racial bias against women-identifying learners and professionals, and suggests methods to provide optimal support for this integral part of the health care workforce.

LEARNING OBJECTIVES

1. Become familiar with the data around pay disparities and lack of professional advancement of those in academic medicine who identifying as women.
2. Describe the effects of implicit and explicit bias and work-life challenges on those persons in GME who identify as women.
3. Develop strategies to improve the experience and career progression of those who identify as women physicians.

Case Study

Dr Monique Thomas is excited to come back to her workplace as an academic pediatrician. She just finished four weeks of maternity leave and has mixed feelings about leaving her infant daughter, Nicole, at daycare. Dr Thomas is also nervous that her husband, an officer in the United States military, is leaving in three days for a yearlong deployment. Dr Thomas joined her academic practice 11 years ago. Her current academic rank is assistant professor.

Dr Thomas drops her baby off at daycare, holding her a little longer as she knows it is her child's first day away from her mother. She walks into the conference room at 9:03 AM for the 9:00 AM quarterly departmental meeting. Her department chair pauses mid-speech and says, "Dr Thomas, I know you are returning from maternity leave, but you really need to be here on time." Embarrassed, she apologizes and quickly sits down.

Later, Dr Thomas joins her team on the inpatient pediatrics service at the hospital. They walk into a patient's room, and she greets the patient's parent. "You?" the parent eyes her warily. "I didn't know they let people like you go to medical school." There is an awkward silence in the room. Dr Thomas continues, "I completed four years of medical school and three years of pediatric residency, Mrs Jones. Now, I would like to ask some questions." The parent huffs and rolls her eyes.

Once rounds are finished, Dr Thomas sends her department chair a text that she will have to move their meeting from 12:00 PM to 12:30 PM, as she is lactating and needs to pump. Her department chair does not respond. She hurriedly asks a colleague where there is a lactation room. Her colleague laughs and points to the bathroom. Dr Thomas balances herself on the seat of a toilet, pumps for 15 minutes, and then rushes to her department chair's office.

"You really need to get your act together, Monique," he starts. "You have been late twice today." Dr Thomas apologizes profusely, but he does not seem to listen. She gingerly brings up the topic of promotion. "I have been here for 11 years and thought we could talk about promotion," she begins, realizing that she has brought this matter up annually for 10 years and has made no progress. Her department chair cuts her off. "Hmm, maybe we can talk about it in six months, when you're back on track," he replies curtly. "Could you explain what you mean by 'back on track'?" she asks him. He changes the subject.

Case Discussion

Dr Thomas' case illustrates the complexities of being a woman in academic medicine. She will soon function as a single parent and will need the support of colleagues, learners, and leadership. Her uncomfortable encounter with a patient's parent is an example of the bias faced by women with intersectional identities. The ensuing silence of her team members after the parent's remark further underscores the need for education and training on how to address such situations proactively and productively, whether as the target of the attack or as a bystander. The stern reprimand about her tardiness and lack of empathy from her department chair, who knows she is returning from maternity leave, and the lack of lactation support, illustrate the need for organizations and leadership to provide support and accommodations for parents. Dr Thomas' lack of headway with her department chair in her conversations about promotion after 11 years of service highlights an opportunity to address women's lack of progression in promotion and leadership at the departmental and organizational levels. While reading this chapter, consider how variations in the social, racial, ethnic, religious, or other intersectional identities of each person in the case study may have an impact on how the story unfolded or how each person is perceived. Think of ways in which you could have supported Dr Thomas as her resident, colleague, or department chair, and what changes you would want to make in your organization to address her challenges. Finally, consider how the environment in which Dr Thomas practices may impact the experience of resident and fellow physicians (or other learners), particularly women, in the program.

DIVERSITY AND INCLUSION FOR WOMEN IN MEDICINE

Women-identifying students have made great strides in narrowing the gender gap in medical school admission,[1] and while they have comprised a large proportion of graduates for decades, they still face many barriers. Certainly, there has been tremendous progress for women in medicine, but many inequities persist and affect women at all stages of their education and careers. For example, one study demonstrated that women remain less likely to be promoted to full professor or chair of a department than men.[1] Even more concerning, the study showed no progress on these metrics over the past 35 years. Women whose identity is intersectional with other marginalized characteristics, including but not limited to those who identify with underrepresented racial and ethnic groups or with minoritized sexual orientation or gender identities (SOGI), often face higher levels of bias and discrimination.[2] Issues of bias and discrimination disproportionately affecting women are common not only among faculty members, but also in medical education to the point that it affects women medical students' choice of specialty.[3]

Importantly, no specialty stands out as being a model for gender equity. In fact, specialties with large proportions of women, including pediatrics, obstetrics and gynecology, and dermatology, continue to struggle with many gender-related disparities, such as promoting women to the highest-level leadership positions. The fact that disparities exist even when women comprise the majority of a specialty has refuted the theory that critical mass is sufficient[4]; this theory postulates that things will change for the better on their own when there are enough women (ie, 30% or more) in a specialty. Because we cannot count on things changing simply by diversifying medical school classes, some experts have encouraged people to become "critical actors" and focus on driving change strategically and intentionally.[4]

ACHIEVING FAIR PAY AND A SAFE AND SUPPORTIVE WORK ENVIRONMENT

Gender-related pay disparities disfavoring women have been documented in all specialties and many subspecialties of medicine. The pay disparities occur for women even when accounting for other variables, such as productivity and time off from work. These disparities begin when women seek their first job after completing a residency or fellowship, and last throughout their careers, even when they achieve high-level leadership positions, such as chair of a department.[5] National surveys, such as those conducted by Doximity and Medscape, as well as some peer-reviewed studies, have shown that women with intersectional marginalized race and ethnicity identities experience greater gaps in pay than men or White women.[6] The struggle is not limited to women physicians, as learners are also plagued by financial hurdles. Further complicating the financial stress equation is education debt, which is disproportionally carried by Black learners.[7]

HARASSMENT

A landmark report published by the National Academies of Science, Engineering, and Medicine (NASEM) describes **sexual harassment**, which is pervasive for women in medicine, and defines it as "a form of discrimination that consists of three types of harassing behavior: (1) **gender harassment** (verbal and nonverbal behaviors that convey hostility, objectification, exclusion, or second-class status about members of one gender); (2) **unwanted sexual attention** (unwelcome verbal or physical sexual advances, which can include assault); and (3) **sexual coercion** (when favorable professional or educational treatment is conditioned on sexual activity)."[8] The report noted that harassing behavior can be either *direct* (targeted at an individual) or *ambient* (a general level of sexual harassment in an environment), and that both are harmful. The report also stated that the "overwhelming majority of sexual harassment involves some form of gender harassment (ie, affronts that include sexist hostility and crude behavior). Unwanted sexual attention is the next most common form of sexual harassment, and only a small minority of women experience sexual coercion."[8]

An environment free of any form of harassment is considered safe. Yet even in work environments that are psychologically safe, women often must navigate challenges, such as trying to find the time and a dedicated space to pump breast milk when lactating. Some GME programs are paying for wearable breast pumps for women residents and fellows to minimize interruptions and promote ease of pumping, thus offering tangible support. This type of support is not only needed, but it may also enhance residency recruitment efforts when eligible medical students learn of a program's family-friendly work environment. Additionally, women may also be expected to do a greater share of citizenship tasks and invisible work, such as unofficial mentoring, committee assignments, and event planning.[9] Such expectations are referred to in the literature as a **gender tax** or minority tax.[10]

CLIMATE AND CULTURE: MICROAGGRESSIONS AFFECTING WOMEN IN GME

When women are subjected to pay disparities, gender taxes, and lack of accommodations (eg, lactation rooms), the result is an unfavorable climate and culture for all. The term "learning climate" refers to the general atmosphere of a work group intended to support and encourage a learner's involvement. "Workplace culture" is defined as how individuals interact and treat one another in the work environment.[11] A healthy workplace culture and learning climate cultivate work engagement, which results in optimal patient care delivery, fewer medical errors, and enhanced patient satisfaction. Less healthy learning climates are associated with burnout and lower quality of life in health care professionals, particularly in residents and fellows.[12]

The data regarding resident/fellow burnout and mental health are startling. Up to one-third of physician learners have clinical depression, 50% to 70% experience burnout, and 6% to 12% express suicidal ideation by their third year of medical school and residency.[13] Further, suicide rates for physicians are twice that of the general population.[13] Two studies comparing resident and faculty member well-being found that residents, particularly female residents, were more likely to report feelings of sadness or depression and had the lowest probability of scoring above the study population mean for wellness.[14]

What are the contributing factors to unhealthy learning environment, culture, climate, and lack of well-being for women residents and fellows? According to Dr Derald Wing Sue (2020), microaggressions are defined as "verbal and nonverbal interpersonal exchanges in which a perpetrator causes harm to a target, whether intended or unintended," and further, these "brief and commonplace indignities communicate hostile, derogatory, and/or negative slights to the target."[15] Implicit (unconscious) and explicit (conscious) gender and race-based bias often manifest in the form of these very microaggressions, a term originally coined by Dr Chester M. Pierce.[16] A nurse asking a junior male resident what medications he would like to order when a woman senior resident is running the code is one of many examples of a gender-based **microaggression**. The implication is that the male resident is running the code.[16] The cumulative effect of these "one thousand paper cuts" on women, and particularly those who are underrepresented in medicine, include burnout, negative impact on wellness and academic performance, and chronic health conditions, such as anxiety, depression, and hypertension.[16] Think back to our case involving Dr Thomas and her chair. Do you think she is experiencing microaggressions? What impact might her experiences with various forms of bias have on her emotional and physical well-being?

PARENTHOOD AS A WOMAN PHYSICIAN IN GME

Women residents and fellows who are parents also face a myriad of challenges when their academic culture and climate are not conducive to their overall well-being. The Mayo School of Graduate Medical Education's internet-based survey of 269 residents and fellows in their GME programs showed that approximately 40% of respondents planned to have children.[17] The ACGME has included parental leave compliant with applicable laws in its Institutional Requirements since 2003. In addition, since 2021, along with member boards of the American Board of Medical Specialties (ABMS), established a minimum requirement of six weeks of parental leave at least once during residency, which was a promising breakthrough.

A comprehensive review of pregnancy during residency found increased rates of preterm labor and preterm delivery in pregnant residents.[18] In addition, 13 studies identify antepartum and postpartum stress and perceptions of discrimination as a part of the pregnancy experience for residents. Six studies describe colleague and faculty member resentment and perceptions of childbearing as a risk to a department. The intense pressure on resident mothers to return to work from maternity leave was also described.[18] Women who wish to continue to breastfeed face considerable challenges when returning to work. One study showed the primary reason for women residents to discontinue breastfeeding was their work schedule.[19] While 80% initiated and continued breastfeeding during maternity leave, half discontinued on return to work; by six months, only 15% were still breastfeeding. Among the minority who continued breastfeeding after six months, challenges described were insufficient time, no appropriate place to pump at work, and lack of consistent support from faculty members, staff members, and colleagues.[19]

STRATEGIES TO IMPROVE INCLUSION AND BELONGING FOR WOMEN IN GME PROGRAMS

Studies that show little or no progress for many years, even decades, tell us that we need to think more strategically about interventions and devote more resources to improving inclusion and belonging for women in GME programs. For example, reports published by NASEM suggest specific actions for effective mentoring programs (Table 19.1)[20] and reducing sexual harassment (Table 19.2).[8] The authors propose the following

Table 19.1 Recommended Practices for Mentoring and Their Impact on Inclusion for Women in GME

Recommended Practice for Mentoring	Example of How Each Practice May Enhance Inclusion for Women Resident Physicians and Faculty Members in GME
1. Adopt an operational definition of mentorship.	Emphasize the importance of the trusting relationship, investment of time, and bi-directional communication in building successful mentorship relationships across the organization.
2. Use an evidenced-based approach to support mentorship.	Utilize multiple resources and studies highlighted in the *Journal of Graduate Medical Education* and NASEM.
3. Establish and use structured feedback systems to improve mentorship at all levels.	Encourage mentors and mentees to set up regularly scheduled meetings to discuss a mentee's progress in their specific goals; encourage mentees to share feedback on whether their needs are met.
4. Recognize and respond to identities in mentorship.	Develop mentorship programs for Black, LHS+, Native American, LGBTQIA+, and transgender residents.
5. Support multiple mentorship structures.	Structure formal mentorship program events while honoring more informal mentorship relationships.
6. Reward effective mentorship.	Add mentorship to criteria for promotion and tenure; honor mentors with mentorship awards on a regular basis.
7. Mitigate negative mentorship experiences.	Emphasize the foundation of trust in mentorship relationships; establish a reporting system where mentees can disclose negative experiences.

Adapted from Dahlberg ML, Byars-Winston A, eds. *The Science of Effective Mentorship in STEMM.* National Academies of Sciences, Engineering, and Medicine; Policy and Global Affairs; Board on Higher Education and Workforce; Committee on Effective Mentoring in STEMM. National Academies Press (US); 2019.

Table 19.2 Recommended Practices for Reducing Sexual Harassment That Can Be Applied to GME

1. Create diverse inclusive, and respectful environments.
2. Address the most common form of sexual harassment: gender harassment.
3. Move beyond legal compliance to address culture and climate.
4. Improve transparency and accountability.
5. Diffuse the hierarchical and dependent relationship between residents/fellows and faculty members.
6. Provide support for the person who experienced harassment.
7. Prioritize strong and diverse leadership.
8. Measure progress.
9. Incentivize change.
10. Address the failures to meaningfully enforce Title VII's prohibition on sex discrimination.
11. Make the entire academic community responsible for reducing and preventing sexual harassment.

Adapted from Benya FF, Widnall SE, Johnson PA, eds. *Sexual Harassment of Women: Climate, Culture, and Consequences in Academic Sciences, Engineering, and Medicine.* National Academies of Sciences, Engineering, and Medicine; Policy and Global Affairs; Committee on Women in Science, Engineering, and Medicine; Committee on the Impacts of Sexual Harassment in Academia. National Academies Press (US); 2018. doi: 10.17226/24994

strategies that GME Sponsoring Institutions and programs should consider for ensuring that women physicians can thrive in a safe learning and practice environment:

1. *Consistently use gender bias evaluation practices and tools.*

    Gender bias is common in evaluations of students, residents and fellows, and faculty members. For example, in a literature review, 5 out of 9 studies reported gender bias in resident feedback.[21]

    Job descriptions, awards announcements, requests for applications, letters of recommendation, and similar documents may use language that is exclusive, such as words that target a single group (or the preferences of a single group) rather than another. This is a common source of unconscious bias, notably in the recruiting and hiring processes. Authors of these documents[22] must be mindful of language chosen to appropriately represent the skills, talents, and attributes of the person being described. Efforts should be devoted to discussing the potential impact of bias, whether conscious or unconscious, prior to decision-making, such as resident/fellow ranking or faculty member hiring decisions. The Bias Time Out tool[23] is a framework that invites decision makers to consider what bias may impact their decision and discuss opportunities to mitigate that bias prior to making a decision.

2. *Acknowledge, explore, and proactively address interpersonal implicit (and explicit) bias and microaggressions.*

    Women, and particularly women with intersectional marginalized characteristics, are negatively impacted by bias. The authors recommend acknowledging these experiences and providing opportunities to discuss them in open and safe spaces, such as through workshops, teaching sessions, peer mentoring sessions, or educational modules. Further, they recommend adopting frameworks to productively respond to microaggressions and any acts of bias. One method is ERASE: *Expect* mistreatment will occur; *Recognize* mistreatment; *Address* the situation in real-time; *Support* the individual after the event; and *Establish* a positive culture.[24] Establishing an equity support team consisting of trauma-informed faculty members to handle instances of mistreatment in real-time is another strategy to consider.

3. *Track data around systemic microaggressions (gender taxation, "untitling," service expectations, obligation to volunteer) and macroaggressions (awards, pay, institutional policies, academic promotion, leadership selection) to inform policy changes.*

    An analysis of departmental and institutional data can identify areas where women are disproportionally represented in support roles (mentorship, committee service without leadership, volunteer activities that do not advance women's careers) and aim to adjust the contributions of everyone toward these activities.

The tendency to "**untitle**" women, addressing them by their first name in settings where male colleagues are addressed by professional titles, is well documented. Individuals and groups can adopt name-affirming practices[25] that appropriately address all members of the community, using professional titles regardless of gender.

Similarly, there should be a standardized institutional approach to recruitment, selection, and compensation so that the voice and perspectives of all genders and those with intersectional, minoritized, gender identities are represented when decisions are made regarding award nominations, candidate selections, compensation policies and standards, and conference planning.[26]

4. *Establish and enforce parental leave guidelines that optimally support women residents, fellows, and faculty members.*

    It is vitally important to have parental leave guidelines that are easily accessible and separate from general leaves of absence. The ACGME Institutional Requirements and the ABMS member boards have established firm guidelines of a minimum of parental leave. The question remains, is six weeks enough? The optimal duration of parental leave to maximize the well-being of residents and fellows who are parents while allowing them to complete their program requires further study and discussion. Further, organizations must work to create a culture of acceptance and support of parents.

    Regular review of institutional policies and procedures for exclusionary practices that impact those in caregiving roles is vital. Women disproportionally assume caregiving roles given cultural norms and expectations within their own families, and thus face greater work-related conflict when caregiving infringes on professional responsibilities. This is particularly problematic for residents, fellows, and early-career women faculty members when the demands of caring for young children are typically at their highest; yet the experience, expertise, and roles that may allow for career flexibility are not yet established. Institutions should devote efforts to strengthen policies, practices, and processes to better support the productivity and retention of residents, fellows, and early-career faculty members with family caregiving responsibilities.[27]

5. *Establish flexible work arrangements and family-friendly accommodations.*

    For mothers who return from parental leave, flexible rotations with a lighter workload, whether they are residents, fellows, or faculty members, will enhance their well-being and ability to effectively transition back to the workplace. Family-friendly accommodations, to include protected time for pumping and easily accessible lactation rooms for mothers as mandated by ACGME Institutional Requirement III.B.7.d).(4),[28] and Common Program Requirement I.D.2.c),[29] coupled with childcare resources in the form of on-site daycare and back-up childcare, will provide considerable support for parents who are working outside the home.

6. *Leverage the power of allies.*

    There is evidence that both targets and bystanders may experience moral injury in toxic cultures, including when a microaggression occurs. Innumerable opportunities exist to demonstrate active allyship on a daily basis. Importantly, organizational leaders need to develop a positive workplace culture and learning climate in which everyone is treated with dignity and respect. Skills in allyship can be built through individual learning and institutional training, with resources on best practices and exemplar programs available.[30]

> While there has been great progress for women in medicine, multiple inequities persist that affect them at all stages of their education and careers.

> Harassment and racial and gender bias faced by women physicians is taking a toll on their mental health, quality of life, and ability to advance in their careers.

Take Home Points

- Addressing women physicians' lack of advancement in promotion and tenure and leadership must be a top priority for any GME Sponsoring Institution and program.
- Using evidence-based tools to counter micro- and macroaggressions is vital to cultivating a healthy institutional culture and climate for women in academic medicine.
- Data is foundational to informing decisions on modifying inequitable policies, procedures, and practices, such as pay, parental leave, and breastfeeding accommodations.
- Flexible work arrangements and fair parental policies are imperative to optimally support women residents, fellows, and faculty members who are parents.

QUESTIONS FOR FURTHER THOUGHT

1. What data does your institution track that could enable evaluation of gender disparities in leadership, promotion, and pay? How can your institution or program enhance its data collection, tracking, or reporting to address gender equity?
2. What systems does your institution have in place to address and reduce microaggressions and macroaggressions that affect women physicians, including residents, fellows, and faculty members?
3. How accessible and equitable is the current parental leave policy at your institution?

REFERENCES

1. Richter KP, Clark L, Wick JA, et al. Women physicians and promotion in academic medicine. *N Engl J Med.* 2020;383(22):2148-2157. doi:10.1056/NEJMsa1916935
2. Myers AK, Williams MS, Pekmezaris R. Intersectionality and its impact on microaggression in female physicians in academic medicine: a cross-sectional study. *Womens Health Rep (New Rochelle).* 2023;4(1):298-304. doi:10.1089/whr.2022.0101
3. Stratton TD. McLaughlin MA, Witte FM, Fosson SE, Nora LM. Does students' exposure to gender discrimination and sexual harassment in medical school affect specialty choice and residency program selection? *Acad Med.* 2005;80(4):400-408. doi:10.1097/00001888-200504000-00020
4. Helitzer DL, Newbill SL, Cardinali G, Morahan PS, Chang S, Magrane D. Changing the culture of academic medicine: critical mass or critical actors? *J Womens Health (Larchmt).* 2017;26(5):540-548. doi:10.1089/jwh.2016.6019
5. Mensah M, Beeler W, Rotenstein L, et al. Sex differences in salaries of department chairs at public medical schools. *JAMA Intern Med.* 2020;180(5):789-792. doi:10.1001/jamainternmed.2019.7540
6. Association of American Medical Colleges. Promising practices for understanding and addressing faculty salary equity at U.S. medical schools; 2019. Accessed June 12, 2024. https://store.aamc.org/promising-practices-for-understanding-and-addressing-faculty-salary-equity-at-u-s-medical-schools.html
7. Holaday LW, Weiss JM, Sow SD, Perez HR, Ross JS, Genao I. Differences in debt among postgraduate medical residents by self-designated race and ethnicity, 2014-19. *Health Aff (Millwood).* 2023;42(1):63-73. doi:10.1377/hlthaff.2022.00446
8. Benya FF, Widnall SE, Johnson PA, eds. *Sexual Harassment of Women: Climate, Culture, and Consequences in Academic Sciences, Engineering, and Medicine.* National Academies of Sciences, Engineering, and Medicine; Policy and Global Affairs; Committee on Women in Science, Engineering, and Medicine; Committee on the Impacts of Sexual Harassment in Academia. National Academies Press (US); 2018. doi:10.17226/24994
9. Armijo PR, Silver JK, Larson AR, Asante P, Shillcutt S. Citizenship tasks and women physicians: additional woman tax in academic medicine? *J Womens Health (Larchmt).* 2021;30(7):935-943. doi:10.1089/jwh.2020.8482
10. Kamceva M, Kyerematen B Spigner S, et al. More work, less reward: the minority tax on us medical students. *Wellness.* 4(1). doi:10.55504/2578-9333.1116

11. Tanaka P, Hasan N, Tseng A, Tran C, Macario A, Harris I. Assessing the workplace culture and learning climate in the inpatient operating room suite at an academic medical center. *J Surg Educ*. 2019;76(3): 644-651. doi:10.1016/j.jsurg.2018.09.014
12. Lases LSS, Arah OA, Busch ORC, Heineman MJ, Lombarts KMJMH. Learning climate positively influences residents' work-related well-being. *Adv Health Sci Educ Theory Pract*. 2019;24(2):317-330. doi:10.1007/s10459-018-9868-4
13. Ey S, Moffit M, Kinzie JM, Brunett PH. Feasibility of a comprehensive wellness and suicide prevention program: a decade of caring for physicians in training and practice. *J Grad Med Educ*. 2016;8(5):747-753. doi:10.4300/JGME-D-16-00034.1
14. Raj KS. Well-being in residency: a systematic review. *J Grad Med Educ*. 2016;8(5):674-684. doi:10.4300/JGME-D-15-00764.1
15. Sue DW. *Microaggressions in Everyday Life: Race, Gender, and Sexual Orientation*. Wiley; 2010.
16. Molina MF, Landry AI, Chary AN, Burnett-Bowie SM. Addressing the elephant in the room: microaggressions in medicine. *Ann Emerg Med*. 2020;76(4):387-391. doi:10.1016/j.annemergmed.2020.04.009
17. Blair JE, Mayer AP, Caubet SL, Norby SM, O'Connor MI, Hayes SN. Pregnancy and parental leave during graduate medical education. *Acad Med*. 2016;91(7):972-978. doi: 10.1097/ACM.0000000000001006
18. Finch SJ. Pregnancy during residency: a literature review. *Acad Med*. 2003;78(4):418-428. doi:10.1097/00001888-200304000-00021
19. Miller NH, Miller DJ, Chism M. Breastfeeding practices among resident physicians. *Pediatrics*. 1996;98 (3 Pt 1):434-437. PMID: 8784369
20. Dahlberg ML, Byars-Winston A, eds. *The Science of Effective Mentorship in STEMM*. National Academies of Sciences, Engineering, and Medicine; Policy and Global Affairs; Board on Higher Education and Workforce; Committee on Effective Mentoring in STEMM. National Academies Press (US); 2019.
21. Klein, R, Julian, KA, Snyder, ED, et al. Gender bias in resident assessment in graduate medical education: review of the literature. *J Gen Intern Med*. 2019;34:712-719. doi:10.1007/s11606-019-04884-0
22. Madera JM, Hebl MR, Martin RC. Gender and letters of recommendation for academia: agentic and communal differences. *J Appl Psychol*. 2009;94(6):1591-1599. doi:10.1037/a0016539
23. Calder G, Boyd C, Calhoun C, Capozzalo G, Pollart S. The Bias Time Out: a practical tool for advancing in the health care space. *Manag Health Care*. 2023;7(4):301-318. https://hstalks.com/article/7854/download/?business
24. Goldenberg MN, Cyrus KD, Wilkins KM. ERASE: a new framework for faculty to manage mistreatment of trainees. *Acad Psychiatry*. 2019;43(4):396-399. doi:10.1007/S40596-018-1011-6
25. Olson EM, Dines VA, Ryan SM, et al. Physician identification badges: a multispecialty quality improvement study to address professional misidentification and bias. *Mayo Clin Proc*. 2022;97(4):658-667. doi:10.1016/j.mayocp.2022.01.007
26. Arora A, Kaur Y, Dossa F, Nisenbaum R, Little D, Baxter NN. Proportion of female speakers at academic medical conferences across multiple specialties and regions. *JAMA Netw Open*. 2020;3(9):e2018127. doi:10.1001/jamanetworkopen.2020.18127
27. Jagsi R, Jones RD, Griffith KA, et al. An innovative program to support gender equity and success in academic medicine: early experiences from the Doris Duke charitable foundation's fund to retain clinical scientists. *Ann Intern Med*. 2018;169(2):128-130. doi:10.7326/M17-2676
28. Accreditation Council for Graduate Medical Education. Institutional requirements. Accessed June 12, 2024. https://www.acgme.org/globalassets/pfassets/programrequirements/800_institutionalrequirements2022.pdf
29. Accreditation Council for Graduate Medical Education. Common Program Requirements (Residency). Accessed June 12, 2024. https://www.acgme.org/globalassets/pfassets/programrequirements/cprresidency_2023.pdf
30. Melaku TM, Beeman A, Smith DG, Johnson WB. Be a better ally. *Harv Bus Rev*. 2020. Accessed February 22, 2023. https://hbr.org/2020/11/be-a-better-ally

20

Transgender and Gender-Diverse Patients, Physician Learners, Clinicians, and Staff: Improving Inclusion, Equity, and Belonging

Keisha Bell, MD, FAAP, FCCM, Associate Professor of Pediatrics, Vice Chair of Inpatient Operations, Department of Pediatrics, Chief, Division of Pediatric Critical Care, Director of Diversity, Equity, and Inclusion for Department of Pediatrics Medstar Georgetown University Hospital, Medstar Georgetown University Hospital, Washington, DC

Monique Gary, DO, MSc, FACS, FSSO, Breast Surgical Oncologist, Adjunct Associate Professor, Health Equity, Dartmouth Institute for Health Policy and Clinical Practice, Dartmouth Geisel School of Medicine, Hanover, NH

CHAPTER SUMMARY

Health care for gender-diverse patients has historically been poor in both quality and delivery. This community is often marginalized within the health care space. In many circumstances, both patients and physician learners in graduate medical education (GME) programs who are transgender, non-binary, or otherwise gender-diverse have experienced bias and mistreatment because of their gender identities. Recognition of the need for health care-related competence focused specifically on transgender and gender-diverse (TGD) people has been well documented. We will present case-based learning that highlights best practices for health care delivery and aids in fostering an affirming environment for patients, residents, fellows, faculty members, and staff. In addition to reviewing fundamental concepts, we will explore unique cultural and societal considerations that place this community at risk, with the intent to provide physician learners with strategies to promote equity within both the medical encounter and the work environment.

LEARNING OBJECTIVES

1. Review basic terminology and demographics of transgender and TGD people.
2. Review the historical context and current landscape of health care focused on TGD people.
3. Explore strategies to improve the learning environment for physician learners of all gender identities and enhance institutional equity practices.

Case Study

Sal, a transgender man who is a third year cardiology fellow, presented to the breast center with a complaint of breast pain. He was referred for diagnostic imaging, but delayed presentation for 4 months because not only is he a busy fellow, but also because he was nervous about being a patient in his own institution. Sal's roommate,

(continued)

Dana, had an embarrassing experience last year in the emergency department of the same health system and came home crying, untreated for the original concern, vowing never to return to the place that treated them so disrespectfully.

In the process of registering at the center, Sal was given a bright pink gown with his pink intake form. From there, he was sent behind double doors where a member of the environmental staff immediately stopped him, saying, "Sir, are you lost? This area is for women only." Sal shyly replied, "I'm here for a mammogram," to which the staff member replied, "Oh, yes, sorry." A technician then came to meet him and led Sal to a private dressing room where he undressed and waited to be taken to mammography. As the mammogram was being performed, the technician repeatedly instructed him with canned phrases like, "Ok, ma'am, please hold your breath" and "One more set of films, ma'am, and we're all done." Upon completion, Sal was taken back to the waiting room where, minutes later, the ultrasound tech knocked on the door saying, "Sal, we need to examine you further with ultrasound by a physician."

During the wait, Sal wondered many things: *Does this condition run in my family?* He was no longer in communication with his family, so he was unable to ask. He also wondered: *Who will take care of me? How much work will I have to miss? How much is all of this going to cost?*

Sal's concerns grew during the 5-minute wait. After the ultrasound, which seemed to go well, he was told that the breast doctor could see him today for a clinical exam since the ultrasound only showed dense breast tissue and clinical correlation was recommended. He was instructed to dress and was escorted down the hall to a surgical clinic where, after registering at the front desk, Sal was shown to another exam room. The medical assistant seemed flustered and said, "Ok ma'am…um, sir, uh, please change into this gown and wait for the doctor."

The doctor entered the exam room hurriedly. She seemed to have been running behind, or was in a hurry. She looked at the intake form and said, "Ok, sir, looks like you have breast pain. Did you have imaging? Gynecomastia is very common in males and can be a source of breast pain." When the doctor looked up, she saw the confused look on Sal's face, and said, "Oh, I'm sorry. Let's begin again. I think we've got this all mixed up…"

Case Discussion

This case highlights some of the complexities encountered by all stakeholders in the health care landscape that can ultimately impact patient care and, potentially, health outcomes. Set against the backdrop of the uncomfortable health care experience of Sal's roommate, the vulnerability of the fellow as a patient in the scenario is evident. What could be the impact of being misgendered by the technicians, environmental staff, and the attending physician? Further, the attending physician makes assumptions about the nature of the clinical concern based upon Sal's presumed gender. What might be the consequence of this clinical error for Sal and how might it impact his ability to feel supported by his health system? As you consider this scenario, what steps can the breast specialist take moving forward, now having recognized the error, to assure Sal that he is being appropriately managed? What system-wide initiatives could be implemented to address this issue, the clinical environment, and the patient experience across departments? What initiatives have you observed in your medical experience as either a patient or as a learner?

INTRODUCTION

Western culture has long associated one's gender identity with one's sex designation. When these two attributes are congruent for a person, or the same, it is also known as being **cisgender**. While this congruence is true for most people, in this chapter, we will discuss **transgender and gender-diverse (TGD)** people, that is, those for whom their gender identity and/or expression of their gender identity are not congruent with their assigned or designated sex. They include people who are transgender and **non-binary** and those with **gender-diverse** identities or expressions.

As a society, we are beginning to understand what others around the world have known for millennia: gender is not what we thought it was. One's internal, deeply held sense of self is now widely accepted as a better definition of gender. This concept is counter to our traditional framework of **gender identity**.[1] Our social and institutional structures have been modeled to support gender identity in a binary, boy-girl construct with few exceptions. Despite this fact, for the past 100 years or so, TGD populations have sought care from the medical establishment. In the early 20th century, clinicians observed that there were men who enjoyed dressing as women. In the 1910s, the term transvestite was coined for this population by Magnus Hirschfeld.[1] In the mid-20th century, the term transsexual was created by psychiatrist David Cauldwell and then popularized by Dr Harry Benjamin.[1,2] The term was used to describe the many patients seeking medical care who wanted to live a life that corresponded with their experienced gender as opposed to their designated, assigned gender. Over the past few decades, the term transgender has emerged and has been widely adopted as the umbrella term used for TGD people. The term "gender expansive" may also be used when referring to the TGD population.

In the United States, there are approximately 1.6 million transgender adults (~0.5% of the population). When youth 13 years and older are added to the adult population, the overall percentage increases to 0.6% of the population, as openly identifying transgender people tend to be younger within the population, with a lower mean age than cisgender people. The rates are similar across racial/ethnic groups (categorized as White, Black, Asian, American Indian/Alaska Native, Latinx, or Multiracial/Biracial/Other). Regardless of the age group or region evaluated, this population remains a small minority across age and location and for at least the last decade, rates of those identifying as transgender or gender-diverse have remained stable.[3]

For thousands of years, cultures around the world have observed, acknowledged, accepted, even *celebrated* TGD people (Figure 20.1). For example, the Navajo identified multiple genders, including those who in today's world would be identified as transgender people (see Figure 20.1).[4]

FIGURE 20.1 Gender-diverse cultures throughout the world (Reprinted by permission from Independent Television Service. A map of gender-diverse cultures. Last modified October 2023. https://www.pbs.org/independentlens/content/two-spirits_map-html/. Map data ©2025 Google.)

In the context of graduate medical education (GME), understanding TGD identities is critical for two primary reasons: (1) to support, recruit, and retain residents and fellows, faculty members, and staff who themselves are TGD, and (2) to improve health care and reduce health inequities experienced by TGD patients.

It is not well known how many residents, fellows, and practicing physicians are TGD. In a 2014 review of LGBT surgery residents, it was found that one of the 388 people in their sample was transgender (0.2%).[5] In June 2022, a TGD-focused study of physicians in the United States was published which reported that 1.2% of matriculating medical students in 2021 were TGD. The authors were able to identify 24 physicians who were TGD, 14 of whom were attending physicians and ten of whom were resident physicians; 50% of them worked in academic medicine.[6]

THE DEVELOPMENT AND SCIENCE OF GENDER

When studying cisgender children, it has been found that most are able to identify their own gender and use pronouns fairly well by 3 years of age, demonstrate strong preferences to play with children of the same gender at this same age, and exhibit preferences for gender-typed toys and clothing throughout this preschool into middle childhood.[7] A combination of influences has been theorized to explain this development, including prenatal hormone exposure, the child's own gender cognition/self-socialization, and cultural socialization. For cisgender children, their **assigned sex at birth**, socialization, and their own gender identity are aligned. Gülgöz et al studied over 300 transgender children and found that their gender development and coherence very closely aligned with that of cisgender children.[7] Indeed, while both cisgender and transgender children appear to follow similar paths of gender development in this study (and can be observed anecdotally with many trans people), it is becoming clearer that gender identification may have different trajectories for different people. Proposed trajectories could include early incongruence and early transition, early incongruence with delayed transition, and a later experience with gender dysphoria, although these trajectories will require further research.[8]

The etiology of gender development has not been well-elucidated. However, there are some clues in the scientific literature about disorders of sexual development that suggest possible avenues for further research: intersex individuals not identifying with the gender to which they were assigned; animals and human fetal exposure to pre- and post-natal androgens (ie, biologic females with virilizing congenital adrenal hyperplasia) with higher rates of masculine identities; higher rates of twin concordance for transgender identity; and post-hypothalamic changes in transgender men and women which mirrored others with the same gender identity, but notably, not similar to those with whom they shared sex assignment at birth.[1]

TRANSGENDER AND GENDER-DIVERSE INDIVIDUALS

In 2019, the World Health Organization (WHO) replaced its previously classified term "transsexualism" with gender incongruence and removed it from being classified as a mental disorder. This change was an effort to use more appropriate and less stigmatizing language within the WHO's International Classification of Diseases (ICD) which serves to provide a platform for TGD individuals seeking and receiving medical care worldwide.[9]

Transgender is an umbrella term that is used for people whose gender identity is not congruent with their assigned sex. It is commonly experienced in a binary way, such that a person might be "boy on the outside, girl on the inside," hence, transboys and transmen, who are assigned female at birth but are boys in their gender identity, and transgirls and transwomen, who are assigned male at birth but are girls in their gender identity. However, it is not uniformly true that every transgender person will experience "the opposite" gender. For many gender-diverse people, their sense of gender is outside of this binary, and they are often referred to as "non-binary." Non-binary people may be both a man and a woman, neither a man or a woman, somewhere in between, or may fall completely outside these categories. They may use terms such as enby, queer, gendervoid, **agender**, **genderqueer**, or gender fluid and may use pronouns such as they/them, ae/aer, ze/zir, etc. The Williams Institute estimates that a one-quarter of adults who are transgender are **gender non-conforming**.[3]

Although use of gender non-conforming as a term could describe this population that we are portraying as non-binary or TGD, it may not be the best choice. Non-conforming creates a "standard" of conforming behavior/existence and affirms that these individuals are not conforming or not "normal." The use of the term non-conforming has potential to be a means of othering that is not inclusive.

People who are **gender fluid** may not always have a fixed gender. They may experience more than one gender or various combinations of gender identity at different periods in time.

How a person shows their gender to the world is their **gender expression**. Such expressions can include their name, hair, clothes, speaking voice, use of pronouns, behavior, etc. It is different from and may not at all reflect a person's gender identity. For example, a person can be transgender (internal identity) and not show the world in any way that this is the case. They may never change their clothes, hair, etc. to "match" their identity. Conversely, there are cisgender people whose expression is different, even "opposite" of what society expects of their gender (ie, a cisboy who prefers dressing in skirts, heels and may have long, styled hair). Those TGD people who do take the steps to have their gender expression match their identity are engaging in a process known as **transition**. Social transitions are often the first steps taken by people, both children and adults, to live an affirmed life. Changes that one might include in a social transition include name, hair, clothing, behavior, etc.

GENDER-AFFIRMING CARE AND MEDICAL TRANSITIONING

Gender-affirming care does not begin in clinical encounters. Rather, it begins with their family, of origin or chosen, and social structure surrounding the TGD person long before they ever seek therapeutic support from mental and medical health professionals. Such care includes believing and validating their gender identity and allowing them use of personal descriptors (clothing, naming, pronouns, etc.) that affirm them. The importance of this early gender-affirming care cannot be overstated.

MEDICAL TRANSITIONING

Medical transitioning is the use of medication and/or surgery to better align one's body with their identity. As puberty begins, many transgender people are faced with the reality that their bodies will further develop into a being that does not represent who they are. Thus, puberty can be a very distressing time that, unmitigated, will leave transgender people with several irreversible changes, that is, voice changes, bony structure changes, etc. Many people have benefited from having the opportunity to suspend puberty and its effects at the start of puberty (Tanner Stage II). The medications best suited for this purpose are long-acting GnRH agonists which have been safely used and FDA-approved for over three decades in children with precocious puberty, popularly known as puberty blockers. The benefits of this therapy include full reversibility of their effects and the opportunity for a longer diagnostic and therapeutic window for confirmation of the child's gender diversity. The medical risk of using these medications include an increased risk of reduced bone mineralization, potentially compromised fertility, and unclear effects on brain development.[2] Despite these potential risks, the benefit of having a child being able to blossom into their identity, for most families and patients, heavily outweighs these potential risks.

Hormonal support is available to both prepubertal and postpubertal TGD individuals. While the timing of these medications may vary depending on access, resources, and shared decision-making, the outcome is that patients have the option to receive hormones which are consistent with their gender to yield changes that are more aligned with their identity. Hormonal support should be tailored to the individual based on their exposure to puberty and their desired outcome. Medical care should include these considerations as well. As noted in the case at the beginning of this chapter, Sal and his breast concern could be such an example. Gender medicine specialists may serve as a valuable clinical resource to help patients and other clinicians understand the options of medical therapy including the benefits and risks of the various therapeutic interventions.

SURGICAL TRANSITION

Tremendous progress in gender-affirming surgical techniques and strategies have been made in the last decade. While not everyone chooses surgical intervention, recent guidelines recommend providing comprehensive support and evaluation to those who express interest.[10] **Gender-affirming surgery** is not always available to everyone who desires to have it and this discrepancy represents one of the ways that TGD people can face inequity in care.[11] However, for many patients, being able to receive wrap-around care inclusive of hormonal replacement and surgical intervention have improved their overall well-being. The Endocrine Society and the World Professional Association for Transgender Health both recommend that the patient's mental health professional and clinician are part of the readiness assessment for this intervention.[9,10]

The following surgical interventions may be used to better align TGD persons' bodies with their identity: gonadectomy, penectomy, neovagina creation, breast augmentation, laryngeal surgeries, facial feminization, oophorectomy, vaginectomy, hysterectomy, neopenis creation, and mastectomy.

Not all TGD people desire outward gender affirmation. One might have interest in some, all, or no parts of transitioning. For safety and survival, some TGD people have felt the need to change their outward appearance to align with their assigned sex such as those who may be incarcerated, in need of a public shelter, or in need of obtaining and retaining employment.[11] Participation and interest in transition activities are very individual and cannot be used to determine the authenticity of someone's identity.

DETRANSITIONING

Detransitioning is a process whereby a TGD person decides to outwardly present as their sex assigned at birth. In the 2015 survey by the National Center for Transgender Equality (NCTE) transgender, 8% of TGD individuals in their survey had detransitioned at some point, more transwomen than transmen.[11] When queried, detransitioning was most often attributed to pressure from a parent, other family members, spouse/partner, harassment, discrimination, and trouble obtaining employment. Five percent of those who detransitioned did so because they no longer felt that they were gender-diverse (representing 0.4% of the entire sample). At the time of the survey, 62% of those who had previously detransitioned were currently living full time in a gender different than the gender they were thought to be at birth, in other words, had retransitioned.[11] The pressure to **detransition** can also be viewed as one of the psychological stressors related to their gender identity.

THE CLINICAL EXPERIENCE OF THE TGD PERSON

Encounters with the healthcare system for TGD people have been historically fraught with challenges. Physicians have played a significant role in the marginalization of this population. This cultural, de facto marginalization set the stage for how vast swaths of the medical community have treated TGD people. The Diagnostic and Statistical Manual of Mental Disorders (DSM) did not address gender diversity at all in its first two editions. By the third edition, transsexualism was added to the list of conditions, which prompted the WHO to add this diagnosis to the ICD. In the fourth DSM edition, gender identity disorder was substituted for transsexualism with the hope of decreasing stigma. In the most recent iteration (DSM 5-TR), gender identity disorder was updated to gender dysphoria. **Gender dysphoria** is the condition of being in distress about one's gender identity. Not all TGD people are distressed, yet they may still want medical support to better align their bodily presentation with their identity.

Throughout these iterations of progressive diagnostic name changes and the social movements that drove these changes, the medical community was largely silent. By far, one of the most significant roles that medicine has played has been its participation in and long-held silence regarding **conversion therapy**. Conversion therapy is the process by which a mental health professional, medical clinician, or religious leader attempts to change the gender identity (or **sexual orientation**, a topic covered separately) of a person. Statistics tell us that individuals subjected to these futile, but harmful, interventions have significantly higher rates of suicidality and post-traumatic stress disorder (PTSD).[12] According to a 2023 survey from The TREVOR Project, the rate of attempted suicide in those threatened with or subjected to conversion therapy was 28% versus 11% in those not subjected to conversion therapy.[13] In the 21st century, most major medical societies have renounced all conversion therapy as harmful. These organizations include the American Medical Association, American Academy of Pediatrics, American College of Physicians, American Psychiatric Association, American Academy of Child and Adolescent Psychiatry, and American Psychological Association. The practice has been outlawed in 20 states and in Washington, DC.

Those living in states that have not banned conversion therapy will continue to subject between 10,000 and 20,000 minors each year to the practice, continuing to add to the trauma that this community faces.[14] TGD people have faced mistreatment, medical voyeurism (people watching/examining parts of patients' bodies unrelated to the visit), refusal to treat, mockery, and in rare cases, physical roughness, physical assault, or even sexual assault in the clinical setting.[11,12,14 15] Patients have also noted communication casualties (verbal and non-verbal cues that the patient identifies as uncomfortable, judged, or not having their concern addressed) and bigotry in disguise (providers exhibiting implicit or explicit negative attitudes and behaviors).[16] The result of this mistreatment can be that patients *anticipate* bias during encounters. The 2015 NCTE survey results showed that one-third of respondents who had seen a health care provider within the year prior to the survey experienced having had at least one negative experience relating to their gender identity such as verbal harassment, refusal of treatment, and/or having to teach the provider about transgender patients.[11] In addition, 23% of the over 27,000 respondents reported that they did not see a doctor when needed for fear of being mistreated.[11] Health inequities for TGD people include higher likelihood of not being insured, higher rates of suicidality, higher rates of HIV, depression, and psychological distress.[11]

KEY CHALLENGES EXPERIENCED BY TGD PHYSICIAN LEARNERS

While there is a paucity of data regarding the lived experience of LGBTQIA+ medical students, residents, fellows, and attending physicians, a recent study of self-reported clinicians revealed that 88% have overheard disparaging remarks from coworkers, 30% experienced discrimination from patients, 60% of LGBTQIA+ surgical residents reported mistreatment at work and had a higher likelihood of leaving a GME program.[17] LGBTQIA+ residents, fellows, and physicians face higher rates of suicidality as compared to heterosexual/cisgender colleagues. Another study highlighted the evidence that disclosure of LGBTQIA+ status on the part of physicians could have deleterious effects on patients' willingness to keep them as their doctor or even to remain in the same practice.[5] In light of this reality, 40% of LGBTQIA+ medical students were advised to hide their sexual/gender status during their undergraduate medical education and only 57% of them planned to disclose their LGBTQ+ status during the residency application cycle.[18]

Wetafer et al published a focused review on transgender and gender-diverse resident, fellow, and attending physicians and their lived experiences.[6] They grouped their experiences into categories of emotional distress, dominance of the binary gender paradigm, and structural factors. Emotional stressors included fear and anxiety related to anti-trans sentiment from colleagues, fear of or actual loss of jobs/privileges, being misgendered, and the stress of being "stealth" (not having their identity known publicly). Furthermore, dominance of the societal binary gender paradigm caused difficulty and erasure if one fell outside of the binary (ie, non-binary people). Lastly, structural factors impacted TGD physicians who needed safe physical spaces for changing clothes and using the bathroom. One participant recounted the stress of having to find a single stall bathroom while spending the day in the operating room because finding an available single stall could add so much time to their needed breaks. During oral board examinations, professional societies often gave instructions for how men and women should dress, not leaving an opportunity for those TGD physicians who may not have notified the organization that their expressed gender was different than it had been in the past.

INTERSECTIONALITY OF TGD PERSONS WITH OTHER MARGINALIZED IDENTITIES

Intersectionality, a concept created by the legal scholar Crenshaw, is the framework in which one person may have multiple parts of their identity, with each part having the potential to mitigate or exacerbate marginalization.[19] Certain subgroups of TGD people face multiple axes of marginalization, including racial and ethnic minorities, those possessing migrant status, those who are impoverished, and incarcerated individuals.[12] While incarcerated, TGD people have an up to 6-fold increased risk of being physically assaulted and up to 9-fold risk of being sexually assaulted than the general incarcerated population.[12] In rural areas, TGD people may also face isolation and difficulty in finding affirming and competent health care professionals.[20]

Lett et al noted that Black TGD individuals were more likely to have a lower annual income, and less likely to be married or coupled, own a home, or be employed.[21] Black and Brown TGD people, particularly transwomen, are subjected to higher rates of violence including murder, higher rates of HIV and chronic medical conditions, and homelessness. Kattari published data that showed that TGD people of color were at increased risk of receiving discriminatory treatment from physicians and paramedics.[22]

MAKING IT RIGHT: STRATEGIES TO IMPROVE THE HEALTH CARE AND CLINICAL LEARNING ENVIRONMENT OF TGD INDIVIDUALS

While we do not have control of societal stigma and the ensuing societal devaluation that can make life challenging for the TGD population, those of us in the medical profession have significant power over the spaces in which we provide care. Within our medical ecosystem, on interpersonal levels and through community engagement, we can have an important, tangible impact. By optimizing inclusive and validating spaces, not only do we have the capacity to improve healthcare outcomes and mitigate inequities, but we can foster environments that hopefully assist in reversing internalized stigma that some TGD people may have absorbed over time.

Systemically, an organization can employ many strategies to become welcoming and inclusive. Examples include displaying visible signage that the office/hospital is welcoming, prominently displaying non-discrimination policies, using electronic medical records which are inclusive and accommodating to those who may not have had the means nor interest in formally changing their names/pronouns, removing gender assumptions from intake forms, and using a standardized bodily parts checklist which separates an association with gender. Additional steps include training all persons who work in the clinical space (eg, environmental support staff, nursing, medical assistants/patient care technicians, staff, and front desk staff), engaging their local LGBTQIA+ communities to build relationships, advocating for the presence of patient advocates, and ensuring that physician learners, faculty members, and staff are provided support in their work environments.[15,23]

SUPPORTING TGD MEDICAL STUDENTS, PHYSICIAN LEARNERS, AND ATTENDINGS

Immediate steps that can be taken to create a more affirming environment for physician learners and attendings include:

- making language as gender expansive and inclusive as possible;
- using gender neutral endings or non-gendered terms, that is, chairperson instead of chairman;
- actively avoiding gender stereotypes and bias by specifying gender only when it is known, relevant, and necessary; and,
- acknowledging, apologizing, correcting, and moving on if you make a mistake in identifying gender or using pronouns.

Institutions and GME programs may consider the use of formalized training such as SafeZone for all faculty members, clinicians, and front-facing staff, thereby providing opportunities for system-wide change.

Several strategies have been identified by LGBTQIA+ physicians as helpful for their TGD colleagues. In the study by Lee et al, many of the LGBT residents reported that seeing an openly LGBT resident or attending in a GME program made it more likely that they would rank their program more highly.[5] TGD physicians reported the following actions that encouraged inclusion and mitigated their emotional distress:

- active allyship (interrupting microaggressions such as misgendering and anti-transgender sentiment in real time);
- proactive pronoun use (everyone introduces themselves with pronouns, use of pronoun badges);
- valuing representation in faculty members and staff;
- education being provided by someone other than them to avoid their paying the "minority tax"; and,
- receiving tangible support from leadership in these efforts.[6]

> In 2021, a study of almost 35,000 LGBTQIA+ youth found that having *just one accepting adult* or *just one accepting peer* decreased their risk of suicidality by *39% and 45%, respectively.*[1]

> Pronouns should not be referred to as "preferred," since they do not represent preference (ie, suggesting that identity is a choice). Rather, pronouns represent who individuals are and should be used when referring to them. One way to ask about pronouns is, "What pronouns do you use?"

CONCLUSION

Our review of the lived experience of TGD physician learners, faculty members, staff, and patients has shown the myriad opportunities we have to further the inclusion and acceptance of this population. The purpose for engaging in these opportunities is to maximize our ability to create platforms for optimal personal and professional growth and clinical environments of safety, inclusivity, and belonging for colleagues and patients. Belonging can look like acceptance, belief in the patient or colleague, intentionally engaging the LGBTQIA+ community-at-large, and systemically offering education about LGBTQIA+ people.

Lastly, and importantly, recognizing and undoing the pathologizing of TGD people and reversing the trend of medicine's tradition of mistreatment toward the TGD community are core elements of creating a health care environment that fully embraces and cares for gender-diverse patients, trainees, health care professionals, and staff.[15,16]

Our charge in medicine is best characterized by a 2020 Tweet from Dr Tedros Abhamon Ghebreyesus, the then-Director-General of the WHO: "Ultimately our fight is not against a single disease. Our fight is against a world in which people get sick and die simply because they are poor, or female, or young, gay, transgender, sex workers, use drugs, or are in prison. Our fight is for #Healthforall."[24]

Take Home Points

- Gender minorities experience unique challenges in health care environments due to the intersection of their gender identity with other social identities, impacting their overall well-being and access to equitable care.
- Systemic barriers, including lack of provider education on gender-affirming care, contribute to the marginalization and inadequate health care of gender minorities.
- Incorporating gender minority health into medical education is crucial for improving health care outcomes, promoting cultural competence, and ensuring that future health care providers are equipped to deliver inclusive care.
- Strong institutional policies and support systems are essential in creating a safe and affirming environment for gender minority patients and health care providers, fostering equity and reducing health disparities.

❓ QUESTIONS FOR FURTHER THOUGHT

1. When was the first time you remember experiencing your gender?
2. Can you recall a clinical scenario which reflected a lack of acceptance or even discrimination against a gender-diverse colleague or patient?
3. In what way is your clinical learning environment inclusive of gender-diverse patients, physician learners, staff, and clinicians? Are there opportunities to improve the environment for this population?

Acknowledgments
The authors would like to thank Kamela Hayward-Rotini, PhD, and Ellen Kahn for their insightful reviews of this chapter.

REFERENCES

1. Korpaisarn S, Safer JD. Etiology of gender identity. *Endocrinol Metab Clin North Am.* 2019;48(2):323-329. doi:10.1016/j.ecl.2019.01.002
2. Hembree WC, Cohen-Kettenis PT, Gooren L, et al. Endocrine treatment of gender-dysphoric/gender-incongruent persons: an endocrine society clinical practice guideline *J Clin Endocrinol Metab.* 2017;102(11):3869–3903. doi:10.1210/jc.2017-01658 Published correction appears in *J Clin Endocrinol Metab.* 2018 Feb 1;103(2):699 Published correction appears in *J Clin Endocrinol Metab.* 2018 Jul 1;103(7):2758-2759
3. Herman JL, Flores AR, O'Neill KK. How many adults and youth identify as transgender in the United States? 2022. University of California at Los Angeles School of Law: The Williams Institute. Accessed June 19, 2024. https://williamsinstitute.law.ucla.edu/publications/trans-adults-united-states/
4. Jacobs SE, Thomas W, Lang S. *Two-Spirit People: Native American Gender Identity, Sexuality, and Spirituality.* 1st ed. University of Illinois Press; 1997.
5. Lee KP, Kelz RR, Dubé B, Morris JB. Attitude and perceptions of the other underrepresented minority in surgery. *J Surg Educ.* 2014;71(6):e47-e52. doi:10.1016/j.jsurg.2014.05.008
6. Westafer LM, Freiermuth CE, Lall MD, Muder SJ, Ragone EL, Jarman AF. Experiences of transgender and gender expansive physicians. *JAMA Netw Open.* 2022;5(6):32219791. doi:10.1001/jamanetworkopen.2022.19791
7. Gülgöz S, Glazier JJ, Enright EA, et al. Similarity in transgender and cisgender children's gender development. *Proc Natl Acad Sci USA.* 2019;116(49):24480-24485. doi:10.1073/pnas.1909367116
8. Doyle DM. Transgender identity: development, management and affirmation. *Curr Opin Psychol.* 2022;48:101467. doi:10.1016/j.copsyc.2022.101467
9. Macdonald V, Verster A, Mello MB, et al. The World Health Organization's work and recommendations for improving the health of trans and gender-diverse people. *J Int AIDS Soc.* 2022;25 (suppl 5):e26004. doi:10.1002/jia2.26004
10. Coleman E, Radix AE, Bouman WP, et al. Standards of care for the health of transgender and gender diverse people, version 8. *Int J Transgend Health.* 2022;23(suppl 1):S1-S259. doi:10.1080/26895269.2022.2100644
11. James SE, Herman JL, Rankin S, Keisling M, Mottet L, Anafi M. *The Report of the 2015 U.S. Transgender Survey.* 2016. National Center for Transgender Equality. Accessed June 19, 2024. https://transequality.org/sites/default/files/docs/usts/USTS-Full-Report-Dec17.pdf
12. Streed CG Jr, Anderson JS, Babits C, Ferguson MA. Changing medical practice, not patients—putting an end to conversion therapy. *N Engl J Med.* 2019;381(6):500-502. doi:10.1056/NEJMp1903161
13. The Trevor Project. 2023 U.S. National Survey on the Mental Health of LGBTQ Young People. 2023. Accessed June 19, 2024. https://www.thetrevorproject.org/survey-2023/
14. Mallory C, Brown TNT, Conron JT. Conversion therapy and LGBT youth. 2019. University of California at Los Angeles School of Law: The Williams Institute. Accessed June 19, 2024. https://williamsinstitute.law.ucla.edu/publications/conversion-therapy-and-lgbt-youth/
15. Garcia AD, Lopez X. How cisgender clinicians can help prevent harm during encounters with transgender patients. *AMA J Ethics.* 2022;24(8):e753-E761. doi:10.1001/amajethics.2022.753
16. Casanova-Perez R, Apodaca C, Bascom E, et al. Broken down by bias: healthcare biases experienced by BIPOC and LGBTQ+ patients. *AMIA Annu Symp Proc.* 2022;2021:275-284. PMID: 35308990

17. Elko A, Agarwal S, Erkmen C. Confronting the scope of LGBT inequity in surgery. *J Am Coll Surg.* 2022;234(5):959963. doi:10.1097/XCS.0000000000000101
18. Madrigal J, Rudasill S, Tran Z, Bergman J, Benharash P. Sexual and gender minority identity in undergraduate medical education: impact on experience and career trajectory. *PLoS One.* 2021;16(11):e0260387. doi:10.1371/journal.pone.0260387
19. Crenshaw K. Demarginalizing the intersection of race and sex: a black feminist critique of antidiscrimination doctrine, feminist theory and antiracist politics. *Univ Chicago Legal Forum.* 1989;1989(1):139-167. http://chicagounbound.uchicago.edu/uclf/vol1989/iss1/8
20. Renner J, Blaszcyk W, Täuber L, Dekker A, Briken P, Nieder TO. Barriers to accessing health care in rural regions by transgender, non-binary, and gender-diverse people: a case-based scoping review. *Front Endocrinol (Lausanne).* 2021;12:717821. doi:10.3389/fendo.2021.717821
21. Lett E, Dowshen NL, Baker KE. Intersectionality and health inequities for gender minority blacks in the U.S. *Am J Prev Med.* 2020;59(5):639-647. doi:10.1016/j.amepre.2020.04.013
22. Kattari SK, Walls NE, Whitfield DL, Langenderfer-Magruder L. Racial and ethnic differences in experiences of discrimination in accessing health services among transgender people in the United States. *Int J Transgend.* 2015;16(2):68-79. doi:10.1080/15532739.2015.1064336
23. Grasso C, Goldhammer H, Thompson J, Keuroghlian AS. Optimizing gender-affirming medical care through anatomical inventories, clinical decision support, and population health management in electronic health record systems. *J Am Med Inform Assoc.* 2021;28(11):2531-2535. doi:10.1093/jamia/ocab080
24. @DrTedros. Ultimately our fight is not against a single disease. Our fight is against a world in which people get sick and die simply because they are poor, or female, or young, gay, transgender, sex workers, use drugs, or are in prison. Our fight is for #Healthforall. https://x.com/DrTedros/status/1333880892083810304. Posted December 1, 2020.

Inclusion and Health Equity for Sexual Minorities

Nelson Sánchez, MD, Associate Professor of Medicine, Weill Cornell Medicine & Memorial Sloan Kettering Cancer Center, New York, NY

Tyree M.S. Winters, DO, Program Director, Pediatric Residency Program, Goryeb Children's Hospital/Atlantic Health System, Morristown, NJ

CHAPTER SUMMARY

The term sexual minority refers to individuals who do not identify as straight or heterosexual. They may identify as gay, lesbian, bisexual, queer, or something else. The Association of American Medical College (AAMC)'s Graduation Questionnaire reports nearly 10% of medical school graduates self-identify as a sexual minority, and similar proportions likely enter residency. This chapter aims to help programs improve their efforts to recruit, retain, and support residents and fellows with sexual minority identities. It will highlight key challenges and opportunities for graduate medical education (GME) programs and institutions to embrace the personal and professional skills and knowledge within this community and provide suggestions to improve inclusion and equity.

LEARNING OBJECTIVES

1. Identify common yet underrecognized health concerns for patients who are sexual minorities and key challenges experienced by residents, fellows, and practicing physicians who are sexual minorities.
2. Describe strategies to support a welcoming clinical environment for residents, fellows, and faculty members who are sexual minorities.
3. Develop strategies to prepare residents, faculty members, and leadership in GME on clinical care resources for sexual minorities.

Case Study

Sam is a first-year resident who self-identifies as a gay man. He has shared his identity with some of his professional colleagues but is not sure if everyone in his program knows how he self-identifies. He approaches his program director after a disturbing conversation with his continuity clinic preceptor, Dr Smith.

Sam shares that he recently saw a 28-year-old patient, Ms C, who identified as cis-female and lesbian, for her annual visit. During the visit, Ms C shared that she had been sexually active with three separate partners who all identify as female. Ms C had missed her last several annual appointments and did not undergo routine sexually transmitted infection or cervical cancer screenings. During his clinical precepting conversation with

(continued)

Dr Smith, Sam discusses his plan to screen Ms C for cervical cancer with a pap smear. Dr Smith informs Sam that screening for cervical cancer was not necessary since Ms C identifies as lesbian and only had sexual activity with individuals who identify as female. Sam shares his concern that Ms C was still at risk for cervical cancer despite her sexual orientation; however, Dr Smith dismisses this concern based on Ms C's sexual behaviors. Dr Smith also tells Sam, "She would be a good patient for your future practice, being from the gay community." Dr Smith evaluates Ms C and discharges her from the clinic without a recommendation for cervical cancer screening.

Sam believes that Dr Smith demonstrated implicit bias to Ms C and himself based on their sexual identities, but does not feel comfortable approaching his continuity clinic preceptor with his concerns. Sam shares his concern with his fellow clinic residents and is advised to speak with his program director to receive guidance on how to address his concerns with Dr Smith.

Case Discussion

Sam's experience illustrates an opportunity for GME to improve the environment for LGBTQIA+ health education and health professional career development. A knowledge gap currently exists in Dr Smith's understanding of sexual minority sexual behaviors, cancer risks, and appropriate cancer screenings. Consider strategies to address LGBTQIA+ health knowledge gaps for both residents and faculty members. Additionally, Sam is unaware of how best to address bias in health care environments, both short-term to ensure patient safety and long-term to ensure corrective workplace measures. Finally, Dr Smith's comment about Sam's professional future based on his sexual identity may negatively impact Sam's sense of value in his residency program and career in medicine. This case raises important concerns about health equity, health education, and workplace inclusion. In reviewing this chapter, consider what could have gone differently in this scenario, and what systems are in place at your institution for residents to address concerns about the learning environment.

NATIONAL SEXUAL MINORITY REPRESENTATION

The term **sexual minorities** refers to individuals who do not identify as straight or heterosexual. They may identify as **gay, lesbian, bisexual**, queer, or something else. Some may also identify as a member of the **LGBTQIA+** community, which encompasses sexual and gender minorities. Terminology within the community is constantly in flux and will continue to evolve over time. It is most important to support an individual's chosen identity and understand what the term means for that person.

A 2022 Gallup poll revealed that individuals who self-identified as LGBTQIA+ comprised 7.2% of the US population, with representation highest among bisexual (4.2%), gay (1.4%), or lesbian (1.0%) communities (Figure 21.1).[1] Additionally, US census data have shown that same-sex households exist in almost every county, representing urban, suburban, and rural communities.[2] Health disparities among sexual minorities have been well-documented, including marked disparities identified in health care access, sexually transmitted infections, mental health, and cancer care.[3] For example, although lesbians have the same risk of cervical cancer as their heterosexual counterparts, research has shown poorer access to cervical cancer screening among lesbians when compared to their heterosexual peers.

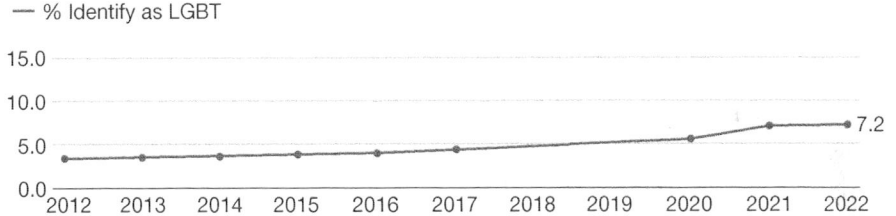

FIGURE 21.1 Self-identification as LGBTQIA+ based on Gallup Survey Results (https://news.gallup.com/poll/470708/lgbt-identification-steady.aspx).

Sexual minority representation among academic faculty, residents, and fellows remains unclear as there is currently no systematic national data collection. However, the American Medical College (AAMC) does collect sexual identity data from medical students during administration of the Matriculating Student, Second-Year Medical Student, and Medical Student Graduation questionnaires. Data have shown that sexual minorities represent as much as 9.3% of graduating medical students, reflecting current trends in national representation, particularly among younger generations.[4] While the representation of sexual minorities in GME has not yet been studied, this cohort of residents and future faculty members represents a unique workforce that could address sexual minority health equity. Their lived experiences may inform their awareness of and preparedness for the health issues facing sexual minorities. They also represent a workforce that needs tailored mentorship and professional support for career development.

CHALLENGES THAT INFLUENCE INCLUSION OF SEXUAL MINORITIES IN GME

Research has unveiled poor inclusion of LGBTQIA+ health education in medical school and residency education.[5,6] Gaps in clinician knowledge and clinical communication skills can lead to subpar clinical care for sexual minorities, including deferred sexual health prevention, sexual health treatment, and cancer screenings. **Barriers** to sexual minority health education include a paucity of educators who feel comfortable teaching the material, space in the curriculum for LGBTQIA+ health education, and leadership advocating for and supporting LGBTQIA+ health education and learner evaluation. In this chapter's case study, didactic presentations and small group discussions on sexual minority health concerns, including a review of sexual behaviors and appropriate cancer screenings, should improve access to the patient's cervical cancer screening and sexual health counseling.

The US Supreme Court's 2020 ruling prohibiting workplace discrimination based on sexual orientation or gender identity (*Bostock v. Clayton County*) offered new legal protections for LGBTQIA+ employees and allies and new opportunities for academic medicine to advance LGBTQIA+ inclusion in its institutions.[7] The ruling helps to support employees who openly champion LGBTQIA+ initiatives at their academic health centers. As a result, more LGBTQIA+ employees and allies can serve as role models, mentors, and champions for residents and fellows, expanding opportunities for their academic, professional, and personal development. Employees are also now better protected when they press their institutions to clearly state and enforce antidiscrimination policies that protect LGBTQIA+ employees, physician learners, and patients. Moreover, out leadership at graduate health schools, national medical societies, and accreditation bodies are better protected to advocate for LGBTQIA+ patients, staff members, residents, fellows, and institutional faculty members.

Research has also shown that LGBTQIA+ health professionals face numerous obstacles in their career development.[8] Poor support for LGBTQIA+ scholarship, LGBTQIA+ discrimination, lack of mentorship, and feelings of isolation are some barriers known to impede LGBTQIA+ health professional interest in academic careers. In the case study involving Sam, Dr Smith exhibited examples of conscious or unconscious LGBTQIA+ discrimination by dismissing Ms C's potential health concerns based on her sexual identity and sexual behaviors. Dr Smith also missed a unique opportunity to mentor Sam. He could have supported Sam's clinical concern for Ms C by recommending a literature search on the topic of cervical cancer screening for lesbians or supervising a resident-led presentation on lesbian health concerns. This type of mentorship can support future scholarship and could have facilitated Sam's sense of belonging at his residency program.

The presence or lack of curriculum to address sexual minority health issues is a signal to sexual minority residents and fellows that speaks to their programs' supportiveness of LGBTQIA+ community members. When individuals who are sexual minorities report a concern or complaint related to mistreatment or sexual minority care, if the report is addressed in a meaningful fashion, the person who reports may be more likely to seek professional advice from their preceptor, engage in scholarly activities, and pursue a career in academia.

STRATEGIES TO IMPROVE INCLUSION AND EQUITY FOR SEXUAL MINORITIES IN HEALTH CARE AND GME

1. *Collect sexual orientation and gender identity data among residents, fellows, faculty members, and patients.*

    Many academic medical centers have implemented sexual orientation and gender identity (SOGI) data collection for their patients, including in their electronic health record systems. These data can be used to identify sexual minority patient health care needs and to develop and deliver tailored sexual minority health services. The AAMC also collects SOGI data from the nation's medical students to monitor trends in enrollment and student satisfaction. Similar methods can be implemented to track sexual minority representation among resident physicians and faculty members. These data could then be used to track and evaluate progress in sexual minority employee recruitment, workplace satisfaction, retention, promotion, and advancement.

2. *Partner with LGBTQIA+-affirming organizations for recruitment of residents, fellows, and faculty candidates.*

    Academic medical centers and program directors can partner with national LGBTQIA+-affirming organizations to facilitate recruitment of sexual minorities to their GME programs. National organizations, such as Building the Next Generation of Academic Physicians (BNGAP) and GLMA: Health Professionals Advancing LGBTQ Equality, have robust programming supporting LGBTQIA+ student career development and they maintain large listservs of LGBTQIA+ students. BNGAP also partners with student organizations that represent learners from racial and ethnic minoritized groups, such as the Latino Medical Student Organization, the Student National Medical Association, the Association of Native American Medical Students, and the Asian Pacific American Medical Student Association, to support diverse physician learners' career interests in academic medicine. Some students from these organizations also self-identify as sexual minorities; thus, it is important to be mindful of intersectionality and the multiple marginalized groups with which a resident or fellow may identify. Additionally, the American Medical Student Association and the American Medical Association have LGBTQIA+ student interest groups that may also serve as recruitment resources for LGBTQIA+ residents and fellows, and journals such as *LGBT Health* and the *Annals of LGBTQ+ Public and Population Health*, can serve as advertising resources.

3. *Organize LGBTQIA+ health education lectures and small group discussions to improve all physician learners' preparedness to care for this patient population.*

    Program directors can lead efforts to support sexual minority health education at their respective programs. Dedicating time for didactic lectures and small group discussions in each year of a resident's educational program can serve as regular continuing education activities for residents. Additionally, infusing sexual minority patients in routine objective structural clinical examination (OSCE) cases and case reports will support normalizing sexual minority identities and stories. MedEdPORTAL is a free, open access medical education curriculum journal that includes an excellent repository of peer-reviewed LGBTQIA+ medical education innovations. Many materials can be downloaded by faculty members for use with their residents. Faculty members can also invite MedEdPORTAL authors to lead presentations if they are uncomfortable teaching the material themselves. Additionally, residents with an interest in sexual minority health and teaching could facilitate sexual minority curricula under appropriate program director supervision.

4. *Update institutional clinical guidelines to ensure that disease screening recommendations include sexual minorities.*

    Program directors should work with their primary care and subspecialty faculty members to review their institution's disease screening recommendations and ensure they are inclusive of and up-to-date for sexual minorities. The Centers for Disease Control and Prevention and Fenway Institute are two national resources with regularly updated LGBTQIA+ health recommendations.[9]

> Seventy-six percent of US medical schools report having three or fewer learning activities such as a lecture or group discussion focused on LGBTQIA+ themes in their medical curriculum, according to a 2017-2018 AAMC Curriculum Inventory.

> In 2017, a prospective cohort study showed that medical students who had favorable contact with LGBTQIA+ faculty members, residents, students, and patients, and who perceived preparation and skills to provide care to LGBTQIA+ patients, had associated lower explicit bias against gay men and lesbian women.

5. ***Review non-discrimination hospital patient policies and human resources policies to ensure that sexual orientation is explicitly protected.***

    Program directors should review their institution's non-discrimination and human resources policies to ensure there is equitable treatment for their sexual minority patients, faculty and staff members, residents and fellows. The materials should be easily available and visible to all patients, faculty and staff members, and physician learners.

6. ***Be responsive to reports of bias and discrimination.***

    The authors recommend programs take steps to deter discrimination, create reporting pathways that are easily accessible, act quickly and be responsive to all reports, support residents and fellows who experience or witness discrimination, ensure safe reporting, be accountable for their safety, and be ready to improve policies and practices.

7. ***Support scholarly work related to sexual minority health.***

    Program directors should support physician learner and faculty member participation in sexual minority health scholarship such as through development and production of sexual minority health curricula, attendance at regional and national health conferences where participants can present posters and oral presentations pertaining to sexual minority health, and submission of sexual minority health publications to national medical journals.

8. ***Support mentorship efforts for LGBTQIA+ residents and fellows.***

    Program directors should identify and support networking opportunities and mentorship programming for LGBTQIA+ residents, fellows, and faculty members. Identity concordance is not always necessary for successful personal and professional development, but research has shown that LGBTQIA+ physician learners and faculty members desire opportunities in which they can meet and network with concordant health professionals.

Take Home Points

- Sexual minorities reside in all US communities, including urban, suburban, and rural areas. All physcian learners should stay up to date on the health concerns of sexual minorities and be prepared to administer and process an inclusive sexual history.
- Surveying one's academic environment for inclusive sexual minority health education and professional development is an important way to assess whether the institution is creating an educational setting in which a diverse group of learners can belong and thrive.
- Strategies to improve recruitment and inclusion of sexual minorities in GME should focus on educational and clinical interventions to improve clinical care for sexual minorities through curriculum and resources and creating learning environments that support residents and fellows through mentorship, scholarly work, and partnerships with LGBTQIA+–affirming organizations.

QUESTIONS FOR FURTHER THOUGHT

1. Physician learners and faculty members in GME programs who identify as sexual minorities often experience microaggressions in clinical settings by colleagues and patients. Can you think of a few tangible actions that would help create safe and supportive environments in the field of medical education?
2. Sexual minorities can use terms to identify themselves that may not conform to that term's widely accepted definition. How can we ensure that we understand our patients' and our colleagues' unique identity correctly?
3. What data does your institution currently collect regarding sexual orientation of residents, fellows, faculty and staff members, and patients, and how can it be improved?

REFERENCES

1. Jones JM. U.S. LGBT identification steady at 7.2%. Gallup. Published February 22, 2023. Accessed June 15, 2023. https://news.gallup.com/poll/470708/lgbt-identification-steady.aspx
2. Walker L, Taylor D. Same-sex couple households: 2019. American Community Survey Briefs. ACSBR-005. United States Census Bureau; 2021. Accessed June 15, 2023. https://www.census.gov/content/dam/Census/library/publications/2021/acs/acsbr-005.pdf
3. Institute of Medicine (US) Committee on Lesbian, Gay, Bisexual, and Transgender Health Issues and Research Gaps and Opportunities. *The Health of Lesbian, Gay, Bisexual, and Transgender People: Building a Foundation for Better Understanding*. National Academies Press (US); 2011. Accessed June 15, 2023. https://www.ncbi.nlm.nih.gov/books/NBK64806/
4. Obedin-Maliver J, Goldsmith ES, Stewart L, et al. Lesbian, gay, bisexual, and transgender-related content in undergraduate medical education. *JAMA*; 2011;306(9):971-977. doi:10.1001/jama.2011
5. Bunting SR, Goetz TG, Gabrani A, et al. Lesbian, Gay, Bisexual, Transgender, and Queer (LGBTQ+) Health Education in primary Care Graduate Medical Education Programs: A National Survey of Program Directors. *Ann LGBTQ Public Popul Health*. 2022;3(4). doi:10.1891/lgbtq-2021-0027
6. Sanchez NF, Rankin S, Callahan E, et al. LGBT trainee and health professional perspectives on academic careers—facilitators and challenges. *LGBT Health*. 2015;2(4):345-356. doi:10.1089/lgbt.2015.0024
7. Streed CG, Siegel J, Davis JA. Keeping our promise to LGBTQ+ patients. *AAMC News Viewpoints*; 2019. Accessed June 18, 2023. https://www.aamc.org/news/viewpoints/keeping-our-promise-lgbtq-patients
8. Sánchez NF, Kennedy L, Spigner ST, et al. LGBTQ+ worker protections: implications for academic medicine today and in the future. *Acad Med*. 2022;97(11):1597-1604. doi:10.1097/ACM.0000000000004672
9. Phelan SM, Burke SE, Hardemen RR, et al. Medical school factors associated with changes in implicit and explicit bias against gay and lesbian people among 3492 graduating medical students. *J Gen Intern Med*. 2017;32(11):1193-1201. doi:10.1007/s11606-017-4127-6

22

Creating Inclusive Working and Learning Climates for Residents and Fellows with Disabilities in Graduate Medical Education

Michael S. Argenyi, MD, MPH, MSW, Addiction Medicine Physician, HealthRIGHT 360 San Francisco, San Francisco, CA; Assistant Professor, Department of Family Medicine & Community Health, University of Massachusetts Chan Medical School, Worcester, MA

Jasmine R. Marcelin, MD, Vice Chair for Equity and Inclusive Excellence, Department of Internal Medicine; Associate Professor, Division of Infectious Diseases; Associate Program Director, Internal Medicine Residency, University of Nebraska Medical Center, Omaha, NE

Nichole Taylor, DO, Former Dean of Student Affairs, Clinical Associate Professor, Department of Anesthesiology, Wake Forest University School of Medicine, Winston-Salem, NC

*****Christopher J. Moreland, MD, MPH,** Professor of Medicine, Associate Residency Program Director, Department of Internal Medicine, Dell Medical School at the University of Texas at Austin, Austin, TX

*****Lisa M. Meeks, PhD, MA,** Associate Professor of Learning Health Sciences and Family Medicine, University of Michigan School of Medicine, Ann Arbor, MI; Executive Director, Docs with Disabilities Initiative

CHAPTER SUMMARY

Individuals with disabilities are an essential and valuable part of our health care workforce—with the potential to improve health care for all and reduce disparities for patients with disabilities through informed experiences and disability humility. In appreciation of the value of this population, medical associations have put forward varied levels of guidance to support disability inclusion, including the ACGME Program and Institutional Requirements that require a disability policy, accommodations for residents and fellows, and a plan for the recruitment and retention of diverse residents and fellows. However, despite a clear commitment to increasing access for disabled physician learners, barriers persist, such as ableist policies, unclear processes, and fear of stigma and bias. These barriers contribute to non-disclosure of disability, which places learners at risk of poorer educational, professional, and mental health outcomes. In this chapter, we review the guidance for disability inclusion and offer recommendations for improving practices. Recommendations are crystalized through case examples, allowing the reader an opportunity to apply the lessons in the chapter to frequent disability interactions in graduate medical education (GME).

LEARNING OBJECTIVES

1. List the ACGME Program and Institutional Requirements for disability policy and reasonable accommodations for physician learners.
2. Describe the benefits of educating and employing individuals with disabilities.
3. Identify effective strategies to evaluate GME program and institutional practices regarding disability policy and accommodation requests.

---

*These authors share co-senior status and contributed equally to the formation and guidance of the chapter.

A NOTE ABOUT DISABILITY LANGUAGE

Language is constantly evolving, and our chapter uses person- and identity-first language to honor and respect both preferences within the disability community.

Case Study

Rae is a third-year resident in a pediatrics program. She was diagnosed with secondary progressive multiple sclerosis (MS) in her first year of residency. Over the last 2 years, symptoms have been relapsing and remitting; however, each relapse worsens neurologic function. Rae noticed that she was more fatigued with overnight calls and long cases that require significant standing but currently she has no other symptoms. When Rae was initially diagnosed, she searched the program website for a disability accommodation policy but could not find one. Her program director referred her to Human Resources (HR) which advised Rae that there was nothing they could offer; staff encouraged her to return when/if she developed functional disability symptoms.

Lately, Rae has been more symptomatic and, as a result, has returned to HR to discuss reasonable accommodations. During the meeting with HR, Rae was told to speak directly to her program director to ask for accommodations since HR does not understand the responsibilities and expectations of a pediatric resident. Rae was very frustrated with what seemed like an uninformed and unhelpful process, and she was hesitant to disclose the symptoms from MS to her program director. However, she wanted to investigate the availability of accommodations to mitigate the impact of MS on her education and ensure the best patient care, so she approached the program director to explain the impact of her disability on her effective functioning as a resident. She requested a reduced call and case schedule, which are the accommodations most likely to reduce her symptoms. The program director advised Rae to "just ask for help in the clinic when you need it."

Rae is committed to becoming a pediatrician but is concerned about her education and training experience and the inevitable board certification examinations. Given that no disability accommodations policy or standardized practice exists within her pediatric residency program, she is not sure how to proceed and is not comfortable with the vague "just ask for help" response from the program director. Rae is frustrated by a lack of clear guidance and specific accommodations from the institution and is unsure how her progressing disability will affect her future as a pediatrician.

Case Discussion

Rae's experience is not unique. Indeed, residents and fellows struggle to find clear pathways to requesting accommodations. GME program leaders, regardless of specialty, share the goal of increasing diversity in medicine. This includes creating accessible, supportive spaces for all learners, including those with disabilities. To realize the goal of diversifying the physician workforce, GME programs and institutional leaders must engage with the latest data and guidance on building inclusive and welcoming programs. As part of this engagement, program and institutional leaders should review ACGME Institutional and Common Program Requirements for maintaining an institutional disability policy and providing accommodations to residents and fellows in accordance with the institutional policy. They should also consider the Association of American Medical Colleges (AAMC) and American Medical Association (AMA) recommendations to employ a highly skilled and qualified person familiar with medicine and the Americans with Disabilities Act (ADA) that can result in a more informed interactive process to determine accommodations and serve as a skilled facilitator of learner, program director, and Human Resources (HR) discussions (see Table 22.1).

Disclosing a disability and requesting accommodations can be anxiety-provoking for a learner as noted in Rae's case. For Rae, the lack of both clear policies and processes and an informed HR contact increases her anxiety. Like so many learners, Rae was hesitant to disclose personal information to her direct supervisor fearing that this information could lead to bias and stigma and might even impact her performance review. The response to just "ask for help" in the clinic left Rae feeling unsupported and placed her in the awkward position of having to disclose multiple times over, to several of her colleagues, in the absence of reliable supports in place. Rae also fears that she will have limited access to items as a function of providing the best—and safest—patient care. Making sure that she can access all the items needed for patient care and procedures is paramount. The nebulous approach used by Rae's program to address disability inclusion leaves her anxious; she expends a considerable about of cognitive energy thinking about her access needs. Eventually, this level of anxiety leads to an increase in her depressive symptoms. Not wanting to draw further attention to herself or have anyone question her ability, Rae decides not to engage in help-seeking. For Rae, the energy she expends to manage her symptoms and negotiate training with barriers in place takes up all her spare time. Even if she wanted to seek therapy—when would she have the time? Rae finds herself wishing she'd matched to another program and approaches residency as a task to "get through" instead of an opportunity to learn and thrive.

As you review the chapter, consider whether residents and fellows with disabilities like Rae, would feel comfortable disclosing disability in your program and if they could easily locate and follow a process for requesting accommodations. Additionally, you will want to reflect on the specialization and knowledge base of the office overseeing the process—often HR. How would HR personnel respond to this inquiry? Are they connected to national resources to be able to see how other programs have addressed access for learners with chronic health- related disabilities? If processes do not exist for your program, also consider engaging your GME office and how you might build disability policies as part of your institution's equity and inclusion efforts.

INTRODUCTION TO DISABILITY IN THE UNITED STATES

Approximately 27% of people in the United States have a disability,[1] defined as a physical or mental impairment that substantially limits one or more major life activities. Individuals with disabilities are at risk for poorer health outcomes when compared with people without disabilities,[2] as well as significant health care disparities and inequities, including challenges in accessing the health care system.[3] These disparities are due, in part, to inaccessible health care facilities and perceptions of the type of care needed and result in less evidence-based health care screening and treatment due to barriers that are complex and multi-pronged including communication access and physical barriers.[4] It is understandable, then, that these patients are often less satisfied with their care.[5]

People with disabilities also face high levels of ableism in medicine, including stereotyped beliefs about disability and low levels of disability competency among physicians.[6-9] National studies suggest that three-quarters of physicians believe that people with disabilities experience an inferior quality of life, while less than half of physicians report feeling qualified to treat patients with disabilities and admit to providing ineffective, if any, accommodations for disabled patients.[10-12] In one study, primary care physicians expressed explicit bias towards patients with disabilities, including de-prioritizing health maintenance screenings,[13] refusing accommodations, and discharging patients with disabilities from their care.[12] These attitudes stem, in part, from insufficient education about disability and lack of exposure to people with disabilities during their education.[14,15] Additionally, physicians are not educated about the civil rights protections associated with the Americans with Disabilities Act (ADA), their responsibilities to provide reasonable accommodation, or the duty to ensure that their practices are non-discriminatory.[11,16]

DISABILITY INCLUSION AS A MECHANISM OF REDUCING BARRIERS

Discussions and initiatives related to justice, equity, diversity, inclusion (JEDI), and access in medicine have historically excluded disability. Disability researchers and scholars, in addition to physicians with disabilities, suggest that disability-informed medical education and care may serve to reduce the aforementioned barriers.[16-22] Based on their study and experience, these experts believe that a disability-focused curriculum, informed by and provided alongside disabled people, may challenge stereotypes and reduce disparate outcomes through increasing disability consciousness and improving culturally humble care.[14-26] At the same time, increasing the number of people with disabilities from differing backgrounds in medical education may combat ableist belief systems about disability through the tenants of contact theory, whereby stereotyped beliefs are reduced when people work closely together in equal status roles toward a shared goal.[27,28] Impacting health care through the inclusion of disabled physicians requires a coordinated commitment to disability inclusion and an understanding of disability as a valued part of diversity.

Additional training on disability or culturally humble care is not enough, as demonstrated by a longitudinal series of education experiences and lectures on disability. Immediate gains in empathy and positive attitudes are not sustained over time.[29,30] Considering the minimum of 3 years of graduate medical education (GME), preceded by 4 years of undergraduate medical education, studying and training alongside peers with disabilities is likely to be an effective strategy for maintaining empathy and positive attitudes toward people with disabilities in the long term.[19]

A SHIFT TOWARD DISABILITY INCLUSION

Workplace Accommodations in GME: Accreditation Requirements

The ACGME approved an institutional requirement in 2007 that specifies that all Sponsoring Institutions must have a policy, "not necessarily GME-specific, regarding accommodations for disabilities consistent with all applicable laws and regulations." (IV.I.4.)[32] In 2021, as part of its effort to ensure a healthy and safe clinical and educational environment for all physician learners, the Institutional Requirements were updated to add that accommodations must be made for residents and fellows with disabilities consistent with institutional policy. Subsequently, in conjunction with the Institutional Requirements, the ACGME approved a Common Program Requirement (I.D.2.e),[31] applicable to both residency and fellowship programs regardless of specialty/subspecialty, that ensures accommodations for disabilities must be available at the program level, consistent with institutional policy. In addition, both the Institutional and Common Program Requirements also address the need to increase the diversity of ACGME-accredited programs.[31,32] Finally, while not specific to disability, the ACGME also states that it is the responsibility of the program, in partnership with the Sponsoring Institution, to address the well-being of residents and fellows, by requiring that they must be given the opportunity to attend medical, mental health, and dental appointments, including those scheduled during work hours (VI.C.1.d).(1)).[31] (See Table 22.1 for a summary of the ACGME Requirements.)

Table 22.1 — Summary of Available Guidance and Regulations for Disability Inclusion in GME

Source: ACGME. Common Program Requirements (Residency).[31]		Expectation
ACGME Common Program Requirements	I.D.1. The program, in partnership with its Sponsoring Institution, must ensure the availability of adequate resources for resident education. (Core) [I.D.2. The program, in partnership with its Sponsoring Institution, must ensure healthy and safe learning and working environments that promote resident well-being and provide for:] I.D.2.e) accommodations for residents with disabilities consistent with the Sponsoring Institution's policy. (Core)	Required
ACGME Common Program Requirements	VI.C.1.c).(1) Residents must be given the opportunity to attend medical, mental health, and dental care appointments, including those scheduled during their working hours. (Core)	Required

Source: ACGME. Institutional Requirements.[32]		Expectation
ACGME Institutional Requirements	[III.B.7.d] The Sponsoring Institution must ensure a healthy and safe clinical and educational environment that provides for:] III.B.7.d).(6) accommodations for residents/fellows with disabilities, consistent with the Sponsoring Institution's policy. (Core)	Required
ACGME Institutional Requirements	III.B.8. The Sponsoring Institution, in partnership with each of its programs, must engage in practices that focus on ongoing, mission-driven, systematic recruitment and retention of a diverse and inclusive workforce of residents/fellows, faculty members, senior administrative staff members, and other relevant members of its GME community. (Core)	Required
ACGME Institutional Requirements	IV.I.4 Accommodation for Disabilities: The Sponsoring Institution must have a policy, not necessarily GME-specific, regarding accommodations for disabilities consistent with all applicable laws and regulations. (Core)	Required

Source: Meeks LM, Jain N. *Accessibility, Inclusion, and Action in Medical Education: Lived Experiences of Learners and Physicians with Disabilities* AAMC.[33]		Expectation
AAMC Lived Experience Report	**Conduct a programmatic assessment.** Make systemic changes, beginning with an assessment of services by an outside expert and/or through soliciting feedback from existing community members with disabilities.	Consideration

(continued)

Table 22.1	Summary of available guidance and regulations for disability inclusion in GME (*continued*)		
AAMC Lived Experience Report	**Set a welcoming and inclusive tone.** • Make a statement about valuing diversity (including disability) in the residency program to reduce the stigma around disclosing disability. • Ensure that interview activities and spaces are accessible to applicants with disabilities. • Include a clear statement about how to request accommodations in invitations for interviews, including a specific contact person. State what measures you have already taken to ensure access for interviewees (eg, all interview spaces are wheelchair accessible).	Consideration	
AAMC Lived Experience Report	**Conduct awareness training that highlights successful physicians with disabilities.** Make residents aware of networks for physicians with disabilities (see Appendix B). Work toward full accessibility for clinicians, learners, and patients.	Consideration	
AAMC Lived Experience Report	Provide professional development training for faculty, residents, and staff on multiple topics.	Consideration	
AAMC Lived Experience Report	Consider accessibility for residents and physicians with disabilities in planning orientation and onboarding events and activities.	Consideration	
AAMC Lived Experience Report	**Have a clear process for requesting accommodations that does not involve direct disclosure to a colleague or supervisor.** Residency programs can use the University of Connecticut GME policy as a template for developing communication to applicants.	Consideration	
AAMC Lived Experience Report	**Employ someone with knowledge of disability, disability rights law, and accommodations in a clinical setting to facilitate the interactive process.**	Consideration	
AAMC Lived Experience Report	**Develop and disseminate a clear understanding of the financial obligation to provide accommodations and ensure that accommodations are adequately funded.**	Consideration	
AAMC Lived Experience Report	**Integrate disability into diversity initiatives, efforts, and language.** • Ensure that diversity initiatives explicitly include disability as an aspect of diversity valued in institutions. • Meaningfully integrate disability into diversity training. • Count individuals with disabilities in diversity measures, identify trends in the number of staff with disabilities, and use these metrics as an indication of improved efforts for inclusion. Create an environment where disabilities are acknowledged and respected.	Consideration	

Table 22.1	Summary of available guidance and regulations for disability inclusion in GME (*continued*)	
AAMC Lived Experience Report	**Make wellness services and programming visible.** Make sure residents and employees are aware of the available support services through employee assistance programs (EAPs) or specialized wellness programs for residents.	Consideration
AAMC Lived Experience Report	**Acknowledge the challenges of residency and medical practice and normalize help-seeking behavior.** Acknowledge that residency and medical practice are difficult and emotionally exhausting. Residency program directors should normalize help-seeking behaviors and provide a positive learning and working environment that encourages work-life balance. Lead by example by engaging in wellness activities and encouraging residents to do the same and highlight the resources available to residents.	Consideration
AAMC Lived Experience Report	**Improve opportunities for coverage.** Residents should have the option of taking time off, as needed, without the added weight of burdening their colleagues. The use of nurse practitioners or physician assistants, in lieu of a jeopardy system in which residents cover for each other, can remove the guilt that keeps many residents working through crisis and would encourage help-seeking behavior.	Consideration
AAMC Lived Experience Report	**Integrate wellness into the residency curriculum and workplace culture.** Discuss mental health and provide opportunities for residents and employees to share stories and support one another. Provide time for wellness in the curriculum, and reward residents and employees for taking time to attend to self-care.	Consideration
Source: Council on Medical Education. A study to evaluate barriers to medical education for trainees with disabilities. American Medical Association.[34]		**Expectation**
AMA CME Report	That our American Medical Association (AMA) urge that all medical schools and graduate medical education (GME) institutions and programs create, review, and revise technical standards, concentrating on replacing "organic" standards with "functional" standards that emphasize abilities rather than limitations, and that those institutions also disseminate these standards and information on how to request accommodations for disabilities in a prominent and easily found location on their websites.	Recommendation

(*continued*)

Table 22.1	Summary of available guidance and regulations for disability inclusion in GME (*continued*)	
AMA CME Report	That our AMA urge all medical schools and GME institutions to a) make available to students and trainees a designated, qualified person or committee trained in the application of the Americans with Disabilities Act, Section 504 of the Rehabilitation Act of 1973, and available support services, b) encourage students and trainees to avail themselves of any needed support services, and c) foster a supportive and inclusive environment where students and trainees with disabilities feel comfortable accessing support services.	Recommendation
AMA CME Report	That our AMA encourage research and broad dissemination of results in the area of disabilities accommodation in the medical environment that includes: the efficacy of established accommodations; innovative accommodation models that either reduce barriers or provide educational approaches to facilitate the avoidance of barriers; impact of disabled learners and physicians on the delivery of health care to patients with disabilities; and research on the safety of established and potential accommodations for use in clinical programs and practice.	Recommendation

Guidance from Professional Associations

In 2018, an Association of American Medical Colleges (AAMC) report, "Accessibility, Inclusion, and Action in Medical Education: Lived Experiences of Learners and Physicians with Disabilities,"[33] identified the following four key barriers to disability inclusion in GME: (1) absence of individual and institutional knowledge regarding the benefits of disability inclusion; (2) poorly defined policies and procedures for disclosure; (3) absence of a knowledgeable and identifiable point person; and (4) an insufficient understanding of the legal requirements to accommodate learners with disabilities under the ADA.[33] In light of these barriers, the AAMC proposed considerations for GME (Table 22.1). Five years later, this AAMC report was buttressed by a similar report from the American Medical Association (AMA)[34] that identified similar barriers across the continuum of medical education. Its findings included: (1) a lack of informed decision-making about accommodations in medical school and residency; and (2) barriers to accessing timely decisions for accommodations on the licensing board examinations, including those administered by the National Board of Medical Examiners and the National Board of Osteopathic Medical Examiners. The AMA called for continued research to understand the most effective accommodation mechanisms in medical education and to create more inclusive learning environments (Table 22.1).[34]

KEY CHALLENGES FACED BY LEARNERS WITH DISABILITIES IN GME SETTINGS

Despite calls for action in medicine, barriers continue to contribute to low representation and significant attrition of learners with disabilities along the medical education pathway to practice. Research using parallel questions from the AAMC Year Two (Y2Q) and Graduation Questionnaires (GQ), The National Sample Survey of Physicians (NSSP), and the University of Michigan Intern Health Study allowed researchers to capture representation across the training-to-practice pathway. These studies demonstrated a steady and significant decline as trainees with disabilities move through training, with 9.3% of graduating medical students identifying a disability,[35] 9.3% among resident physicians,[36] and 3.1% among practicing physicians.[37]

Program Access

Program access plays a critical role in helping residents and fellows with disabilities to thrive. Learners are thought to have program access when disability barriers in the learning and working environment are removed, usually through reasonable accommodation.[38] Program access includes strategies beyond individual accommodations which tend to be reactive to an individual's needs (and may even be thought of as existing only while that disabled resident is in the program). Other strategies included in the concept of program access include applying universal design principles to curricular and environmental design so a certain barrier may not exist in the first place. Lack of program access can result from more than a lack of accommodation; program access may be stymied by attitudinal barriers, the culture or climate of an institution that renders the environment unsafe for disclosure of disability. Under these conditions, residents and fellows opt out of the accommodation process because the cost-benefit analysis suggests more harm by disclosing and engaging in the process of requesting accommodations.[36]

Non-Disclosure of Disability and Associated Consequences

Indeed, physician learners may choose not to disclose their disability. Recent research suggests that upwards of 50.6% of residents do not disclose disability.[36] The main drivers of non-disclosure are fear of stigma/bias followed by a lack of a clear institutional process for requesting accommodations. This finding is highly problematic given that program access for residents and fellows is significantly associated with self-reported medical errors and increased depressive symptoms in disabled learners.[38,39] In this same study, for the physician learners whose access needs were met, no differences were noted in depressive symptoms and medical errors.[38] These studies, in addition to the guidance and requirements offered by varied associations and organizations, provide programs with a map highlighting a path to improved access and inclusion for disabled learners.

Lack of Funding Structure and Understanding of Responsibility

Another challenge encountered by physician learners with disabilities is the lack of funding to support needed accommodations. Let us examine a hypothetical case of a resident physician, Colette, who is experiencing this problem:

> Colette is six months into her pediatric gastroenterology fellowship. She previously worked alongside a dedicated team of sign language interpreters in medical school and residency, and when she moved for fellowship, they were unable to relocate. When she approached the hospital's disability office about interpreter coverage, the specialist stated, "We determined that interpreters are only reasonable when you are doing procedures. We are looking into technology and acquiring additional clear masks to fill in for your needs." Colette feels dismissed. After seven years of medical training, Colete understands her needs; she experienced high levels of success when she had a team of designated interpreters affording her access to all facets of training, both those that were patient forward and educational experiences like grand rounds, research team meetings, and conferences. Colette also understands the critical nature of accurate communication and fears that in the absence of designated interpreters, her ability to provide safe and effective patient care will be impacted. Given the decision of the Sponsoring Institution, Colette has only worked with interpreters during her procedure clinic hours. As a result, she has not had access to the other elements of the fellowship and has struggled with navigating these responsibilities and missed several opportunities, particularly inpatient consults. Colette sent an e-mail advocating for additional coverage but was told that there was no identifiable department funding available in the budget and that they would have to re-evaluate her accommodations during the next fiscal year.

Learners have difficulty asking for any accommodation, and when they do ask, they are generally knowledgeable about what works and have utilized these accommodations in previous educational experiences. Here, Colette took the proper steps to outline her needs, was proactive in addressing access barriers, and was dismissed. Worse yet, she was told that financial constraints were keeping her from having full access to the program, her patients, and her career.

Budget concerns are often cited as the issue keeping learners from accessing communication-based accommodations like captioning services or interpreters. Discussion of funding restraints with learners is not appropriate and places an inordinate amount of stress on the learner. Such discussions about financial considerations can lead to the perception that access is a burden for the institution. Discussing financial matters may also create a culture where learners accept subpar accommodations rather than asserting themselves to gain full program access and to maximize their potential. Case law suggests that the cost of the accommodation is an institutional responsibility and that evaluation of whether an accommodation expense is an undue burden should be made using the entire budget of the institution or hospital system, not just the budget of the department. For Colette, the uncomfortable interaction left her feeling like she was not an important part of the program and that her ability to provide patient care was not a priority.

Access and Inclusion

When the institutional culture does not consider accessibility and accommodations as part of its standard practice, individuals with disability can experience a sense of othering and exclusion that threatens their ability to thrive in their GME community. This experience is exacerbated when a physician learner is also part of a minoritized population which increases the odds of experiencing burnout.[40] Let's explore the case of Aaron:

> Aaron is a new family medicine resident at a large academic medical center. Aaron identifies culturally as Afro-Caribbean hailing from Jamaica and completed his undergraduate medical education in the Caribbean. He has paraplegia resulting from a car accident in adolescence, propelling him to enter medicine after his extensive time in rehabilitation. The institution has proactively created wheelchair-accessible clinical spaces, and his program director has collaborated with physical medicine and rehabilitation faculty members about additional modifications. The first day's orientation includes a carpool trip to multiple clinical sites for a tour and to a locally owned restaurant for a social dinner. His program director turns to Aaron, "I know you've got an accessible car you're able to drive. I have the addresses for each site for you. I figured you could drive yourself." When he arrives at the third site, he realizes that his co-residents have started to bond while in the shared van. He initially thinks, "I'll make it up over dinner." However, when Aaron tries to enter the restaurant, he finds out there are a few steps to enter the building, and the only other entry with no barriers is through the back. His co-residents and faculty members are already inside. He debates asking his colleagues to assist him inside but does not feel like this is appropriate to ask on the first day and doesn't know if he will be able to navigate his wheelchair inside either. He also hesitates to ask the team to relocate to a more accessible location as he hasn't bonded with them. As he enters the back entry, his colleagues do not know how to respond, creating an awkward and non-inclusive outing.

GME leadership plays a vital role in building an inclusive culture. In Aaron's case, while the program director may have thought that acknowledging his accessible car and providing the addresses sufficed for being inclusive, the exclusion was miscalculated, when Aaron was required to drive to the restaurant on his own, and when locations that lacked adequate wheelchair accessibility were selected. If the program director had instead chartered an accessible van to accommodate all the residents, (a small example of universal design), they would all have had that opportunity to bond with Aaron. Furthermore, if the program director had consulted with Aaron before planning the event, they might have brainstormed some inclusive activities together instead of trying to plan something on his own without understanding Aaron's needs. Being direct with people with disabilities and not assuming their needs or desires can build trust, foster community, and solidify leadership and learner as a unified team.

STRATEGIES TO IMPROVE INCLUSION OF LEARNERS WITH DISABILITIES IN GME

While the ACGME requires GME programs and Sponsoring Institutions to maintain a policy that addresses the accommodation of needs of residents and fellows with disabilities, these requirements do not provide specific guidance about how to create inclusive and welcoming policies. In what follows, we offer several recommendations from the GME literature to help program leaders, designated institutional officials (DIOs), and other advocates take meaningful steps toward creating inclusive educational and clinical environments.[41,42]

1. *Review existing policies for physician learners and faculty members with disabilities to ensure they are inclusive and portray welcoming language that encourages people to disclose and request accommodations.* The policies should be posted to the program and institutional websites and should be available in all house staff communication and handbooks. The process should be clear, and all content should be accessible (eg, accessible PDFs).
2. *Identify the office tasked with making accommodation decisions within your institution, that is, the "ADA Designee."* This office may be located within Human Resources (HR), Occupational Health, or the ADA office. At least one person or office at the institution should be identified as the Disability Resource Professional (DRP)/ADA Specialist, who oversees managing requests related to disability. Within this role, individuals making determinations about disability should have knowledge of medical education and disability law.
3. *Use an interactive, iterative process to discuss and refine potential accommodations related to disability.*

    Optimally, institutions will employ a DRP and will engage the learner in a process whereby all parties discuss and refine potential accommodations; this is known as the **interactive process** (Figure 22.1).[43] The process is confidential and should begin with a neutral party, such as the institution's DRP. The learner is responsible for contacting the ADA designee for this consultation. The process begins with a confidential consult between the learner and the ADA designee. This is a critical step as the learner is the best source of information about their disability and the historical use of accommodations. If the learner decides to pursue accommodations, the designee will involve the program director to begin the interactive process. Documentation may be necessary if the disability is not readily apparent, but it should not delay discussions of potential accommodations and should be stored confidentially, and details are not shared with the program director. To assist the ADA designee in making an accommodation decision, the program director and/or Designated Institutional Official (DIO) will communicate essential functions required for the GME program and will engage in a discussion about potential accommodations and modifications. Then, the program director, the ADA designee, and the DIO may seek outside consultation to determine potential creative solutions and best practices, and an accommodations plan

8 Step Process

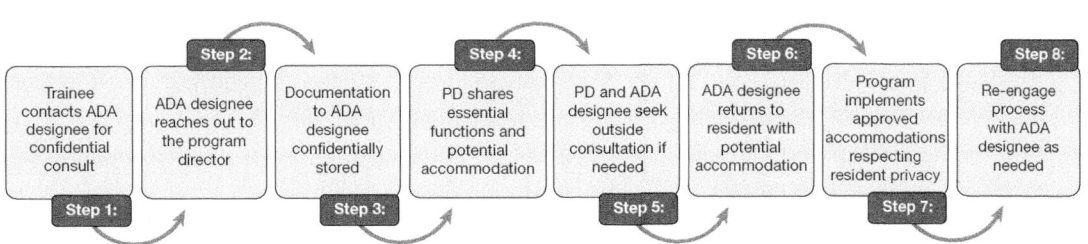

FIGURE 22.1 Eight step iterative, interactive process for determining disability accommodations. (Source: Meeks LM, Taylor N, Moreland CJ. *Disability accommodation in GME.* Learn at ACGME: Equity Matters Video Library, Module 10. Accreditation Council for Graduate Medical Education; 2022. Accessed June 23, 2024. https://dl.acgme.org/learn/learning-path/equity-matters-video-library)

will be presented to the learner. The final part of the process is the implementation of accommodation, usually overseen by the program. The process is interactive and iterative, meaning the institution and program must collaboratively and continuously re-evaluate the accommodations plan for effectiveness.

4. *Incorporate themes consistent with a culture of disability inclusion throughout the organization, including the overall mission statement and practices pertaining to recruitment, selection, curriculum, and bias reporting.*

Given the limited proportion of physicians with disabilities in medical education and practice, increasing representation is a critical starting point for GME programs. Applicants exploring a residency or fellowship program should be able to review its mission, vision, and values, and identify themes consistent with a culture of disability inclusion. Such inclusion incorporates the development and identification of accommodation policies and resources for learners with disabilities. Curricula should be infused with themes addressing microaggressions, language use, bystander/upstander engagement, and functional mechanisms to report mistreatment of people with disabilities (learners or patients). The FAM (Flexibility, Accommodations, Modification) framework has been suggested to improve access to and participation in STEMM (Science, Technology, Engineering, Mathematics, and Medicine), allowing a flexible approach to organization of the workplace environment, creative accommodations, and modifications to essential duties or time requirements, all of which help to address varying needs and encourage inclusion of people with disabilities.[44]

> Ensure your program and institution actively welcome residents, fellows, and faculty members with disabilities and encourages them to disclose.

> Communicate your commitment to diversifying the workforce, and your understanding that physician learners with disabilities increase workplace diversity, promote inclusivity, and bring attention to access and health care needs among patients with disabilities.

Take Home Points

- GME programs should be aware of the institutional policy for disability inclusion, requiring constant reassessment and revision and make it readily available to learners.
- GME program and institutional leaders should identify their institutional DRP/ADA expert and accommodation request workflow.
- Involve physician learners in an interactive process that engages with them as experts in their own disability and in accommodating their needs.

? QUESTIONS FOR FURTHER THOUGHT

1. What institutional or program policies do you have related to disability? Can potential residents easily locate them?
2. If you were a resident or fellow with a disability, to what extent would you feel comfortable disclosing a disability in your program, and would the process for requesting accommodations be clear?
3. How can you improve practices to create a welcoming environment where learners feel safe disclosing a disability?

Acknowledgments

The following guidance is informed not only by researchers and leaders on disability but, importantly, by a myriad of disabled learners who bravely share their stories and experiences so that we can improve the educational environment. Individuals with disabilities are the most important source of information about their needs. For this reason, we acknowledge and dedicate this chapter to learners and physicians with disabilities.

REFERENCES

1. Varadaraj V, Deal JA, Campanile J, Reed NS, Swenor BK. National prevalence of disability and disability types among adults in the US, 2019. *JAMA Netw Open.* 2021;4(10):e2130358. doi:10.1001/jamanetworkopen.2021.30358
2. Krahn GL, Walker DK, Correa-De-Araujo R. Persons with disabilities as an unrecognized health disparity population. *Am J Public Health.* 2015;105(Suppl 2):S198-S206. doi: 10.2105/AJPH.2014.302182
3. Agency for Healthcare Research and Quality. 2010 national healthcare disparities report. 2011; last reviewed 2013. Accessed November 8, 2021. https://archive.ahrq.gov/research/findings/nhqrdr/nhdr10/index.html
4. Reichard A, Stolzle H, Fox MH. Health disparities among adults with physical disabilities or cognitive limitations compared to individuals with no disabilities in the United States. *Disabil Health J.* 2011;4(2):59-67. doi:10.1016/j.dhjo.2010.05.003
5. Iezzoni LI, Davis RB, Soukup J, O'Day B. Satisfaction with quality and access to health care among people with disabling conditions. *Int J Qual Health Care.* 2002 Oct;14(5):369-81. doi: 10.1093/intqhc/14.5.369
6. Smith DL. Disparities in health care access for women with disabilities in the United States from the 2006 National Health Interview Survey. *Disabil Health J.* 2008;1(2):79-88. doi:10.1016/j.dhjo.2008.01.001
7. Iezzoni LI, Kurtz SG, Rao SR. Trends in mammography over time for women with and without chronic disability. *J Womens Health (Larchmt).* 2015;24(7):593-601. doi:10.1089/jwh.2014.5181
8. Story MF, Schwier E, Kailes JI. Perspectives of patients with disabilities on the accessibility of medical equipment: examination tables, imaging equipment, medical chairs, and weight scales. *Disabil Health J.* 2009;2(4):169-179.e1. doi:10.1016/j.dhjo.2009.05.003
9. Agaronnik ND, Lagu T, DeJong C, et al. Accommodating patients with obesity and mobility difficulties: observations from physicians. *Disabil Health J.* 2021;14(1):100951. doi: 10.1016/j.dhjo.2020.100951
10. Iezzoni LI, Rao SR, Ressalam J, Bolcic-Jankovic D, et al. Physicians' perceptions of people with disability and their health care. *Health Aff (Millwood).* 2021;40(2):297-306. doi: 10.1377/hlthaff.2020.01452
11. Iezzoni LI, Rao SR, Ressalam J, et al. US physicians' knowledge about the Americans with Disabilities Act and accommodation of patients with disability. *Health Aff (Millwood).* 2022;41(1):96-104. doi:10.1377/hlthaff.2021.01136
12. Lagu T, Haywood C, Reimold K, DeJong C, Sterling RW, Iezzoni LI. 'I am not the doctor for you': physicians' attitudes about caring for people with disabilities. *Health Aff (Millwood).* 2022;41(10):1387-1395. doi:10.1377/hlthaff.2022.00475
13. Iezzoni LI, Wint AJ, Smeltzer SC, Ecker JL. Effects of disability on pregnancy experiences among women with impaired mobility. *Acta Obstet Gynecol Scand.* 2015;94:133-140. doi:10.1111/aogs.12544
14. Smeltz L, Havercamp SM, Meeks L. Aspiring to disability consciousness in health professions training. *AMA J Ethics.* 2024;26(1):E54-E61. doi:10.1001/amajethics.2024.54
15. Havercamp SM, Barnhart WR, Robinson AC, Whalen Smith CN. What should we teach about disability? national consensus on disability competencies for health care education. *Disabil Health J.* 2021;14(2):100989. doi:10.1016/j.dhjo.2020.100989
16. Agaronnik ND, Pendo E, Campbell EG, Ressalam J, Iezzoni LI. Knowledge of practicing physicians about their legal obligations when caring for patients with disability. *Health Aff (Millwood).* 2019;38:545-553. doi:10.1377/hlthaff.2018.05060
17. Meeks LM, Herzer K, Jain NR. Removing barriers and facilitating access: increasing the number of physicians with disabilities. *Acad Med.* 2018;93(4):540-543. doi:10.1097/acm.0000000000002112
18. Meeks LM, Maraki I, Singh S, Curry RH. Global commitments to disability inclusion in health professions. *Lancet.* 2020;395(10227):852-853. doi:10.1016/S0140-6736(20)30215-4
19. Singh S, Meeks LM. Disability inclusion in medical education: towards a quality improvement approach. *Med Educ.* 2023;57(1):102-107. doi:10.1111/medu.14878
20. Shakespeare T, Iezzoni LI, Groce NE. Disability and the training of health professionals. *Lancet.* 2009;374(9704):1815-1816. doi:10.1016/s0140-6736(09)62050-x
21. Doebrich A, Quirici M, Lunsford C. COVID-19 and the need for disability conscious medical education, training, and practice. *J Pediatr Rehabil Med.* 2020;13(3):393-404. doi: 10.3233/PRM-200763
22. Gupta R. I solemnly share. *JAMA.* 2018;319(6):549-550. doi:10.1001/jama.2017.22135
23. Adashek J. Invisibly disabled. *JAMA Oncol.* 2016;2(10):1265-1266. doi:10.1001/jamaoncol.2016.0117
24. Herzer KR. Moving from disability to possibility. *JAMA.* 2016;316(17):1767-1768. PMID: 27802549
25. Swenor B. Losing vision and gaining perspective. *JAMA.* 2019;321(5):455-456. doi:10.1001/jama.2019.0076
26. Schwarz CM, Zetkulic M. You belong in the room: addressing the underrepresentation of physicians with physical disabilities. *Acad Med.* 2019;94(1):17-19. PMID: 30157092

27. Jaregui J, Strote J, Addison C, Robins L, Shandro J. A novel medical student assistant accommodation model for a medical student with a disability during a required clinical clerkship. *AEM Educ Train.* 2019;4(3):275-279. PMID: 32704599
28. Pettigrew TF. Intergroup contact theory. *Annu Rev Psychol.* 1998;49:65-85. doi:10.1146/annurev.psych.49.1.65
29. Meeks LM, Poullos P, Swenor BK. Creative approaches to the inclusion of medical students with disabilities. *AEM Educ Train.* 2019;4(3):292-297. doi:10.1002/aet2.10425
30. Cecchetti M, Last J, Lynch J, Linehan C. Evaluating the longitudinal impact of a disability education intervention on medical students' attitudes towards persons with a disability. *Disabil Health J.* 2021;14(3):101092. doi:10.1016/j.dhjo.2021.101092
31. Accreditation Council for Graduate Medical Education. Institutional requirements. 2022. Accessed April 22, 2024. https://www.acgme.org/globalassets/pfassets/programrequirements/800_institutionalrequirements2022.pdf
32. Accreditation Council for Graduate Medical Education. Common program requirements (residency). 2023. Accessed April 22, 2024. https://www.acgme.org/globalassets/pfassets/programrequirements/cprresidency_2023.pdf.
33. Meeks LM, Jain N. *Accessibility, Inclusion, and Action in Medical Education: Lived Experiences of Learners and Physicians with Disabilities.* Association of American Medical Colleges; 2018.
34. Council on Medical Education. A study to evaluate barriers to medical education for trainees with disabilities. American Medical Association. In: CME Report 4-A-20, November 2021. https://www.ama-assn.org/system/files/n21-cme02.pdf. Accessed November 20, 2021.
35. Association of American Medical Colleges. Graduating questionnaire survey results 2022. Accessed April 22, 2024. https://www.aamc.org/data-reports/students-residents/report/graduation-questionnaire-gq
36. Pereira-Lima K, Meeks LM, Ross KET, et al. Barriers to disclosure of disability and request for accommodations among first-year resident physicians in the US. *JAMA Netw Open.* 2023;6(5):e239981. PMID: 37166801
37. Nouri Z, Dill MJ, Conrad SS, Moreland CJ, Meeks LM. Estimated prevalence of US physicians with disabilities. *JAMA Netw Open.* 2021;4(3):e211254. doi:10.1001/jamanetworkopen.2021.1254. Erratum in: *JAMA Netw Open.* 2021;4(4):e2110025. PMID: 33856480. Erratum in: *JAMA Netw Open.* 2022;5(8):e2232194. PMID: 33710286
38. Meeks LM, Pereira-Lima K, Frank E, Stergiopoulos E, Ross KE, Sen S. Program access, depressive symptoms, and medical errors among resident physicians with disability. *JAMA Netw Open.* 2021;4(12):e2141511. doi:10.1001/jamanetworkopen.2021.41511
39. Meeks LM, Pereira-Lima K, Plegue M, et al. Disability, program access, empathy and burnout in US medical students: a national study. *Med Educ.* 2023;57(6):523-534. doi:10.1111/medu.14995
40. Nguyen M, Meeks LM, Pereira-Lima K, et al. Medical student burnout by race, ethnicity, and multiple disability status. *JAMA Netw Open.* 2024;7(1):e2351046. PMID: 38198142
41. Meeks LM, Taylor N, Case B, et al. The unexamined diversity: disability policies and practices in US graduate medical education programs. *J Grad Med Educ.* 2020;12(5):615-619. doi:10.4300/JGME-D-19-00940.1
42. Meeks LM, Jain N, Moreland C, Taylor N, Brookman JC, Fitzsimons M. Realizing a diverse and inclusive workforce: equal access for residents with disabilities. *J Grad Med Educ.* 2019;11(5):498-503. doi:10.4300/JGME-D-19-00286.1
43. Meeks LM, Taylor N, Moreland CJ. Disability accommodation in GME. Learn at ACGME: Equity Matters Video Library, Module 10. Accreditation Council for Graduate Medical Education; 2022. Accessed June 23, 2024. https://dl.acgme.org/learn/learning-path/equity-matters-video-library
44. Mattison SM, Gin L, Abraham AA, Moodie M, Okanlami F, Wander K. Community voices: broadening participation in science, technology, engineering, mathematics, and medicine among persons with disabilities. *Nat Commun.* 2022;13(1):7208. doi:10.1038/s41467-022-34711-w

Remaining Inclusive of and Supporting Non-traditionally Aged Residents

Ngozi F. Anachebe, PharmD, MD, Vice Dean for Educational Affairs, Associate Professor, Wright State University Boonshoft School of Medicine, Fairborn, OH

Leila E. Harrison (née Diaz), PhD, MA, MEd, Vice Dean for Admissions, Student Affairs, and Alumni Engagement, Assistant Professor, Washington State University Elson S. Floyd College of Medicine, Spokane, WA

CHAPTER SUMMARY

Non-traditionally aged resident physicians (hereafter referred to as "non-traditional residents") who bring with them diverse experiences and perspectives, are an important cohort of our physician learners in graduate medical education (GME). They may have and continue to experience ageism and stereotype threat in the learning environment which may contribute to burnout. Non-traditional residents have significant life experiences that can positively add to their medical teams' efficacy and help improve their rapport with patients and patient outcomes. Residency programs should harness these residents' rich lived experience, create a respectful and active learning environment, provide opportunities for graded responsibility, and give timely, effective feedback. We propose strategies to improve the education of non-traditional residents, enhance faculty development, and build an inclusive learning environment for all residents.

LEARNING OBJECTIVES

1. Define non-traditional residents in GME and use this definition to compare with data from their organization.
2. Identify key challenges and barriers faced by non-traditional residents as well as the benefits and value they add to GME learning environments.
3. Differentiate primary intersections to be understood about non-traditional residents.
4. Develop some organization-specific recommended strategies to enhance inclusion and equity for non-traditional residents from the perspective of leadership, within the workforce and workplace, and for patients.

Case Study

Dr Tom Smith is a first-year family medicine resident in the fifth month of his program. He has enjoyed each rotation and feels he is on track with his learning. However, he has felt isolated. Each medical team he joined seemed unsure how to interact with him initially; some even asked if he was the attending. He assumed these suppositions must be due to his greying hair. On his ambulatory family medicine rotation, his resident

(continued)

colleagues seemed to distance themselves. They did not invite him to their social outings which he heard about after-the-fact. He wondered if this exclusion was from the resident orientation icebreaker when he shared that he is married with two young children.

He was excited about his 4-week obstetrics (OB) rotation at a level I county hospital, specifically looking forward to gaining experience managing uncomplicated pregnancies on the labor and delivery floor. He heard from the family medicine residents that the OB rotation was demanding and hectic. He worked hard to meet their expectations, arriving early to see his assigned patients before morning report. He was always available on the floor to assist residents with patient care duties. However, he felt like an outsider. The OB residents and attendings seemed to ignore him and focus on the medical students and lower-level OB residents. Despite this, he remained encouraged.

Dr Smith consistently reached out to the OB resident to whom he was assigned, asking to see patients waiting in triage, which was well-received. He just wished his team would include him like they included the other residents and medical students.

During the last week of this rotation, a post-op patient coded on his floor. The OB residents and the attending were in a C-section on the same floor a few rooms away from the distressed patient's room. Dr Smith was near the patient's room when he heard the patient's nurse calling for help. He ran in and began the resuscitation of the patient. He was in his element. He had been certified for advanced cardiovascular life support (ACLS) for many years, had run codes many times before, and even taught the ACLS class at one point. As members of the health care team arrived, Dr Smith calmly told them what tasks to handle. Within a few minutes of the overhead page, his attending for the day, who is almost 2 years out of her residency, and the OB team, ran in to discover Dr Smith calmly and accurately handling the code. Even the anesthesiology attending physician who arrived after the OB team was impressed with Dr Smith's composure and competency in handling the situation.

Dr Smith's attending and the OB team began to acknowledge him by asking him about his background and his perspectives. During a debrief with the OB team after the code, the attending asked how he mastered running a code. He shared his background as a registered nurse for over 10 years and his work as an Air Force medic in Afghanistan. Dr Smith began to feel seen and valued for the life experiences he brought to the team. He found himself enjoying his work on the OB rotation. Until this point, the attending had not thought much of Dr Smith, viewing him as an older, and likely average resident, a new physician-in-training without much clinical experience.

Case Discussion

Medicine is a hierarchical profession with those in higher positions typically being older than the rest of the team. Each member of the team, however, has varied backgrounds and experiences and may have hidden skills and talents. For some, medicine is a second career. Those leading medical teams will miss these residents' rich lived experiences and perspectives if they make assumptions and fail to learn about their backgrounds. The interactions of the medical team should be guided by mutual respect and intentionality in addressing bias regardless of position in the medical hierarchy.

Non-traditional residents may experience exclusion due to assumptions about their background and/or skills which may disadvantage them if team leaders fail to learn about each team member, thereby missing out on the opportunity to fully engage or value the unique skills these non-traditional residents bring to the learning environment. Performance may suffer when any team member feels unheard, unseen, and unvalued; they may become dissatisfied with their work which can led to burnout. Team cohesion is important for team effectiveness. As you review this chapter, consider how Dr Smith's learning environment as a resident could have been more inclusive and how that would benefit Dr Smith, his colleagues, faculty members, and patients.

REPRESENTATION OF NON-TRADITIONAL RESIDENTS IN GRADUATE MEDICAL EDUCATION

The term **non-traditional age** is commonly used in medical education to identify medical students who are 25 years or older at the time they matriculate into medical school.[1] By extrapolation, residents of non-traditional age begin their residency at age 29 years or older. According to the 2022 Association of American Medical Colleges (AAMC) Graduation Questionnaire (GQ), a survey administered to all graduating US allopathic medical school seniors, 44.9% of the 16,901 respondents were aged 27-29 years, 11.7% of the respondents were aged 30-32 years, and 5.3% of the respondents were older than 32 years.[2] Table 23.1 shows how these numbers have changed over the past 5 years.[2] In 2021, 55.3% of active physicians, all specialties combined, were younger than 55 years compared to 46.7% who were over the age of 55.[3]

KEY CHALLENGES AND BARRIERS, BENEFITS, AND VALUE-ADDED

We live in an era of changing landscapes for undergraduate medical education (UME) and GME. Following the broad adoption of the holistic review framework in UME, residency programs have begun applying the framework into their selection processes. **Holistic review**, officially developed by the AAMC, is a framework that identifies an applicant's life experiences and personal attributes that are aligned with the program mission as well as identified academic metrics.[4] Importantly, holistic review is designed so that experiences, attributes, and in GME, competencies, are balanced with an applicant's

Table 23.1 Age at Graduation from US Allopathic Medical Schools 2018–2022[3]

	All Allopathic Medical Schools				
	2018 (%)	2019 (%)	2020 (%)	2021 (%)	2022 (%)
Under 24	0.4	0.3	0.3	0.4	0.3
24 through 26	39.9	39.5	39.5	37.6	37.8
27 through 29	41.7	42.6	42.8	44.2	44.9
30 through 32	12.0	12.0	11.7	11.8	11.7
Over 32	6.0	5.6	5.7	6.1	5.3
Number of respondents	16,223	16,657	16,630	16,611	16,901

Source: Association of American Medical Colleges. Active physicians by age and specialty, 2021. Accessed June 25, 2023. https://www.aamc.org/data-reports/workforce/interactive-data/active-physicians-age-specialty-2021

more traditional academic metrics (eg, US Medical Licensing Examination [USMLE] scores, clerkship grades, academic honors, and class ranking), the latter of which have had greater influence in making selection decisions. The use of this framework has been shown to increase the broad diversity of UME cohorts, one of which is age.[5] For GME, this means some of those entering residency have rich lived experiences outside of the educational context. These individuals may come into medicine as a second career, may have previously served in the military, may have various leadership experiences, and may have personal experiences managing complex life demands (eg, children, increased financial debt).

The most recent AAMC Matriculating Student Questionnaire (MSQ)[6] indicates that 17.1% of those enrolling into medical school are 26 years old or older, 8.2% are married, have a common law or civil union, are divorced, separated, or widowed, and 2.5% have dependents. In terms of life experience, 23.9% were out of college for more than 3 years when they enrolled in medical school, 23.3% come into medical school with $15,000 or more in educational debt, and 7.2% with $10,000 or more in consumer debt. Table 23.2 shows how these factors have changed over the past 3 years.[6]

Residency programs understand the need to recruit broadly qualified residents who not only align with their mission but also whose demographics and experiences reflect the patients they serve. Non-traditional residents add value to the medical teams they join, bringing significant skills, expertise, and unique perspectives from their prior careers and lived experiences. If they have families and/or came to medicine later in life, they may have greater empathy, be better listeners, easily relate to their patients' struggles, and be better able to establish rapport with their patients. In one study, non-traditional students were found to leverage their prior work experiences, thereby increasing autonomy, initiative, and confidence in the clinical context, and they adapted to patients' needs and felt more confident interacting within the hierarchy of medicine, including with faculty members who may be of similar age.[7]

Despite the many potential advantages non-traditional residents may bring with them, they may experience bias. Their supervising physicians may not feel comfortable relating to them and may unintentionally create a non-inclusive and non-affirming learning environment. Such unintended discrimination may begin during the residency interview when interviewers may pose biased and legally off-limit questions referencing the applicant's age. For example, non-traditional applicants may be asked "How old are you? Is it even worth our time to train you if you only practice 10 years?" Some applicants may be asked about their plans to start a family. Clearly, such questions do not speak to the applicant's abilities as a resident and are off limits.

Once matched to a residency program, these non-traditional residents may experience continuing **microaggressions**, **ageism**, and **stereotype threat**, which over time could impact their learning, lead to

Table 23.2 Matriculating Allopathic Medical Student Data from 2020-2022[6]

	2020 (%)	2021 (%)	2022 (%)
Age 26 years or older	16.2	16.9	17.1
Married, common law/civil union, divorced, separated, or widowed	7.6	8.1	8.2
Has dependents	2.4	2.6	2.5
Out of college for 3+ years	22.2	23.7	23.9
$15,000+ in educational debt	24.7	24.4	23.3
$10,000+ in consumer debt	6.6	7	7.2%

Source: Association of American Medical Colleges. *Matriculating Student Questionnaire (MSQ): 2022 All Schools Summary Report.* AAMC; 2022. Accessed June 25, 2023. https://www.aamc.org/data-reports/students-residents/report/matriculating-student-questionnaire-msq

underperformance, and contribute to burnout. Non-traditional residents have previously shared feelings of being judged, of being considered incompetent, and of experiencing isolation.[8] Having a learning and work environment that is inclusive of all fosters positive connections, both in and outside of the learning and working environment, and results in improved communication which is critical in the clinical environment.[9]

Non-traditional residents may have experienced academic performance issues while in medical school due to an overestimation of their learning abilities. Their past experiences and current circumstances may detract from their ability to fully apply themselves in residency.[10] For some non-traditional residents, the extra responsibilities of raising families or caring for older parents may limit their time for studying and affect their academic performance in their program and on licensing exams. Non-traditional medical students are more likely than their younger classmates to have repeat attempts at the USMLE Step 1 exam and earn lower passing scores on the USMLE Step 2 Clinical Knowledge exam.[11] Those with more time between college and medical school had higher negative perceptions of the learning environment,[12] which has shown to negatively impact performance on the USMLE Step 1 exam compared with those who perceived the learning environment more positively.[13] Non-traditional learners may experience complex life circumstances and bias which may impact their experience in the learning environment as well as their performance. This These factors should not influence the perceived value this group adds. Superior grades and exam scores are not all-encompassing in determining a physician's quality, compassion for patients, or ability to work within their medical teams. This information may help faculty better understand how to support non-traditional residents.

Primary Intersections to Be Understood for Non-traditional Residents

Non-traditional resident cohorts enrich the diversity of the learning environment. Many come to medicine after pursuing other careers and have a deepened passion for medicine. They may have laudable humility, grit, and the ability to rebound from adverse outcomes. The non-traditional resident has a complex background with primary intersections between their life, family, and age. They may have a family to support and additional financial pressures. Their unique rich background may include previous work as nurses, emergency medicine technicians, military veterans, or other equally meaningful professions that have helped them develop the skills and knowledge valuable in medicine.

To ensure these valued members of the medical team thrive in residency training and reach their true potential, we propose that those who supervise their training incorporate adult learning theories into their teaching. Adults are independent learners whose life experiences serve as a learning resource and they value learning which is associated with life demands. Adults are internally motivated and apply problem-focused approaches to the learning situation.[10] Adults learn best when they are actively engaged in the experience, can practice what was learned, understand the relevance to their work, and have a supportive environment where self-assessment and feedback are respected.[10]

RECOMMENDED STRATEGIES AND SOLUTIONS FOR INCLUSION AND EQUITY

Implementing the following strategies to support non-traditional residents is a win- win for the entire GME learning environment and beyond.

1. ***Employ an adult learning approach to teaching and learning that benefits all residents.***
   Inclusion, mutual respect, trust, collaboration, and support for sharing ideas and experiences should characterize the learning environment and be modeled by upper-level residents and attending physicians.[10] Team leaders must act intentionally. Seek to get to know non-traditional learners rather than make assumptions about their life or skills. Ask about their prior work histories, education, and skills which may yield unique assets to the team.
2. ***Acknowledge the life experiences, strengths, and skills of non-traditional residents and value how these characteristics enhance their ability to provide excellent patient care.***
   Supervising physicians should acknowledge their non-traditional residents' rich life experiences which may provide insight into the hidden strengths and skillsets. If these residents are open to sharing

> The United States celebrates youth, even though age is one of the "protected" classes in employment law as is gender, religion, race, color, disability status, and national origin. Notwithstanding this fact, older individuals may be marginalized and excluded from experiences.

> GME is demanding, and the hierarchical nature of medicine may add to the stress experienced by non-traditional residents if they are not included or valued for the lived experiences they bring and are misunderstood or not supported if they have complex personal lives.

their backgrounds and life stories, the supervising physicians should take an interest in their dynamic life circumstances or prior careers. GME programs must be proactive and seek to better understand how to support their non-traditional residents, especially those with families. Such an effort may take the form of surveys asking residents for input into some of the personal issues they face and how best their programs can support them. While residents' needs differ, programs that are open to learning about their residents may find some common themes emerge as to what their residents need to thrive.

3. *Incorporate faculty development to address bias in resident supervision and assessment processes*

    Ongoing faculty development of those who supervise residents and residents-as-teachers programs are imperative to help all those who supervise residents to acquire effective teaching and assessment skills. There are several pedagogical models in use by those who supervise residents and physicians. Two examples are the One-Minute Preceptor,[14] which lends itself to supervising residents at ambulatory sites, and the SUPERB model,[15] which is best for inpatient supervision. The SUPERB model asks the supervisor to *S*et expectations, explain what the resident should do if they are *U*ncertain about any aspect of their patient care work; describe *P*lanned communication such as time for the resident and supervisor to catch up; assure the resident of the supervising physicians' *E*asy availability; and *R*eassure the resident's fears. Finally, the model provides the resident with *B*alanced supervision and autonomy tailored to the resident's level of experience and competency.

    Moreover, having the non-traditional resident evaluated by individuals with whom these residents have significant interactions and having a long-term mentoring relationship with a faculty member in the program may help mitigate bias.

4. *Incorporate ageism and age discrimination as elements of professional development for residents and faculty members.*

    Our final recommended strategy involves including professional development in GME programs to include a robust diversity, equity, and inclusion component with participation by everyone involved in GME, including the residents themselves and those responsible for the selection and hiring of new residents. This training should incorporate teaching the impact of ageism, bias, and age discrimination.

    GME programs are committed to their residents' success and well-being and must continue to improve the clinical learning environment so that all residents, regardless of their age or other demographic identities, feel welcomed, valued, and can thrive during their education and training.

Take Home Points

- Residents of non-traditional age may experience subtle discrimination, bias, and exclusion from the medical team.
- Residents of non-traditional age bring untapped knowledge, experience, and personal attributes which, if harnessed properly, will enrich and improve team dynamics and communication, patient care, and clinical outcomes.
- Professional development of faculty members, GME leaders, and residents will help equip them with the tools and skills to create a welcoming and affirming learning environment for residents of all ages.

QUESTIONS FOR FURTHER THOUGHT

1. What is your knee-jerk reaction when you first encounter a resident who looks older than the average resident?
2. What is your initial reaction when a resident makes a shift time request due to immediate family responsibilities?
3. How does your institution or GME program currently include age in its non-discrimination employment policies or in the professional development/training offered about microaggressions or bias?
4. What opportunities exist to enhance or more explicitly address age bias in your program or institution?

REFERENCES

1. Rothes A, Lemos MS, Goncalves T. Motivational profiles of adult learners. *Adult Educ Quarterly.* 2017;67(1):3-29. doi:10.1177/0741713616669588
2. Association of American Medical Colleges. *Medical School Graduation Questionnaire: 2022 All Schools Summary Report.* AAMC; 2022. Accessed June 25, 2023. https://www.aamc.org/media/62006/download
3. Association of American Medical Colleges. Active physicians by age and specialty, 2021. Accessed June 25, 2023. https://www.aamc.org/data-reports/workforce/interactive-data/active-physicians-age-specialty-2021
4. Addams AN, Bletzinger RB, Sondheimer HM, White SE, Johnson LM. *Roadmap to Diversity: Integrating Holistic Review Practices into Medical School Admission Processes.* Association of American Medical Colleges; 2010. Accessed June 25, 2023. https://store.aamc.org/downloadable/download/sample/sample_id/195
5. Harrison LE. Using holistic review to form a diverse interview pool for selection to medical school. *Proc (Bayl Univ Med Cent).* 2019;32(2):218-221. doi:10.1080/08998280.2019.1576575
6. Association of American Medical Colleges. *Matriculating Student Questionnaire (MSQ): 2022 All Schools Summary Report.* AAMC; 2022. Accessed June 25, 2023. https://www.aamc.org/data-reports/students-residents/report/matriculating-student-questionnaire-msq
7. Jurjus RA, Butera G, Abdelnabi M, Krapf JM. Comparing the experiences of mature-aged and traditional medical students in the clinical setting: a qualitative approach. *J Acad Dev Educ.* 2017;7(7):1-32. https://www.researchgate.net/publication/312000483
8. Peterson EB. Re-signifying subjectivity? A narrative exploration of 'non- traditional' doctoral students' lived experience of subject formation through two Australian cases. *Stud High Educ.* 2014;39(5):823-834. doi:10.1080/03075079.2012.745337
9. Stucky CH, De Jong MJ, Kabo FW. Military surgical team communication: implications for safety. *Military Med.* 2020;185(3-4): e448-e456. doi:10.1093/milmed/usz330
10. Knowles MS. *The Modern Practice of Adult Education: From Pedagogy to Andragogy.* Cambridge University Press; 1980.
11. Gauer JL, Jackson JB. Relationships of demographic variables to USMLE physician licensing exam scores: a statistical analysis on five years of medical student data. *Adv Med Educ Pract.* 2018;9:39-44. doi:10.2147/AMEP.S152684
12. Smith SD, Dunham L, Dekhtyar M, et al. Medical student perceptions of the learning environment: learning communities are associated with a more positive learning environment in a multi-institutional medical school study. *Acad Med.* 2016;91(9):1263-1269. doi:10.1097/ACM.0000000000001214
13. Wayne SJ, Fortner SA, Kitzes JA, Timm C, Kalishman S. Cause or effect? The relationship between student perception of the medical school learning environment and academic performance on USMLE Step 1. *Med Teach.* 2013;35(5):376-380. doi:10.3109/0142159X.2013.769678
14. Neher JO, Gordon KC, Meyer B, Stevens N. A five-step "microskills" model of clinical teaching. *J Am Board Fam Pract.* 1992;5(4):419-424. PMID: 1496899
15. Farnan JM, Johnson, JK, Meltzer, DO, et al. Strategies for effective on-call supervision for internal medicine residents: the superb/safety model. *J Grad Med Educ.* 2010;2(1):46-52. doi:10.4300/JGME-D-09-00015.1

GLOSSARY

Ableism: Stigma and discrimination against people with disabilities resulting from the belief that typical abilities are superior.

Ad hoc interpreter(-ting): A person serving...situation arises in health care; the act of engaging in untrained interpretation in a language-discordant situation.

Ageism: Discrimination based on age.

Agender: Not having or lacking the experience of having a gender.

Alaska Native: A person or people belonging to the Indigenous tribes and villages of Alaska.

Allyship: Active support for the rights of a minoritized or marginalized group without belonging to the same social identity group.

American Indian: A person or people belonging to the Indigenous tribal communities of the continental United States.

Antiracism: The range of ideas and political actions meant to counter racial prejudice, systemic racism, and oppression of specific racial groups; the process of actively identifying, opposing, confronting, and dismantling racist systems.

Asian, Pacific Islander (API), Native Hawaiian or Pacific Islander (NHPI), and API American: Umbrella terms that emerged during the civil rights movement identifying distinct ethnicities, languages, and cultures of southern Pacific origin.

Assigned sex at birth: The sex (male or female) designated to a child at birth, based on the child's anatomy; also referred to as birth sex, natal sex, biological sex, or sex.

Barrier: An environmental, structural, or procedural component that limits the ability of a person to fully achieve an objective.

Bias reporting mechanism: A tool or system designed to anonymously record comments or actions driven by prejudice targeting individuals' identities.

Biological racism: The pseudoscientific belief in the existence of empirical evidence for races as biologically distinct entities.

Bisexual: An identity for persons who are sexually and/or emotionally attracted to some men and some women.

Blood quantum: A product of federal assimilationist policy that assigns various degrees of "pure Indian blood" to American Indian (AI)/Alaska Native (AN) individuals enrolled in or descended from enrolled members of federally recognized Tribes.

BridgeUSA: A program operated by the US State Department's Bureau of Educational and Cultural Affairs that facilitates the cultural exchange programs under the J-1 (Exchange Visitor) Visa, including J-1 physicians, that designates, monitors, and partners with US organizations to administer the program; previously known as the US State Department's Exchange Visitor Program.

Cisgender: Gender identity that corresponds with the sex registered at birth; not transgender.

Clinical Competency Committee (CCC): A required body within an ACGME-accredited graduate medical education program comprising three or more members of the active teaching faculty, including at least one core faculty member, that is advisory to the program director and reviews the progress of all residents or fellows in the program.[1]

Coloniality *(also known as coloniality of power)*: The set of attitudes, values, ways of knowing, and power structures upheld as normative by western colonizing societies and serving to rationalize and perpetuate western dominance.

Complaint: An allegation that a Sponsoring Institution and/or graduate medical education program accredited by the ACGME is non-compliant with ACGME accreditation or recognition Requirements.[1]

Concern: An issue identified as an impediment or potential impediment to learning in the graduate medical education environment; may be reported through avenues within residents' and fellows' ACGME-accredited programs and Sponsoring Institutions, and to the ACGME anonymously through its Office of the Ombudsperson.

Conversion therapy: The process by which a mental health professional, clinician, or religious leader attempts to change a person's gender identity or sexual orientation.

Correctional health care: Health care provided through jails, prisons, and juvenile detention facilities.

Critical consciousness: An approach to understanding the world positing that the thinking subject exists in relationship to the world; requires reflective awareness of differences in power, privilege, and inequities embedded in social relationships; fosters a reorientation of perspective toward commitment to social justice.[2]

Critical mass theory: A concept that proposes inequities will improve on their own when enough people in a certain group are present.

Cultural humility: A life-long process of self-exploration and self-critique combined with a willingness to learn from others; learning about another's culture by examining one's personal beliefs, values, and cultural identities.[3]

Deferred Action for Childhood Arrivals (DACA): A US immigration policy issued by President Barack Obama in 2012 to offer temporary immigration relief to children who were brought into the country without proper documentation and reside in the country unlawfully; offers work authorization and a temporary stay of deportation.

Detransition: The process by which a transgender person who has already transitioned realigns with the gender with which the person originally identified, deciding to no longer live as an outwardly presenting transgender person.

Disability: A physical or mental impairment that substantially limits one or more major life activities; persons with a record of such impairment, even if they do not currently have a disability diagnosis.

Disciplinary action: In the context of graduate medical education, an action including suspension, non-renewal, non-promotion, or dismissal that may be taken by an ACGME-accredited Sponsoring Institution, subject to due process, in response to subpar performance by a resident or fellow.

Due process: In the context of graduate medical education, refers to the fair and consistent treatment of individuals pursuant to established policies and procedures by the ACGME-accredited Sponsoring Institution in accordance with the ACGME Institutional and Common Program Requirements intended to protect and enforce the private rights of a resident or fellow if a disciplinary action is initiated against the resident or fellow.

Educational Commission for Foreign Medical Graduates (ECFMG): A private nonprofit 501(c)(3) organization that evaluates the qualifications of physicians worldwide through primary source credentials verification; evaluates and supports international physicians who enter US graduate medical education; and supports world-wide medical education and regulatory communities in assuring the qualifications of physicians.

Eid: Two religious holidays in Islam that include festivities and celebrations, exchange of presents, large gatherings, and holiday prayer; *Eid Al-Fitr* occurs at the end of Ramadan and *Eid Al-Adha* occurs approximately two months and ten days after *Eid Al-Fitr*.

Equity: The assurance of the conditions for optimal health for all people, which requires valuing all individuals and populations equally, recognizing and rectifying historical injustices, and providing resources according to need.

Essential function: Fundamental job responsibility performed in a position.

Exurban: A district outside a city, particularly a prosperous area beyond its suburbs.

First Generation and Low Income (FGLI): The first family member to obtain a bachelor's degree, often also coming from a lower income background compared to peers whose parent(s) possess a college degree.

Frontier: A geographic area with a population of less than six people per square mile.

Gay: An identity most often used by men who are attracted sexually and/or emotionally to some other men; some lesbians may use the term to define themselves.

Gender-diverse: Umbrella term used to describe gender identities that demonstrate a diversity of expression beyond the binary framework.

Gender dysphoria: Distress experienced by some individuals whose gender identity does not correspond with their assigned sex at birth; manifests itself as clinically significant distress or impairment in social, occupational, or other important areas of functioning; not every transgender person presents with this DSM-5 diagnosis.

Gender expression: The manner in which a person dresses, speaks, and behaves that is socially associated with gender and does not necessarily correspond to assigned sex at birth or gender identity.

Gender fluid: Description of a person whose gender identity is not fixed and may sometimes feel like a mix of genders, as well as more one gender some days than other days.

Gender harassment: Verbal and non-verbal behaviors that convey hostility, objectification, exclusion, or second-class status about members of a certain gender.

Gender identity: A person's internal, deeply held sense of one's own gender.

Gender non-conforming: A gender expression that differs from a given societal norm for males and females; no longer used favorably, since it connotes a "standard" or "conforming" performance of gender.

Gender tax: Non-promotable work, such as event planning, taking notes, or unofficial mentorship, aligned with gender stereotypes.

Gender-affirming care: Social, medical, and/or surgical support that assists individuals in expressing their gender.

Gender-affirming surgery (also known as *gender confirmation surgery*): Surgery used to modify one's body to be more congruent with one's gender identity; historically referred to as sex reassignment surgery.

Genderqueer: Description of a person whose gender identity falls outside the traditional gender binary; related terms sometimes used include gender diverse, gender expansive, agender, gendervoid, etc.

Halacha: Jewish law; the complete body of Jewish religious laws, including biblical commandments, commandments instituted by rabbis, and binding customs.

Halachic: Pertaining to Jewish law.

Harassment *[see also Sexual harassment]:* Unwelcome conduct, whether verbal, physical, sexual, or visual, against a person and based on the person's protected status.

Health disparities: Racial or ethnic differences in health care not due to access-related factors, clinical needs, patient preferences, or the appropriateness of the intervention.

Health equity: Assurance of the conditions for optimal health for all people.[4]

Health Professional Shortage Area (HPSA): Geographic population or facility-based definition where a shortage of primary, dental, or mental health care professionals exists.

Hijab: An Islamic religious practice of modesty in which a Muslim woman covers her hair, neck, and body up to her wrists and ankles so that only the hands, face, and feet can be exposed; a headscarf intended to cover a woman's hair.

Holistic review: A selection framework developed by the Association of American Medical Colleges for applicants, that balances the consideration of an applicant's life experiences, attributes, and academic metrics in seeking to develop a mission-aligned and diverse applicant cohort.

Implicit bias: A personal, sometimes unreasoned judgment that occurs automatically and unintentionally, that nevertheless affects judgments, decisions, and behaviors.

Imposter syndrome: Internalized perception of persistent self-doubt, characterized by questioning one's skills and abilities.

Indigenous: An international term referring broadly to first or aboriginal people native to a place which has been colonized and settled by another ethnic group.

Injunctive relief: Discretionary power of the court which restrains a party from doing certain acts or requires a party to act in a certain way.

Institutionalized/structural racism: Policies and procedures existing throughout a whole society or organization that result in and support a continued unfair advantage to some people and unfair or harmful treatment of others based on race or ethnic group.[5]

Internalized racism: Internalized belief in negative messages about one's race and/or culture, particularly about one's own abilities and intrinsic worth; not believing in others who look like oneself.[5]

International medical graduate (IMG): A physician who has graduated from a medical school outside of the country where the physician intends to practice; in the United States, a graduate from a medical school located outside the United States and Canada.

Interpreter *(Medical):* A person who verbally changes the words from one language to another; professional medical interpreters ensure language-appropriate care during language-discordant situations (ie, when the clinician and patient are unable to effectively communicate in the same language).

Intersectional identities: A concept describing the complex convergence of how an individual can hold multiple social identities including but not limited to gender identity, race, ethnicity, nationality, language, class, and sexual identity; the effect on any of these various identities can be multiplicative.[6]

Intersectionality: A conceptual framework that highlights the complex and interwoven identities of individuals and describes how various systems of oppression may differentially impact marginalized individuals and populations.

J-1 visa *[see also Bridge USA; Educational Commission for Foreign Medical Graduates (ECFMG)]:* A temporary exchange visitor nonimmigrant visa offered through BridgeUSA; a program within the US Department of State's Bureau of Educational and Cultural Affairs; ECFMG designated by the US Department of State as a BridgeUSA sponsor for J-1 exchange visitor physicians enrolled in accredited graduate medical education programs or advanced research programs (involving primarily observation, consultation, teaching, or research).

Justice-involved populations: Persons who are or have been convicted; are or have been incarcerated in jail or prison; are or have been detained in a juvenile facility; or are being supervised in the community under probation or parole.

Kashrus (or Kashrut): The Kosher status of a food.

Kosher: Food that has been prepared according to requirements of Jewish law and is considered permissible for consumption for Orthodox/observant Jews.

Language coaching: A longitudinal educational model whereby learners (eg, a resident, fellow, or other clinician learner) receive personalized coaching to advance their language skills while being supervised and supported in providing language-appropriate clinical care by a team of faculty members, medical interpreters, and staff.

Language concordance: Descriptor for those encounters when a clinician and patient can communicate directly in the same language.

Language-appropriate: Descriptor for those encounters when a patient's language preferences are appropriately considered in health care communication.

Latino, Latina, Latinx, Latine, Hispanic, or of Spanish origin (LHS+): Umbrella term used to describe the heterogeneous group of people who trace their ancestry to Latin America or Spain; who may share Spanish language heritage or ancestry and speak different languages; and who have various national, territorial, or ethnic group origins (eg, Colombian, Afro-Latina, Mayan); recognizes historical terms used on standardized surveys (eg, Hispanic, Latino) and emerging non-binary terms (eg, Latinx, Latine).[7]

Lesbian: An identity for women who are attracted sexually and/or emotionally to some other women.

LGBTQIA+: Initialism for Lesbian, Gay, Bisexual, Transgender, Queer (or questioning gender), Intersex, Asexual,+ (all other identities not encompassed in the initialism)

Linguistic discrimination: Prejudicial treatment of persons due to linguistic attributes such as accent.

Loctician: A natural hair stylist; someone who specializes in the starting, maintaining, caring, and styling of dreadlocks.

Medical language course: A classroom-based educational model (virtual or in person), led by a faculty member, that centers on enhancing oral communication (speaking and listening) for dialogue with patients in the target language.

Medical language proficiency: An individual's skill level in using a language for medical communication; commonly used with regard to a clinician's oral language skills (speaking and listening) for direct communication with patients.

Medical language proficiency testing/certification: A language proficiency examination that evaluates how well a clinician can independently perform clinical responsibilities with patients in a given language.

Medical transitioning: The use of medication to better align a person's body with the individual's gender identity; also referred to as cross-sex hormones.

Medically Underserved Area (MUA): A geographic area having a shortage of primary health care services.

Micro/macro aggressions: Everyday subtle statements and behaviors directed at individuals or at groups – such as verbal, nonverbal, environmental slights, snubs, or insults – that communicate disregard, insensitivity, isolation, and otherness, whether intentional or unintentional, that minimize the existence of discrimination or bias and often repeat or affirm stereotypes about minoritized groups.

Multilingual: Having skills in more than one language.

Native American: A person or people native to the United States and its territories; includes Native Hawaiians, Chamorros, and American Samoans, as well as persons from Indigenous communities in Mexico and Central and South America who are US residents.

Non-binary: A gender identity that may reflect both man and woman, neither man nor woman, or be completely outside of a binary framework.

Non-English language preference: Descriptor for an individual or group who prefers to use a language besides English in a particular context; proposed to replace the deficit-oriented construct of limited English proficiency and more accurately define individuals who prefer a non-English language with respect to health care.

Non-traditional age: Age 25 years or older when matriculating into medical school.

Parole: The early supervised release of a prison inmate.

Passover: A week-long biblical holiday occurring in March or April that celebrates Jewish redemption from Egyptian slavery.

Pathway program: A program directed at students from middle school through college that aims to support their becoming qualified applicants to a medical school or, depending on the level of the program, to another health professions program or a science/technology/engineering/mathematics (STEM)/biomedical graduate program.

Personally mediated/interpersonal racism: Prejudice and discrimination where prejudice means differential assumptions about the abilities, motives, and intentions of others according to their race, and discrimination means differential actions toward others according to their race; can be intentional as well as unintentional and includes acts of commission as well as omission.[8]

Pioneer syndrome: A characteristic combination of opinions, emotions, or behaviors that elicit reactions to newness of an experience, the historical absence of previous experience, the need to learn quickly from mistakes, and the need to develop relationships to strengthen performance.

Prejudice: Differential assumptions about the abilities, motives, and intentions of others according to their characteristics, such as race, ethnicity, religion, immigration status, etc.

Probation: A sentence, usually for persons serving short jail terms, whereby a convicted individual is released from confinement but remains under court supervision; can be given in lieu of a prison term or can suspend a prison sentence if the convicted person has consistently demonstrated good behavior.

Professional Identity Formation (PIF): Integration of the knowledge, skills, values, and behaviors of a profession with one's preexisting identity and values.

Program access: The concept that disability barriers in the learning and working environment are removed or avoided, usually through reasonable accommodation for a person with a disability or through proactive policies, procedures, and universal access design.

Psychological safety: An emotional state supported by an environment of trust and respect that allows individuals to feel able to ask for help, admit mistakes, raise concerns, suggest ideas, and challenge ways of working and the ideas of others on the team, including the ideas of those in authority, without fear of humiliation, and the knowledge that mistakes will be handled justly and fairly.

Queer: Denoting or relating to a sexual identity that does not correspond to established ideas of sexuality, especially heterosexual or other societal norms; historically a derogatory term not used by all members of the LGBTQIA+ community.

Race-based algorithms: Decision-making tools that misuse race as a proxy for biological or genetic ancestry.

Race-based discrimination: Differential actions toward others according to their race.

Racial battle fatigue: The effect of cumulative subtle and layered verbal and nonverbal insults, based on one's race, color, gender, class, sexuality, language, immigration status, phenotype, accent, or surname, directed at people of color, often automatically or unconsciously.

Racism: A system of structuring opportunity and assigning value based on the social interpretation of how one looks (referred to as "race").

Ramadan: The holiest month of the year in the Islamic calendar during which observant Muslims fast from dawn to sunset, abstaining from food, drink, and water.

Reasonable accommodation: A modification or adjustment to a job and employment practice or the work environment that makes it possible for a qualified individual with a disability to experience an equal employment opportunity and does not create a direct threat or undue hardship.

Redlining: A historical phenomenon, heavily thought to be influenced by segregation, where governmental agencies assigned credit worthiness to different communities that ultimately determined allotment of federally backed mortgages; lending organizations and realtors used a red line to circumscribe those communities deemed to have the lowest credit worthiness.

Re-entry: The transition from life in jail or prison to life in the community.

Retaliation: Adverse action taken against an individual or group perceived to have engaged in an adverse action directed at the recipient individual or group.

Rosh Hashana: The Jewish New Year; a high holy day of observance occurring in September or October; the first two and last two days involve restrictions of *Yom Tov* for Orthodox/observant Jews in all countries except Israel.

Rural: Any area outside of a Metropolitan Statistical Area (MSA) as identified by the US Office of Management and Budget.

Sexual coercion: Unwanted sexual activity as a result of pressure, trickery, threat, or physical force, often from an authority figure having power over an individual; occurs when favorable professional or educational treatment is conditional upon sexual activity.

Sexual harassment: A form of discrimination that consists of unwanted conduct based on gender, unwanted sexual attention, and sexual coercion.

Sexual minority: Individuals who do not identify as straight or heterosexual; they may identify as gay, lesbian, bisexual, queer, or another identifier and/or as a member of the LGBTQIA+ community encompasses attraction and sexual behaviors; does not include gender identity and associated terms

Sexual orientation: The manner by which people characterize their sexual and emotional attraction to others, including but not limited to, bisexual, gay, heterosexual (straight), lesbian, and pansexual.

Shabbos (or Shabbat): The Jewish Sabbath, which begins at sundown on Friday and ends at sundown on Saturday; some observant Jews do not drive or work on the Sabbath.

Social vulnerability index: An index intended to identify those communities with deep resilience for external disruptions, such as the COVID-19 pandemic, or those communities that have great vulnerability.

Social/structural determinants of health: The conditions under which people in society are born, grow, live, work, and age.

Sponsorship: A step beyond mentorship in which the mentor actively advocates for mentees by leveraging resources and networks in order to increase visibility and provide mentees with experiences that will support future career success.

Stereotype threat: A socially premised psychological intention to inflict pain or hostility that arises when one is in a situation or engaged in an activity for which a negative stereotype about one's group applies.

Structural bias *[see also Structural racism]*: A system in which public policies, institutional practices, cultural representations, and other norms work in various, often reinforcing ways to perpetuate inequity based on a group's identity or characteristics, such as race.

Structural racism *[see also Structural bias]*: Emphasizes the role of the structures (laws, policies, institutional practices, and entrenched norms) that serve as systemic scaffolding in reinforcing racial group inequity.

Structural violence: The social structures—economic, political, legal, religious, and cultural (eg, racism, poverty) – that stop individuals, groups, and societies from reaching their full potential.[9]

Substantial impairment: A significant limitation or restriction on a major life activity such as hearing, seeing, speaking, breathing, performing manual tasks, walking, caring for oneself, learning, or working.

Sukkot: Known as the Festival of Tabernacles; multi-day biblical holiday occurring in September or October during which observant Jews dwell in a *sukkah* (a temporary dwelling); the first two and last two days of the holiday involve restrictions of *Yom Tov* for Orthodox/observant Jews in all countries except Israel.

Supplemental Offer and Acceptance Program® (SOAP®): The process by which eligible unmatched, or partially unmatched, applicants may apply to programs with unfilled residency positions and receive offers through the *National Resident Matching Program® (NRMP®)* Registration, Ranking, and Results (*R3®*) system.

Systemic racism: A form of racism pervasively and deeply embedded in and throughout systems, laws, written or unwritten policies, entrenched practices, and established beliefs and attitudes that produce, condone, and perpetuate widespread unfair treatment of racially marginalized individuals; sometimes used interchangeably with structural racism, however, in comparison, emphasizes involvement of whole systems, and often all systems (eg, political, legal, economic, health care, school, and criminal justice systems; including the structures that uphold the systems).

Talmud: Texts of Jewish tradition that record the legal and religious discussions of thousands of rabbis, central to Jewish religious law and Jewish theology.

Timely access: The ability to obtain care when care is needed, typically within one hour when care is emergent, within one to two days when urgent, within 10 days for non-urgent primary care and mental health care, and 15 business days for specialty care.

Transgender: An umbrella term used for people whose gender identity is not congruent with their assigned sex at birth; occasionally abbreviated as "trans."

Transgender and gender-diverse (TGD): A composite term/initialism used to describe transgender and gender diverse people.

Transition: The process of expressing one's gender identity, most often referring to the period when a person makes social, legal, and/or medical changes, such as changing clothing, name, gender designation, and using medical interventions.

Unconscious, unrecognized, or conscious biases and stereotypes: Biases that may lead to disparities based on race, ethnicity, gender, socioeconomic status, or other characteristics.

Underrepresented in medicine: Racial and ethnic populations that are fewer in the medical profession relative to their numbers in the general population.[10]

Undocumented immigrant: A foreign-born, non-citizen who is not a legal resident of the United States and who likely entered the United States without inspection or remained in the United States after the non-citizen's temporary immigration status expired.

Untitle/untitling: The act of addressing some persons without their professional title in settings where the standard is to address persons by their professional title.

Unwanted sexual attention: Unwelcome verbal or physical sexual advances, which can include assault.

Urban underserved area: An urban geographic area with a lack of access to primary care services.

Well-being: The extent to which persons experience happiness and satisfaction and are realizing their full potential.

White emotionality: A concept describing how discussing race and racism often conjures up emotions of guilt, shame, anger, defensiveness, denial, sadness, dissonance, and discomfort for White people.[11,12]

Whiteness: A social construct that assigns social value and privilege to being White which is not just a structure, but a perspective and way of behaving in the world.[13]

Yom Kippur: The Jewish Day of Atonement and the holiest day on the Jewish calendar, involving a one-day fast and occurring in September or October, with all the restrictions of the Sabbath.

Yom Tov: The biblical Jewish holidays of Rosh Hashana, Yom Kippur, Sukkot, Passover, and Shavuot; the 39 categories of creative work that are forbidden on the Sabbath are also forbidden, except those related to cooking; observance of these holidays involves restrictions for Orthodox/observant Jews in all countries except Israel.

Zabiha Halal (**or** *Halal*): The manner in which an animal is slaughtered according to Islamic law; also includes abstinence from alcohol, and pork/pork products that have not been slaughtered according to religious practice.

REFERENCES

1. Accreditation Council for Graduate Medical Education. ACGME Glossary of Terms. June 24, 2024. https://www.acgme.org/globalassets/PDFs/ab_ACGMEglossary.pd2
2. Kumagai AK, Lypson ML. Beyond cultural competence: critical consciousness, social justice, and multicultural education. *Acad Med.* 2009;84(5):782-787. doi:10.1097/ACM.0b013e3181a42393
3. Yeager KA, Bauer-Wu S. Cultural humility: essential foundation for clinical researchers. *Appl Nurs Res.* 2013;26(4):251-256. doi:10.1016/j.apnr.2013.06.008
4. Jones CP. Systems of power, axes of inequity: parallels, intersections, braiding the strands. *Med Care.* 2014;52(10, Suppl 3):S71-S75. doi:10.1097/MLR.0000000000000215
5. Jones CP. Levels of racism: a theoretic framework and a gardener's tale. *Am J Public Health.* 2000;90(8):1212-1215. doi:10.2105/ajph.90.8.1212
6. Disch LJ, Hawkesworth ME, eds. *The Oxford Handbook of Feminist Theory.* Oxford University Press; 2017.
7. Sánchez JP, Rodriguez D, eds. *Latino, Hispanic, or of Spanish Origin+ Identified Student Leaders in Medicine.* Springer; 2028.
8. Jones CP. Levels of racism: a theoretic framework and a gardener's tale. *Am J Public Health.* 2000;90(8):1212-1215. doi:10.2105/ajph.90.8.1219
9. Farmer PE, Nizeye B, Stulac S, Keshavjee S. Structural violence and clinical medicine. *PLoS Med.* 2006;3(10):e449. doi:10.1371/journal.pmed.00304410
10. Association of American Medical Colleges. Underrepresented in medicine. Accessed August 15, 2024. https://www.aamc.org/what-we-do/equity-diversity-inclusion/underrepresented-in-medicin11
11. Matias CE, Leonardo Z. *Feeling White: Whiteness Emotionality and Education.* Sense;20113.
12. Badenhorst, P. Raced encounter on a hilltop: a call for soulful justice alongside social justice work. *English Education.* 2019;51(2)200-208. https://www.jstor.org/stable/26797031
13. Frankenberg R. *The Social Construction of Whiteness: White Women, Race Matters.* University of Minnesota Press;1993.

INDEX

Note: Page numbers followed by *f* and *t* denote figures and tables respectively.

A

AAMC. *See* Association of American Medical Colleges (AAMC)
Ableism, 23, 25, 219
ABMS. *See* American Board of Medical Specialties (ABMS)
Academic leadership, 91–92
Academic learning, 68
Accelerated aging, 127
Accreditation Council for Graduate Medical Education (ACGME), 61–62, 139
   Clinical Learning Environment Review, 47
   Common Program Requirements, 18–19, 36, 63, 67, 179, 219, 221*t*, 220
   due process requirement
      considerations for program directors, 68–70
      considerations for resident and fellow physicians, 65–68
      institutions' implementation of, 63–65
      for residency programs, 63
   Institutional Requirements, 67, 191, 193, 221*t*, 220
   Program Requirements, 68
ACGME. *See* Accreditation Council for Graduate Medical Education (ACGME)
Action Collaborative for Black Men in Medicine, 26
Ad hoc interpreter, 156, 161
Ad hoc medical interpreting, 156
ADA. *See* Americans with Disabilities Act (ADA)
ADA Designee, 227
Adult learning approach, 235
Affinity groups, 111
Age discrimination, 236
Ageism, 235, 236
Agender, 201
Aging
   accelerated, 127
   incarcerated population, 127
Alaska Native. *See* American Indian and Alaska Native (AI/AN)
Allies, power of, 193
Allyship, 100
AMA CME Report, 223–224*t*
AMCAS. *See* American Medical College Application Service (AMCAS)
American Board of Medical Specialties (ABMS), 191, 193
American Indian and Alaska Native (AI/AN), 79–80
   financial barriers, 84
   historical trauma and cultural assimilation, 83
   key challenges to recruitment, selection, and retention, 83
   lack of mentorship, 84
   othering of, 84
   recommended opportunities and solutions, 84–85
   representation, 81–83, 82*f*, 82*t*
   terminology and identity, 80–81

American Medical Association, 146, 213
American Medical College Application Service (AMCAS), 93
American Medical Student Association, 213
Americans with Disabilities Act (ADA), 223
   interactive process, 55
   residents for employer's violation, 55
   steps to comply with and limit liability under, 55
   Title IX Regulations, 56
Anti-Asian racism, 94
Antiracism, 17–18, 94
   Asian, 94
   in Whiteness, 118, 119–120
API. *See* Asian, Pacific Islander (API)
API American, 90
   in GME and academic leadership, 91, 91–92*f*
   intersectional identities influencing inclusion, 92–93
   strategies to improve inclusion and equity for
      bias and discrimination, reports of, 94
      departmental and institutional data, 94
      disaggregate data, 93
      name-affirming practices, 94
      policies and practices, 93
      recruitment and selection, institutional approach to, 93
Appeal hearing, 64
Appointment renewal, 63
Area Deprivation Index, 9
Asian, Pacific Islander (API), 90
   in antiracism, 94
   in GME and academic leadership, 91, 91–92*f*
   intersectional identities influencing inclusion, 92–93
   strategies to improve inclusion and equity for
      bias and discrimination, reports of, 94
      departmental and institutional data, 94
      disaggregate data, 93
      name-affirming practices, 94
      policies and practices, 93
      recruitment and selection, institutional approach to, 93
Asian Pacific American Medical Student Association, 213
Asr, prayer, 166
Assigned sex at birth, 200
Assimilation, cultural, 83
Association of American Medical Colleges (AAMC), 110, 137, 146, 224
   Action Collaborative for Black Men in Medicine, 26
   Graduation Questionnaire, 224, 233
   Lived Experience Report, 221–223*t*
   Matriculating Student Questionnaire, 234
   sexual identity, 212
   Year Two (Y2Q), 224
Association of Native American Medical Students, 213

B

Barrier, 32, 176
  disability inclusion as mechanism of reducing, 220
  educational, 92
  by FGLI learners, 137–138
  financial, 36–37, 84, 92
  to IMG, 148–149
  non-traditionally aged residents, 233–235
  Orthodox Jewish Learners, 176–177
  to sexual minority health education, 212
  social, 92
  structural, 26, 93
  systemic, 26
Beard, 167–168
Bias, 112, 189, 214, 236
  explicit, 192
  gender, 192, 193
  implicit, 112, 192
  racial, 193
  reporting mechanism, 112
  support groups and, 169
Bidirectional exchange, 68, 68t
Biological racism, 16
Bisexual, 210–211
Black, 98
  demographic data and learners in medicine
    bystander vs. upstander support, 100
    community building beyond medicine, 103
    Imposter Syndrome to Pioneer Syndrome, 102
    inclusive professionalism, 101
    issues, 99–100
    micro and macroaggression, 100–101
    timely and constructive evaluation, 101–102
  recommendations for GME programs, 103
Blood quantum, 80
BNGAP. See Building the Next Generation of Academic Physicians (BNGAP)
BridgeUSA, 145
Building the Next Generation of Academic Physicians (BNGAP), 111, 213
Bystander/upstander approach, 100, 120

C

Career progression, 16, 17f
CCC. See Clinical Competency Committee (CCC)
Centers for Disease Control and Prevention, 213
Chicago Community Areas, 35–36, 35f
Cisgender, 199
Civil Rights Act of 1964, 53–54, 58
CLER. See Clinical Learning Environment Review (CLER)
Clinical Competency Committee (CCC), 64
Clinical learning environment
  assessment of, 45f
  culture of, 43, 44f
Clinical Learning Environment Review (CLER), 47
COCA. See Commission on Osteopathic College Accreditation (COCA)
Coloniality, 110
Commission on Osteopathic College Accreditation (COCA), 81–82

Communication, effective, 66
Community building, 103
Complaints, 67
Concerns, 67
Conversion therapy, 202
Correctional facilities, 125–126, 128
Correctional health care, 127
COVID-19 pandemic, health disparities, magnified, 10
Critical actors, 189
Critical consciousness, 112
Critical mass theory, 189
CROWN Act (Creating a Respectful and Open World for Natural Hair), 101
Cultural assimilation, 83
Cultural humility, 112
Culture and belonging, 24–25

D

DACA. See Deferred Action for Childhood Arrivals (DACA)
Deferred Action for Childhood Arrivals (DACA), 93, 94, 146
  applicants, acceptees, and matriculants with status 147t
  challenges, 148
  contributions of students and physicians, 148
  recipients, 146–147
  strategies to mitigate barriers to, 148–149
Designated Institutional Officials, 49
Detransitioning, 202
Dhuhr, prayer, 166
Diagnostic and Statistical Manual of Mental Disorders (DSM), 202
Dietary accommodations, Muslims, 168–169
Disability, 26, 218–219, 220
  accessibility, 226
  consequences, 225
  defined, 219
  inclusion, 226
    barriers to, 224
    challenges faced by learners, 224–226
    culture of, 228
    guidance and regulations for, 221–224t
    as mechanism of reducing barriers, 220
    shift toward, 220–224
    strategies to improve, 227–228, 227f
  lack of funding structure and understanding of responsibility, 225–226
  non-disclosure of, 225
Disciplinary actions, 63, 64
Disclosure of LGBTQ+, 203
Discrimination, 15, 189
  linguistic, 157
  religious, 175
Dismissal, 63, 70
Disparities. See Health disparities
Distressed Communities Index, 9
Diversity, 70
  in leadership, 169
  linguistically diverse physicians, 158–161
  strategies to support, 10t
  for women in medicine, 189
  workforce, 16, 17f

DSM. *See* Diagnostic and Statistical Manual of Mental Disorders (DSM)
Due process requirement
　Accreditation Council for Graduate Medical Education
　　considerations for program directors, 68–70
　　considerations for resident and fellow physicians, 65–68
　　institutions' implementation of, 63–65
　　for residency programs, 63

E

ECFMG. *See* Educational Commission for Foreign Medical Graduates (ECFMG)
Education Amendments of 1972, Title IX of, 54
Educational Commission for Foreign Medical Graduates (ECFMG), 145, 146
Effective feedback and evaluations, critical role of, 68–70
Eid Al-Adha, 167
Eid Al-Fitr, 167
Electronic Residency Application Service (*ERAS*), 93, 147–148, 155, 157
Endocrine Society, 202
Equal Employment Opportunity Commission, 68
Equal Employment Opportunity policy, 53
Equitable space, building, 119–120
Equity, 46, 70
　linguistically diverse physicians, 158–161
　strategies and solutions for, 235–236
　strategies to improve, 213–214
　Whiteness, 120
ERAS. *See* Electronic Residency Application Service (ERAS)
Essential function, 55, 56, 227
Ethnicity, 99
Eugenics Sterilization Program, 111
Exurban area, 31
　developing pathway of learners from, 36
　opportunities for, 36
　solutions to reduce disease and mortality gaps in, 36–38

F

Fair pay policy, 189
Fajr, prayer, 166
FAM framework. *See* Flexibility, Accommodations, Modification (FAM) framework
Family and Medical Leave Act (FMLA), 57
　remedies, 58
　steps to comply with and limit liability under, 58
Family-friendly accommodations, 193
Fasting, Muslims, 167
Federal employment laws, 51–52
　Americans with Disabilities Act, 55–56
　Family and Medical Leave Act, 57–58
　Pregnancy Workers Fairness Act, 57
　Title VII of Civil Rights Act of 1964, 53–54
Fenway Institute, 213
FGLI backgrounds. *See* First-generation college graduate and low-income (FGLI) backgrounds
Final appeal, 65
First-generation college graduate and low-income (FGLI) backgrounds, 135–137
　barriers of, 137–138
　defined, 137
　strategies for improving inclusion, 138–139, 140*t*
　strengths of, 138–139
Flexibility, Accommodations, Modification (FAM) framework, 228
Flexible work arrangements, for women, 193
Flexner Report, 7
FMLA. *See* Family and Medical Leave Act (FMLA)
Foreign national physicians, 143–145
　Deferred Action for Childhood Arrivals. *See* Deferred Action for Childhood Arrivals (DACA)
　International medical graduates. *See* International medical graduates (IMGs)
　J-1 physicians, 145
Friday prayers, 166
Frontier area, 31–33
　developing pathway of learners from, 36
　opportunities for, 36
　solutions to reduce disease and mortality gaps in, 36–38
Funding structure, lack of, 225–226

G

Gay, 126, 210–211
Gender. *See also* Transgender; Transgender and gender-diverse (TGD) individuals
　-diverse cultures, 200*f*
　development and science of, 200
　identity, 22, 99, 189, 199, 212, 213
　interactions and physical exams, 168
Gender-affirming care, 201
Gender-affirming surgery, 176, 202
Gender-based microaggression, 190
Gender bias, 192, 193
Gender diverse individuals. *See* Transgender and gender-diverse (TGD) individuals
Gender dysphoria, 202
Gender expression, 201
Gender fluid, 201
Gender harassment, 189
Gender non-conforming, 201
Gender tax, 190
Genderqueer, 201
Geography
　as determinant of health, 29–38
　with disparate health outcomes, 34*f*, 35–36
　intersection of, 33–34
　on mortality, 33, 34*f*
Geriatric age, 127
GLMA: Health Professionals Advancing LGBTQ Equality, 213
GQ. *See* Graduation Questionnaire (GQ)
Graduation Questionnaire (GQ), 224, 233

H

Hadith, 169
Halacha, 175–176
Halachic, 176
Harassment, 53, 189, 193
　gender, 189
　sexual, 189, 192*t*

Healing ARC framework, 17–19
Health care
  access to, 31
    poverty on, 33–36
    universal, 37
  segregation, 16
  strategies to improve inclusion and equity for sexual minorities in, 213–214
Health Care Quality Improvement Act, 63
Health disparities
  COVID-19 pandemic magnified, 10
  defined, 8
  in heart failure, 5–6
  in justice-involved populations, 126–127
    aging incarcerated population, 127
    improving GME to reduce, 128–129
Health equity, 10
  in Whiteness, 118
Health Professional Shortage Areas (HPSA), 31
Hearing, 64–65
Heart failure, 5–6
HeLa Cells, 7
Hidden knowledge, 138, 139
Hijab, 167, 168*f*
Historical trauma, 83
Holistic review, 26–27, 120, 233
Home Owners' Loan Corporation, 8
Hospitalization, 5–6
HPSA. *See* Health Professional Shortage Areas (HPSA)

I

Identity, 26. *See also* Gender, identity
IHS. *See* Indian Health Services (IHS)
IMGs. *See* International medical graduates (IMGs)
Implicit bias training, 112
Imposter Syndrome, 102
Incarcerated population. *See* Justice-involved populations
Inclusion
  considerations, 70
  of disability. *See* Disability
  linguistically diverse physicians, 158–161
  Muslim residents and fellows
    beard, 168
    dietary accommodations, 168–169
    diverse representation in leadership, 169
    fasting and holy month of Ramadan, 167
    gender interactions and physical exams, 168
    hijab, 167, 168*f*
    prayers, 166–167
    religious holidays, 167
    social gatherings, 169
    support groups and bias, 169
  strategies and solutions for, 235–236
  for women in medicine, 189, 191–193, 191*t*
Inclusive professionalism, 101
Independent of race, 9
Indian Health Services (IHS), 82
Indigenous, 80–81, 85
Inequity, Whiteness and, 117
Injunctive relief, 53, 54

Institutional culture, 42–43
  effects of, 43
  equity, 46
  humility, 112
  key indicators of, 48*t*
  learning environment, 43–46
  prioritizing delivery of quality care, 46–47
  safe and equitable, 48*f*
  of safety, 47–49
  well-being, 46
Institutionalized racism, 15, 118
Interactive process, 227, 227*f*
Interagency Language Roundtable for health care scale (ILR-H), 159
Internalized racism, 15, 118
International medical graduates (IMGs), 145, 157–158
  challenges, 146
  contributions of, 146
  J-1 physicians, 145
  strategies to mitigate barriers to, 148–149
Interpersonal racism, 15
Interpreter (Medical), 156
Intersectional identities, 112
Intersectionality, 24*f*, 99
  as aspect of holistic review, 26–27
  defined, 23–24
  GME strategies to support in professional identity formation, 24–27
  linguistically diverse physicians, 157–158
  transgender and gender-diverse individuals, 204
  trauma informed care and, 25
Invisibility factor, 84, 139
Isha, prayer, 166
Islam. *See* Muslims

J

J-1 BridgeUSA program, 145
J-1 physicians, 145
J-1 visas, 145. *See also* BridgeUSA; Educational Commission for Foreign Medical Graduates (ECFMG)
JEDI. *See* Justice, equity, diversity, inclusion (JEDI)
Jewish Physician Network (JPN), 180
JPN. *See* Jewish Physician Network (JPN)
Judaism. *See* Orthodox Judaism
Justice, equity, diversity, inclusion (JEDI), 220
Justice-involved populations, 123–125, 125*f*
  defined, 125
  health disparities in, 126–127
    aging incarcerated population, 127
    improving GME to reduce, 128–129
  justice-involved youth, 125–126
Justice-involved youth, 125–126

K

Kaiser Permanente Clinician Cultural Language Assessment, 159
Kashrus (or *Kashrut*), 176
Kosher, 175, 176

L

Language-appropriate health care. *See* Linguistically diverse physicians
Language coaching, 160
Language concordance, 153, 155
Language-concordant care, 112
Latino, Hispanic, or of Spanish origin (LHS+), 107–108
    groups, 109t
    obstacles to advancement, 110–111
    race and ethnicity as related to, 109–110
    representation within academic medicine, 110
    trainees, opportunities to improve learning and working environment for, 111–112
Latino Medical Student Association, 111
Latino Medical Student Organization, 213
LCME. *See* US Liaison Committee on Medical Education (LCME)
Leadership
    academic, 91–92
    diverse representation in, 169
Learning climate, 190
Lesbian, 210–212
LGBTQI youth, 126
LGBTQIA+ community, 210, 211f, 212–214. *See also* Sexual minority
Life expectancy, 31, 33, 35
Linguistic discrimination, 157
Linguistically diverse physicians, 153–154
    intersectionality, 157–158
    multilingual physicians, challenges of
        discrimination, bias, and mistreatment, 157
        overburdening learners, 156–157
    representation of, 155–156
    strategies to improve, 158–161
Loctician, 100

M

Macroaggression, 100–101
Maghrib, prayer, 166
Marginalization, 204
The Match, 178, 179
Matriculating Student Questionnaire (MSQ), 234
MCAT. *See* Medical College Admission Test (MCAT)
MedEdPORTAL, 213
Medical College Admission Test (MCAT), 92, 137
Medical interpreter, 156
Medical language courses, 159, 160
Medical language proficiency, 156
    testing/certification, 159
Medical Organization for Latino Advancement, 111
Medical transitioning, 201–202
Medically underserved areas (MUA), 31
Mentorship, lack of, 84
Microaggressions, 100–101, 112, 192, 235
    defined, 190
    gender-based, 190
    systemic, 192–193
Minority tax, 156
Mistreatment, language-related, 156–157, 161
MSQ. *See* Matriculating Student Questionnaire (MSQ)
MUA. *See* Medically underserved areas (MUA)
Multilingualism, 155
    challenges of
        discrimination, bias, and mistreatment, 157
        overburdening learners, 156–157
    multilingual skills, 158–161
Multiple identities, 26
Muslims, 163–164
    challenges, 165–166
    demographic landscape of, 165
    strategies to improve inclusion
        beard, 168
        dietary accommodations, 168–169
        diverse representation in leadership, 169
        fasting and Holy month of Ramadan, 167
        gender interactions and physical exams, 168
        hijab, 167, 168f
        prayers, 166–167
        religious holidays, 167
        social gatherings, 169
        support groups and bias, 169

N

National Association of Medical Spanish, 111
National Center for Transgender Equality (NCTE), 202
National Hispanic Medical Association, 111
National Practitioner Data Bank (NPDB), 63–64
National Sample Survey of Physicians (NSSP), 224–225
Native American, 80–81
Native Hawaiian or Other Pacific Islander (NHOPI), 90
    in antiracism, 94
    in GME and academic leadership, 91, 91–92f
    intersectional identities influencing inclusion, 92–93
    strategies to improve inclusion and equity for
        bias and discrimination, reports of, 94
        departmental and institutional data, 94
        disaggregate data, 93
        name-affirming practices, 94
        policies and practices, 93
        recruitment and selection, institutional approach to, 93
NCTE. *See* National Center for Transgender Equality (NCTE)
NHOPI. *See* Native Hawaiian or Other Pacific Islander (NHOPI)
Non-binary people, 200–201
Non-discrimination, 214
Non-English language preferences, 155
Non-traditional age, 233
Non-traditional residents, 231–232
    in graduate medical education, 233, 233t
    key challenges and barriers, benefits, and value-added, 233–235, 234t
    primary intersections to be understood for, 235
    strategies to support, 235–236
NPDB. *See* National Practitioner Data Bank (NPDB)
NSSP. *See* National Sample Survey of Physicians (NSSP)

O

Objective structural clinical examination (OSCE), 213
One drop rule, 81

One-Minute Preceptor, 236
Orthodox Judaism, 173–175
  barriers of, 176–177
  challenges of, 176
  Jewish holidays, 177*t*
  Sabbath observance and, 177–178, 178*t*
  strategies for accommodation, 178–180
    accommodations by residents/fellows, 179
    considerations to achieve clarity, 179
    program approach, 178–179
    Sabbath observance and The Match, 179
    suggestions and references to facilitate, 180
OSCE. *See* Objective structural clinical examination (OSCE)

P

Parole, 127
Passover, 177*t*
Pathway programs, 111–112
Pay disparities, gender-related, 189
Peer support groups, 169
Personally mediated racism, 15, 118
Physician Oral Language Observation Matrix, 159
PIF. *See* Professional identity formation (PIF)
Pioneer Syndrome, 102
Poverty
  on access to care, 33–36
  intersection of, 33–34
Prayers, Muslims, 166–167
Pregnancy, 191
Pregnancy Workers Fairness Act, 56
  employer violations of, 57
  steps to comply with and limit liability under, 57
Prejudice, 15
Probation, 64, 127
Professional identity formation (PIF)
  defined, 24
  GME strategies to support intersectionality in, 24–27
Professionalism in medicine, 24
  redefining, 26
Program access, 225
Program directors, considerations for, 68–70
Psychological safety, 46
Puberty blockers, 201

Q

Quality care, 46
Queer, 126, 201, 210

R

Race-conscious approach, 120
Race/ethnicity, 6–7. *See also* Racism
  case study, 5–6
  COVID-19 pandemic, 8
  health disparities, 8
  historical events, 7–8
  history and consequences of, 9, 9*t*
  intersection of, 33–34
  on mortality, 33, 34*f*
  as related to LHS+, 107–108
  social risk in communities, examining, 9
Racial battle fatigue, 120
Racial bias, 193
Racial health inequities, 19
Racial identity, 25
Racism, 6–8
  antiracism, 94
  antiracist change, strategies for, 17–18
  biological, 16
  defined, 14
  health care segregation, 16–17
  institutionalized, 15, 118
  internalized, 15, 118
  interpersonal, 15
  levels of, 15–16
  naming, 118
  naming, 14–15, 15*f*
  operation of, 118–119
  personally mediated, 15, 118
  structural, 14, 15–17, 118
  in Whiteness, 118–119
  workforce diversity and career progression by, 16, 17*f*
Ramadan, 167
Re-entry population, 128
Reasonable accommodation, 55–56, 57
Reasonable modifications, 56
Redlining, 8
Religious discrimination, 175
Religious Holidays, 167
Religious identity, 26
Residency programs, 63
Resident and fellow physicians, 65–68
Resident promotion, 63
Retaliation, 54
Rosh Hashana, 177*t*
Rural areas, 30, 31–33, 32*f*
  developing pathway of learners from, 36
  opportunities for, 36
  solutions to reduce disease and mortality gaps in, 36–38

S

Sabbath (*Shabbos*/Shabbat), 174–180
Sabbath observance, 177
  learners, 178–179
  resident/fellow, 178–179, 180
  suggestions for creating match opportunities for, 178*t*
  and The Match, 179
Safety
  culture of, 47, 48*t*
  psychological, 46
Sexual attention, unwanted, 189
Sexual coercion, 190
Sexual harassment, 189, 192*t*
Sexual minority
  barriers to health education, 212
  defined, 209–210
  guidelines to screening recommendations, 213–214
  inclusion
    challenges, 212

strategies to improve, 213–214
national representation, 210–212
scholarly work related to health, 214
Sexual orientation, 189, 202, 212, 213–214
Shavuot, 177t
Shomer Shabbos, 177, 179–180
    Medicine Network, 180
    Residency, 180
SHPEP. *See* Summer Health Professions Education Program (SHPEP)
SOAP. *See* Supplemental Offer and Acceptance Program (SOAP)
Social and structural determinants of health, 31
Social construct, 9
Social determinants of health, 9
Social gatherings, 169
Social transitions, 201
Social vulnerability index, 9
Sponsoring Institution, 37, 47, 63–70, 128, 180, , 220, 227
    leadership, 52, 136t, 139, 140t
    and programs, 43
    strategies for, 24–27
Sponsorship, 138
Stereotype threat, 235
Structural bias, 8, 6. *See also* Structural racism
Structural racism, 14, 15–17, 118. *See also.* structural bias
Structural violence, 111
Student National Medical Association, 213
Substantial impairment, 55
Sukkot, 177t
Summer Health Professions Education Program (SHPEP), 99
SUPERB model, 236
Supplemental Offer and Acceptance Program (SOAP), 102
Surgical transition, 202
Systemic racism, 15, 25

T

Talmud, 175
TGD individuals. *See* Transgender and gender-diverse (TGD) individuals
Timely access, 3, 31–32, 34f
Title VII of Civil Rights Act of 1964, 53–54
    employer's violation of, 53
    steps to comply with and limit liability under, 53–54
Title IX of Education Amendments of 1972
    steps to comply with and limit liability under, 54
    violation of, 54
Train to remain strategy, 36
Transgender, 126, 197, 21–22. *See also* Transgender and gender-diverse (TGD) individuals
Transgender and gender-diverse (TGD) individuals, 197–198, 200–201
    attendings, supporting, 204–205
    celebrated, 199
    clinical experience of, 202–203
    detransitioning, 202
    gender-affirming care, 201
    hormonal support, 201–202
    intersectionality with other marginalized identities, 204
    medical students, supporting, 204–205
    medical transitioning, 201–202
    physician learner
        key challenges of, 203
        supporting, 204–205
    strategies to improve healthcare and clinical learning environment of, 204
    surgical transition, 202
Transsexualism, 200
Trauma informed care
    intersectionality and, 25
    principles of, 25
TREVOR Project, 203
Trusted support network, 65–66
Tuskegee experiment, 7

U

Unconscious, unrecognized or conscious biases and stereotypes, 102
Underrepresented in medicine, 109
Undocumented immigrant, 147
Undue hardship, 57, 175
University of Michigan Intern Health Study, 224–225
Unwanted sexual attention, 189
Upstander, bystander *vs.*, 100
Urban areas, 31
    developing pathway of learners from, 36
    emergency department, 30–31
    opportunities for, 36
    solutions to reduce disease and mortality gaps in, 36–38
Urban underserved area, 36–37
US Liaison Committee on Medical Education (LCME), 81
US Medical Licensing Examination (USMLE) scores, 146
USMLE scores. *See* US Medical Licensing Examination (USMLE) scores

W

Well-being, 46
White emotionality, 120
White institutional spaces, 116–120
White Racial Frame, 120
Whiteness, 115–117
    antiracism in, 118, 119–120
    confronting, necessity of, 118
    creating and maintaining inequity, 117
    defined, 117
    health equity in, 118
    racism in, 118–119
Women in academic medicine, 187–188
    climate and culture, 190
    diversity and inclusion for, 189
    harassment, 189–190
    hijab, 167, 168f
    microaggressions affecting, 190
    parenthood as, 190–191
    pay disparities, 189
    safe and supportive work environment, 189
    strategies to improve inclusion and belonging for, 191–193, 191–192t
    untitle, 193

Workforce diversity, 16, 17*f*
Workplace
   culture, 190
   in graduate medical education, 220
   for LHS+ trainees, 111–112
World Professional Association for Transgender Health, 202

Y
Yom Kippur, 177*t*

Z
Zabiha Halal, 168